Maya Heath

The Book of

Stones & Metals

Merlyn Press
630 S. Huttig
Independence MO, 64053

LIBRARY OF CONGRESS CATALOGING-IN-PUBLICATION DATA
LIBRARY OF CONGRESS #99-70134

HEATH, MAYA 1948-
THE BOOK OF STONES & METALS / MAYA HEATH
ISBN: 0-9651554-2-0

PUBLISHED BY: MERLYN PRESS
            630 S. HUTTIG
            INDEPENDENCE, MO 64053
            (816) 836-1182

INTERIOR ILLUSTRATIONS: PAM STEELE

COVER ILLUSTRATION AND DESIGN: MIKE AXEN

ACKNOWLEDGMENTS

This book has been many years in the writing and preparation and it would be impossible to thank all those who have contributed to the effort of turning it from concept to reality. Nonetheless, there are those exceptional few without whose help it would never have happened. My greatest thanks go to my publisher and long time friend Bob Isaac who has been so extraordinarily patient, supportive and encouraging in bringing this book to completion. To Margaret Utter for technical consultation on the scientific and gemological nature of minerals. Great thanks to Jamison Utter for extraordinary technical support in keeping the computer not only running but expanded ever better so seamlessly. Trace Bunker and Charlotte McGee have my sincerest gratitude for stepping in at the last moment to edit and refine the manuscript. To my daughter, Adrienne, for her patience and good humor, and to Chris and Larry for keeping the place together while all this was in progress.

DEDICATION

To my husband, Bob, who has shared
in this work and supported this dream
since its inception...........all my love.

TABLE OF CONTENTS

ACKNOWLEDGMENTS III
DEDICATION III
AUTHOR S NOTE XIV
CHAPTER 1 - THE PATH OF PREPARATION 1
   PHYSICAL HEALTH & PREPARATION 8
   THE GREAT DANCE 9
   BEGINNING THE INNER WORK 12
      ❀ - BEGINNING EXERCISES 13
   DANCING ON THE RIVER OF LIFE 14
   CENTERING 17
      ❀ - MEDITATION ON CENTERING 18
   SHIELDING 18
      ❀ - MEDITATION ON SHIELDING ------------------------------ 20
CHAPTER 2 - THE HUMAN ENERGY SYSTEM COMPLEX 22
   RED & ROSE / BASE 26
   ORANGE - GOLDEN / BELLY 28
   YELLOW / SOLAR PLEXUS 29
   GREEN / HEART 30
   BLUE / THROAT 31
   INDIGO / VIOLET / BROW 32
   PURPLE / DIAMOND WHITE / CROWN 32
      THE ANALOGY OF THE ROSE 35
  BALANCING THE CHAKRAS 36
   THE BALANCE OF LIFE FORCE 38
   THE BALANCE OF PERSONALITY, KARMA & TIME 39
   THE BALANCE OF EXPRESSION & ACTION 40
   THE COORDINATION OF THE HEART CENTER 41
   THE HORIZONTAL AXIS OF THE BODY'S ENERGY FIELD 42
   IMPAIRMENT AND RESTORATION OF THE BODY'S ENERGY FIELD 43
   STATES OF AWARENESS 43
   ENERGY STATES 46
      ❀ - CHAKRA MEDITATION 47
CHAPTER 3 - CONDITIONS OF LIGHT 54
  THE BASIC MECHANISM 56
   CLEAR STONES 57

❀ - MEDITATION ON CLEAR (QUARTZ) 59

DARKNESS & LIGHT - (WHITE & BLACK) 61

WHITE 61

WHITE STONES 61

❀ - MEDITATION ON WHITE - (QUARTZ) 62

BLACK 64

BLACK STONES 64

❀ - MEDITATION ON BLACK - (TOURMALINE - SCHORL) 66

THE SPECTRUM OF CRYSTALS 68

INTENSITY OF COLOR 69

RED STONES 70

ROSE STONES 71

❀ - MEDITATION ON RED / ROSE - (GARNET / RUBY) 72

ORANGE STONES 74

❀ - MEDITATION ON ORANGE - (CITRINE) 74

YELLOW STONES 75

GOLDEN STONES 76

❀ - MEDITATION ON GOLDEN/YELLOW - (TOPAZ) 77

GREEN STONES 78

❀ - MEDITATION ON GREEN - (EMERALD) 80

BLUE STONES 82

❀ - MEDITATION ON BLUE (SAPPHIRE) 83

PALE BLUE STONES 85

❀ - MEDITATION ON PALE BLUE (AQUAMARINE) 86

VIOLET/INDIGO STONES 88

❀ - MEDITATION ON VIOLET (AMETHYST) 89

PURPLE STONES 90

❀ - MEDITATION ON PURPLE - (TOURMALINE - SIBERITE) 91

CHAPTER 4 - WORKING WITH CRYSTAL ENERGY 93

BASIC TECHNIQUES OF STONE USE 93

LIFE STONES 94

HEALING STONES 94

STONE ELIXIRS 95

STONE TALISMANS OF POWER 96

THE LAWS OF HARMONIC RESONANCE 97

THE LAW OF PARALLEL RESONANCE 98

CONFIGURATION OF CRYSTALS 99

AXES & TERMINATIONS 100

MATRIX & BASE ROCK 101
DOUBLE TERMINATION 102
TWINNING 102
INCLUSIONS 103
GHOSTING 104
GENERAL GUIDELINES 105
PREPARATION & INTERACTION 108
CLEARING 108
COLOR CHANGES 110
INTENTION & CLEARING 110
❀ - MEDITATION ON INTENTION & CLEARING 111
CHARGING 114
THE INITIAL CHARGE 115
❀ - MEDITATION ON CHARGING 116
SELECTING YOUR STONES 117
WEARING & PLACEMENT OF STONES 118
OVERLOADING A STONE 119
WHEN THE WORK IS DONE 119
A RAINBOW OF EXPERIENCE 119
CHAPTER 5 - JOURNEY OF THE SPIRIT 121
ETHICAL PRINCIPLES 122
SHIELDING 124
LEVELS OF SHIELDING 124
HEALER'S SHIELDS 127
SEER'S SHIELDS 129
MAGE'S SHIELDS 129
WARDED SPACE 129
KARMA AND ENERGY WORK 132
THE ENERGY PATTERNS OF RELATIONSHIPS 134
NEUTRALIZING KARMA 137
KARMA & THE CHAKRAS 138
IMPLANTS 139
KARMIC INJURIES 140
TIME, PERCEPTION & EVENT WAVES 143
MACROINTERACTIVES AND POWER 145
THOUGHT FORMS AND PROJECTED INTENTION 149
THE PRACTICE OF CREATING A THOUGHT FORM 152
FETCHING 153

Chapter 6 - Energy Work With Stones & Talismans 155
Healing by Placing Stones on the Body 155
Simple Healing with Carved Images 160
Chapter 7 - The Energies of Metal 163
Iron & Steel 163
Copper 166
Bronze168
Gold 170
Silver 171
Electrum 173
Platinum 173
❁ - Meditation on Metals 174
Chapter 8 - Complex Talismans 178
Elements of Complex Talismans 178
Primary 179
Qualifier 181
Driver 181
Setting the Talisman 183
Specific Construction 184
Stone Choice Specifics 184
The Dreamer's Talisman 186
Balancing the Stone Combinations 188
Talismans of Singular Power 190
The Seer's Talisman 190
Talisman of the Planet's Energy 191
Chakra Talisman 192
The Grand Talisman 196
The Vajra Talisman 197
Chapter 9 - The Callings & Their Talismans 199
Purpose & Configuration of the Talismans 202
Dual Resonances 206
Artisan & Smith 206
Warrior 209
Dancer 211
Healer 212
Seer / Teacher 215
Monarch 216
Priest 218

SIMILAR PROPERTIES 219
TALISMANS OF TOGETHERNESS 220
CHAPTER 10 - GROUP WORK & THE GREAT GATHERING **221**
FULL GATHERING OF THE CALLINGS 225
GATHERING OF SINGLE REPRESENTATIVES 227
APPRENTICE CALLING STONES 231
COMPLETING THE PROCESS 231
CHAPTER 11 - TALISMANIC REGALIA **233**
JEWELRY 233
WANDS, ORBS, BLADES & STAFFS 236
WANDS 236
ORBS 238
BLADES 238
CLEANSING & CHARGING BLADES & OTHER METAL OBJECTS 239
CHARGING A MASTER BLADE 240
WEARING BLADES 242
CUPS, VESSELS, & LAMPS 243
THE DREAMER'S CUP 244
THE CUP OF JOINING 245
BOXES & STORAGE CONTAINERS 245
LAMPS & BRAZIERS 246
SCRYING MIRRORS & BOWLS 246
ARMOR 247
MASKS 249
TALISMANS OF NOBLE HOUSES 250
PART 2 - STONE FAMILIES AND TYPES **253**
ARTIFICIALLY COLORED AND SYNTHETIC STONES 254
QUARTZ 255
WHITE 256
SMOKY & BLACK (MORION) 257
RED 258
ROSE 259
ORANGE (CITRINE) 260
THE TALE OF THE GOLDEN LION 261
CHLORITE INCLUSIONS 261
GREEN 261
GREEN CITRINE 262
VIOLET (AMETHYST) 263

AMETHYST QUARTZ 264
BLACK AMETHYST 264
RUTILATED QUARTZ 265
STAR QUARTZ 266
MICROCRYSTALLINE QUARTZ (CHALCEDONY) 267
WHITE 268
BLACK (ONYX) 268
ORANGE (CARNELIAN) 269
MOSS AGATE 270
GREEN 270
CHRYSOPRASE 271
GREEN AVENTURINE 272
BLUE (SIDERITE) 272
CAT'S EYE QUARTZ 273
HAWK'S EYE 273
TIGER'S EYE 273
JASPER & OPAQUE CHALCEDONIES 274
JASPER 275
RED 275
YELLOW 275
GREEN (HELIOTROPE) 276
BLUE 276
OPALS 276
FIRE AGATE 278
OPALS AND IRON 278
GARNET 279
BLACK & BROWN GARNET (MELANITE) 281
RED 282
ROSE 283
ORANGE (CINNAMON) 284
GOLDEN & YELLOW 284
GREEN 285
PURPLE 286
THE ZINC GROUP 287
ZINCITE 287
HEMIMORPHITE 288
SMITHSONITE 288
TOPAZ 290

Topaz as a Primary 291
Clear 291
Smoky 292
Rose 292
Yellow & Golden 293
  The Tale of the Warrior's Torch 294
Green 295
Blue 295
Beryl 296
Beryl as a Primary 297
Red and Rose (Morganite) 298
Yellow (Heliodore) 299
Green (Emerald) 299
Pale Blue (Aquamarine) 301
Corundum Group 302
White Sapphire 303
Ruby 303
Orange (Pad Parajah) 304
Yellow 304
Green 305
Blue 305
Violet 306
Black 306
Star Sapphire 307
Tourmaline 308
Tourmaline as Primary 311
White and Clear (Acrhoite) 312
Black (Schorl) 312
Yellow/Brown (Dravite) 312
Red and Rose (Rubelite) 313
Yellow (Dravite) 314
Golden (Dravite) 315
Green (Verdelite) 315
Blue (Indicolite) 316
Purple (Siberite) 317
Watermelon Tourmaline 318
Diamond 319
Colored Diamond 320

WIDE SPECTRUM CRYSTALS 321
  KUNZITE 321
    SECONDARY QUALIFYING STONES 323
    DRIVERS AND KUNZITE 323
  KORNERUPINE 324
  SERAPHENITE (GEM CLINOCHLORE) 324
  KYANITE 327
THE FELDSPAR GROUP 327
  SUNSTONE (AVENTURINE FELDSPAR) 328
  MOONSTONE 329
  LABRODORITE (SPECTROLITE) 331
  AMAZONITE 331
STONES OF CLARITY, REGENERATION AND RENEWAL 331
  PERIDOT 332
  ZOISITE 332
  EPIDOTE 333
  TANZANITE 335
JADE 336
  JADEITE 336
  NEPHRITE 336
  ACTINOLITE 336
PERSONAL DEVELOPMENT AND TRANSFORMATION 338
  ZIRCON 338
  SPINEL 339
LIGHT REACTIVE STONES 341
  ALEXANDRITE 343
  ANDALUSITE 343
  IOLITE 343
CRYSTALLINE IRON / HEMATITE, MAGNETITE, PYRITE, MARCASITE 343
NON-CRYSTALLINE STONES OF POWER 345
THE COPPER GROUP 346
  TURQUOISE 346
  AZURITE 346
  CHRYSOCOLLA 348
  COVELLITE 348
  MALACHITE 349
  EILAT STONE 349
MANGANESE GROUP 350

RHODONITE 350

RHODOCHROSITE 351

STONES TO REBALANCE THE ENERGY SYSTEM COMPLEX 352

LEPIDOLITE 352

SUGULITE 353

CHAROITE 353

THE SEER'S STONES 354

LAPIS LAZULI 355

SODALITE 355

THE CALCIUM GROUP 355

FLUORITE 357

APATITE 357

CALCITE 359

SELENITE (CRYSTALLIZED GYPSUM) 359

ALABASTER & MARBLE 359

DIOPSIDE 360

LIFE FORMS & FOSSILS 362

JET 362

CORAL & PEARLS 362

AMBER 363

CORAL 365

PEARLS 365

FOSSIL ANIMALS & PLANTS 365

APPENDIX A 366

INDEX 374

Author s Note

This book is derived from a variety of sources. It began as a transcription of material that exists as a multi-dimensional multiple access reference codex that may be scanned from any point in its existence. The original entries were made in what the book describes as the Ancient Days and placed under certain access codes in the records with the intent that only students at certain points in their educational and spiritual development could reach them. This record was also designed to collect and store any further information that responded to the pre-existing codes, and it recorded any major event that had reference and bearing on the material already available. The entries in it have been made over the course of many thousands of years and contain the collected wisdom and experience of many hundreds of practitioners. The wealth of information recorded in this archive is literally incalculable, and it contains information on philosophy, social behavior, history, mythology, physics and physiology, as well as the expected information on the energy properties of stones and metals. It began recording its information in the dim recesses of Time before current history began and the most recent entry ends about 1927 c.e.

In order to put this basic material into a linear readable form accessible by the modern reader, I have worked in connection with a group of beings who identify themselves as the Teacher/Guardians, to provide commentary and background information. It is their intention as well as my own to help as many people as possible gain the developmental level necessary to make the transition into the coming age. Their message and intention is one of great love and concern for the inhabitants of this planet and this physical plane. Their contribution has been of enormous value in making this work something of contemporary use and relevance.

Spirit guides and channeling are subjects that have received a lot of attention in the past few years. And there seems to be a large variance of opinion about who or what they are and what importance should be attached to the information received from them. Sometimes I hear the terms Guardian Angel, sometimes Ancestor Spirit - there are so many different ways of describing and perceiving these intelligences depending on your worldview, religion and cultural perspective. I believe that in order to make this form of communication comfortable the subconscious mind gives it a shape and form that the receiver can understand and be receptive to. Depending on your cultural orientation you might perceive this in any one of many different ways. You might call it your intuition. You might have dreams or see your dead grandmother. You might be as I've heard Thomas Edison was - he'd have a problem, take a 20 minute nap, and wake up with the solution. Or you might actually see glowing spirits of whatever kind. In our generation brought up on Hollywood horror Bmovies you might visualize these entities as ETs - either for good or for ill – because that is what you expect to see or that is what your subconscious is comfortable with. It is our minds that give shape, form and context to beings of energy whose existence has no shape or form or context that we can understand from our physical view point.

But there is a much more personal aspect to consider. Every individual is a part of a greater spiritual whole of which he or she may be completely unaware. There is the individual person, anchored here in the time/space continuum by the chakra energy code etc. Then there is "Higher Self", the archetypal person regardless of the context of incarnation and temporary personality. If you can imagine a person sticking their big toe into a bathtub - higher self is the person and you here and now would be the toe. We are all connected to our Higher Selves by what we call the subconscious. This is the corridor that leads from our limited present physical universe perspective to the much wider world in which we embrace a much fuller and richer identity.

From that higher self there is the group of beings of which we are a part - sort of like relatives/family only much more closely knit. Its a group consciousness that is woven from the combined consciousnesses of a group of spirits/beings. These can also appear as spirit guides. This appearance of "self" as different and separate from "others" is a time/space differentiation implying distance. On other planes this sort of perception is not so well defined or is not present at all. The point behind this is that the channeler and the entity being channeled are quite often one and the same entity. They are different parts of the same higher intelligence. Often when we channel it is to translate knowledge from our own higher selves. This should not be a point of arrogance or a claim of omniscience, but rather an acknowledgement that our present time conscious self is only one small aspect of a much greater whole. To acknowledge and allow that connection in this frame of existence is to begin bridging the gap in our understanding of our own natures. It is to begin to see ourselves as part of the spiritual whole of which this universe is only one small aspect. Channeling can be an expression of the connection of any one of these things.

Because this material has been translated from non-physical sources, the language is sometimes difficult and complex. Most of the entries were never rendered into verbal form and translating them into a linear language format has presented many challenges. One particular difficulty has been in the use of gender specific pronouns. These are primarily used to express energy polarity rather than physical gender, but our language does not present the flexibility to express this. The text explains about polarity and that each Calling has a dominant polarity that is expressed as gender. This corresponds to all sorts of other things with dominant energy polarities. It does not imply that only the individual of the dominant polarity can hold a particular Calling. It refers to a Calling by the gender pronoun of its dominant polarity. I have tried wherever possible to adjust the syntax so that a more general reference is made, but some places that was not possible. I apologize in advance for any discomfort this may cause on the part of the student.

To make the best use of this book, that is subject to the limitations of volume format, the reader is advised to read the entire volume through from cover to cover. After you have an overview of the material, then go back and begin at the first, doing the meditations as suggested. In order for the material to be valid as a reference work, you must understand the working forces it refers to and develop a feeling for the individual elements discussed. In the course of the meditations it is suggested that you experiment with single stones and single metals. Work with each type, one at a time until you develop your own personal knowledge of its inner properties. Only when you feel clear on the meanings of the individual stones and metals should you begin to work with combinations. It will also be of great value to the student if this study also includes broader research into the physical science of atomic structure, geology and crystallography. These are integral to the nature of crystal energy as well as healing and energy work in general.

Maya Heath
Parkville, Mo
December 1998

CHAPTER 1

THE PATH OF PREPARATION

As the current age draws to close, Humankind is preparing to undergo a change in conscious awareness, another step of growth toward the return to spiritual identity that is the purpose of all Spirit on this plane. Growing children leave behind toys and games, attitudes and behaviors that they once found precious and relevant. The nature of healthy growth moves them to reach out for new ways of participating in their environment as they leave behind things that are too small or limited in scope. Spiritual growth on this plane of reality is much the same. Each Age offers new challenges and freedoms as Humankind grows and develops.

Long ago this planet was recognized as an environment in which entities could experience many things in order to learn and grow. It provides an extraordinary environment in its unique microcosm of energy patterns. Those that had come far from the knowledge of their spiritual identity and memory of their beginnings could use the energies and energy cycles of this planet for their growth and development towards a return to their full consciousness. Also, those beings newly come into this physical plane and not yet familiar with its nature could use this same planetary energy mechanism as a testing and learning place before translating into the greater experience of this universal plane. Some beings remain here only a short time through one cycle. Others remain for longer periods of time, some because they become trapped within this plane's heavier physical forms, and some from the desire to assist and teach other younger beings in order to ease their passage.

This planet is like a schoolroom. At each turning age, young beings enter for the first time and older ones leave to try a wider world of learning and growth. Also like the schoolroom, there are teachers, guardians, beings who watch over the children to help them in their learning and growth. They are responsible for providing opportunities for both individuals and groups to learn the lessons of this place. These teacher/ guardian entities are working to enhance and ease the transition of Humankind into the coming age by opening areas of information that will stimulate and quicken spiritual growth and development.

One essential step in this growth process is an increasing awareness of Humankind's place in the cosmic order. For many ages past, human beings have seen themselves as separate from the spiritual continuity of the greater universe. They have assumed a role of disinherited stepchildren participating only as suppliants, not as siblings, or equals. Only rarely have individuals gained sufficient clarity of vision to join the greater universal resonance, and achieving such a state of mind and being has always been regarded as the province of the exceptional few. Those with spiritual visions and goals have often thought that these goals could only be achieved in seclusion far removed from the flow of everyday life. In addition, those in the mainstream of physical, mundane life have often regarded spiritual consciousness as a distraction from the daily business of life and survival. This has resulted in a greater and greater schism between these two points of view making each way of life more alien to the other and more difficult to live.

Physical life without union with the spiritual becomes a tyranny of sensuality without meaning or purpose, its cycle without substance or higher reason. Spiritual life without physical reference becomes withdrawal and denial, a renunciation of the challenges and responsibilities that make all experience valuable and enriching. Each must support and nurture the other to have a whole existence. Only when a balance is achieved and the two extremes are rejoined can life on this plane and in this place become what it was intended to be - an experience that strengthens, expands and instructs the individual on many levels of conscious awareness.

So, the teacher/guardians are acting now as guides in a more active role than before in this cycle. At each turning of an age, they are able to enter into closer communication with individuals who have grown personally and spiritually. These guardians are then able to open energies to these individuals that stimulate their awareness of concepts and practices. They are making the way known so that the physical life can be joined with the spiritual one in an attitude of harmony and reunion, an embracing of what is so that this level of living consciousness can be transformed. As the spirit joins with the physical, both will be transformed and the general awareness level be raised and heightened altogether.

This has been happening gradually from age to age throughout human history on this planet. Each age brings its own unique specific vibrations of energy so that the beings living in that time are affected and transformed in tune with them. But at the turning of one age to another, it is most possible for new ideas and awarenesses to come forward and intense growth and transition in all who are sensitive and tuned to it. However, before these new ideas can become established practice, they cause great instability and uncertainty as the old ways are reevaluated and reassessed. At these times, that which was new and vital at the beginning of the age has become old and ritualized, its forms outdated and outgrown. It is no longer a relevant form for growth to continue. New realizations begin to dawn and sweep away the stale dust of old ways and usher in new ideas and forms of putting the coming time's vibrations into physical world form and practice. New forms develop and old forms change so that they will be suited as vehicles for the new vibrational energy. Many ideas and practices are tried and discarded until the vibration of the age clarifies itself and becomes steady. This is the nature of the time that you are living in. It should be understood that these new ideas and attitudes are the result of the individual consciousness interacting with and being affected by the changing energy matrix of the environment. Energy patterns of both the planet and the reality plane deeply affect the individuals who are a part of them. Then these individuals articulate and dramatize the nature of this energy matrix and react to its changing nature.

A growing child becomes restless and dissatisfied in the time of transition as one stage is outgrown but the new one is not fully realized. Toddlers learning that the world is greater than they have known want to embrace it but have not the size or strength to do so. Stripling adolescents are too young to live on their own, but are old enough to sense their own wider goals and purposes. At these ages, tantrums and depressions result from these changes and the frustrations they cause. In the same way, Humankind becomes restless at each changing and upheavals of every sort happen. Riots and revolutions flourish as groups and nations demonstrate their dissatisfaction with old forms and the dawning awareness that better things are possible. Expanding awareness creates a desire to demonstrate this new spiritual condition in the physical environment while older rigid forms resist this change. Plagues and diseases spring up that have never been known before as the energy level of the spirit changes and causes instability in the energies of the body that houses it. They become out of harmony with one another and the energy fields are no longer sufficient to protect the energy system from unaccustomed imbalances. These diseases and maladies serve to change the physical form in minute genetic ways so that it is more able to achieve the harmony and resonance of the coming age. One is part of the other; the change brings about its own adaptation. Just so war, riot, and genocide, while being great and grievous evils, serve a duel purpose, one of allowing a great number of new spirits to try physical forms briefly and interact with this place. By this interaction they integrate their energies and are then released from them quickly so that they may evaluate and adjust to this plane. Great slaughter also serves to stimulate social conscience and moral outrage that such activity should exist, causing reevaluation of practices and personalities and stimulating reactions against them. It also provides a magnitude of intense experience that allows individuals the opportunity of facing many issues in a short period. This clears them for further development.

All of these events reflect the instability of outgrowing the old age and preparing the way for the new. This imbalance causes people to take down, discard, and remove the old ways. In this manner, the way is opened and space is made to receive the new. This is the pruning of the orchard so that new and vigorous growth can occur and the trees bear fruit. It is only after they are put aside that space is made to receive the new. A child must leave the parent's house in order to establish his or her own place. Although he or she may return with love and welcome, he or she only achieves independent identity by breaking the old pattern. At this time, the same thing is happening to Humankind. The downfall of governments, ancient monarchies and nation states is clearing the way for newer group identities to emerge and newer forms of government that reflect the changing awareness of peoples and groups. New forms of social custom are replacing the old ways as social awareness expands. Castes and practices are put aside as new institutions are brought into being that reflect the hopes and goals of the coming time.

There is concern and consternation, also, that religions are, in some cases, reorganized and in other cases put away altogether. This causes great fear and insecurity leading to great backlash in many areas and an outcry to return to what is seen as purer roots of faith. Many people will feel the loss of rigidly conventional form and dogmas. However, this removal of rigid forms leaves the way open for individual spiritual awareness. When the rituals and trappings of dogmatic religion are released, the way is made for a newer level of individual experience, responsibility, and enlightenment. The individual spirit can then reach outward beyond previously held beliefs to approach and recognize the divine nature of the universal consciousness by acknowledging and celebrating the divine nature within. The greater and the lesser are connected being part of one another. It remains but for the individual to recognize and fully acknowledge this. Then the spirit grows to a greater conscious awareness and comes closer to rejoining the universal conscious continuum.

We see this. We know this. We watch you and care for you. It is the purpose of the teacher/guardians to assist this process by making information available to the emerging consciousness of Humankind. The time of transformation is again at hand. Therefore, we are opening the way for information to come to Humankind that will assist in this transformation. Long dormant consciousness and sensitivities are awakening in many individuals. There are many beings on this world that are returning in awareness to the recognition of their identities and natures. They are hearing their own inner voices and the voices of the universe beyond. We place the keys to better understand and facilitate this change in the way for any who are able to receive and benefit from them. Therefore, we are opening the way to the ancient wisdom recorded in these records.

This cycle of the knowledge of spectrum energies was well known in many cultures of great antiquity. Wise and powerful healers and technicians used these principles to harness forces that performed miracles of healing, teaching and power technology that are still recalled in whispered legends, thousands of years after those people have passed into dust. But while the physical remnants of those civilizations may long ago have passed into ruin and oblivion, the ancient ones left a more lasting artifact that has remained unknown and undiscovered until your time. They were able to record much of this information in an energy construct that holds not only the basics of their teaching, but expands with time as new information is gathered and put into use. In their age, this energy lattice recording made it possible for anyone of the appropriate level of training and development to access the information at any time they wished to do so. It has remained in place for all the ages waiting other individuals who could key into this information.

You current civilization is paralleling these ancient ones in many significant elements of its development. Great technology and great knowledge of the physical laws of your plane have put great power into the hands of many. This has allowed many luxuries and leisure time that have provided the opportunity for personal development on a scale that has been unknown for many ages. This has enabled many individuals to develop their inner potential and reach a level at which they can access and make use of this ancient knowledge. In this time, it is also the life purpose of many to redeem what they recall as failures and tragedies in these ancient times. Their purpose in this cycle is to put right what went wrong and failed with such catastrophic results. With the intention of assisting these individuals we are making a way for these ancient records to be opened and the basic information brought to light so that many people can reclaim what was believed lost. As we proceed in this work, we will include many of the ancient tales and concepts along with more contemporary commentary and clarification so that the wisdom of the past may hopefully be brought forth to stimulate wisdom in the future. It is for this reason that the following text will seem to speak with many voices, because many hearts and minds contributed to its information.

In the following sections that describe the many properties and manifestations of color, we will first give a brief commentary and explanation. Then, the appropriate sections from the ancient records will be quoted at length. The language in many cases is difficult for the contemporary reader and the student must keep in mind that the days when these entries were recorded are long past and the human organism has gone through a great deal of change and development. We have retained their original content as closely as possible because the ideas these entries discuss are often best expressed in this fashion.

The universe as Humankind perceives it is built from basic energy archetypes. These come together in a variety of patterns and combinations to form the energy lattices that hold this universe together and give it its form, context, and continuity. They exist as fundamental units of both the greater external universe and the individual internal one. The inner spirit awakens through the stimulation and development of these internal energies. Because of this stimulation, these energies begin to resonate in harmony with their counterparts in the greater external universe. The best way to begin this process of growth is to study these fundamental energy forms in the most accessible way, that is, as they exist within the individual and as they are externally exemplified in the energy structures of physical forms known as crystals.

Crystals provide the clearest and least complicated expression of these pure energy forms and are an ideal example of these energies as they reside, not only in the macrocosm of the universe as a whole, but also in the microcosm of each life form living within it. They provide excellent material for teaching preparation of the body and spirit and the principles of working with power and energy. Because they exist in isolated form, crystals have an almost pure energy that is not interrupted or obscured by surrounding forms or complex biological or mechanical interaction. They contain objective information for the student to experience and learn with that, at the same time, stimulate and trigger the student's receptive centers and raise his/her attunement level to correspond with the work at hand.

This work can be used in two ways. The first is as a learning guide to assist individuals of this age to return to a fuller awareness of their abilities and potential. This is done by reading this work thoroughly from front to back, and making sure at every step that the information is understood on all levels and can be utilized on all levels. By all levels, we mean that this work requires more than a mental or intellectual understanding of words and concepts. Human beings exist on four levels of consciousness simultaneously – mental, emotional, physical and spiritual. Each of these levels has its own full and uniquely valid range of perceptions of the world in which that individual lives and moves. The individual experiences all things as a combination of all these levels of consciousness and perception and their interelationship. No study or practice can be learned without integrating its principle on all four levels. This is what we mean by making something part of your total experience. These levels of perception are operating all the time in all circumstance, but very often one or another of them is discounted and ignored as being inappropriate to a given situation. Emotions are disregarded; physical stimuli ignored; analytical facts put aside; spiritual essence unrecognized. However, it is only when these four work in harmony that a concept is fully understood. This is know as intuition - inner teaching. It is only when the individual is in balance with all the inner selves that this inner teaching can take place and a higher level of understanding achieved.

We must constantly encourage you to cultivate intuition and instinct, just as in the mental/physical world you acknowledge and act upon information brought to you on that level. This joins the rational/physical process with the emotional /spiritual one. Intuition is the result of spirit's learning process. Action is the way in which spirit unifies the learning process and meshes with this universe. Intuition without action is incomplete. It is through acknowledgment and practice that discretion and degree are developed. In this way, higher influence on all levels results.

A practice of understanding should also take place on the physical level through attention to health, exercise, diet, and rest. To this end, we have included many meditations that are guided journeys through the matrices of specific energy configurations and manipulation practices. Participation in these meditations is essential to the development of sensitivities to specific energy forms based on the direct experience of them.

This book may also be used as a general reference work, once the initial procedures have been completed. When referencing a stone, first read the color, then the general family type, then the section regarding the stone itself. It is not possible in one reference work or indeed in one lifetime to record a reference on all possible stones and their combinations. At this time, we have opened the records of those crystals and stones that are most closely associated with the fundamental energies of this plane and planet. These stones hold the signature patterns that Humankind most needs at this time to stimulate the needed growth and awareness to evolve into the pattern best suited for the coming age. These stones are readily available. They are also the principal energy signature patterns associated with healing the individual on many levels of being and with initializing the reintegration of those levels so that a whole and harmonious consciousness can be achieved. As your growth and study progress you should be able to develop sensitivity to the nature of stones, in general. Even if a specific type is not listed, you should be able to experience its properties and sense its uses by working with it and through it. We encourage you to reach out and experiment with a variety stones and crystals apart from those mentioned in this work, using your developing intuition and sensitivities as a guide. There is no energy form found in the earth that does not have some beneficial aspect.

PHYSICAL HEALTH & PREPARATION

Preparation for this work should proceed along two paths, one in tune with the other. The first path is that of the physical preparation that allows the body and spirit to integrate harmoniously and engage in the work. The second is that of the inner way, the development of the abilities to perceive and comprehend the energy fields presented by matter and within it. Let one proceed with the other. Each has merit, but cannot be fully realized without its counterpart. The physical and spiritual should be kept in balance with each other because that is the nature of this universe and of the life in it. Spiritual work should not lead the individual to abandon or misuse the body. Nor should the physical care and health ignore the spirit that the body houses. They must proceed together so that the benefit to both can be realized. The body that houses your spirit should be well cared for. Let the body be kept well rested with sleep, for fatigue dulls the way in which these energies are transmitted, causing resistances that will hinder both the understanding of the information and the ability to act upon it. Eat what is necessary to meet the body's requirements, primarily relying on fruits and grains, for heavier protein substances, such as red-blooded meat will cause certain resistances in the nerve channels that will cause the work to proceed without clarity. We do not mean to abstain entirely from animal proteins, for it is the nature of the physical form that they are generally required if the body is to function properly. Fish is an excellent protein as is fowl.

Eat in accordance with necessity; be aware of cravings for food, for the body will know its own needs. In this, each individual will differ one from another, for as all forms differ, so will the needs of each form differ. What is healthy and appropriate for one person may be excessive or inadequate for another. Also, at different points in your work and development your body's needs will change as a result of the varying demands that the higher energies put on it. As the nature of your activity varies, so will the body's requirements. Be sensitive to this. Fasting and denial for their own sake have neither merit nor benefit. There is much said in this time regarding various dietary habits that might be required for spiritual clarity and growth. We would say that each individual must be the judge of his own body's needs and his own spiritual values. To be a vegetarian is not always the wisest course for everyone. Physical bodies differ in their requirements for nutrients and in the forms these nutrients should take.

We should also clarify this by saying that you should regard the way in which life has evolved on this planet. Each form survives and grows by consuming other forms. This is true of the plant kingdom as well as of the animal. It is in the nature of your evolution even to the cellular level. Consuming any life is neither a bad thing nor a good one, but a necessity of physical survival. There is no one form of life more worthy of respect than any other, or more worthy of being consumed than any other. Whatever you decide should be part of the diet, whether plant or animal, let it be consumed with gratitude and respect for whatever organism it is. Acknowledge the place of all forms in the cycle of life in this place.

THE GREAT DANCE

In this time and age, sexual activity is much misused and misunderstood, and Humankind has turned away from the knowledge of this blessing. Consider the lower forms, the animal life. Their mating is spontaneous and dictated by instinct, quickening the womb with offspring, and regenerating the energy flows of the body. This is as true for humans as for butterflies or fish or any living creature that is aware of itself. Instinctive behavior is dictated by various energy flows and should be examined with care, for there are many levels to its validity. Among spirits and beings such as Humans whose nature is spiritual as well as physical, there is the instinct to seek the partner and mate. This happens on all the conscious levels: on the mental level, one seeks companionship; on the emotional level, joy and comfort; on the physical, desire and passion, and on the spiritual, balance and rejoining of the spiritual whole. When carried out as an expression of the joining with the partner and the fulfillment on these levels, sexual activity is a great blessing and benefit. Sexual activity and loving should include all these levels. Let the partners dance the dance and make love gently and with grace to bring forth the balance within themselves, within each other, and with the greater universe surrounding them.

Caring for the body and spirit includes respect for the need for sexual expression. When this activity is allowed to flow freely and without tension, it brings forth the body's energy centers, enlivens the lights of the body, refreshes the spirit and results in the pleasant out flowing of energies in accord with the true nature of spirit. Do this in the attitude known to you as Love, for it is much more than you realize. By the union of loving and compatible partnership interaction all forms of energy resonance are expressed in harmony. The body is gratified, the musculature is invigorated, the flow of blood is encouraged, and there is great benefit in this for both the body and spirit. In addition to this, as the lights and flows become balanced, blocked energy flows are released, and energies, that would solidify and become harmful if released, are transmuted and released, causing relaxation and health both to the body and spirit. As blocked flows are released, impurities and incongruities are transmuted into useful flows and swept outward in the release of energy.

Again, we say that this should be done in the attitude of Loving, and this is most important. It is by their unions and their harmonious interactions that the truest nature of spirit is revealed, for it is the nature of spirit to unite with spirit in joy and blessing. It is the greatest expression of giving and the greatest magnitude of receiving. It is the true expression of the unified polarities by which this universe was formed.

As with food and rest, be aware of the energy demands of the body. Physical sexuality is not always in keeping with the demands of the work. Just as we urge you to be sensitive to your dietary needs, so also you should be responsive to these needs and proceed with sensitivity and respect. Different levels of work and activity require different levels of physical attention. Your work should lead to acknowledgment of this.

This is the Dance together in harmony with the flowing of the Great River of Life. By its power, great healing and benefit can be achieved for all parties, along with great union of love and spirit and great power for the cause of all workings. However, let this be said in warning lest harm result: all parties participating in this should do so as equals in the levels of power achieved. One participant should not overdrive the other beyond their capacity to assimilate and balance the energy. All must be done with mutual willingness, joy, and consideration for the well being of those involved, for if this is not done, there will be no lasting benefit derived from it. Whatever momentary gain is seemingly achieved will be nullified by the harm that is inevitable in such a case of imbalance.

Let the singular Dancers come together. Let them raise their energies together with their breath. Let the breath pass between them and through them and let this then raise their basal fires. As each dancer raises his or her own capacity and power of his or her own nature, this energy should be transferred to the other or others by means of the fingertips and palms of the hands, until they have raised themselves and one another to the pinnacle they can achieve of this separately. Then let them join in physical union and bring forth the Great River, or Great Chi as it is called, in their coupling as sexual union occurs. In this manner, all the centers will become energized from this combined force as the river flows through both together, and they stand as one united center of light in its fiery stream. This is the true Dance of Light and Life and Union.

This may be used as a form of healing as well. Let one who is strong raise his or her powers by the Dance. By the Dance, we may also mean metaphorically, for as practice continues, it requires but a moment to bring oneself into conscious alignment with the flow of all things and power. Then he or she shall come to the one whose life force has waned and it will be revitalized by this joining. This practice may not require actual physical union of the parties, but may be accomplished by the touching of hands and the breathing of Life between them so that the life force is renewed. Breathing may also be understood as a metaphor for focused and directed intention of energy. However, the breathing exercise raises and intensifies this awareness and activity.

We speak of dancers together, and there is no greater means of manifest power than this. They are the two whose life energies, when raised together, make one song. Theirs is the union of their rhythms together in harmony with the rhythm of the great flow. They are separate no longer but are one with one another, and with the universe as a whole, and their power is unified. This can not be sustained indefinitely. The participants should realize that no being here is inseparable from any other and each is unique and individual. This must be realized truly, for it is the union of these two realized individuals which enables the power flow to be enhanced beyond the level of either one's singular capabilities. Do this reverently, in Love and joy for each other. Do not attempt this for working power unless both parties are separately adept in the expression of their own will and rhythm in the flow. This may be attempted for the simple joy of its blessing at any time and is most beneficial whether in the renewal of life forces after some great exertion or in the sharing of the joy of life together. However, let the prohibitions spoken of here be taken into account for whatever purpose it is done. This and all these exercises should be practiced wisely, well and with respect for the proper balance and maintenance of the centers and their interrelating flows.

BEGINNING THE INNER WORK

Before beginning a difficult physical task, it is necessary to prepare the body so that it will be able to endure the demands placed on it. Its strength must be patiently developed before the work begins or the burden will be too great and lasting damage can result. The same is true of spiritual work. The spirit, mind, emotions, and physical body must be strengthened and toned carefully and patiently. The groundwork must be prepared so that the individual can adapt to the types of energy that will be presented, otherwise, pain and damage can result from too much power moving through a channel that is not clear and strong enough to bear it. This could have manifestations on any of the four levels of your awareness. So we will begin with basic exercises and meditations that will prepare you for the work that will follow. These are as important, if not more so, than the intellectual or mental study of this work. For without developing the inner vehicle, any such mental exercise would be wasted. Therefore, knowledge of the self should be built with discipline and meditation and knowledge of ethical behavior, as well as a true commitment to the work. We will begin with a basic course of self-preparation so that the best use may be made of the information and techniques presented in this work.

The preparation of the spirit must be done carefully and patiently in order to abide the work, for both the body and spirit have long been unaccustomed to the work and, therefore, the form is unready to receive it. All organs are in place for this work and development, but they are not yet fully developed to receive these energies. In the coming days, form will evolve itself again and become more attuned to the fullness of this existence. It was ordained by those who developed the pattern of these bodies that it would develop in this way when its centers were keyed by the energy flows of the awakening spirits. This evolution will take less time than you realize. Before a thousand years have passed, this new capacity will be achieved. That is yet to come, and in order for this development to take place, care must be taken that the initial steps be taken properly.

The brain will be affected, as it is the repository of great power. It is the focus and storage place, the center of direction and control of great electrical and magnetic energies, which are sometimes referred to as Chi. As the work is manifested and developed, new areas of the brain that have been dormant will be energized and awakened. As they are new to this task and have not been developed throughout childhood by proper conditioning, their flows will be uneven. In the adult who has not had the training of the Temple, as was done in ages past, this effect is unavoidable. A certain amount of discomfort where the Chakras are expressed may result, also dizziness and occasionally dysphasia and dyslexia. Should this occur, slow the pace of the work and abstain from eating the flesh of red-blooded animals until these symptoms have passed and, at least, one sleep cycle has elapsed. Then let the work proceed in a slower fashion until the physical development catches up with the spiritual drive. In this text, we shall give certain meditative exercises that will aid in this initialization, so that the body may be properly prepared considering these limitations.

As for the exercises themselves, set aside at least an hour per day so that the fullest benefit of the work can be achieved. The place chosen for your work should be peaceful and free from undue distraction. If incense is used, let it initially not be made from flowers, but from spices, particularly, from sandalwood which is a most ancient and holy herb of greatest virtue. Do not use music, for this will interfere with the energizing of the signature flows of the spirit and the secondary flow of the information and the learning experience. Each thing has its own resonance and song. However pleasant or helpful the music may seem to be, it will not be the same vibration as what is being received and will interfere with its benefit. In all things, let the surroundings be in agreement with the context of this activity. Be sure that the body is comfortable and free from duress of external demands of any kind. Also, let the body be fed well, but not too much, so that it has sources of energy to draw upon.

❊ - Beginning Exercises

While seated in a comfortable chair, feet on the floor, hands on the knees and eyes closed, begin breathing deeply and slowly from the base of the lungs, for proper oxygenation is very helpful in clearing the body centers and releasing blocked energies. Draw several measured breaths in this fashion, and gradually become aware that the breath draws not only from your mouth and nose but also from the soles of your feet. As you inhale to breathe, also inhale energy from the earth. Draw the force of the earth upward as each breath is drawn inward, and as the breath is expelled, reverse the flow of this force and flow it outward from you with the breath through the crown of your head. Envision yourself as a conduit through which this energy passes clearly and cleanly. Draw it through your feet with the intake of breath and flow it outward through the crown.

This should be done often and not just in meditation, for this practice establishes the constant flow of renewing energy on all levels. This can be done in a moment whenever the opportunity presents itself. It will clear the senses and center the energies. It will both relax and revitalize the form. This attitude of clearly flowing energy is an essential factor in this work.

When the flow is comfortably established, begin the cycle of energy through your hands, cycling it through your heart. Place the palms of your hands together in front of you at approximately the heart level. Envision the energy flowing from your heart, down your right arm, passing between your palms and hands, then upward through the left arm and returning to the heart. Feel the energy cycle around and around. With each cycle, it grows brighter and stronger until your heart, arms, and hands feel like a circle of light and power. Feel the heart strengthen and clear, radiating comfort and strength. As the flow of energy strengthens, you can draw your palms slightly apart and feel them warm and tingling as the energy passes across them. Feel the channels of your body clear and balance through this exercise as it brings all energies into harmony. Do this slowly and harmoniously with an attitude of renewal and relaxation. Repeat this process daily until, with only a breath or two, the flows balance in harmony and accord. It is through this meditative cycling that the healing energies are raised and channeled and that power in all forms is put into useful manifestation. It brings all the energies are brought into accord, and physical and mental overload is avoided to a great degree. Even when overall balance is not possible and one center's needs overrides the needs of the others, doing this they can balance and bring them into harmony and with each other if this is practiced consistently.

DANCING ON THE RIVER OF LIFE

The second step in the preparation of the body is the singular dance within the rhythm of the Universe. Its purpose is to bring the spirit into harmony with the natural flow and rhythm of the energy of this Universe by incorporating motion and rhythm. It will encourage your sensitivity to the flows of the earth's energy through your body's centers. It also clears and strengthens the flow of energy through the body by making it a part of the experience of all motion. Be aware that participating in the flow of universal energy is not an occasional exercise happening only during meditation or spiritual work. It is a constant state of being. It is the way you are always in union with the greater universe. You are strengthened and revitalized on all levels by connecting to the source of all wisdom and flowing power so that from moment to moment you are clarified and renewed in the way. These exercises are intended to clear the channel through you to strengthen and clarify this flow and heighten your awareness of it and unity with it so that you can more easily access it as the source of great power, harmony, peace and healing energy.

Begin by cycling the energy upward through your feet through the spine and out the crown. When you are comfortable with this flow, connect the cycle through your hands and heart. This is the energy current known as the Small Chi and is the awareness of the body's own flow in accord with itself and its own energy centers. Place the feet slightly apart, with the knees gently flexed so that the legs are not locked but springy at the joints of the knees and hips. As the breath rises, feel the earth beneath the feet and how the feet are supported by it. While inhaling, draw the force not only from the base of the spine but from the earth that supports you. Feel how the power flows upwards and sustains the basic energy of the body and spirit flow, just as the physical earth supports the feet. With each indrawn breath, feel this connection reaching ever deeper into the earth-flow below, and with each exhaled breath, feel the energy disperse through and outward from the body through the crown, for there is fire within the center of all things which is the living fire and energizes all who realize their connection with it.

Once the base of this flowing fire is realized and all is in peaceable accord, step lightly then to the ball of one foot or the other. Allow the weight of your body to shift into balance with this movement and be aware of this as it is done. Notice that the flow of the fire is not interrupted by this, but shifts and modulates to accommodate this shift. You are part of this flowing fire and it is the very song and essence of true life. Step gently onto your other foot, and feel the rippling flow modulate through and from your body. As each step is taken, feel this grounded connection between heaven at the crown and earth at the base. Feel how you are suspended safely and in harmonious accord with the flow of the Universe. Now, as the fires flow through you feel their context and consistency. Let them flood the senses. Savor their textures and continuities; in this is a subtle and powerful song. Their pulse beat is kin to that of the heart song. Feel how you resonate with it as one string of a harp resonates to the note of all the other strings. Move gracefully within this flowing song. Allow it to enter you and become one with it. Flow it generously outward from you until you have become a center of radiance along its path. You are suspended like a child within its mother's womb in complete accord with the greater flow of her body. Know that this never ceases.

Only the awareness of the condition may be overlooked. This is the true access of channeled power, the earth magic, and what is called by some the Dragon's Back. Repeat this process consistently. Do this daily as a part of your preparation, resting afterwards, to unify the flow of energy and bring about balance both within the self and in continuity with the greater whole. In directed work, this flow of energy may be cycled through the hands via the heart center as has been explained to be both the balm of the healer and the weapon of the warrior.

As power is drawn upward and through the body, it is raw energy having no identity or form. It is by the will of the spirit alone that it is channeled, formed, and directed. As you raise this force and dance to its song, practice this modulation of the will. Envision changing its color as it passes between your hands and outward through your head. Envision it as warmer or cooler. Hear with your mind's ear how it can hum softly or crackle with static. Experiment with changing its texture and form until you can do this comfortably with little or no effort.

This is the Dance upon the River of Life. As you partake of its flow, you also contribute to and join with it, realizing that you are in harmony with it, for the River of Life is the ongoing and ever-renewing song of creation. The Song of the River is the blending of all various songs and notes of the energy helixes in this creation. Your body is part of this stream as is your spirit, for material reality is created from the knowledge and reality of spirit. All things are part of all other things in this way.

Mastery of this practice will not be accomplished in a moment but is a result of disciplined growth through work and practice. Let this growth take place gradually within you on a daily basis within the course of your meditations. Each day raise these energies gently to the point at which they are comfortable and harmonious within you, otherwise, the centers become overworked. Practice until changing the shape and color is an effortless joy attained without force, gracefully, as a dance within the flow of music. As this force passes through you, it cleans out resistance and left over energies in the course of its flow. Should this process cause excessive fatigue or pain in any measure, unpleasant headaches, or dizziness, slow the pace of the work. Return to the first exercise until the weariness is passed, for these symptoms are indicative that the vital centers of the body are being over driven and to continue without heed would be to court harm. However, it is not unnatural to experience a gentle light-headedness or giddiness that soon passes. This is the natural result of the clearing process that unaccustomed lightness and vitality return to the functions of the body and spirit. Do not misunderstand and try this newly found strength too much. There is the tendency to want to do mighty deeds with this. Instead, integrate this strength into your daily pattern of activities so that this invigoration will be sustained and have its fullest healing and developmental influence.

CENTERING

Imagine the hub of a wheel. The spokes of the wheel extend from it and attached to them is the rim. As the hub turns the spokes are in constant motion and the rim is in contact with the ground, so that the vehicle moves forward along the ground. However, the hub is relatively still. It is its firmness as the center point of this motion that allows the rest of the motion and transference of energy to take place and travel to result because of the action of the wheel. Your center is the hub of your wheel. It is from this center that the motion of your work must originate while the center itself remains fixed. If the action of the wheel were to originate from any other point than its center, the entire motion and resultant action of the wheel becomes eccentric and uneven; forward motion is greatly impeded.

All things begin from the center. Just as any dance must move outward and around the dancer's center of balance, so your energy work will always extend from your inner center. It is not a location or place of physical nature, but a point of consciousness. This place inside of you is immovable and unchangeable. It is the core of your being that is pure identity without personality, emotion, or other qualification. It is the spark of light within you that is the extension and reflection of the universal light. Because it is part of the universal light, it cannot be changed, altered, diminished, or damaged. We often hear the term "having lost the center" or "not working from the center." This happens when an individual is working from some other position in his or her reality. It can come from allowing the emotions to rule the actions. It can also happen when the intellect rules the actions. It can happen when the individual accepts another individual's reality other than his own. Emotions, intellect, physical perception, and conflicting reality are all spokes on the wheel, rather than the hub. They can be large, moving, and impressive while the hub is small and still. Because of these things, they appear to be much more important and valid than the small, still hub. Nevertheless, it is the hub alone that is the transfer point of all energy to the wheel and consequently it is the hub alone that is ultimately responsible for the forward motion of the vehicle.

Integrity of the center is an important concept to recall in daily life as well as in any working practice. It is easy to become swept away by the force of feelings, the dictates of logic, the demands of the physical or the force of someone else's needs or opinions. We are not saying that you should not consider someone else's feelings or opinions, nor are we saying that you should disregard you own state of mind, feelings or body. We are saying that these are only elements or extensions of a greater and more central reality and it is this reality that powers your work. It is important to maintain the quiet and powerful center within you so that sensory, emotional and informational input can be evaluated while being kept in perspective and proportion.

Your center is an important concept as you begin your journey as a practitioner. You will be working with energies and concepts that can arouse powerful reactions within you. It would be easy to allow yourself to be swept away with the intensity of these reactions and lose sight of the focus and purpose of your work. For example, as a healer it is necessary to have compassion for the subject you are healing. However, it is important to maintain an objective distance so that the impaired energies of your subject do not become entangled with your own energies. As a healer or practitioner, you should not absorb the negativity or damage of your subject. You may manipulate those energies; you may cleanse them, and use your own energies to bolster them and their supporting systems. Empathy is a valuable tool to use to perceive the cause of your subject's unwellness, but you should never merge with the one you are aiding in a total blending of energy patterns. Perception does not mean absorption or symbiosis. It requires objectivity that is inherent in working from your own center.

❀ - MEDITATION ON CENTERING

(Note: To accommodate the difficulties of a written text, marks have been placed at each point where a pause is necessary. --- At these points, the student should pause and make certain that the information given has been experienced and understood. Take as long as you like or feel necessary at each of these points so that the full benefit may be gained from these guided journeys. Before beginning, read each meditation carefully making sure that you understand what will happen and all of the words that will be used. Also, know that none of these meditations will take more than one hour of time and that when this time has elapsed you will awake and be fully conscious, rested, and alert.)

Return to the beginning section on the breathing. From a sitting posture go again to the singular dance of balance and breathing. Intensify this exercise. Feel the energies you are raising surround the body, as they flow around and through you in harmonious balance. Be aware and observe these energy flows. See how they are as the petals of the flower having the center at the heart. Be aware of your physical center of balance and how it coincides as well as how it differs from the energy center of balance. Now, as you move within this flowing force, see yourself as surrounded by a sphere of glowing white light. It is thinner than cloud yet stronger than lightning. This is your personal area of power radiation. It surrounds your immediate area of influence as the skin of your body surrounds your flesh. Now become aware that around you there are other energy spheres. Some are larger, some smaller. Concentrate on the difference between your own and the others. You reach out and encounter them with this energy as though testing bath water with the tip of your finger. Observe their qualities. Some are dense; some are pleasant. Some are thin and fragile. Some are almost opaque in their degree of intensity. Notice how easy it is to alter these spheres by the extension of your intentional flows. Darkness here or there can be lightened and brought into harmony with itself. Notice that another one has a spot too bright which can be smoothed and soothed to blend with itself. Notice that although you may interact with these things, you yourself are not altered by them. They pass near you, but not through you. They touch you, but do not join you. Know that this is the true nature of interactive energy. It is only through your own volition that these things may encounter and interact with you. You need not allow interaction or invasion unless you wish it. You are singular and separate. It is your nature and healthy state of being to be aware of this state of separation or individual integrity. You may interact as you choose. You are only interacted with as you permit. The lights and flowing energy that surround you are yours alone and are not the purview of any other except yourself. See yourself as a whole and completely at peace within yourself. See your energies as belonging to you and under your control and direction. It is true that you may allow this energy field to be interacted with if you wish. You need not allow your integrity to be violated. You have been and are continuing to develop your senses to be aware of interactions in order to judge them according to their true nature and to alter them according to your own needs and the demands of any given situation.

Thus, you see yourself as you dance with the breath - whole and harmonious, aware and in control of your energies and your perceptions. Repeat this exercise whenever it is possible. Recall these procedures when interacting with groups of people. Reinforce your own ability to turn away energies that are invasive or impinging, and to manipulate in a positive manner those that are in need of assistance. Accept those which are positive in nature for the pleasure and strength in them. Let them flow with you but do not internalize them except for those which you truly wish.

SHIELDING

As you begin to work with the stones and energies, you will find yourself becoming increasingly aware of energies on many levels. Some of these energies are pleasant, while others are not whether they are the random impulses of other people's thoughts and emotions, the chaotic energy of an urban environment, or the deliberate intrusion of someone else's intentions. It is necessary to have the ability to shield oneself from unnecessary or unwanted energies. You should be able to hold these energies at a distance so that you can examine or manipulate them if you need or wish to, or deflect them back to their source or to the universal pool of energy. This process has been described as shielding, but this term is misleading. To manipulate energy, you must be able to meet it and not hide or seal yourself away from it. In this way, you will remain at peace with yourself, the work, and the world around you. This is an extension of centering and this knowledge and ability to work from your inner integrity is the keystone and foundation of safety and inner peace.

We will begin with a practice of centered breathing. Remember that this centered breathing should be continued on a daily basis all the time. This centering and shielding on a regular basis will be pivotal to the health and well being of the spirit and the flesh which houses it and we do encourage its practice most strongly.

❀ - MEDITATION ON SHIELDING

While in the process of meditating and embarking upon the field of clouds, see yourself as surrounded by the light of which the clouds are made. This may be very pleasant for it is soft, cool, and soothing to the touch. Draw forth from the clouds the rainbow as you drew it forth before. This is a pleasant and resilient flow of color and energy that is the same as the energy within you. You feel the answering kinship within yourself as though a familiar friend greets you. — As you draw these energies forth see it become a shining sphere in your hands that grows larger and larger as you blow your breath upon it. — It stretches and grows until it is as transparent as a soap bubble. It is as light as a whisper. It flexes and glimmers in the light of the surrounding clouds. — Now draw it around you so that you are within the rainbow bubble. You may stand, sit, or stretch at length whichever is most comfortable. Let the bubble conform to your posture. — Feel how pleasantly it buoys you up. You may ride within it and direct it wherever you wish. Feel how flexible it is. — Now you see a light. You draw towards the light to find out what it is. As you draw nearer, you find that it is growing hotter and hotter. The warmth you feel is unpleasant. — You still wish to examine the light source, but its excessive heat drives you away.

Now you examine your bubble. What can it provide you with? You begin to manipulate it until the side towards the light begins to become denser and a little darker like the back of a mirror and yet still perfectly transparent - like a pair of dark glasses. You notice the temperature inside has immediately grown cooler and is now quite pleasant. The light is no longer painful in its intensity. You are aware of its colors and its ever shifting, rippling nature but it does not burn you or blind you as you grow closer to its source. You are almost upon it now. Its radiance is beautiful and lively in its variations. You can see how the clouds roll and turn around it as though churned by its intensity, but you feel no discomfort at all. The bubble is constantly conforming to shelter you from its unpleasant effects while remaining clear and supple to allow examination. — Now reach your hand through the skin of the bubble. You want a little piece of the light to examine and experience. Not the whole thing which seems too large to be dealt with. Just a tiny piece to look at. See how easily the skin of the bubble parts to allow your hand to pass through it as you quickly take one little piece of the light and draw it back inside. Yes, that is better. This small piece is warm but it does not burn; it is bright but not blinding. It is large enough to study but small enough to handle. Now you may manipulate it and play with it. See how it flutters around the ball like a butterfly. See its shades of color in all their variety. Smell its perfume. Feel its flickering texture with your fingertips. Let it ripple in your hands like water. When you are through looking at it, put it back through the wall of the bubble. Now look around you. It has left no changes, no residue, no odor, and no energy of any kind.

The changing rainbow bubble may protect you as long as you maintain its existence. Know that it is there even when you arise from your meditations. It acts as a shield automatically and is always subject to your conscious control as long as it is in place by your conscious will and intention. Its rainbow light is as your own internal rainbow white light and is subject only to your own will. Reinforce this meditation as you desire, but always be sure that this thought is in place with you. Meditate again, but instead of fire, using the image of ocean waves, and depths; use also torrents and gusts of wind, depths of earth and bedrock. All things are subject to your will in this realm. Do this exercise until you are assured of your center of protection. For always this rainbow shield radiates from the light center at your heart Chakra. It will become as an inherent part of your nature. It will never cut you off and away from that which you wish to feel and experience. It will only provide a sort of buffer which may protect you from unwanted overwhelming stimuli until you wish to change your intake perceptions. You will be aware of everything you need and wish. You will not, however, be violated nor impinged upon by those things that you do not wish. Nothing can creep up on your "blind side" for the bubble has no "blind side", being a perfect sphere and uniform throughout.

CHAPTER 2

THE HUMAN ENERGY SYSTEM COMPLEX

At the center of all things, there is one singular Prime Source that is all without differentiation. As the Prime became self aware and manifested itself, Universes were created as reflections of it. All Beings are its reflections, and all things within all Universes no matter how great or small. It does not matter how simple or complex, each entity or spirit is a unique reflection of the Prime Potential. Each Universe is different, and it is the nature of each separate Universe that determines how the Prime will manifest within it. When Spirit enters this Universe, it manifests as pure energy. It is complete and contains within itself all possible expressions of that energy. In this Universe, energy manifests as vibration, that is, frequency and wavelength. As this energy manifests as physical matter, it slows and changes its vibration. As this occurs, it is broken into its component separate energy signatures behaving very much like light striking a prism and spreading into a rainbow or spectrum containing all the basic colors contained within that clear light.

The degree of stimulation/resistance the energy encounters is determined by the nature of the physical form the spiritual energy inhabits and the resulting diversification of vibration is caused in two ways. One way is determined by the nature of the form itself, for example, whether the form is a stone, an earthworm, a plant, or a human being. The physical form slows the energy down, changes it, and causes the energy to adapt itself to the constraints inherent in any substance existing within the laws of this universe. This gives the energy its basic pattern. The second way that follows the first depends on the general state of being of that form, that is, its physical well being, its perception of its surroundings, if any, and also its mental and emotional conditions resulting form these perceptions.

Color is the way these energy signatures can be best described. Color is a function of wavelength and frequency and is, therefore, a form or expression of energy. Color is the expression of energy without form, it is pervasive, and it exists, whether optically perceived or not, as an operant force. It acts on and reacts with the body, mind, and spirit according to the nature of its expression. This determines the strength, clarity, and balance of each center both in itself alone and in its relation to the other centers.

In human beings, the pattern of energy signatures is called the chakra system and the levels of awareness. Other forms will have other patterns according to their nature.

Every individual is a channel for conducting the universal power and life force. As you practiced and observed in your beginning meditations and exercises, the body and its energy systems act as a channel for the constant flow of this universal life energy. On this plane, the individual exists at a balance point between the slower moving, denser energies of the primal life forces that activate the physical drives, and the faster moving vibrational energies of the spiritual etheric energies. The slower moving energies enter the main flow of the energy system at the base of the spine. They are transferred along the spinal axis, and accelerated by each successive chakra center until they emerge through the crown center at the higher spiritual vibration rate to connect with the greater celestial/spiritual life force. At the same time, the faster moving etheric energies are entering through the crown and are modulated, slowed and condensed. They pass downward along the same channel until they pass out of the base of the spine and connect with the primal life fire. This double cycle flow is in constant motion, forming the double helix energy system around the human form. This is a balanced system allowing each individual to exist in harmony with this universe. Is connects each individual to the basic life force that drives and maintains each life form on this plane. No matter how simple or complex each organism is, each derives its vitality from the primal fire energy, and the spiritual energy that is the life force of all creation.

These energy centers are known as chakras. The number of chakras depends on the nature and complexity of the organism. In living creatures that have a central spinal column, they are located along its length at the points where the major energy meridians intersect. The energy centers of the human body are the manifestation of the spectrum of spiritual energy refracted through the physical form. The presence of the centers is an active indication of the Life Level of that organism. Their pattern is an indication of the way in which that organism is attached to the primal energy sources of the Universe and the strength or weakness in the way the individual relates to that energy. It is the clarity and balance of these centers that determines the individual's strength, health and state of mind.

The power of these centers can be used to heal the body and the spirit that resides within it; they can also be used to express power from the energy system of the body to act on the world around the individual. To the degree that an entity differs from or fails to manifest a total balance of spectrum energy, he or she becomes separated from the Prime. This is seen as illness or insanity on many levels. The purpose of healing is to realign this individual so that he or she returns to the fullest potential to exist within the unrestricted flow of this universal life force.

We want to make it very clear about the chakras and the nature of their energy as it pertains to the conscious awareness of all living beings. The combination of the seven chakra points makes up an individual's distinctive energy harmonic pattern. No two are alike and it is the art and science of working to adjust and clarify these seven singular energy centers and the way in which they make a harmonic resonance pattern that we refer to as healing. This harmonic resonant pattern gives the individual his or her location in the physical world, much in the same way a combination of lines drawn from side to side in a box determine a specific point or location within it. It is this harmonic signature that shapes the way that an individual moves on all levels of consciousness and gives him or her the tools necessary to confront his or her karma and move towards his or her life purpose and ultimate destiny. It is the pattern of this harmonic that in turn forms either a further harmony or dissonance with other individuals so that a variety of associations such as love and hate are formed. This has a great deal to do with the recognition signature patterns that are the way individuals recognize and identify one another from one lifetime to the next. It is through this harmonic interaction with persons and circumstances that an individual adjusts and moves in this world and, in response to these complex stimuli, the individual's own harmonic energy is changed. This is called learning and growth.

It is through this harmonic that individuals remain synchronized into this Universe's framework of linear time and sequential physical experience. It is by the information here we hope to give you the tools you need to be a more active participant in your own growth and, hopefully, your evolution. However, we also want to clarify that this harmonic pattern is the signature of the individual's location and relationship to this universe. This is similar to your address and telephone number. It gives you the coordinates of the physical vehicle you are using to relate to this universe but it is not your identity any more than your address or your telephone number are your identity. They are the way you locate your residence. The chakra system is the way you locate yourself in time as well as space.

In this universe, there is a scale of perception of Time. Nothing exists outside of perception here. The state of absolute existence is not relevant to this topic. So there is the scale in which you perceive time. At one end is the absolute infinity of pure spirit. This extends throughout creation as immortality, and infinity of awareness, pan-determinism. Then at the other end of the scale there is the absolute finite, the single locus point of consciousness, an absolute concept of Now. This corresponds to your crown and base chakras respectively. Time in these states cannot be perceived. However, as the states change through the chakras, the nature of the perception of time changes. Time appears to slow and become compressed. This perception is determined by the vibration states of the chakras. Time actually does not change in this case, but your perception of it does, as if seeing the same scene through differently shaped lenses. This is where energy states touch on the waveform of time here and it is at the point where the two touch that perception is possible. Of course, since the energy state of each chakra is different, the perception will vary. Time itself becomes compressed and appears to be fluid. It is at each of these points that the relationship of time and matter becomes discernable. It is by the density of time that the state of matter will vary according to the perception dictated by the nature of the separate chakra centers. Consequently, as your perception of it changes so does your concept/construct of reality, and therefore your ability to manipulate and exist with the reality.

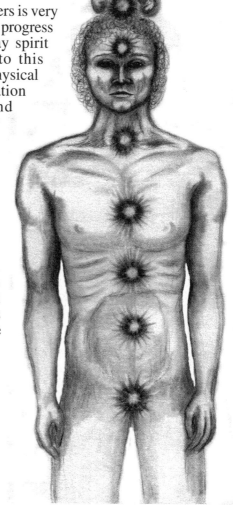

Understanding of the chakra centers is very important in the development and progress of your work. They are the way spirit connects to and interrelates to this universe. The chakras govern physical health and well being, information gathering and processing and emotional health. They are your key to the awareness of time, memory and change that are the critical elements of the cohesion of this universe and your relationship and place in it. Without the chakra centers, spirit has no means by which to fully interact with part of this universe and can only observe without action. The chakra centers are also the way in which Humankind expresses itself, relates and is connected to the world outside the body.

RED & ROSE

BASE – PRIMAL

CREATION / SURVIVAL

I AM

As energy enters the system at the base of the spine, it corresponds to the vibration of the color red. Its energy is the primal life force that drives and maintains physical substance and dictates connection to a specific form of short duration. It is the entry point of the Earth Fire and the vital connection to healing energy, strength, and vitality. If this source is limited or impaired, the general health and stamina of both the body and spirit is limited. We say both because it is through the awareness and vitality of the physical form that spirit interrelates with this universe and, as the body is impaired, so is the spirit impaired from interaction through it. In addition, no matter how well made a machine may be, if its source of fuel and energy is limited, constricted, or damaged, then the machine will not function to its capacity. This center manifests as instinct for survival, self-preservation, and procreation. At this center, there is no consciousness of time. There is no realization of cause and effect - no sense of other outside the self. All experience through it exists in the constant Now without awareness of past circumstance or future consequence.

The red ray is often misunderstood and is characterized as primarily aggressive, assertive, and sexual. However, its primary function is intensely life affirming. This is a joyful center involved with creativity and creation. The base chakra is the entry point of the body's system for the life sustaining energies of the planet and the Universe. It is the seat of the physical energies of health and well being. It is the power center behind all actions of healing and renewal, for without this primal life drive, there would be no will to live, no birth, and no healing.

The essential quality of the red ray is creation for it is at this point that unspecified energy enters the visible spectrum and achieves the form of color. In this same way, it enters the physical sphere of the body and manifests as the Primal Life Drive. In all species, this manifests as the drive to procreate and defend the self, which is to sustain and continue physical existence. In sentient forms it manifests further as the drive to create, form and change the environment. This is also a form of self-defense, for by adapting the environment to suit specific needs, the individual secures more stable and benevolent surroundings in which to live. Creation is an act that is assertive and aggressive because it recognizes no boundaries. Its business is expanding what is possible. Its aspect is the curiosity of invention and the realization that all things are possible.

Red is the first manifestation of light in the visible spectrum. This is forthright, aggressive and assertive energy manifesting as pure power in action unqualified by other considerations. It does not recognize boundaries or restrictions. In all expressions, this may be said to be the most powerful of the Life Rays, for it is pure action and assertion of survival. The red current flows at the heart of the Tree. This is Primal Life in its purest form, the power of both the Creator and the Destroyer, the Blood of Being. Its purpose is to explore the limits of what is possible. In its negative form, its aggressive nature is exhibited as anger, rape, and rage.

The red ray does not draw on reason but on primal drive of impulse for survival. It is by this force that the badger defends her young and also why the hounds pursue her. This is the creature that turns at bay, whether stag or Man, and knows no denial or defeat save that of Death.

Do not let your heart manifest this ray without the balance of others, for without Love and Reason, this is the ray most prone to destruction. This is because energy at this point of the self is not aware of others either in the sense of objective cause and effect or in the broader sense of compassion. All drives at this point center on the self and the will to survive. With the mediating qualities of the higher self, it is the power of the moment of birth. By it, the female brings forth her young and by it, the Spirit is bonded to the Flesh. This alone enables survival. Use this ray wisely, for there is no other so potent in any working or power. However, know and never forget that in excess this will destroy you. This is because its pure force is ungoverned, and the will that drives it to the exclusion of all others or that uses it as the primary carrier will, in turn, be burned by it and, in the end, be fit for no other purpose. Rare is the spirit that can turn from this path, and grievous are its wounds to heal in this event. This is true not only of the Destroyer, but of the Builder as well, and for this reason must the Warrior forever strive to perpetuate the balance of his nature and practice the disciplines both of forbearance and of healing and creation. Consider this in our discussions of the path of the True and Perfect Knight and thus you shall know that the Arts of Grace in this path are not without reason. Great good may be done with this ray, but recall always that this is a path of great danger.

ROSE

The color rose is closely allied to the red ray but with some subtle differences. It also centers in the base chakra and represents a slightly different manifestation of its vibration. The nature of the rose colored ray is the primal drive expressed as the Urge to Life. This is not only overt sexuality, although that is its most obvious manifestation.

More completely, this energy pulses from the ever-flowing stream of life energy that is the sustenance of the Universe. It is drawn through the soles of the feet and may be guided to energize and strengthen all other centers. It originates where a connection is made to the source of life and energy and power. Through the channels of sexuality, this energy may be guided to enliven the Life Force of the Being when all other means have been exhausted, because this is the base and beginning of self-awareness. It is also the crucible of consciousness and it is on this drive that all others have their foundation. It is through this focus that Man has perpetuated himself as a race both physically and emotionally. Through this channel, Love, as well as Life is first expressed. This is primitive instinct in its basic form but should not be denied, for that basal entity is always within the body and spirit from its beginnings to its finish. All these expressions are resident within the individual. This ray is unique in that it may be the channel of the charging of the other centers. As its life gives life to the whole Tree, it does not alter or slant the nature of these centers or channels but strengthens them according to their own nature.

Be aware that in focussing this ray the practitioner must take responsibility for all manifestations of its strength. There is great power in it to heal and to harm. Its effects may be great or subtle, and its force must be wisely used and with circumspection. Note also that, to the degree that one takes, one must also give. The full cycle of energy must be achieved for this energy to remain in healthful balance for all parties involved. When balanced in harmony with green, this may be a highly potent force, charm, and one of great honor. Recall this as the Analogy of the Rose

---

ORANGE - GOLDEN

BELLY

CAUSE & EFFECT

I ESTABLISH / I DEFEND

The second chakra resides in the belly slightly below the navel. It corresponds to the vibration of the color orange. This is the seat of individual identity and self-assertion, because it is at this point that a recognition and realization of others occurs. While the base chakra mandates self-defense and preservation, the belly chakra motivates the defense of others whether they be offspring, mate, family or village. It is at this point that an awareness of time begins, of consequence of action and of cause and effect.

Orange is the color of the archetypal sun that banishes the darkness in Man's beginning and the heart's darkest night. This is the brave heart of the Lion in defense of her young. This is the energy of hearth and home, the love of young, and the safety of the dwelling. This is the Right Courage of the Warrior when his cause is just. It is, therefore, the true joy of selfless sacrifice to a just and noble end, not mean pointless sacrifice. In this ray lies purification and renewal.

YELLOW

SOLAR PLEXUS

INSTINCT

I ANTICIPATE / I ADAPT

The third chakra centers at the solar plexus and corresponds to the vibration of yellow. The energy at this center defines the intuitive/instinctive response to external stimuli. In animals, this center appears as herd or pack awareness. It is not a rational center. It determines reaction before conscious thought. This is combined with the intuitive/instinctive reaction to subliminal stimuli - that is, stimuli that are received in a non-rational form, the input of the many senses by-passing the analytical functions of mind. It is here that change is anticipated through sensitivity to rhythm and flow. This is the first sense of predictability and anticipated affect of cause. In higher life forms with more complex rational processes, this center also processes the reaction to aesthetic stimuli. The reaction to art forms, color, sound, and rhythm that translate as emotional responses begins here. Conversely, the impulse to translate emotional states into static forms, that is, art forms rhythm and music, is a correspondent harmonic of this center.

Yellow is the color of sunshine and joy. This is the ray of the Eternal Child at play. The light banishes the darkness of the spirit and brings forth the day of new beginnings. This is the power of laughter in the heart and mind, because yellow anticipates change by drawing on knowledge of previous patterns of stimuli. This is not memory in the conscious sense, but an awareness of cycles of change that, in turn, predicates that no condition is static. In this way yellow anticipates and adapts. It is through this center that the organism can hold the consciousness of the light even in times of darkness, knowing that this is part of the cycle of experience.

Do not underestimate its virtue nor take it lightly, for its healing power is great indeed. It is the sovereign charge against sore harm caused by grief and fear. It is the natural enemy of all things that dwell in darkness, and its image is the laughing youth arising in glory as fair as the Dawn. This is the heart of Dancing and Song - not its creation for that lies elsewhere - but the spirit that engenders it. Its power, when expressed, can burn in brightness as the lightening, and its strike may be as quick and sure. Yet, its influence may be as gentle and sweet as the breath of a morning breeze. Indeed, the yellow ray is the Power of Hope expressed as the power of the Mind. This influence and power often leads to change and in this it is manifested as inventiveness and all things most clever and the joy of the Spirit in those things which are unique. It is curiosity in its most positive sense, and all those capacities of mind that see the world as new and fresh. Its dangers are indulgence and superficiality, and this tendency to lightness should be balanced with other energies to give it strength, depth and durability.

GREEN

HEART

COMPASSION

I COORDINATE / I UNIFY

The fourth chakra rests at the heart and resonates to the vibration of the color green. It has a strong secondary harmonic to the rose and purple vibration. It is through the heart that the impulses and information of all the other centers are balanced and processed. It stands at the center, poised between the lower chakras of instinct and animal, physical vitality, and the upper ones of the higher reasoning and spiritual identity. The heart center stands between them, mediating between their functions and allowing them to communicate. The voice of the heart center is love and compassion. The heart is unique in the function and ability to heal or harm the system and the other chakras in it. It expresses energy as well as modulates it. It is through the heart that this work progresses.

Green is the ray of coordination. Its position in the body's spectrum is the heart chakra where it stands at the center midway between the Animal of the lower centers and the Angel of the upper. It is the combination of the yellow ray bringing the reactive awareness of the lower centers into anticipation and adaptation and the blue ray of the seer and teacher that relates the higher orders of vision and analytical intelligence with the world on this plane. The green center is where all energies meet and join so that they can be experienced and expressed on this plane. Green is the essence of healing because all forces meet within it and are harmonized by it. All things may be resolved here because this is experience without judgement - the true essence of compassion.

Green is the ray of regeneration on both a spiritual and physical level. This may be true in many ways, for the heart draws all energies and potentials of the individual into one harmonic expression. It is the hub of the balance of these expressions generating the ever-springing force rebirth and renewal. This is the ray of selfless nurturing - creativity without possessiveness. At this point, the higher self experiences life in its fullest sense through the physical mechanisms of the body. Most often, it is attributed to artists and gardeners, as theirs is the green ray in its purest form. They participate in the ongoing unfolding of the beauty of the Universe, aiding Creation while releasing their works spontaneously to become new parts of the Universal Whole. They attain and amplify life in many aspects as they do this. These agents most closely mirror the primal energy - first Creation, first Postulate of Being - and in this activity most closely recalls their purpose as Beings interacting in this Universe. It is the nature of life to bring forth life and to manifest itself through Creation.

This is the ray of the Mother and may thus be extrapolated to be the ray of the Earth for it connotes the ever-renewing bounty of the physical world. This ray will restore and renew all that draw on its bounty. It is the fullest expression of Spirit united with Form.

BLUE

THROAT

COMMUNICATION

I SEE / I ENVISION / I TEACH

The fifth chakra is positioned at the throat level. Its vibration corresponds to the color blue. As the solar plexus center focused response to subliminal physical stimuli, so the throat expresses the reaction to mental and spiritual stimuli and perception. It is through this center that mediumship and divination find their voice being the expression of higher information translated into language. This center is also the vehicle of the mind translating processed input of the critical and logical facilities into communication. It assembles; it responds; it processes as expression. Thus, it is also the seat of expressed will and intention, carrying the force of higher personality manifesting the impulse of the connection to spirit. It instigates manipulation and control of the environment brought forth by the will to mediate circumstance.

Blue describes the essence of communication by seeking to bridge the gap between two points. This creates a shared awareness. It is the means by which the spiritual essence of the higher chakras is first introduced into the physical world by speech. It is the power of the Seer because it is the vision of the higher planes translated and made available on this plane. It is the essence of the teacher because it is the highest level of interaction. Speech is as powerful an act as any other on this physical plane. It causes changes in the energies by the initiation of sounds that are physical vibrations, and by being the carrier of the mental and spiritual realities of the individual. Blue is the first point on the upward journey of energies that truly reaches beyond the insular self and connects with the ranges of mental and spiritual energies. It brings knowledge of the higher planes and the greater self into articulated form. Blue puts into communication and structured rationality both the inarticulate impulses of the lower centers and the spiritual and analytical essence of the higher ones. It is the path by which reality is shared and cultivated.

Speech represents a joining. It serves to mediate, to unify, and to provide a means of concrete expression. It is the first way that Spirit expresses itself in the form of sound in the physical universe.

INDIGO / VIOLET

BROW

MEMORY & THOUGHT

I ANALYZE / I COMMAND

The sixth chakra is seated in the brow, vibrating in correspondence to the color violet. This center focuses the functions of consciousness, logic, and reason. It is the center where spirit analyses the data of this universe. It articulates the input of the physical senses, and in its critical capacity evaluates and governs. Here, also, are the keys to stored memory. This is not the actual place where true memory is kept, but it is the gateway where it is accessed. It is through the mind center that memory is brought into consciousness and used as a rational tool to evaluate current circumstance. Consequently, it is said that time is a function of this center and is the anchor of spirit in this universe.

The violet ray performs the analytical sorting function. It processes sensory information into a form that the spirit can sense and by doing so creates a platform to enable both memory and response. It is through this structure that spiritual vision and instinctual impulse become ordered and it is in this way that objective extrapolation and memory are enabled. This is the spirit's key to time and collective resonance of linear experience. This is the first internal physical center and it is only natural that spirit should use this as its portal to organize its experience in accordance with the structure that binds this universe - Time.

This center not only initializes the spirit's anchor to the body by putting it in synchronization with the physical realm. It also entraps the spirit with the illusion of linear time. In an effort to use time as the sorting function of experience, linearity is imposed, thereby denying a viewpoint of seeing experience as simultaneous rather than cumulative. Although this provides a convenient link to data derived from experience, it limits the viewpoint of the individual to only what can be seen and experienced from one point at a time.

Violet is the union of the Purple of Majesty and the Blue of Will. This is the ray of understanding those matters that extend from and deal with the higher self and its relation to the Multiverse. The voice of the true inner self reaches the conscious self, and makes its knowledge available to the individual personality by this path. The voices of those resident on other planes may reach and communicate with those of this world by this path. This is the light of conscious understanding by which all things are made known.

It is not advisable to use the brow chakra as a portal to enable the spirit to leave the body, even for short periods. This portal should be established where the harmonic circuit of the energy is complete and conscious, that is, at the crown or the heart. It will overdrive the system and result in lengthy periods of imbalance. Use of this ray without total balance will overload the true system balance, for Man is a creature integrally interwoven with the energy systems of this universe. Should he attempt to mingle with those others without proper grounding here, he will loose his hold on the life energies of his body and thus bring his work to nothing.

The violet ray is the access to the combined recorded energy forms of the power workings of this universe and thus the gateway to others. Its access is as simple as the others for all things are ready and available to the Seeker. It should be accessed by reaching upward and outward from the base through the brow and crown rather than the reverse. Use this ray as a path by which to expand outward, not as a mechanism to bring things down and inward as is the tendency. If it is rightly used, the knowledge found will become a true component of the active understanding. If it is used incorrectly, the knowledge accessed will remain outside of the being, seen but not integrated into the frequency capabilities of that being.

PURPLE / DIAMOND WHITE

CROWN

CONNECTION

I AM

The highest center is located on the crown of the head slightly about the physical body. It corresponds to the vibration of purple with a secondary harmonic as white or clear. This is the entry point of pure spiritual energy into the physical universe, as the base chakra connects to the life fire that unites all physical creation. It is the seat of the godhead and the attachment to the immortal spiritual identity that is indefinable. It can reside in an infinite number of forms, states of manifestation, and has not yet reached the limitation of time. Its nature is infinite change through infinite stability. Not being limited by time or space, it can assume a higher viewpoint beyond the physical. It requires the physical as its vehicle and as its vehicle of expression and learning.

Just as the red ray exists in an area outside the range where the individual is cognizant of time, so its balancing counterpart, the purple ray, also exists in its own consciousness and existence in the awareness of the perpetual now and eternity. The red ray is the center of the individual self and the purple is the awareness of perpetual union with the greater universe. It is through the essence of this ray that a connection is made with the energies of other levels of being. It is also through this ray that the individual maintains his or her connection with the higher self, the group soul or consciousness and the greater beings on many other levels.

It is as necessary to the individual's survival, consciousness and well-being on all levels that this connection is clear and uninhibited as it is for the lower ray and centers to connect with the primal earth fire. The purple ray is the gate of spirit. Purple is the color of power and balance for it is the perfect joining of red, the primal animal drive, and blue, the pure expression of evolved higher will. Both are rays of great force and singular identity and, when joined in equal proportions, the force is balanced and complete. This may be understood as the metaphor for spirit incorporate in flesh, uniting the beast with the angel in perfect accord and balance. By purple, we mean royal red violet. It sits at the center and can work from both passive and active poles. It is as much dark as light, cool as warm, perfectly centered between white and black and all the rest revolve around it.

The Analogy of the Rose

*This is the great analogy and shall stand in place of much explanation
of many concepts which seem to differ but which in actuality do not. In
the Garden of Life, there is a rose that opens its blossoms to the light
of the sun and extends its perfumed splendor about the stirring air.
This radiant blossom sits on a bush that holds it upward into the glory
of the sun. From the green leaves and stems, the essence of life passes
into the blossom and from the darkness of the earth is this richness
drawn. By the blossom, the fruit is made and thus the continuation of
the plant is assured on the earth. Thus, the continuing unity is made
between heaven and earth, for without the sun's radiance the earth
brings forth nothing and thus is left only the light which burns without
purpose and the earth which is barren stone. The flower is also like
this. Without the bush the blossom receives no nourishment and falls to
the barren earth unfulfilled, and so the bush without the flower
achieves no continuance but lives for the season only and then passes
from creation.*

This is the eternal dance. This is the great mystery.

BALANCING THE CHAKRAS

Chakras are often discussed singly, as though they were completely separate from one another and had no interrelationship. This is extremely misleading. One center alone can not be adequately discussed or understood without including its relationship to the entire energy system. The centers are similar to individual organs of the body in that each has its unique function within the whole, but none exists alone unto itself. The healthy function of each one depends on the health and strength of the others in order to operate in balanced unity. The chakra centers represent significant events in a continuous flow of energy through the organism. It must always be kept in mind that each center is both a point on the complete flow of energy that connects every organism to the universal life force and a point within the internal harmonic of the body's internal balance. It is a sense of balance and proportion that we encourage. Rejoice in what you are as well as in what you would become.

In order to fully channel and manifest the Universal Life Force, the chakra centers and the channels that connect them must be open and in balance and harmony with this life force and with each other. All spirits manifesting on this plane exist within this flow of Life. To the degree that there is resistance to and blockage of this flow, an individual will fall out of resonance with the Life and will sicken and lose control of himself and the Universe in which he dwells. Most of the time this may be generally improved and remedied. An understanding of these energy centers is essential to any healing procedure and, indeed, to any working of power.

Imagine the human body as a helix of energy, a spiral that ascends, sometimes from the feet, but most usually from the base of the spine, centering in the heart and proceeding outward through the crown of the skull. The process of healing is the process of restoring the balance between and within the fields which has been lost through shock, injury, or illness, therefore, the complete field must be taken into account with equal consideration. Generally, trauma occurs on all levels at once. The purpose of healing is to raise each center to power and balance with all the others so that the entire system is one harmonious balance. Because of this strengthening and balancing process, an individual's awareness and sensitivity to the specific energy of each center will develop. Then, as mastery of this balance comes about, the energy of each separate center can be amplified and focused by the conscious will of the individual. The individual can work from the point of view of a particular center to manifest its energies and to express itself in that way.

Each Universe demands to be dealt with on its own terms and all events within that universe must behave within the parameters of its laws. In this Universe, the focused seat of the spirit is the body, for without physical means, the spirit has no means of expression. The spirit occupies a larger space than the body. In a healthy individual it permeates and surrounds the body like a cloud. Its emanations, its non-physical "senses", extend outward from it appearing like nested energy fields. This interaction between physical, emotional, mental, and spiritual perceptions is accomplished constantly one with the other. As the body fares, so the other levels of consciousness are affected. An injury, shock, or illness to the body causes the spirit to withdraw from the negatively charged currents of the affected area. This causes unbalanced power fields, impaired action, perception, and capabilities. The body, being deprived of the life energy of the Spirit, fails to heal fully and renews itself slowly and imperfectly. Without aid, this becomes a cyclical condition and must be causatively remedied to avoid severe and/or lasting impairment.

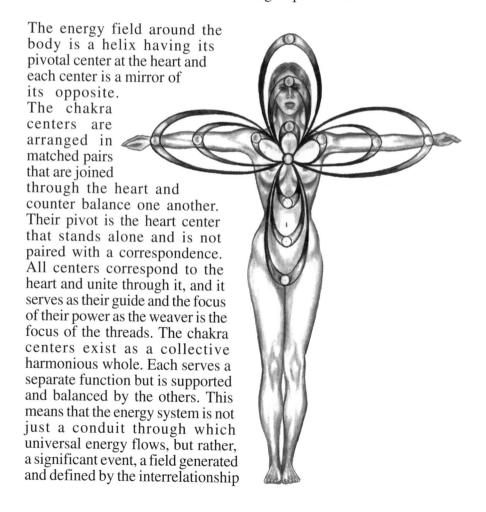

The energy field around the body is a helix having its pivotal center at the heart and each center is a mirror of its opposite. The chakra centers are arranged in matched pairs that are joined through the heart and counter balance one another. Their pivot is the heart center that stands alone and is not paired with a correspondence. All centers correspond to the heart and unite through it, and it serves as their guide and the focus of their power as the weaver is the focus of the threads. The chakra centers exist as a collective harmonious whole. Each serves a separate function but is supported and balanced by the others. This means that the energy system is not just a conduit through which universal energy flows, but rather, a significant event, a field generated and defined by the interrelationship and interplay of these component smaller fields.

To understand this system fully and to be able to work with its complex energies, it is always necessary to remember this. If a chakra seems to be blocked closed or stuck open, impaired or excessively energized, one must also consider how the centers on either side of it are effected and how its corresponding opposite must function in the balance.

THE BALANCE OF LIFE FORCE

Envision the feet as rooted to the ground by tendrils of light which come together at the heart, then three tiers of petals radiating from the heart in each direction. The base chakra at the base of the spine is the center of the primal will, that which is basal and instinctual, the fire of existence and procreation, the energy and survival. It corresponds to and counterbalances the crown chakra that is the highest seat of awareness that connects in the highest evolution to the primal light of the spiritual survival. As they are unified at the heart center, the resultant balance could be described as the Beast uniting with the Angel and a whole being is revealed. These two survival energies should balance each other to make up the composite whole definition of the individual's life force. This is because their combined level defines the survival level for the organism as well as the being's degree of connection to the physical vehicle and, consequently that being's effectiveness in interacting on the physical plane.

The analytical insight of the brow, joins with the assertive identity of the belly center. These two centers link the individual to the flow of linear time. Each center is involved with the understanding of cause and effect, and when unified by the heart center, the combination of the two results in active creativity and problem solving. Also, the combination of the qualities of the belly center that dictate assertion of the individual identity with those of the brow center defining individual perception together with the linear time linkage of both define the framework for specific individual personality. With this in mind, it becomes easy to see how the chains of karma are bound from one lifetime to another. By taking the resonance frequency of the personality as an anchor, the connection is stimulated across the time frame. Each lifetime that had a sufficiently similar resonant harmonic is stimulated. As the individual grows and changes with life experience, the resonance pattern is altered and different patterns are formed.

THE BALANCE OF

PERSONALITY, KARMA & TIME

In most individuals, the principle dominant pattern formed by these centers remains consistent, that is, the personality remains constant, and little change occurs on any deep level. This also gives the individual a consistent connection to those other lifetimes that resonate to a similar frequency and pattern that had no resolution or closure. This lack of resolution causes what could be described as a dissonant harmonic with the current lifetime pattern. When an individual reaches a peace, an understanding, a closure of these patterns, they cease to be held apart from that individual. As these patterns resolve, the energy that has held them in place releases and returns to the conscious control of the individual in the focal point lifetime. Nevertheless, as long as they are unresolved, these energy patterns remain. The brow is called the seat of memory only in part because it corresponds with the physical location of the brain. True memory exists outside the physical body and is accessed by the minute shifts in the individual's fields caused by the active stimulation of nerves and brain cells. This is how memory is carried from one lifetime to another. There are many variables to this degree of connection. More often than not, the individual is not consciously aware of being connected to these other patterns. However, with intention and meditation these connections can become activated to the point that they are living links of memory on a conscious level. The energy patterns are attached to sensory images containing information regarding the nature of the conflict. By using the essence, that is, the energy of the resonant connections, and by manipulating this energy and then by changing its nature through conscious will, the individual can unlock the energy that is bound up in these connections.

This is a complex issue, and one to which we will return in the course of this work, for there are many strands of energy binding individuals across their consideration of time and space. Certainly not all are dark and filled with extreme unresolved emotional states. Some are pleasant and constructive, but all are bound together. Time is a continuum. Other lifetimes that are activated in this way are reflections of the current focal point lifetime as are the endless reflections of paired mirrors replications and potential distortions of the central object that is reflected.

What we are saying is that a sufficiently similar resonant pattern will awaken the individual's awareness of the other lifetimes in which there were difficulties that remain unresolved. It is a function of memory whether it is on a conscious level or on an unconscious one. It is partly a means of survival awareness that this function exists. The individual carries these patterns across lifetime in an attempt to avoid painful situations and in order to learn how to resolve them. It is partly a function of learning and growth. When the conflict is resolved, the energy bound up in holding the pattern in place returns to the energy field of the focal lifetime. This also allows for the release of whatever fears, inhibitions, impairments, or limiting emotional, mental, spiritual, and physical states it has caused.

THE BALANCE OF EXPRESSION & ACTION

When the expression of the throat center is brought together with the adaptive rhythmic sense of the solar plexus center, it allows for the expression of feeling, the articulation and communication of emotion. This allows for the instinct to join the rational process and for a greater understanding to result from the interaction of individuals. That is, not only the ability to extrapolate results, but to plan for their execution. The combination of these two centers represents the individual's adaptation and interaction with the present time circumstance. This is his or her focal point. It is the anchor in current events and in the present lifetime of which all others are reflections. These centers represent the tools that the individual uses to interrelate on a real-time basis with surrounding conditions, individuals, and events. The solar plexus dictates anticipation and sensitivity to currents and causes. The throat dictates actions, will power, and self-assertion in the form of articulation. The throat is not only speech, but also the way in which the individual moves forward into life and society, connects, and expresses his or her nature, opinions, and feelings. It is the fountainhead of manipulation of surrounding circumstance. The solar plexus center provides the sensitivity of feeling to guide the throat. The throat provides the expression of action in response to this anticipation and sensitivity. The first pair is life force; the second is personality; this third pair is the way in which life force and personality move forward into the world and act on karma and learned information. Learning does not take place if the lesson cannot be practiced. It is through this pair that this practice takes place and invention acquires form.

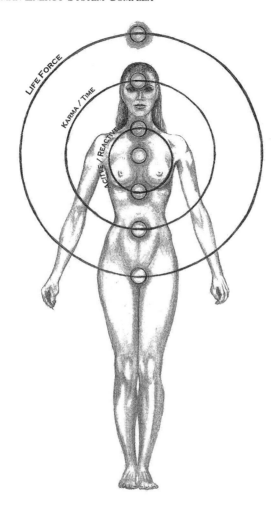

THE COORDINATION OF

THE HEART CENTER

The heart stands at the center of all energies and unifies the being into an integral whole. It acts much in the same way as the center of a gyroscope does. It is the point around which all these energies turn. An impairment of the heart chakra will adversely effect all the other centers. A clearing of the heart chakra will improve the interaction of all the other centers.

In general, when the practitioner intends to adjust the energy levels of one or more centers, it is advisable to observe the interaction of these centers with one another. When working to relieve headaches, it is also advisable to observe whether or not there is impairment in the belly center or base chakra. An impairment of the speech/will center can lead to stomach cramps and nervous digestion because as the ability to act according to feeling and instinct is limited or conflicted this sets up a nervous reaction. The solar plexus energies will try to override the blockage or impairment as its messages are seemingly ignored by its twin center. In another example, excessive concentration on the higher centers will inevitably result in a loss of function and sensitivity of the lower ones, just as an excessive concentration of gratification of the lower centers will eventually result in a clouding and impairment of the upper ranges.

However, this is not a situation that will result as an immediate cause. Many times, it takes a great deal of time for these results to manifest themselves as serious physical damage. This is why we recommend that the energy system be maintained by healthy habits on all levels. Good diet, exercise, meditation, and rest combined with pleasant and stress-free an environment as is possible within the limits and constraints of one's daily life - all these elements are important to the healthy maintenance of all levels of awareness.

THE HORIZONTAL AXIS OF
THE BODY'S ENERGY FIELD

There is a second helix that runs cross to the first, also centering in the heart and having its paired centers in the shoulders, elbows and the hands. The hands are twinned in the same manner as the poles of the vertical energies. They are opposite in their polarity and are the means by which the vertical force is translated into manifestation. The left hand (in right handed bodies) is the perceptive, intake, negative pole - passive and gentle used to steady and draw forth, while the right translates and broadcasts power, expressing energies in dexterity on all levels being the active instrument of the heart's generated light. These axes - horizontal and vertical - are not separate from each other. They are like the spokes of the wheel - separate but indivisible when considering the wheel itself as a whole. This is the horizontal axis - the shoulders, elbows, and hands.

At this time, as the age changes, humankind is returning in evolved awareness so that this axis is developed in many people, whereas in Ancient Days, only a few could use this power and were known as true priests, saints, and angels in honor of this miracle. Now, as Humankind is evolving with the stimulation of the new energies that are coming to this planet, many individuals will have the potential of developing the power of this axis as a completion of this balance. The development of the vertical axis alone is not enough to teach the balance and true expression of this power. However, cleanse and balance the vertical axis first so that the individual will be healthy, sane, and whole, then the horizontal power can become functional. The focused power of the vertical axis through the heart flows outward into use at the hands and appears as wings, to the second vision and can be directed according to the individuals intention.

IMPAIRMENT AND RESTORATION

OF THE BODY'S ENERGY FIELD

A body need not be physically perfect in order to evolve in the work. This may be a point in the being's Karma to overcome. This addresses the question of those with withered or missing limbs, excessive scar tissues about the brain and spine, organs damaged or missing altogether due to misadventure or deficiencies of birth, those who are blind, deaf, mute, or impaired in any other physical senses. By meditation and healing of the aura, that is, of the energy fields of the body, the Spirit may reenter and "recreate" the afflicted areas. Every individual is connected fully to the universal life force. An impairment of the physical body changes the arrangement and intensity of the nerve/energy centers involved, but on a deeper level, the continuum of life force remains unharmed. It remains, therefore, to acknowledged and intensify the connection with and consciousness of this greater force. This may not be easy because, not only is this an area of great memory of pain and shock, but also because the spirit has no reference point on which to base itself and establish this relocation. Take great care and love in this meditation. Flow the heart's power in the form of golden light as sparkling water into the affected area. Constantly reinforce this both in meditation and in daily waking consciousness, until the Spirit dwells constantly and consistently in wholesome balance. This will cause regeneration on all levels not only to restore spiritual power but to build physical health as well. This meditation may also be done in healthy persons to maintain their wholesome balance, because it relaxes and renews on all levels. It opens these power channels and realigns the position of the spirit with respect to the physical vehicle.

STATES OF AWARENESS

We have spoken briefly before about the levels or states of awareness and at this point we feel that we should clarify what is meant by this expression and expand on its significance. In addition to the series of chakras forming the individual's energy lattice, every individual is surrounded by a series of layered energy fields. These are sometimes referred to as auras and are perceived by sensitive individuals as radiant halos of light. They are the perceivable fields generated by the individuals connections to the physical plane and their state of brilliance, strength and continuity are direct indicators of how well that individual communicates and relates to the physical plane and its many stimuli. There are four different types of these energy shells - the physical, emotional, mental and spiritual level. Each can manifest a different pattern of light/energy depending on the state of health and well being of the individual. Each should be examined independently of the other before assessing the condition of the individual. Each affects and is in turn affected by the others in a continuous interaction and together they represent the ways in which the individual perceives and evaluates himself and his relationship to his surroundings. These four awareness states represent levels of sensory perceptions that allow the individual to orient himself, live and move about in, interact with and learn from the environment he or she inhabits. They encompass the states of reason, empathy, intuition, and instinct.

You should also understand that although these states of awareness seem ephemeral and subjective, they manifest in a physical way in the physical world both electromagnetically and bio-chemically. There is a tendency to regard the mental and spiritual states as higher or nobler than the emotions or the physical. This is so because these two states seem much more orderly and controllable than the others do. This perception is not necessarily correct and leads to a great deal of suppression and negligence of the needs of the body and the emotions while denying many of their subtle benefits and the essential state of their health. It requires all four levels of awareness and sensitivity working in balance and harmony with one another to provide the individual with a whole and balanced vehicle with which to operate on this plane. None of these states should be regarded as higher or nobler than any of the others. It is the use to which the individual puts the information received that is worthy of evaluation on that level. They are the tools with which you survive in your world. It is the quality of that survival that is the issue at hand.

The most basic of these fields is the aura of the physical body. It reflects the condition of the body's general state of well being and health and the state of its parts, that is, the organs and limbs. This field indicates the base-line level of health and survival. It is also the receptor for other energies and fields on that level. This is the seat of the information that prompts instinctive behavior and reaction. It is also this field that is refined and amplified to produce the physical healing energies. An injury to the body will be reflected in this field because it causes the field energy to flow unevenly and imperfectly as the energy withdraws from the afflicted area and then returns to prompt the body's healing functions. Physical illness is also reflected at this level by a more general dampening of the field. This field is often referred to as the vital life force, and without it the body is only so much bone and tissue without vitality. This is the animating force.

The emotions are the senses of the spirit, just as the body holds the senses of the mind. It is these senses on both levels that provide the information and stimulation that lead to growth and expansion. The two levels - spirit and body - reflect one another, and in this world walk hand in hand. The emotions are often strong enough to rule the individual with their intensity and as a consequence are misunderstood and sometimes feared. Just as well as intense pain and sorrow can overwhelm the individual and override the reason, so can intense joy or pleasure. An individual can easily allow him or herself to be swept away by feelings. Intense emotions can be as entrapping and beguiling as intense physical ones and the drive for emotional gratification can be as compelling as physical addictions. This is so because the emotions are transmitted within the physical individual in the physical form of biochemical reactions. The body's sensual stimulations also effect the spirit. Great emphasis is put on their control but very little attention is paid to what information they hold. Emotion is a tool for learning just as physical feeling and sensation are. Emotions are the way in which spirit experiences interaction with this plane. They can be even more potent than physical sensations but they should not be feared or avoided. Only by acknowledging the feelings can the individual come to know them and understand the nature and content of the information they bring. Only by accepting the range of what they are can spirit learn what they have to teach.

The mental body is the data gathering and processing facility. It collects, stores and organizes the impressions relayed to it by the senses of the body, emotions and spirit, thus rendering this information into a useful format. This mind is a tool for observation and calculation that learns by building conclusions from the analysis and categorization of this information. However, there is a tendency to give it too much credit and therefore excessive latitude in directing the course of action and the state of the feelings and emotions. This leads the individual to deny the validity of the other levels. The mental body can be overdriven by being asked to make decisions it is not qualified to make. It is not emotion; nor is it instinct, nor is it spirit. Yet, it is often pressed to act in their place. This causes stress from imbalance and as a result of this stress, overload. Like the physical and emotional bodies, the mental body can be overstimulated and overwhelmed. States that cause stress to the mental body lead to imperfect calculations and conclusions. This causes loss of memory or reliance on faulty conclusions. This gives the individual a darkened and distorted view of his or her surroundings.

The spiritual body is the most ephemeral of all and the least understood. This is because it is beyond the ability of the more physical senses to observe or describe. The best that can be done by the other three levels is to observe the results of its interaction in terms of feelings, sensations, and impressions. It reflects the connection point between the individual as he or she exists on the physical plane and the rest of that individual that exists on different planes and dimensions and the higher gestalt of spiritual entity that exists elsewhere and coincides with the physical plane. Spirit is the observer of the other three levels and is the communication transfer vehicle by which information regarding this plane is transmitted to the individuals other concurrent states. Spirit is also the interface that allows these states to interact on this plane.

ENERGY STATES

The chakra system creates the energy lattice that is the specific vibrational frequency of the individual. Each chakra in any given individual vibrates at a frequency that, while within the parameters for that center, is particular to that individual. The combination of all seven frequencies creates a harmonic that is equivalent to the key signature pattern of that individual. This is the individual's anchor parameter that holds him or her in place and in alignment with this plane. This is what gives that individual a particular locus in this plane allowing access the various energy states specific to this plane and enabling the state referred to as life here. The states of awareness represent the senses and communications vehicle of his or her specific vibrational energy state. Together they form the framework by which the individual exists on this plane and at any giving specified point of consciousness. The seven chakras manifest in each of the four levels of awareness giving a total of twenty-eight related energy levels. The combined harmonic pattern of these twenty eight levels is known as the energy system complex and its vibrational pattern is unique to the individual. This is referred to as the individual's key signature vibration.

You have wondered about reaching the other spiritual states to which you are connected and about bridging through time - which is a relative state dependent on the energy state of the observer. We have explained how time perception and orientation resides as a function of the higher chakras. It remains for the individual to alter the vibration pattern of one of those chakra centers beyond what is specific for this plane - shift it beyond this scale. By altering these states even by so small a degree beyond what it this universes anchor parameters, this allows the individual to move beyond the lattices known as time and dimension. It does not take much of a shift. The range is quite small. All you have to do first is release the belief in the absolute limitation of this state. Time and dimension are not prison bars, they are only the result of your current energy state. You do not even have to change it all. One node or two is enough when also altering the connection focus. What we mean by connection focus is that it is perfectly natural to be focused on the physical plane. That is, after all, what you are all about and why you are here. However, you tend not to move freely from one state of awareness or observation to another. Just because your attention is directed towards walking forward does not mean that you cannot divert your attention to what is behind or to the sides of you. Shift your attention to the spiritual mode for a moment and change the energy of the time sensing parameters that are already in place. You will be surprised at the ease of the shift and perhaps will be led to deny the validity of that shift because it was too easy. Think about this for a while, then come back to it.

✿ - *CHAKRA MEDITATION*

Relax and begin with deep breathing, as with the previous meditations. Place the body in a comfortable position, preferably reclining. Use a space that you have prepared that is free of discord and distraction. Be certain that you are well fed and well rested. Breathe deeply from the belly, draw the air into the body via the belly expel it slowly, and completely feeling the tension and cares of the exterior world drain out of the body. Breathe again deeply and exhale slowly and the unwanted thoughts and cares of the daily life unwind and disperse from the surface of the mind. Again breathe and exhale slowly and in measured rhythm. Feel how a pleasant stillness is growing within your mind as all cares and discomforts become distant and unimportant. With each breath, the body responds to this pleasant quiet. Continue breathing deeply and as you release each breath more of its tensions and fatigues unwind and disperse. The body becomes relaxed, at peace, more healthy and comfortable. ---

As the breathing continues and the body and mind relax, you know that it is safe and right to leave it for the moment. Begin your journey into the spirit and the energies within. --- You feel yourself sinking deeper and deeper as a pleasant comforting darkness surrounds you, cushions you like velvet. --- You drift pleasantly on the cushion of quiet darkness. ---

You slowly become aware that this darkness feels alive. You begin to feel moving currents within it. Look around you and see shimmers of pastel light. --- You listen to soft strains of music. --- You hear vague murmurs of voices. --- The darkness is growing lighter now and all around you is a softly luminescent glow. --- As you pause to experience the life and textures of this place, you see before you a large mirror whose surface is dark. This is the Glass of Seeing and on its surface may be reflected anything which you wish to look on. It may reflect events at any timeand in any place. It may speak with many voices. It is your reference point and focus at this time. Remember this Mirror, for you may return to it at any time for any purpose you wish. ---

Now, the surface of the mirror begins to glow and become clear, the mist across it thins and vanishes to reveal the figure of a human body standing erect and facing you. As you look closer, you realize that this is a reflection of your own body. --- See how it moves slightly as though alive and waiting at rest, for all things which are alive exist in constant quiet change from moment to moment. --- Now notice how this image is surrounded by a faintly shimmering glow. It is rather like a misty halo surrounding the entire form. This is the appearance of the current of life that surrounds and infuses all living things. You know that, because it is a reflection of your own body. It is the glow of life that surrounds you. ---

Now the body seems to grow transparent as though made of supple, flowing glass so that you may see inside it. --- Look there at the center how the heart beats in regular rhythm pumping blood through its structure. Watch how the blood flows through the tissue of the lungs and is infused with life giving air. Watch how it flows all through the body, through the arms to the fingertips, through the legs and feet. See how it returns again and again to the heart and lungs. Feel how it flows through the face and scalp. Feel the flow of healthy warm blood pulsing throughout the entire body, through the tissues of the muscles and the fabric of the organs. See how even the bones are energized and fed. And you know that, as this is a reflection of your own body, this is how your body works and functions and you feel the pleasant stimulation of the life giving blood feeding and cleansing throughout your own body's system. ---

Now, see the bones within and how they frame and support the body. You watch the body move and you notice how elegantly the skeletal frame is fashioned, how it is hinged at the joints and how each joint is cushioned with cartilage. See how freely and gracefully they move, how strongly they support, how balanced the mechanism is. --- As you watch the body and its systems, you know that at any time you wish to use this means of seeing, it is available to you, whether it is you own body or that of another or of any living thing. See also how, with this image of the body, you can easily focus on any level of its activity you wish. You may move it or turn it so that you may examine it thoroughly and observe all its mechanisms and workings. --- You may focus on the hand for a closer view and there it is before you, fully visible. See the flow of blood, the muscles, and tendons. See how the nerve endings appear to be like tiny points of light across the surface. They are white lights now, but in the case of damage or distress, they will change color so that you may know the nature of what they are registering. They will glow red for pain; they will show blue for cold. They will radiate blackness for other injury or illness. Know also that you will know and recognize what the colors in the image reflection mean when you look at it. You may follow these nerve endings all the way into the brain to trace the progress of their activity. You may watch within the brain to see how thought and energy are transferred. You may look within the eye. All aspects of the body are now clear for your examination and study. ---

Let us now change the perspective of our viewpoint. Move back slightly so that you may once again view the body as a whole. Turn your attention to the soft halo of light that surrounds and infuses it. You see how it moves and changes with the body like a gently glowing second skin. This is the light of life that surrounds all living things, all plants, all animals, and all living creations of whatsoever nature. Examine it carefully. --- Notice that it is brighter in some areas and less bright in others. It is thicker and wider in some areas such as the head. See how it surrounds the head like a shimmering orb resting on the shoulders; how it lies closer to the arms and legs. Notice that it is softly colored. Areas that are healthy have a white shimmering appearance. Perhaps your feet were tired when you began this exercise; the feet would appear darker. If this fatigue is painful, there might be no light at all, only a cloudy darkness. Perhaps this body has been recently injured and the area is irritated and painful. If that were so, the light would seem to be drawn back from the area of injury and replaced by darkness. Registering the pain, there might seem to be a haze of red outlining this darkness. Suppose there had been an injury but the healing process is fully established. There might be a mist of green replacing the darkness and the light pressing around it to fill the void once again.

Look at it carefully remembering that this is your own body. Examine the life lights surrounding you. Now from your viewpoint you reach outward from yourself as you have done before. You reach with the light and energy of your true self. You touch and encounter the image in the mirror with your intention. You adjust the lights around the form, knowing that as you do so you are healing and renewing the body that this image represents. You add light to places where there seems to be insufficient luminosity. You gently soothe any areas that may appear irritated and inflamed. You carefully adjust the life lights until they are once again soft, shimmering and balanced. Now you may move your perspective deeper, past the muscles and into the internal structure. Again, you will into action this healing process. As you do so, you become aware of areas that need adjustment, and you realize precisely what needs to be done. Somewhere perhaps, you see a muscle that is somewhat strained. Move gently and bind the fibers together with healing light, soothe away the tension and the irritation, withdrawing only when you are satisfied that the proper actions have been taken and that all will be well. As you do this, you know without any doubt that what you are doing will be effective. The healing and enlivening process will take place on all levels of reality. You feel the healing power go forth from your hands and into the form. As you do this, you become aware that the energy you are drawing from it is the infinite energy of the Universe. There is no limit to this strength or its uses. It flows through you to do your bidding and leaves you feeling refreshed and invigorated. It flows upward through the soles of your feet, through the spine and outward through the hands directed by the intelligence of the head and the energy and compassion of the heart. It is the raw material of the healing force and refreshes the healer even as he uses it to heal.

See how the figure in the mirror shines and glows. See how freely it moves, relaxed and vigorous at the same time. Know that when you at last return to your body, you will feel the benefit of this work. You will feel healthy and rested, alive and relaxed. Let us now examine this flow of life energy that you have just used. You have only partially realized this interesting phenomenon before. Just as the flow of energy within and around a crystal has been demonstrated to you, so also is that true of organic life forms. Each takes the life force within itself and emits this life force, allowing it to pass through. In its passage through the organism, this life force invigorates and enhances the resident energies of that life form maintaining it within the continuity of this Universe and within the continuity of all Life.

Watch the figure before you and the energy flowing within and around it. You perceive this energy as a soft white glow around the figure. See how the energy seems to be flowing, passing upward through the soles of the feet, traveling upward through the legs and converging into the base of the spine. Notice the pattern of the light as it enters and travels upwards through the spine. See how it appears to be not a single stream but rather two streams twining together in a spiral. This is the helix of life that is mirrored in all living organisms and in all the singular elements of those organisms from the largest creature to the smallest cell and even unto every atom of every cell. ---

Now we shall examine the individual energy nodes within the figure and how this life flow affects them. Regard now the base of the spine. See how as the flow of light encounters this area, you may perceive a glowing red light just at the point of the tailbone. It appears as a rosy red flower like shape within the body. You also notice that it is rotating slowly in time with the beating of the heart's blood, clockwise as you see if from the back. Now feel the energy from this center; feel its primal energy. This is the center of basic life and is the driving force of the physical survival of the organism. It is the center of both procreation and of creation on many levels of awareness whether the most primal or the most spiritual. ---

Allow your awareness to travel slightly upward now and you become aware of the point just slightly lower than the navel. This node is illuminated with a vigorous orange light. This center is also rotating slightly this one in a counter-clockwise direction. This is the center of defense and of justice. It is the first level of perception and is the initial gateway to the evolution of life in consciousness. It is the point of nurturing. ---

Now allow your awareness to travel upwards again to the point of the solar plexus and its bright yellow flower turning clockwise. This is the point of expression and dexterity. This is the point of changing and the point of maintaining balance and grace throughout the course of change. The energy passes upwards through it and into the heart which appears as a shining white sphere composed of a thousand tiny petals and it appears to rotate gently on an axis from left to right. The energy passes upward to the throat and a green flower may be perceived rotating in a clockwise manner. This is the center of conscious translation, of speech and persuasion and communication; the force of will and manifestation in many forms. As your awareness travels upward, on the brow you perceive a royal blue flower of light. This is the seat of both pure intellect and the origination of will and identity. It rotates gracefully counterclockwise. ---

Now your awareness reaches the highest point in the spiral. The violet light resting on the crown of the head. See how it has the appearance of a candle flame or the tapering bud of a flower. This is the seat of spiritual awareness and consciousness and it rotates slowly as does the heart. ---

Regard the image that has been shown here. Move your perception until the entire form can be seen. Study the flow of energy and the lights of the body. See how the lights blend with one another, how the patterns of their luminosity and motion compliment one another in gracious harmony. Notice how easily and cleanly the energy flows within the body and how it passes again through the crown of the head and outward returning to the Universe in completion of this cycle. --- Now regard the figure again and see that the pure white energy of the heart seems to reach outward

and move down the outstretched arms of the figure. It flows outward
unto the hands. The helix pattern in this is slightly less pronounced but it
is still quite visible. The helix crosses once at the elbows then flows
outward into the hands, where again you may observe a flower made of
light. Only this time the lights are not of one certain color but of the
potential of all colors. Now bring the palms of the hands toward each
other until they are but a few inches apart. Notice how the energy streams
outward from the palm of the dominant hand and how it is received by
the palm of the recessive hand. Feel how this cycles and flows the energy
within the system. Let us examine this. The heart acts like a pump/
generator in the cycle of the hands energy. Feel how the energy may be
slowed or accelerated by the intention of the heart center. Feel how its
color and intensity may be changed and manipulated. Notice that although
the manifestations of this light may be many, always the glow of the
flowing energy and the balance of the helix pattern remain the same and
constant. Now take a few moments to work with the energies around the
figure. Experience through the figure the feelings and potentials of these
energies. If there are imperfections in the flow, smooth them out. Replace
darkness with light as you have previously done. --- Watch the patterns
of the lights and helixes as the figure moves and turns. When you are
finished with your observations, know that as this is your image, your
body and your spiritual energy will benefit from this and become more
vigorous, more healthy, and more able - more aware of all life and all
things.

When you have become satisfied with your experience with these energies
of the body, begin the return to the body that you have left resting
peacefully. --- You withdraw from the place of the mirror knowing that
at any time you wish to use it, it shall be there for your experience and
use. You are returning gracefully now, and reentering the body. You feel
its breathing; you feel the blood beating in its veins. You become aware
of its weight and you begin to become aware of the small sounds and
feelings of physical life. You are aware now of a pleasant change that has
taken place. Feel the renewed vitality of the physical vehicle, its elasticity,
and its energy. You know that this is a direct result of the work that you
have just done with its functions. You are not yet fully awake. Let us
remember truly that whatever you wish may be accomplished in this
manner. You may heal yourself as well as others. You may speak with
other beings corporeal and noncorporeal. You may gain whatever
knowledge you require in this fashion. In addition, whenever you use
this method you will return to your physical form feeling rested, refreshed,
and renewed in all systems of energy. ---

Now, you are fully awake. Go forth from your resting-place and
experience these newly found gifts. Examine the people around you and
experiment

with these energies and skills. Repeat this exercise on a daily basis until you are fully familiar and comfortable with these methods and experiences. You may do this as often as you like and no ill will befall either you or your body. You should use this technique often to explore the ranges of your abilities skills and perceptions. Remember that whatever you do at this level of energy is a valid action. Great care and responsibility must be taken with it just as you take care and responsibility with the actions of your physical form, lest harm unwittingly result to any.

CHAPTER 3

CONDITIONS OF LIGHT

As we have mentioned, light begins in this universe as a pure clarity, a radiant luminescence. It is a quality that permeates all things. When we speak of the space between worlds and galaxies, we mean that this space is filled with universal radiance. It only appears as darkness to your eyes because it is completely without color or qualification. In order for light to become visible to your eyes, its wavelength and frequency must be lengthened or shortened to bring it into your range of the perceivable. This does not mean that it is not there. It means that your are not physically able to perceive it. Clear is unqualified, unbounded, and unlimited. It is therefore essence without form, and potential without boundaries.

In the same way we have seen how the pure clear light of spirit is changed - slowed or accelerated - and modulated in the physical form so that it is in such a state that it manifests in the physical universe. In addition, as its nature is manipulated and changed by the action of the physical prism, it manifests as the rainbow of the energy field of the body. The body and the spirit that inhabit it are a microcosm - a miniature reflection of the universal life essence that composes all things. In order to realize and develop our awareness of that light and an existence as a part of it, it will be convenient to use a tool. Your own internal energy states are often too close, complex, and many layered for objective examination. Therefore, we need a way to examine and experience the pure energy key signatures apart from their internal existence. It is helpful to find a tool to help adjust and manipulate these internal energies so that they can be more in harmony with each other and with the purpose of the individual. We need to find a source of these energy signatures where they exist as stable energy models. This would allow us to examine them outside the individual's complex and ever changing energy system complex as well as use them in connection with the body's own energies. Crystals are an excellent way of doing this. Because of their structure, they are the source of well-defined energy signatures. Their nature is such that they are compatible with human energy patterns.

A crystal is defined in the dictionary as "a three-dimensional atomic, ionic, or molecular structure consisting of periodically repeated, identically congruent unit cells." Crystals are composed of molecules nested, layer on layer, in a regular and geometric fashion so that a solid structure is formed wherein, at least to a general degree, the larger structure formed mirrors the structure and arrangement of molecular components. We say "to a general degree" because, ideally, the form would be the perfect image were the crystal to be formed in a pure environment free from any external anomalies. However, natural crystals are formed in pockets deep in the earth. They are consequently subject to the intense external stresses of temperature, gravity and pressure of that geologic matrix, as well as the internal anomalies and changes in the growth medium itself. The way in which they form and grow depends on the way these seemingly random forces combine giving each crystal its own unique pattern of planes, angles, density, and molecular composition.

It is logical and right that at this time in Human history, there is a growing interest in crystals - particularly quartz crystals. Crystals have been a powerful companion of Humankind in many advancing civilizations. Each race or nation that has discovered its higher potential has found its own characteristic way of relating with crystals and relating through them in the course of pursuing their objectives. You see this occurring in the computer and microelectronics industry. This industry is worldwide and is your civilization's vehicle for seeking its advancement because your civilization is in the mode in which it seeks to advance in the physical world on a purely physical basis. So quartz is being used to serve in terms of communications and time measurement and regulation. Its programmable qualities are recognized for information storage and retrieval. But is it not interesting that crystals were used in much this same way millennia ago but instead of the purely physical, they were used to translate psychic/mental/spiritual energies into physical reality? It is an interesting parallel. Two civilizations address the same problems using the same tools like two artists viewing the same subject with the same box of paints, but creating two entirely different paintings. However, while the mainstream of your civilization moves in one direction, there are more and more individuals seeking advancement along more spiritual lines. Many of them are strongly drawn to work with crystals. Also individuals are remembering other ages and civilizations and are finding a desire to rediscover the techniques by which those civilizations advanced themselves so long ago. This is also a time when your linear history is paralleling those other civilizations. In terms of the time fabric, these times are overlaying one another and making their impressions all the more real and vivid. Many individuals are becoming increasingly sensitized to the more subtle energies, and it is those individuals whom we are able to guide to a broader spectrum of crystal working. They are seeking to grow beyond the limitations of the present civilization while preserving what is good and beneficial about it.

THE BASIC MECHANISM

In this section, we will discuss clear quartz as a way of introducing the broader subject of crystal work. The way quartz is configured and the way its energy behaves is typical of crystals in general, while its energy is easily and agreeably accessible. It is a tool that has been invaluable across the ages and, indeed, has proven to be a cherished companion to Humankind. The variety of shapes and configurations of the central axis structure give an almost infinite variety of working resonance patterns and signature frequencies that are then compatible with nearly any individual and configuration of work or purpose. These resonance frequencies are compatible and harmonious with the key signature pattern of Humankind. While other crystal types may require some adjustment on the part of the practitioner to use them to their fullest capacity, the quartz crystal framework comes easily to many with little or no training and remains a tool of value and power to those who have advanced far into the work. But we ask you to remember that as we begin discussing colored crystals in general, we are referring to generalized energy qualities of a wide variety of crystals, any of them having the particular color referred to. It is our way of introducing those energy properties that we will discuss at length and in detail later in the text.

The energy properties of a crystal are defined by the nature of its axis structure. The central axis extends from the tip of the termination to the base. This is augmented by the secondary axes that extend from the angle formed where the sides join inward to the central axis. You can imagine this as though the crystal were divided by invisible walls slicing it into triangular sections all joined at the center. The angles the axes form and their length determines the nature of the energy signature output of the crystal. The specific pattern of these axes along with the ideal configuration of the sides is what delineates and defines each crystal family, each pattern of arrangement being distinctive and specific to one particular family.

No matter what the basic pattern of the axis structure may be, the working mechanism is the same for all crystals. When they come in contact with a current of electricity, their axis structure oscillates at a given frequency that is specific to the crystal type being defined by the axis structure and the atomic structure of the crystal. This oscillation creates a signal similar to both a sonic tone and a radio signal. The energy of this signal is focused and directed by the structure of the crystal itself and the intention of the user as communicated through the atomic lattice and ionic bonding of its surface.

The oscillation of the internal axes gives the crystal its basic character vibration frequency. The ionic bonding of the surface is the actual electro-magnetic field that attaches the molecules together. This determines the "message" and "personality" of the crystal. To a great degree, the quality of the internal axis is fixed and determined by its physical shape and pattern. It is primarily the pattern set by the ionic bonding of the surface that is involved in higher consciousness studies and healing work.

We should point out that, while the primary focus of this work will be on crystals, we will also discuss non-crystalline stones. Although they do not occur naturally in crystalline form, their internal structure is such that they are also useful and beneficial tools for growth and healing. There is a wealth of variety in the mineral world that can be of great value to the healing and growth of Humankind. It is our purpose to use stones and metals of many types in this work. It is also our hope that by using the techniques and exercises presented; the individual student can expand his or her experience into a variety of materials available in whatever form it naturally occurs.

CLEAR STONES

Clear crystals are analogous to an individual's whole energy system. Clear crystals work with the individual as a whole rather than with a specific center within that individual. Clear crystals embody the signature pattern of their kind, for they are without qualification of color or pattern and by their energies the basic structure and nature of their family may be known without consideration or alteration. These stones embody all true potential, for theirs is the ability to throw a full spectrum of truly clear colors and hues without changing their natural integrity or purity. They manifest the rainbow fullness within the single basic nature of the stone. They are not limited to a single ray of energy, but operate in a broad general range dealing with the entire energy system. They are the archetypes of their kind and carry the pure note of the nature of the crystal type undifferentiated by color. They are all-purpose stones and, to the degree that they distribute light, they distribute their power. They can be worn by themselves as potent power talismans and can be tuned to all varieties of work in both intensity and purpose. In this capacity, they provide a good general field of energy that can be directed on many levels. They are excellent meditation tools when used consistently over time. In the same way, they make good personal talismans when an individual wishes to undertake a long-term path of personal growth and awareness. Clear stones are often used in complex talismans in which one or more small stones are combined to a single purpose. The clear central crystal or stone provides an excellent focusing and unifying agent. Depending on their crystal family, they will lend the general nature of this family to the entire assembled piece as they unify the various energies of the multiple components into a single field.

Clear stones can be tuned to a high level of energy making their influence very strong and tightly focused. Like a brilliant beam of specific light, they can be pointed at a specific healing task with powerful results.

Combined with other stones, they will manifest those stones' influence as well as their own and be charms of great influence and value. They may also be worn by those just learning their potential, for they are easily adapted and will not impose specifics on a nature unready to deal with them. Keep in mind that they must be charged to a wide range of vibrations here not to become overly specific.

❀ - *MEDITATION ON CLEAR (QUARTZ)*

Place the body in a relaxed and comfortable position, and be certain that its physical needs have been met before beginning. Choose a place for this where interruptions, threats to the body, or any great change in the sensory stimulation level will not occur to distract the student.

When this has been considered and done, begin breathing with the eyes closed. See the breath as a gentle flame of wind cleansing the body and the mind. Float with this wind until the spirit feels gently disengaged from its body and surroundings. Envision an open plain of clouds filling the view. Watch the clouds as they move and glow with their Inner Light. Experience these clouds of light until you are at peace and one with them. ---

As the clouds move together, you begin to see a more intense light glowing within them - a coalescence of this general fire of energy. The clouds roll and condense on themselves until in their heart you perceive a brightly glowing fire that is the essence of their energy. --- Now, the clouds begin to dissipate and draw away, and you see emerging from them a crystal form. --- Regard its perfect clarity. Feel this clarity fill your senses. --- Feel the harmonious perfection of its angles and planes, the total symmetry of its terminations - the ideal container for the flame heart within it. --- This is the flame that does not consume itself but is ever perfect in its brilliance and radiance. As you perceive this brilliance, you feel it drawing you gently within itself. You feel it calling to that element of your nature that is like itself. You experience the kinship of your natures. It is slowly turning in space - showing you every aspect and angle of itself one face at a time. Watch the light of the surrounding energies reflect on its surface - and as it interacts with this light see how these energies are part of its nature and substance. ---

Now you see tendrils of this light emerge around it slowly, forming spiral patterns around it, interlacing one with the other. This is the manifestation of the pattern of its nature. You feel an inner understanding of these patterns for your patterns are like them and in graceful harmony with them. You feel the peace of this harmony, and this reaffirmation of kinship and life. For this is also a center on the River of Life just as you are. You and the crystal are part of one another. And, as you sense this, you move completely within it. ---

Now from within it you can intimately experience the essence and source of its nature. First feel the center axis - that which extends from point to point, from termination to termination. The spine supports the flow of its energy, just as the spine of your body supports the flow of your body. Now as you feel this center axis, you become aware of the axes extending from it to each angle of its sides. Feel how they radiate outward from it like the spokes of a wheel forming glowing planes of energy throughout their structure. Regard above and below how they intersect at the terminations. They are pulsing with life and energy, as you feel them they are filling you with this life energy. As they glow and pulsate, you begin to hear a tone, a singing, a resonance that you perceive within your heart. It is as though the wind has passed over the single string of a great harp and this string is the center axis, and this center axis is your center axis. This is the song of the stone and it is unique to that single archetypal stone. It resonates throughout your entire being and brings with it peace and great joy and harmony. As the song fills you, so the spirit of the stone fills you and you become more intensely aware of the crystal form. Regard how this is the basic and perfect form of stone. True physical stones are made of this singular building block. This is the cell or seed, the unique singular basic structure of which all organisms are made. Now you become aware of how easily and harmoniously they may be joined one with another, each singing the same true tone/song, coupling its life energy one with another. This is the elemental building block built of purely harmonious energy - complete within itself. It is a whole unit joined to form a greater whole. You are also formed from these units to make a whole and bound together with the same life energy. ---

Now you begin to move out and away from it, you again become aware of your own distinct identity as apart from the crystal form. You are whole and filled with the knowledge of its nature. As you move back and away, you see the glowing clouds move towards it --- They flow around it. --- They obscure it altogether. --- You know it will always be there within those flowing forms when your spirit asks renewal of its energy. ---

Allow your body to partake of its life-giving energy and strength. Know that as you gently return to your physical body, you will feel refreshed, energized and renewed. --- You become aware of your physical body as you settle once more within it. --- It surrounds you and you are comforted by its familiarity. --- It is healed, refreshed, ready for your return. Now you become aware of its breathing, the flow of life energy within it, uniting it with all things. --- The sounds of your world return, --- the smells, --- the sensations. Your eyes open now. Breathe deeply and release the breath slowly. --- Breathe again and feel all systems awaken. --- Breathe deeply a third time and you will be completely awake and refreshed. You are ready to use the knowledge of this experience, fully aware of what you have gained.

Repeat this exercise only once a day. Eat well; sleep well. Go out of your dwelling and experience the reality of your existence. These journeys within the archetypes may be taxing to the untrained. You must maintain great care for your well being as we have explained. Repeat this exercise once a day until it seems easy and natural to you and every step is pleasantly familiar. Then proceed on to the next journey.

DARKNESS & LIGHT - (WHITE & BLACK)

When light enters the visible range, the first awareness that humans have is of the qualities of light and darkness - its presence and absence. Then the colors define themselves and become able to be recognized according to the individual's physical ability to perceive them. Color, however, exists as a form of energy whether it is perceived or not. Having wavelength and frequency, it is a form of energy. This energy operates at all times affecting all things just as other forms of energy do.

WHITE

CALMING

RESTORATIVE

White light is the fullness of the spectrum that is made into one ray of single purpose. It is the centering of the spectrum and the pure focus of its concentrated energy. It draws all of the individual rays into itself and knits them together as whole, supplementing those that are less strong or whole than others. White is spoken of as being related to purity. This is true in that it represents that which lacks nothing and is wholly centered in itself. It is enfolding and uncompromising. It dictates nothing but its manifestation is all things in one. White crystals draw all energy into themselves. This energy is transmuted and balanced, then knit into one whole and given forth again. From the reservoir of energies, the flow is mended and balanced and what is lacking is taken from other energies that are in excess. It is transformed and modified within itself until the ray is given forth again in balanced harmony.

WHITE STONES

White stones are generally those with anomalies that cause them to appear milky. However, the occurrence of these anomalies should be consistent throughout the stone to function to smooth the distribution of their energies. To the degree that the anomaly is consistent and in harmony with the structure of the crystal matrix, it will act as a natural buffer. Do not think that this renders the stone less powerful. This actually enhances its subtle ways and forms a connection with the essential white light energy that descends through the crown chakra. This is the highest ray of power, for it is undiluted with color, but contains all color balanced harmoniously within it. Remember that the color white is known to reserve all colors within itself and thus hold all potential in perfect unity.

White crystals may be used in many of the same functions as grounding stones. This is done in a similar manner to grounding through black stones. When tuned to a purpose, white stones remove all vibrations which are not congruent with the truest purpose of the resonance, whether the wearer's resonances or those of other stones. They have a soothing and harmonizing effect editing out energies that may be harmful to the result of the intended work, leaving only those that are in alignment with the desired. This is not the same way that black and brown grounding stones work, but in many cases the results are the same. This is not a "lowest denominator" phenomenon, for it makes no changes in the waveform pattern. This is how white crystals differ from brown or black ones. This may be a more desirable effect for those whose natures - mental, emotional, and psychic - are delicate or highly sensitized. There are some individual who perceive the action of black crystals as interference and this will trigger automatic defenses which will then in turn again trigger the stone. However, the white will simply focus, which triggers no shields unless in the case of those so mentally unbalanced that all stones should be removed from them except for those of healing purpose. Ideal white stones are those such as white jade, alabaster and white quartz. White jade and alabaster are not found in crystal form, but can be used in either their natural rough state or cut and shaped.

✿ - *MEDITATION ON WHITE - (QUARTZ)*

Begin again to breathe deeply and slowly from the very center of the body, from the very bottom of the lungs. Then allow the breath to escape slowly and with grace. --- Fill the lungs again. Release the breath slowly; allow the tensions and impurities to flow outward from you to return to their beginnings. --- Again breathe deeply and as you do so feel your body relax ever deeper you begin to drift away. As the body breathes you feel yourself beginning to float freer and freer to drift farther away until you are free altogether. --- You turn your attention again to what is around you as you move through the field of clouds. The field expands before you and all around you. It holds you gently; you are suspended on its luminous billows. --- You see them moving into fantastic shapes, turning and rolling gracefully and gently as you gaze around you. --- Now, they begin to rise before you like a column rotating slowly. They begin to thin and fray and to draw away from what is at their center. It is a shining white crystal. --- Look at its surfaces. It is as white and pure as the clouds around it. Light glows from its translucent depths as with the clouds and its song is clear and sweet. It is pure and beguiling as a silver flute. --- You move closer. It is like frost but warm. You move closer still and move within it. You are drawn into its beautiful structure and into its heart. ---

Now look around you. You are again delighted by the grace of the interior structure. Soaring arches reach above and below you. Intricate lattices and expanses of pure white light extend in all directions. --- You float effortlessly within it. See you the light that radiates within it, how each piece no matter how small is composed of light. There are pastel rainbows all around you within the stone. The lights seem to ripple and move, almost of their own accord as though they were alive and glowing. --- As each light passes into the crystal from outside, it is taken and woven into the glowing rainbow framework to become one in harmonious union with the stone. All lights, energies and songs are brought into graceful balance here. Each finds its perfect completion. --- Now you feel yourself beginning to move with the stone's energies, you are part of this balance and completion. Each resonance finds its perfect place in the harmony of the whole and you realize that you are part of that whole. You are a part of the energies and patterns around you. How delightful it is to be part of this living growing developing harmony. --- All things come together here and are made as one, yet all retain their individual nature. --- This is your song and balance as well. You realize that you are the same as this stone. --- You are balanced and complete, ever-changing yet always whole, a moving point in the stream of spiritual evolution. --- You rejoice in the feeling that surrounds you and is part of you. --- You have the sure and certain knowledge that at any time you wish, at any point of your life, you may refresh yourself here and bring yourself once again into balance with the energies around you. --- This is your place and an integral part of your nature. You are comforted and refreshed by this knowledge. It is part of you. ---

You begin to draw away and separate yourself from the stone. You move farther back until you pass out of the stone and you can see it again shining before you. --- Its song is sweet and penetrating in the moving breeze as the clouds rise around it. They roll and turn; rising higher and higher until the stone is finally hidden from view. You know that it is there and will always be there when you have need of its energies. Now you move farther, back across the field of clouds. You float gently moving closer and closer to your body until you feel it again surrounding you. --- You feel it breathe deeply and gently expel the breath. --- You breathe deeply again and you feel the life flow strongly through its veins and tissues. You become aware of small sensations of life as you awake. --- You are perfectly refreshed and relaxed. You breathe again and you are fully awake, renewed in your knowledge and in the energies and strengths of spirit, mind and body.

BLACK

GROUNDING

SHIELDING

Black is the condition of no energy as light whatsoever. Black draws all rays into itself but emits nothing. It is the perfect reservation of all potential. It is whole unto itself. All things are made balanced and level by its nature. As it contains all, nothing is uneven or imperfect within it, for it is the embodiment of balance and order. It is the perfect mask for it has no reflection and reveals nothing except its existence.

BLACK STONES

Black crystals edit out excess, anomalous and erratic waveforms, making the resulting field clear and balanced in its harmonics. When interacting with the human energy field complex, this has the net effect of quieting and calming the individual, whether the anomalies are generated internally by that individual or by an external source. They act in the capacity of a "signal filter". This means that reduces all energy passing through them to its cleanest mean frequency, by editing out the erratic energy forms caused by stress, anxiety, irritation, over stimulation, etc. on any or all four awareness levels. They help clarify the energy pattern of an individual who is excessively prone to empathize or identify with those who are ill or distressed. They do this by clearing the person's energy fields of any external vibrational harmonics that do not originate with him or her. In this way, they are shielding and protective and they can be preprogrammed to fulfill this function when the person using them knows that he or she will be dealing with stressful circumstances.

Black crystals help stabilize the energy patterns of any power working when the procedure must take place under less than ideal circumstance, that is, when there are unavoidable stresses and distractions in the environment. In this case, they should be keyed to the purpose of the work and then the focus of the work should be sent through them as part of the working procedures. Black crystals can be helpful for a novice who is forced to work beyond his or her own estimation of capabilities or training. They can help remove erratic energy patterns and inconsistencies caused by self-doubt and lack of concentration. They will not add power nor solve imperfections of intention, focus, or logic, because only learning and discipline will do that. However, in the case of emergency, the pure black stone will help make the best of the situation.

When choosing a black crystal, take care not to mistake it for a colored crystal that contains so much coloring element that it does not transmit light. Garnets and green tourmalines are particular examples of this. Such stones will behave according to the nature of the coloring agent and not in the grounding and filtering way of black crystals. Evenness of coloration is important. Blotchiness or striations will make the action of the stone irregular and may flaw it as a stone of true general use. Also bear in mind that hematite, pyrite, and other metallic crystals are not black in the truest sense. They are compounds of metal and will behave in the nature of the metal of which they are made. This will be discussed later in this work.

Black stones (and, to a lesser degree, brown ones) are cleared by their own nature as a product of their function. The more they draw and modulate the stronger and more active they become. However, when they are subjected to sudden intense surges or pulses of energy they can become unevenly charged and may develop an unbalanced or variable behavior in later use. Should this occur, they should be taken out and cleared and recharged as you would any other crystal, Then they should be carried in line with a strong and steady field until they are rebalanced and their energy patterns restabilize. This can be done by placing them in a charged container where they can be gradually realigned by the field of the container.

Black tourmaline is an excellent example of this color group. This is true for both dravite (brown) and schorl (true black) formations. Black sapphire is also very powerful because its star is caused by such a regularity of structure that it will act to center and focus the individual while enhancing the basic grounding and clarifying behavior or the stone. Black jade is especially effective in working with emotional instability and with metabolically caused emotional or mental dysfunctions such as pre-menstrual syndrome or the antagonism and disorientation caused by blood sugar disorders. Black onyx is effective in soothing and focusing concentration. These stones also make good companions for meditation because they help edit out the stresses and irritations of the day's tasks and assist in bringing the individual to the calm and peaceful inner state of mind and self desirable in the meditative state. In addition, other stones behave in a similar manner but with some notable differences:

Black quartz (natural morion) and brown smoky quartz have a calmative effect to the degree of their color density. However, be aware of the proportion of the stone that is clear and the whiteness of the base rock, for herein lies the difference. One must regard the crystal as a whole and use its driving/slowing cycle specifically with this quality in mind. The clearer the crystal, the more it will behave in the nature of clear quartz. This can be an extremely useful property when taken into account. The clear base automatically corresponds to the broad energy pattern of the user and can be tuned to harmonize with him or her and the particular purpose of the charm or talisman. When this is combined with the quieting, grounding and shielding properties of the parts of the stone that are in direct harmonic alignment with the clear or white base, the result is a strong balanced and harmonious working crystal that can take high energy load limits and continuously balance and focus the work at hand and the energy field of the wearer.

Smoky topaz is particularly effective in clearing the mental energies. It can be used in complex talismans combined with green jade or malachite to smooth the patterns of the heart, that is, the physical heart. A talisman of this configuration can help a spirit make peace with its own nature when that nature is limited and the spirit chafes against such limitations.

❁ - *MEDITATION ON BLACK* - (*TOURMALINE - SCHORL*)

Let the body assume a comfortable position and begin the breathing as before, harmoniously and deeply inhaling energy and strength with the breath and purging with the exhalation all tension and impurities. Allow the breath to flow graciously in and out in deep rhythmic harmony and as it does so feel its connection to all sources of energy. Feel your linkage with all life and spirit with each breath. As you breathe deeply in this manner, feel yourself drifting gently farther and farther, floating gently and freely. Now again you notice you are within the field of clouds. Feel their texture and their continuity. Allow them to buoy you up, feel how you are part of them. --- You see them moving and drawing together, folding over one another and turning slowly, they do not glow as before but seem dense and smoky at the center. --- As they move they begin to draw back like the petals of a flower. First one layer then the next, thinning and flowing to reveal within their center a shining crystal form. However, this one is different from any you have seen before. All the faces are deepest shiny black. You can see the light flashing from its surfaces and angles as it gracefully turns before you. You hear no music as it turns, only the slight passing of a breeze.

You begin to draw closer to it, intrigued by its difference, and curious about its nature. Although you see no light passing through it, you are able to easily pass within it and merge with its structure. --- Now you feel a little surprised, for while it appeared from outside that it emitted no light,. the inside is very light. You see that what appears to be black and dense is the composite of many tiny strands, lying side by side and bound together. Each strand is composed of all the colors you can imagine. --- You see rays of light entering the crystal from the outer planes and this light is at once drawn into the strands around you, it is bound there, each part of its spectrum put within its proper place along side other colors so that at all times each tiny spectrum segment is complete and whole. --- You begin to realize that no matter what enters this stone it is rendered complete and balanced by the stone's nature. Then this potential is held in readiness within its structure. This is the secret of the stone's apparent silence, the harmonic notes of all resonances are held here as potential as well. --- The stone is light within, for its nature is self-radiance and you know now that it will absorb, rectify and color any energy and resonance rendering it complete. --- You know that this stone can not be overloaded, for its nature is so broad that it embraces all energy of any sort. It also has within it the potential drawn from all energies to supply all that any energy should lack and it is the nature of this form to bring all that it absorbs into a state of completion. --- As you examine it, you begin to realize something else as well. Any energy you wish may be found within it. You recognize that it does indeed emit energy but only as you would tap it and take from it what is needful at the moment. This is a pleasing thought, to have so much balanced potential ready for use.

You also realize something else, that this is part of your own potential nature as well. You are part of the stone and it is part of you. --- You become aware that you are constantly receiving all manner of energy all the time, on all levels of awareness. You receive this energy from other people, from passive energy sources, from the earth and the heavens. --- It passes into you and through you. As it passes through you, you may take its nature and change it as you will. You may reserve part of it. You may use it for whatever potential you desire, for all energy may be transmuted into its component parts and augmented with other energy. It can be edited, and refined for whatever purpose regardless of its source and nature. --- Explore this idea and investigate this potential within yourself. You are beginning to recognize what this means for you and that it is part of your own nature. You can access this any time you wish.

--- Notice also that the stone only absorbs what comes to it naturally. It does not drain nor does it excessively demand what is outside itself. In this sense, it is respectful of the life that surrounds it. Its very nature is integral to the flow of life of which it is a part. ---

Now you begin to draw back from the stone. You feel your energies beginning to disengage from it as you pass out of its structure. You see it before you now. --- It turns gently, cushioned by the silvery clouds which flow around it, rising up its sides to finally cover it and hide it from sight altogether. You know surely that all you have learned will be with you in all levels of life. You retain this potential and this awareness because you recognize it as part of your own nature that you may tap at any time. --- You draw even further from it. You are moving back across the field of clouds even farther. ---

Now you are aware of your body lying peacefully just as you have left it. You are aware of how good it feels, how pleasantly familiar in its shape and weight. You are one with it now. You breathe deeply and feel vitality course through the blood and muscle. --- You breathe again and you feel energy rising all through you. You breathe deeply again and you become fully awake and alert. You are invigorated and renewed.

THE SPECTRUM OF CRYSTALS

The purest form of a stone is clear. By clear, we mean that there is nothing in the molecular/crystalline structure but that pure focus and vibration defined by the atomic structure of the stone. A colored stone retains the basic character of the crystal family it belongs to, but the addition of trace atoms to its basic atomic structure changes the frequency of its vibration and also changes the way in which it refracts light. This change in refraction makes it appear as a colored stone. Not all color is caused by the addition of the same material. For example, not all green stones contain chromium, nor do all purple stones contain manganese. Different crystal structures are configured to admit different atoms and combinations of atoms into their structure. However, the color indicates the frequency of their harmonic vibration.

For instance, in music we could take the key of C. By adding various notes in combination, we can change the character and tone of the basic C note to sound of C major or C minor. We could add many notes to the first one and have a rich range of harmonic tones and qualities, but all would be built around the basic C. Imagine that a quartz crystal stands for the tone C; then, add manganese to the basic silicon dioxide structure. This would be like adding a G note to the C. Now you have a purple crystal called amethyst (or a C major chord). Amethyst is still quartz and has the basic energy properties inherent in quartz, but with the special difference that now it is a quartz that resonates particularly with the violet harmonic.

Even crystals that are not quartz begin as basically clear. They have a resonance that particularly corresponds to one or more of the energy centers and a color that gives them a secondary harmonic. For example, there is the family of crystals known as Beryl. The nature of this family is very gentle and flowing, assimilating. It corresponds to the heart chakra and could be described as the Peacemaker because it encourages all the energies to balance and flow smoothly. A blue beryl is called Aquamarine. Its nature has to do with the throat chakra and expressive, communicative energies. A yellow beryl is called a heliodore. It brings the yellow solar plexus chakra character of adaptation and quickness to the basic mediating nature of the beryl. A green beryl is called an emerald, and brings the regenerative, healing and supportive energies to the beryl nature, encouraging love of beauty and fine surroundings. It is called the principle of its family because not only does the family correspond in energy to a specific center, so also does the color of the stone.

It is too great a generalization to say that all stones of a particular color effect the energy system in the same way. Nonetheless, we will attempt to present the broad outlines of their nature and a brief glimpse into an experience of their resonances.

INTENSITY OF COLOR

Appearances can sometimes be deceiving when judging a color of a stone. The power of a color is in direct relationship to its density, that is, to the level of its saturation. Color in stones is caused by the additions of different materials to the basic atomic structure. Any color can be saturated to the point of appearing black. However, this does not alter the true nature of the color energy. It is not a black stone, but an extremely intense colored stone. For example, in the case of certain types of garnets, red can be saturated almost to the point of black, but this does not make the stone more passive or become a grounding stone. Rather, it's red nature is more intensified, while being subtler in its working. For example, green is generally considered cool and passive, when saturated to the point of appearing black, as in some tourmalines, its focused intensity can drive the wearer almost beyond his own limits and actually cause illness rather than strengthen. Therefore, in color, we speak of power in intensity along with the value of transmitted light, which is an indication of color density. The saturation and darkness referred to here should not be confused with the darkness caused by inclusions that are impurities. This is a different thing entirely.

RED STONES

ENERGIZING

PASSIONATE

Red stones act in harmony with the base chakra, the gateway of the basic life energies of this physical plane. By channeling this vibration, they are powerful healing stones when working with a depressed energy system. They act by reawakening the fires of life and the systems automatic mechanisms that enable survival. They help to renew the will to heal and to live. They encourage the belief in strength on all levels of awareness. Used in a healthy manner, they encourage assertiveness of spirit as well as physical health. They can be highly beneficial when the energy system is under a long-term stress from whatsoever cause. Red stones can be supportive to the system as a whole. The practitioner should be aware, however, that the primal energy of red stones must be balanced through the system as a whole. They have a certain potential to encourage anger and sexual passion that is out of balance with the rest of the systems energies. They can also be harmful if they are allowed to power the system disproportionately to the ability of the other centers to manage and channel the energy. However, used with balance and moderation red stones can serve as a powerful and effective healing tool in a variety of applications from physical healing to counterbalancing the crown chakra.

Red stones embody primal energy and the power of physical survival by raising the life force from the very Earth. They hold great potential force for good or ill. This is the first ray of the formation of the Earth and all others develop after it. First, the red energy must be harnessed before the others may endure and this is the nature of stones of this coloration. By their nature, the lightening may be harnessed to the cause of Victory, and the enemy be struck down and bound away altogether.

Significant examples of the true red vibration in stones can be found in garnets, rubies and particular rubelite tourmalines whose color is a true rich red. Each represents a different aspect of the red energy. Garnet is particularly effective when the Earth-fire energy is required. Its basic nature makes it appropriate for use in physical healing, particularly when this involves energizing and sustaining the physical aura and principal energy structures within the physical form. Ruby attaches to the higher vibrational energy of the brow chakra and can bring these fiery energies through the spiritual aura. The rubelite tourmaline will be automatically keyed by the multi-level energy system with the mental field being its principle seat of activation.

They may be set in gold so that their purpose will be direct and sure. They may be set in silver so that their energies will permeate and surround the body, and flow even. It is appropriate to set them in iron and steel for they will greatly contribute to any works using these artifacts, for the natures of red stones and iron are very compatible. In steel, it is as though this red were mixed with the blue of the harnessed will force. Set in electrum they serve the Mages well and furnish the Artisan with her Talisman. Set in copper they modulate the female polarity and have always been an ancient token in the worship of the Dying God. Set in with platinum they are invincible in their natures and their course always direct and sure.

Rose Stones

Pleasure & Expansion

Rose stones in general encourage the healthy enjoyment of the body, the senses, and the current conscious lifetime. Pleasure is a necessary component of optimal survival. Rose stones act in such a way that the harmonic vibration of the base chakra is resonated and connected through the heart and, sometimes, the crown. This serves the purpose of linking the spirit with the physical surroundings actuated through the heart promoting a sense of love and well being. It is the nature of spirit to delight in harmony, beauty, and pleasure. Because of this connection through these three centers, rose stones can also help the individual connect with the vibrations of other lifetimes that are acting through this present incarnation. It helps the information in these incidents become of value to the individual and assists in healing and coming to terms with incidents in other lifetimes that remain unresolved.

First among the rose stones are rubelite tourmaline and rose quartz, these are followed by morganite beryl and some rubies and garnets, and in some specific occasions, pink jade. These may all serve as most potent charms for the healing and reinforcing of the primal will to live and for the revitalizing of all major life forces when they have been weakened by loss or trauma. They accomplish this effect by reestablishing and reinforcing the connection of the being's life force energies to the universal life force energy. This is not the regeneration of the green ray, but the actual reestablishment of the connection. Once this connection is made, all centers along the being's life flow may then be reenergized according to their natures. It may also be noted here that rose stones are often used in gracious combination with the green. This is because the green energy helps insure that all is kept in balance and harmony and those systems are harmoniously regenerated using the strength of the rose. Rhodochrosite and rhodonite are also powerful stones of the rose vibration appearing occasionally in crystalline form, but more often as microcrystalline formations.

These stones may be set with either silver, gold, electrum or platinum depending on the specific nature and degree of severity of the being's need. Let the healer consider well the nature of the ill before proceeding, and choose a stone of appropriate strength and intensity. It would not serve well for a being whose energies are at a very low ebb should be suddenly charged with the full force of a pink ruby. Consider that a carved charm of rose quartz or pink jade might better serve as an interim step.

These stones are often well worn by temple dancers and others who are celebratory of their sexual energy and thus these stones make joyful and appropriate charms for enjoyment and grace.

✳ - MEDITATION ON RED / ROSE - (GARNET / RUBY)

Begin with the breathing as before. Breathe deeply and slowly, filling the lungs as fully and comfortably as you can and then slowly releasing the breath, letting it flow outward from you. --- As you release the breath, feel it taking with it the tensions of the day. --- Feel it sweeping away all impurities. --- You feel your muscles relax. Your body becomes more comfortable and healthier with this relaxation and comfort. --- You drift farther and farther with each breath until you find yourself once again among the clouds. --- The field of cloud surrounds you and buoys you up. --- You feel free and released. --- You feel invigorated and renewed. You experience a renewed eagerness and curiosity for what the clouds might show you. ---

Now you watch them moving gracefully, forming and reforming into ever changing shapes and patterns. You see them come together and coalesce. --- Then they roll and draw back as before revealing a crystal that is a deep rich red, as deep in color as the reddest rose. Its color is so vibrant that it seems alive. --- You can feel its life reach out to you, it seems to touch you and you respond to it. You extend yourself to it now, joyfully welcoming the knowledge and strength you know you will find within it. Now you move closer still. You feel the energy of the stone welcome and enfold you. You feel it fill you and your energies merge with it. --- It is warm and vital. It is like the everlasting fire. --- It fills you with such energy you feel more powerful that you have ever felt. This energy fills your entire awareness. It flows through your veins and courses through your whole body. This is the power of the fires of primal life. --- This is passion and intensity without thought or content. This is pure joyful energy untrammeled and unformed. It pulses warmly from the base of your spine upward and throughout your whole body. You hear in its song a deep rhythmic pulsing like the beating of a great strong heart. This pulse and rhythm courses through you filling you with its energy and passion. --- It is unlike anything you have experienced before and you recognize it an intimate part of you. --- This energy and force is yours and has always been yours. This is the first song of life that never ends. You know that it is part of you to consciously use and enjoy. --- Its potential of strength will always be within you to aid in whatever you do, for you to draw on at will. ---

Now you are moving back from the stone. You feel your energies disengaging from it, you feel yourself becoming once again separate from it. You still feel the song of life coursing through you. —You can see the crystal clearly now in plain view before you, resting in the swirling clouds. The clouds turn gently around it flowing over and over as they rise higher over it, finally covering it altogether. It is finally hidden from view, its fiery radiance enfolded by the clouds, but you know that at any time you wish it will always be there. Its energies will always be ready should you have need to renew them within yourself.

You move back still further until you feel yourself returning slowly and gently to your physical body. You feel the blood moving in its veins, the breath moving regularly and gently in its lungs. You feel its familiar warmth and weight. --- It is comforting. You also are aware that as you have been absent from it, so that which you have experienced has benefited and revitalized the physical form, as it will always do in these meditations. --- You become aware once again of the small sounds and signs of life around you. You breathe deeply once, feeling your body become more awake. You breathe deeply again and you awaken further. You breathe a third time and you are awake, fully conscious and aware of all the knowledge and strength you have gained.

ORANGE STONES

ASSERTIVE

ENCOURAGING

Orange stones act through the belly chakra in a variety of ways to strengthen and encourage the individual. Their primary focus is self-assertiveness, surety of personal identity and self-esteem from the most positive aspect of these qualities. They stimulate courage combined with intelligence. They bring the courage of laughter, and the foundation of righteous pride. They are the basis of achievement for they have no deterrent. Orange stones serve well as a remedy to fear and weakness of whatever magnitude whether to hearten the Warrior in his just enterprise or comfort the small child who fears the dark. Orange stones bring about self knowledge rising from the individual's own instinct for survival, for self knowledge is the recognition on the most basic levels of that individual's right of existence and triumph. From this knowledge of his rights and value both as an individual and as an expression of the one great Prime Light, courage is generated and formed in truth.

The primary orange stones are citrine and carnelian first, and beside them Pad Parajah, the orange sapphire. They are followed by zincite and sunstone for their healing and strengthening properties. Wear them with gold for gladness and renewal, for these are the energies of laughter and gladness that drive away the darkness of spirit. Set with silver, their fires will permeate even where they are denied and so that they will interact with the consciousness without intrusiveness. It is well suited to be set in bronze and worn on the breast of the Warrior and in the cross guard of his sword.

❈ - *MEDITATION ON ORANGE - (CITRINE)*

Begin this exercise as before with slow regular breathing from deep within. Allow the moving breath to bring life and energy into your body and then slowly release it. Feel with every breath how you are revitalized and renewed. Feel how the breath cleanses the body and moves the mind and spirit into a higher state of consciousness and awareness. Your eyes close and your body is perfectly relaxed. You feel yourself moving again just as before. You are among the great field of clouds and they billow and move around you gently and gracefully. You feel perfectly supported and perfectly free. You move joyfully among them, at ease in your surroundings. --- Now they begin to move together, and coalesce to form and glow within. They are still moving and flowing apart to reveal within their center a perfect orangecrystal. You marvel at its brilliant color and its intense depth. --- You move closer to it. You feel something inside you answering to its harmonic song as it rotates gently before you. Hear it singing. —The song reaches inside you filling you. --- You answer it. You are part of it. The song it is singing is also your song and you feel its answer from deep in your belly. --- As you feel its strength, you feel stronger. The song of the stone is the strength inside you. --- It is like fire and sunlight together. This is the glorious passion of the bursting growth of mid-summer and it is within and around you. This intense strength of energy flows forth from the belly center, surging through you, moving up your spine and down your legs. You feel ready to go forth and claim victory in life. You feel brave and powerful in your joyful strength. --- You are one with the stone's energy and strength. This is the power of the Lion and life within and you know surely that this power has always been within you and will always be within you. It is part of your self to use and enjoy. Feel the orange radiance fill and enliven you. You are one with it. ---

Now you feel yourself moving slowly back from the heart of the stone. You can see it clearly from this distance, turning slowly and filling the air around you with song. --- You move back and back. The clouds are merging and flowing back to obscure the stone, but you can see it glowing within them like a heart of orange fire. --- They have completely covered it now, but you know that it is still there and that at any time you wish, you may tap its boundless source of strength and courage, for it is truly part of you. ---

You are again within your body. You feel its weight, its breath, and you see soft light through the eyelids. It feels good and familiar to you. You are aware of the strength flowing through it. It is a new feeling but somehow familiar. Breathe deeply, releasing the breath slowly. Breathe again slowly and feel all bodily systems awaken refreshed and renewed. Breathe deeply a third time and awaken fully as you release this breath. You are completely aware of the knowledge and strength you have gained on all levels of consciousness.

YELLOW STONES

JOYFUL

CLARIFYING

Yellow stones stimulate uninhibited wit, intelligence, and curiosity. They are constant reminders of the inner joy that is part of every spiritual being. They remind one of the delights in life and surroundings. Their nature is the quickness of laughter and the freedom of exploration. They use this delight as the key to working with injuries of a mental nature both in the sense of physical injury and illness and most especially in mental and emotional distress. By this influence, the sufferer is made well again for they lead the spirit across the barriers of fear and fatigue, and by this influence those barriers are bypassed and shown to be as nothing. Yellow stones encourage adaptability and help in developing a sixth sense to perceive moods and cycles of the world around the individual. Their secondary benefit is in enhancing sensitivity to rhythm and timing. Because they have such a childlike quality of experiencing joy in the newness and originality of things, they encourage adaptability to changes in surroundings and conditions. They also assist in recovery from serious mental and emotional losses in that they gently lead the individual outward from introversion and depression into extroversion and positive interest in the individual's surroundings.

Greatest among the yellow stones for its truest nature is the yellow beryl called Heliodore, stone of the sun. Topaz should also be considered, for it is much more the stone of the intellect and power of the true and archetypal sun, whereas heliodore is the bright young joy of the first day of summer. Take this difference into account in the context of the work to be done and its intended result. Yellow diamonds are generally considered too strong to be used in healing work but are better employed as life stones or focus stones for works of power. Yellow stones can be set in silver or gold equally well, depending on the desired strength and purpose of the work involved.

GOLDEN STONES
TO DRIVE AWAY SHADOWS

Golden stones show the maturity of the yellow ray. As the wit is engaged, so truth manifests itself to the intelligence. As the yellow develops the agility of the mind, so this golden stone ray develops its balance and strength. This is the quality of the mind that does not admit compromise and its strength is based on its integrity. Its Archetype is the Golden Topaz and its secondary is the golden tourmaline. In the tourmaline, it is most often found in nature qualified slightly with green. In such a stone, the green tinting aids slightly in regenerating the practitioner when the stone is used. Golden stones are very powerful in driving away shadows of darkness in the spirit. Their richer color strengthens them if the individual puts a heavy or sudden energy demand on them as in the case of manic depression.

The energy of golden stones is optimized when combined with clear and white ones. If the practitioner wishes to use a primary bodily center in connection with this ray, then the shoulders should be used. Bring the white ray down as in a hood around the head and then merge into the gold as a mantle. Then the energy will be best manifested and generated through the arms and hands to be put to many purposes.

✼ - *MEDITATION ON GOLDEN/YELLOW - (TOPAZ)*

Begin the exercise as before. Breathe deeply while envisioning the great field of clouds. In these clouds feel the flowing fires of infinite life around you and through you. Feel the glowing clouds supporting you and lifting you up and into themselves. You are borne away on the Wind of Heaven and your way is lit, as the clouds are lit, by the Fires of Life. --- The clouds begin to coalesce as before and bring forth the heart of the fire. Emerging from the heart of this radiance is a glowing crystal; its heart is freshly glowing golden yellow like honey wine, clear and sparkling. --- It flashes and sparkles in the light, flickering with fires as bright as laughter and as refreshing. --- Gently and slowly, it turns and revolves showing you every flashing side. --- You move nearer to it, drawn closer to it as the traveler is drawn to a firelit window seeking the warmth of friendship at journey's end. Feel its life reaching out to the life within you. You know, as you move yet closer to it, that like draws unto like and the crystal draws you by the companion warmth inside yourself. --- You move within it, recognizing the center axis pole, and extending from it others going to all of the angles and terminations of the stone. --- You hear it singing in the winds of heaven a clear pure note. The harmonics of the note rise like voices on the wind. As you hear the music and experience the flowing energy of the axes, you know that you are now at one with the crystal. Feeling its nature and hearing its song is to feel this nature and song within yourself as your own. --- When your energies are joined now in mutual recognition, you feel this golden yellow radiance, first at your brow glowing within your head, and then outside as well like a crown of intelligence and joy. --- Your perceptions are clear; all things become bright, with edges sharp and focused. This crown of light shines forth from you illuminating all things on which you direct it. --- Feel the laughter welling up inside you brought from the deepest base and bubbling forth as a clear stream of intelligence and wit and perception. It is the glowing light of the archetypal sun that illumines all and casts no shadows, for it illumines truly from within. Its light causes all things to shine forth with their own unique radiance. As the light flows over and through all things, they are energized by it as the sun brings light and life. This is the archetypal light and life. ---

The sparkling lights of the crystal are within you now. Feel how they bubble through you like water from a fresh flowing spring, leaving all parts of your body tingling and glowing, for the light of this crown is the ever flowing spring of renewal and the sun's energy. It fills you and renews all other systems with its vigor and clarity like the perfect wine. ---

Now you realize you are yourself, separate from the stone, yet joined by the common bond of shared energy. You recognize this force that has always been within you and now has awakened in full awareness for you to draw on at need. You become aware of the crystal's gentle turning motion as you slowly move away from it. As you separate from it, you feel your life forces renewed and unique. --- The clouds move around it once again. They flow around it, and then cover it altogether. ---

Know that its energy will always be there within those flowing forms when you have need to recall its life force and energy. Allow your body to partake of these energies as you return to your body and you feel renewed and revitalized. Now you become aware of your physical body once again. --- Feel how it has been restored and refreshed in your absence. It surrounds you now, and you are comforted by its familiar weight and presence. Feel its breathing, see the light penetrating the eyelids, hear the small noises of daily life around you. Now breathe deeply, releasing it slowly. --- Breathe slowly a second time and feel all systems awaken refreshed. --- Breathe yet a third time deeply and waken fully as you release it. You are completely aware of the knowledge you have gained on all levels of consciousness.

As before, only do these exercises one on each given day. Eat well, sleep well, and restore the physical systems. By doing this, you allow your newfound knowledge to take root within you and become part of your integral consciousness. You should also be aware that excessive use of these meditations and absence from the physical body may become unduly taxing on its structure at this early stage of your work. Your body is not yet accustomed to this process, nor is the conscious spirit. It is necessary for the untrained to proceed slowly and harmoniously into this method of working in order to maintain the health and balance of all systems and on all planes of existence.

GREEN STONES
UNIFY & RESTORE

Just as the heart chakra stands at the center of the individual's essential energy signature field as the hub of interaction of that person's energy fields, green stones stand at the center of the crystal spectrum. They make both excellent healing and working stones because they can greatly facilitate the unification and balancing of the individual's energies as well as developing the health and expansion of the heart chakra itself. As the heart chakra is clear, open, and healthy, the individual's energy is balanced expanded and renewed in its contact with the universal energy sources. This is most important because in the expansion of the heart chakra the individual's consciousness of the all-embracing love of the universe is fortified on all levels of awareness. That individual is then more at peace with his or her nature and more in a position of power to use and command those universal energies.

Green stones produce the highest ray of the quality of dedication whether to a cause or an ideal. They may be worn to intensify both dedication and renewal. The pale green of spring gives forth the energy of beginning in tenderness and joy, and so on through all intensities and variations of color. They may be worn above any chakra of the body to strengthen the vibration of that center. They can be combined with rose stones to open the channels of both physical passion and the higher consciousness love vibration. This is the true and whole meaning of the Analogy of the Rose.

We suggest that the darker intensities (particularly those that appear black) should be worn by those persons of known and integrated purpose. Otherwise, their intensity has the potential to overdrive the individual's nature. By this, we mean that there are many levels of learning and awareness. Each individual must find the place best suited to his or her nature. Some individuals are souls with advanced purpose and awareness, manifesting a high level of dedication to greater purposes. Others have smaller spheres of love and dedication in their lives, but these spheres are appropriate to their growth, development, and karma. It would be damaging to such a person to demand more of the heart chakra than it is given in that life to give. Consequently, we would suggest that dark green stones be used circumspectly in healing. However, in the case of an individual with latent gifts of power and sight, these stones can bring forth unknown reservoirs of creative energy. They can help an individual overcome blocks to creativity and expressiveness. This is because, as he or she opens to the universal love energy and the energy systems become balanced and free flowing, the individual develops more confidence and sensitivity.

In Ancient Times, these stones were often worn by Healers on all levels to aid in the constant renewal of their life giving energies so that they might become a clear and joyful channel for the renewal of life on all planes of their purview. The energy of the clear emerald is the most perfect of these stones. It holds within it all rays of this color and gives what is needed and called for. Be certain that the stone is clear and free from cloudiness. Keep in mind that those anomalies that augment its brilliance add to its blessing and power. These anomalies should be in low proportion to no more than 40% of the total interior volume and not altering at least four of its faces or any of the five intersections of these faces. Its light should be as pure as fresh water. Terminations may be desired as an added focus but are not necessary. Wear this set in silver, copper, or gold. In no instance whatsoever should it be set in or worn with any metal that contains iron even to the smallest degree, for then both stone and spirit must sicken until the iron is removed. Further note on cleansing iron contamination: see section on cleansing and charging, also healing and repair of stones.

Although emerald is the highest archetype of this color energy, any stone that meets the above specifications may be used. The tourmaline is more commonly found and has a pleasing energy, but its automatic quality should be kept in mind, as this may not be desirable to the purpose intended. In addition, peridot and some rare forms of topaz and quartz have similar qualities.

When a Healer decides to use an emerald for a working stone and talisman of his or her Calling, he or she should take great care in its choosing. Until the ideal stone is found, it is better to use a tourmaline in the interim that is strong enough to take the energy load. The choosing of a Life Stone is discussed elsewhere, but in this particular instance, it is most important that the Healer have a stone that will serve the desired strength of the energy load. He or she must be able literally to trust the stone with his or her heart because it is through that heart that he or she will manifest the energies of the Calling. It is therefore understandable that the stone of choice be the ideal one because it is also through that stone that the Healer will be strengthened and renewed after the work is done. It is also preferable but according to the discretion of the Healer, to wear the stones at all times that he or she is practicing the Calling and not to remove the stone until the process of healing and the assimilation of all necessary energies is complete.

❀ - *MEDITATION ON GREEN - (EMERALD)*

Begin the breathing once again --- the deep peaceful breathing of cleansing and renewal. Feel the breath draw life into the body and the spirit also. --- Breathe deeper, and feel the breath draw not just from the air around you, but also from the earth below. Breathe in this earth energy with the breath. Breathe with every pore of the body, allowing the life-giving energies to pour into you and renew both your body and spirit. Let the energy of the earth surround and permeate you. --- Feel it coursing through your veins and surrounding you altogether. --- Continue the breathing slowly, and relax even more. You begin to feel yourself moving gently away from the body. You feel yourself suspended in space, completely free and relaxed. --- Now you move farther still, leaving your body, knowing that in your absence it will be refreshed and renewed in all its systems and perfectly safe until your return.

Now you are moving once again, farther and farther into the field of clouds. --- You are, as always, pleased and refreshed by their intricate shapes and pleasing opalescent colors. See how they form and reform, turning gently and constantly on themselves in an endless dance. You look farther ahead and see them drawn together obscuring something. --- Now they begin to thin and turn transparent as they move gracefully to draw away. They pull back altogether now to reveal a green crystal. --- Look closely at the color and notice the intensity of pure color with which it shines. It is sea green. It is grass green. It is the green of all the leaves in high summer. The color is as deep as it is radiant. --- It is pleasing to the eye, and you feel yourself begin to be drawn into it. You feel yourself pass through the transparent walls and now you are suspended within it held poised among its graceful intricate archways. --- You enjoy the soaring architecture of its interior structure. You feel a slight breeze move through it and hear its structure resonate in answer one note after another. Each tone joins the other like a chorus, and as the breeze slackens, it is quiet again. --- Another breeze stirs the harmonics and as you hear the chorus notes your realize that you are joining with them. You are part of its harmony and this harmony comes from deep within yourself. It is part of you. You feel it in your heart as it vibrates throughout your entire self. It pulses through you with great strength in all directions at once. You are recharged by it and renewed. It sings through you heart and courses through the entire fabric of your being with a great feeling of power and joy. --- All fatigue and discomfort are passing away. --- The resonant song and color are sweeping through you cleansing, renewing and restoring every fiber of yourself. You feel the Center, in your heart, like the hub of a wheel, from which all other systems of your body draw, and modulate this energy. --- As they do so they are drawing this life giving power through them to be restored in turn. --- You are filled with great joy and strength in this newly found energy. You also know that at any time you wish you may draw on this energy to restore yourself on any level of body and spirit. --- You are part of this energy and it is, as always, part of you. ---

Now you begin to move again, back slowly from the stone. You pass outside its walls, farther and farther back, until the stone is completely within your field of vision. You see it turning gently and peacefully. ---

You know that you may touch its power and energy at any time for your renewal and strength. --- The clouds are moving again around it. They curl, roll, and cover it altogether. --- Now you are moving farther and farther away, drawn once again to your physical body. You become aware that you are centered again within it. --- You feel it surround you, and you are comforted by its familiarity. --- You know that the body has also derived great benefit from what you have experienced and you discover this feeling with great pleasure. Now, you breathe deeply in and out and feel its life systems awakening. --- Breathe deeply again and as you release the breath you become aware of all the sounds of life around you. --- Breathe a third time and, as you release the breath, your eyes open. You are fully awake, refreshed, and renewed remembering all you have learned.

BLUE STONES

COMMUNICATION

EXPRESSION

Blue stones activate the communication and expression activity typified by the energy of the throat chakra. They encourage the individual to articulate what the mind envisions and the heart feels. By using these stones, the individual may find the pathway through the darkness of self-doubt. This is the courage of one's convictions, belief in one's own visions, as well as the ability to express and share those convictions and visions with others. This stone also opens the way to interaction with others based on respect and equality, for it encourages the recognition of one's own value. It is excellent when working for balance in relationships whether on a personal emotional or intellectual level and will stimulate the free flow of ideas this type of relationship engenders.

On the spiritual plane, blue stones stimulate and encourage the use of "second sight" and other psychic abilities because they work toward the ability to trust one's own instinct and visions. They allow for expression of these visions whether the visions are in the form of artistic expression or psychic communications. For this reason, many blue stones have the reputation of being a Seer's Stone because they allow for and encourage the expression of visions and intuitions into the physical universe.

We speak here of the pure deep royal blue as the archetypal sapphire, not at all the paler hues of topaz or aquamarine. Occasionally tourmaline will manifest this perfect ray unqualified by green in any degree and this will serve well. When these are worn on the brow center, they will focus the force of the Spirit and open the gateway by which this will is manifested on this physical plane. Worn above the heart at any point on the upper vertical axis it helps the individual to surmount obstacles in life. These obstacles may be the product of the individual's unconscious mind and the blue stone will help the individual focus on the vision or goal, rather than the fear that prevents its realization. It will also help in overcoming obstacles that are generated externally to the individual, because it will enable the individual to interact with the cause of the resistance, and, through the strength of his or her inner belief, rise above it. Never forget that in any undertaking that self-knowledge is a tortuous path and must be trodden slowly and with care. Compassion, right knowledge and teaching are necessary in the preparation of the seeker. Let the indivdual prepare him or herself in all right ways, for self knowledge and great power will come to the strong and wise and will harm the unready. Those who do not have the necessary background for the assimilation of this knowledge and power will surely be harmed and overwhelmed by it, as were those in the Ancient Tales who looked on the face of a God. Go slowly about this, for in the unready, to accelerate this chakra without preparation in teaching, understanding and strength, will bring about headaches and dizziness at the very least. With this as in all others, balance must be maintained for true benefit.

These stones may be set in any precious metal and their benefit will align with the purpose of that metal.

❁ - MEDITATION ON BLUE (SAPPHIRE)

While lying in a relaxed position, breathe deeply and slowly from the very center. Draw the breath within you feeling it enliven and invigorate your entire body. --- As you draw another breath, feel it filling your lungs and then your whole body with life renewing energy. Breathe deeper still again and again, and as you slowly release, feel the tension and impurities draining away. --- You are one with all energy now. You feel it deep within you. You feel yourself centering and expanding. You are aware that you are drawing away from the body now, leaving it safely at rest to renew itself while you are about your business. --- You are floating free now, drifting farther and farther, higher into the field of clouds. Awake and aware, eager for whatever new knowledge and experience awaits you. You feel them support you as though you were a cloud yourself. They turn and move gracefully, moving together like the petals of a flower. They roll and turn, then begin to thin and fold back. You see at their center a glowing stone. It is royal blue, the most intense and vivid blue you have ever seen. --- You feast your eyes on its richness as the crystal slowly turns in its nest of clouds. --- You become aware of its unique and special song. You feel yourself drawn closer and closer to it by the song and by its beautiful color. --- You come closer and closer still until you are drawn within the stone. You pass easily within it. ---

As you pause within the stone, you look around you. See how it arches above you like a great cathedral. See the elegant symmetry of its vaults and arches and how the light from outside penetrates the transparent walls. See how the light is reflected, enhanced, and magnified by the structure within. --- You feel the light around you and within you as part of the song of the crystal. You feel uplifted, joyful, and strong in this feeling. You feel clarified and centered. --- You become aware that you have sure and certain knowledge of the self - yourself. --- You are filled with a sense of the strength of identity and the power that comes from this knowledge. This feeling seems to radiate first from your brow. The feeling centers there like a crown and extends itself to all parts of your awareness. It flows through you, strengthens you, and fills you with a surety that through this center of identity nothing is truly impossible. You feel completely capable both of intuition and of investigation. You know that this is an important key and will be of great use in your studies and your journeys. --- Through this centering you feel yourself focused and complete as though your awareness is becoming fine-tuned and honed sharp. --- You know that this ability has always been with you; you have just never realized it to this degree before. This power and ability are yours. They are brought to your awareness by the nature of the stone. --- You look around you once again and recognize your kinship with this nature. Now this knowledge is yours to use as a tool wherever your path may lead. ---

You feel a great sense of pleasure in this awareness as you draw slowly away from the stone. --- You move farther and farther back from it, sure in the knowledge that whenever you wish to avail yourself of this energy it is available to you. --- You move back farther still and watch the clouds once again roll and cover the shining stone. It is hidden now from your view but you know surely that it will always be there and that you will be aware of its presence when you have need for it. ---

Now you become aware of your body once again, its pleasant warmth, its weight, and its textures. You breathe deeply and release as you reenter it, filling the lungs with life giving air. --- You feel yourself once more enlivened and refreshed as at the end of all your journeys. You become aware of soft light through the eyelids and blood coursing through the frame. You are pleased with your newfound knowledge and know that it is truly yours for all time.

PALE BLUE STONES

FLOW & ADJUSTMENT

Pale blue stones balance the energies of blue will power and communication with the full spectrum adaptability of clear stones. Their luminous transparency combines with the subtle energy of the atomic structure of the blue wavelength to give a clue to their inherent nature. Blue stones encourage balance and flow of energy between the energy bodies and between the energy centers within those bodies. Metaphorically, they are water and by that analogy you may know their activities, for they permeate all but force nothing. They promote understanding from all channels and on all levels. They soothe the troubled spirit by allowing all energies to be put into proper perspective and to distribute those energies to their best balance and benefit. Pale blue acts as a catalyst to bring dissimilar energies together harmoniously so that the individual can find a point of perspective. This can bring peace and harmony of mind, emotions, spirit and body, because those energies that are balanced and those things that are in perspective are considerably less stressful. Less stress on a situation can lay good groundwork for positive and proactive solutions.

This ray is gentle but pervasive and allows approach to all energies. It is not Intelligence in itself, but makes the ways smooth and open for active intelligence to occur. It creates a flow for the balancing and harmonious development of whatever is at hand. In the case of individuals who are prone to extreme emotional outbursts, such as anger or tears, pale blue stones can help them put their emotions into perspective and balance. This also helps clear the way for constructively dealing with the underlying causes of extreme behavior. In individuals whose physical energy is erratic and unreliable, pale blue stones can help the body's energy fields stabilize to clear the path for constructive therapy of rest and proper diet. In all, pale blue stones help all the energies of the individual work together to find a balance.

Blue topaz, aquamarine, and, in some cases, tourmaline are the pale blue stones that most typically demonstrate the activities of this category. They enhance the flow of energies throughout the individual, acting like flowing water as they work subtly and constantly on the energy fields. They are often recommended as life stones to help the individual to integrate the many contrasting elements of their nature and character into a harmonious whole by encouraging all energies to distribute themselves into a balanced harmonious field. This has a long-term calming effect on the spirit and temperament that can greatly help in turning excess or unfocused energy into constructive enterprise. These stones can assist excess energies to translate throughout the energy system in a constant action of rebalancing and refocusing without causing either excessive stress or debilitation on any one center or field. They help the action of other stones they are placed with by distributing their energies throughout the system so that they will reach the areas where they are needed most. Pale blue stones are akin to the darker blue ones in that they can calm the mind and allow the individual to see around blockages that are inhibiting development and growth. It might be said that pale blue stones are the talismans of constructive solutions, for they work in harmony with other rays so that all systems benefit for a harmonious outcome. Pale blue stones also help the individual to see clearly on all levels by "straightening" the path of the mind and spirit so that the voices of inner wisdom and higher awareness can be heard and acknowledged.

These stones are effective in workings of power to enable the wearer to channel energies easily and prevent certain kinds of fatigue and exhaustion. Their energies operate as a broadcasting power stone by aligning their identity patterns with the energies of their wearer. But if they are use in serious power work, they should be put in a secondary energy position to help the primary focus stones balance and sustain their energy. If pale blue stones are place in a primary position, they are likely to burn out and fail. Their nature is to balance and assist, not to take the full burden of concerted power.

Pale blue stones are best set with silver because its natural flowing energy is harmonious and in agreement with the nature and activity of the stones.

✸ - MEDITATION ON PALE BLUE (AQUAMARINE)

Relax your body completely, and as you breathe deeply allow the tension and impurities of the day to flow outward from you. Breathe deeply again, feeling the life and peace flow through you like clear water. --- Breathe deeper still, filling your lungs and your body with health and invigoration as the passing breath cleanses and renews. As you relax and breathe, you feel yourself more and more at peace, at one with yourself and the flowing life within and around you. You are comforted and healed. --- You feel yourself beginning to drift free. You draw farther and farther away from the body, leaving it in peace to rest and renew itself. --- You are floating free now and moving gently within the field of clouds. ---

As before you watch the clouds form and turn, they roll and billow in pleasing and intriguing shapes. They seem to form a flower from their glowing masses. --- Then the petals of the flower begin to thin and turn back revealing within their heart a shining crystal. It is a clear pale blue as the morning sky. The color is so delicate and pleasing that you find yourself drawn nearer and nearer to it. --- Now you are close enough to see inside. Its inner color ripples in the light like a bottomless spring-fed pool. --- You draw nearer still until you pass through the side of the stone and into its heart. Look around you and see how the light passes from side to side. Listen to the bright harplike song of the stone. Enjoy its clarity and the intricate design of its inner architecture. --- You feel yourself becoming one with it. You welcome its influence and energies into yourself. And as you do so, you realize that these are also your own energies that have always been within you. --- You are becoming aware of a difference in yourself. You feel more balanced and calm. You are aware of energies all around you and through you, taking note of their nature and intensity. You notice now that they are flowing easily around and through you. As they do so, they are bringing a balance as they pass. --- All energies seem to work in gentle harmony with one another and with you. Your energy system takes what it needs and passes the rest on, flowing and balancing from moment to moment. --- You feel at once calmed and enlivened. You become cool and bright as the stone itself. There is a feeling of peace and health in unison with the influence of the stone. --- You know that this feeling has always been within your potential and that at any time you wish you may re-experience it by reaching once again for the stone's energy. --- Secure in your knowledge of this stone and its potential you feel yourself moving slowing back from it. ---

You pass outside its structure. You can see it clearly from this distance, turning slowly and filling the air around you with song. You move back and back. --- The clouds are merging and flowing back to obscure the stone. --- They have completely covered it now, but you know that it is still there and that at any time you wish, you may tap its boundless source of peace and balance, for it is truly part of you. --- You come back once again into your body. You feel its weight and its breath. You see soft light through the eyelids. It feels good and familiar to you, you are aware of the strength flowing through it. It is a new feeling but somehow familiar. --- Breathe deeply, and release the breath slowly. --- Breathe again slowly and feel all bodily systems awaken refreshed and renewed. --- Breathe deeply a third time. As you release this breath, you awaken fully; completely aware of the knowledge and strength you have gained on all levels of consciousness.

Violet stones are keys to guidance both from the inner voice of the self and the higher voice of one's guides. They manifest through the brow chakra to help the individual perceive what is real and true on this plane and on others. This is not the connection to spirit of the highest chakra. It is the place where the spirit of the highest center meets the energy of the physical form. These stones can help the individual to see what is real and valuable rather than what they seem to have thrust on them. They allow the individual to make judgements through the awareness of his or her higher nature and to balance this with the necessities and desires of the physical universe. It is through the violet center that physical life is first balanced with spiritual life and for this reason these are known as the stones of the Monarch. It is the Monarch who must rule, and in doing so, balance the daily needs of his or her subjects with the higher needs and purposes of the state. It is through this vision that order and peace are maintained. So it is through violet stones that the individual seeks to come to this balance in his or her own life. They are powerful healing stones in this respect, because they allow the physical to be cared for by the spiritual and the spiritual to be enhanced by the physical.

Amethyst is the archetypal stone of the violet ray and much may be learned of this energy by studying its potential. The amethyst is a great healing stone and one of great strength. Its power lies in its potential to link together the rays of knowledge and make the Being conscious of the nature of the ills. It is a powerful stone for the practitioner, because it has the potential to allow him or her to access all forms of knowledge and energy from other realms along with the sum total of his or her and the general collective knowledge. He or she should not use it as a lever or mechanism, but as a pathway by which he or she may access what is truly necessary to his or her work. Iolites (Cordierites) are violet stones of great strength and usefulness that are often overlooked in this work.

Silver is a good choice of metal for setting violet stones because it helps their energies integrate with the individual's energy system complex gently. This can improve integration of the knowledge and healing gained. Gold renders these stones extremely strong and direct and, when charged properly, provides a talisman of great strength and purpose of action. Electrum provides the qualities of both metals and amethysts particularly are well set in it. Violet stones, and amethysts in particular, may be the key to the inner path of wisdom and understanding. They may open many doors and access many channels. However, it should always be remembered that a true spectrum balance must be maintained across all centers, because Man is not pure Spirit energy, but is resident on many levels simultaneously.

❋ - MEDITATION ON VIOLET (AMETHYST)

Relax again. Let this feeling of comfort and peace fill your whole body as you breathe slowly and deeply. Breathe again and you are filled with a pleasant feeling of health and well being. --- Breathe again slowly and you feel yourself floating farther and farther away, leaving your body behind you to rest and renew itself. You are moving gracefully through the field of clouds. --- You feel the fluffy clouds surround and enfold you, supporting you as you move farther and farther. Ahead of you, you can see the clouds glowing and turning, and you move closer to see what is at their center. --- They begin to turn and roll, and you see they begin to reveal a shiny violet crystal at their center. They move, thin, and then part altogether and you can see how the crystal shines and glows in the light. You move closer and closer to it, and as you do so, you begin to notice that you are filled with a feeling of peace and security. This feeling of serenity fills you altogether as you begin to hear the elegant harmonics of the song of the crystal. ---

You move even closer to it now until you begin to merge with it. You pass inside it, and become part of its shining radiance, its strength, and peace. You feel supported, suspended, and enfolded as though cradled in it. --- You feel its influence flood you with a sense of well being, and, as you accept and welcome this feeling, you begin to explore its source. The source seems to be coming from all around you, from the very song of the stone. It resonates through you and around you. You feel it begin to work on your energies and extend your awareness. --- You are becoming more aware of all that is around you. You are beginning to sense many things on many levels that you have never noticed before. And with this new feeling of heightened awareness, you also realize that it is all making perfectly good sense. --- What you had imagined would be noise and confusion is really a heightened depth of understanding. The source of these feelings is from deep within you. You are being aligned by the song of the crystal, and suddenly things become far clearer than they have ever been before. --- You realize that the energy of this stone may be tapped again and again to aid in bringing to you far greater clarity and awareness. You suddenly understand the healing potential of this stone. As it helps you find your alignment with your own higher awareness, it also helps you find the key to bringing all other energies both spiritual and physical into alignment. You also realize with pleasure that this awareness and perception has always been within you. --- They are part of your nature, and you had only to align yourself in order to perceive them. --- You also know that, at any time you wish, you may avail yourself of the energies of this stone in order to aid in maintaining this alignment and awareness potential. ---

Now you begin to move back from the stone; you move outside of it and look into its peaceful violet depths, feel assured once again that the knowledge you have gained is yours, and you will never lose it. It is part of you. --- You drift farther and farther back as the clouds once again turn and roll and cover the crystal until all you can see is a faint glow at their center. --- You are moving back now, slowly gracefully, filled with a new sense of peace, awareness, and certainty. --- You are becoming aware of your body now. You are aware of all its functions and its familiar texture. You recognize that in your absence the physical form has been rested and renewed. You feel the body breathe deeply now, once, twice and yet again, becoming wide-awake and refreshed on all levels of the body and spirit.

PURPLE STONES

HIGHER AWARENESS

Purple is the color of the vibration of the crown chakra - the center where pure energy of spirit enters physical manifestation. It is the gateway of universal life energy. Purple stones in general enhance this vibration and encourage this universal life energy to flow into the energy systems as they encourage the individual to open to these energies. Purple stones work to establish the connection between the individual and his or her higher self and with beings on other planes who guide and watch over that individual and Humankind as a whole. Purple stones open the way throughout the energy systems for the energy bodies to be renewed and revitalized with the essence of the greater universe. As the individual uses and communicates with these stones, he or she can find his or her own clear path of communication with these higher vibrational energies and through them, raise the vibration of the energy system as a whole.

Purple is the balance stone. A purple stone of great clarity with a perfectly straight center axis hung over the heart chakra will pull all other Chakras on both axes into balance. By this alignment, its focus and power will energize and focus/drive all energies. This is because the purple alignment is the highest extension of the rose alignment/expression of the heart. It may be worn as a healing stone under supervision of an adept and will cure ills of many natures. It is especially useful for treating those ills caused by shocks and sorrows of the heart where the will is prejudiced and the Being becomes crippled with self-doubt and confusion. In this instance, purple stones can help the individual reestablish his or her connection with the greater universe of spirit and the source of universal love and connection to all things. By doing this the individual can recognize and renew his or her sense that he or she are precious, valued and unique in the world, regardless of the temporal sufferings they may have had to endure.

It should be advised that, although the use of purple stones to establish and maintain the higher spiritual connection is greatly blessed and beneficial, the individual is a resident of the physical plane. It is often a temptation to rely solely on this highest vibrational ray and neglect to honor and nurture the full spectrum of the energy system as a whole. Although this practice may initially seem beneficial, it will eventually harm the systems of the body as will relying on any one ray to the exclusion of all others.

Stones of an ideal purple color occur as siberite tourmaline, ruby, or garnet. Siberite tourmaline is the archetype of this ray. This is the Queen of Gems and can be worn causatively by an adept whose energies are already such that its strength can be borne with balance and grace. They should be set in gold, as silver will disperse their energies and this should be worn on a gold chain or band to further direct its benefit. Charoite and sugulite are microcrystalline stones of the purple family. Both of these stones are greatly beneficial in channeling this energy and, because of other elements in their structure, they connect and encouraged a balance of energies with other centers.

❀ - MEDITATION ON PURPLE - (TOURMALINE - SIBERITE)

As before, breathe deeply. Allow the breath to relax and refresh all the systems of your body. Allow the breath to draw gently away and with its passing all tensions and impurities pass away. Allow it to cleanse both mind and spirit. Breathe again and again from the center. As you do so, you drift farther and farther away from the body until once again you are within the glowing field of clouds. You rest in the clouds, floating gently in their soft radiance. Allow yourself to reaccustom yourself to their consistencies and potentials. --- This is the realm of potentials and beginnings and you should be aware of its limitless possibilities. ---

When you are ready, you allow yourself to drift once again. You see them coalescing as before. They condense and come together, then roll back and thin. You see a glow within their center as they become thinner and thinner. --- You see rising from their depths a shining stone. It is deep purple in color and radiant in the richness of its hue. You see it turning slowly and as it turns, the light from the clouds flashes from its faces and the light within it answers the light from without. --- As it turns you become aware of its song. It is rich in harmonics from both the upper and lower tones of the scale blending in harmonious perfection in one ever-changing song. --- You feel yourself drawn to this harmonic. You feel yourself beginning to resonate with it as though you were a part of it and then you begin to realize that this elegant and intricate pattern is your pattern also. --- You are drawn ever closer to the stone by this kinship, then you are drawn within it and enfolded by it. You are suspended in its cathedral like structures by the grace and pleasure of its beautiful singing. You feel enraptured by this blending of the primal life tones and the higher ranges of expressed identity. It is all around you and you know that it is your song too. Allow yourself to experience the ranges and depth of its resonant color. It is a pleasure to the eye of the spirit. ---

Now you begin to draw away from it. You become separate once again from it. --- You know that this song will always be with you because it is also your song and has always been with you and that at any time you wish you may recall it and savor to draw renewed strength and clarity from it. --- You draw back even farther and now you perceive it turning graciously among the glowing clouds. You pause briefly to take pleasure in its song and its structure. --- Then the clouds begin to roll and turn. They drawn up its sides and finally obscure it altogether. You float back and back until now you are once again becoming aware of your body. ---

You see the body lying safely below you but only for a moment and then you rejoin it. You breathe deeply from the center and feel the life giving air flood the lungs. --- You become aware of the smells and small sounds of everyday life. --- You breathe once again and you become aware of the blood pumping through the muscles and the body's familiar weight and shape. You notice soft light coming through the eyelids. You remember pleasantly all that you have experienced. Now you breathe a third time, your eyes are open, and you are fully awake and refreshed. You are aware of your renewed health, vigor, and knowledge.

CHAPTER 4

WORKING WITH CRYSTAL ENERGY

You have begun your journey by experiencing the separate and unique vibration of each energy center of your body and each color of the spectrum. You have furthered your knowledge by exploring how each of these particular energy signatures is represented by the vibrational energy of a particular crystal. The next step is to examine how these energies can be combined with each other to achieve certain goals and purposes. And so we come to a study of using crystals and other stones in the form of charms and talismans that will act in conjunction with the energy centers of the body to bring about certain desired results.

It is important that the student become familiar and comfortable with the technique of exploring energy archetypes through meditation. The very essence of this work is the development of an inner sensitivity to the subtle nature of energy qualities in both the crystals and stones and the energies of the individuals with whom you will be working (even if that individual is yourself). The exercises we have set out will greatly help develop your awareness and sensitivity. We do not expect that any student will achieve instant mastery of this subject, but we do hope that, by beginning with guided visualizations, you will develop a growing openness and acknowledgment of your deeper inner senses. You should begin to trust your instincts and develop your intuition. This is because, at this point, we leave what can be objectively experienced and measured in your time and culture and reach forward into realms of experience that, while no less real, are far more subjective and abstract. It is your inner senses that will be your guide in testing and using the information for further study.

BASIC TECHNIQUES OF STONE USE

It is a basic principal that, if a small current of electricity is put across a crystal, it will vibrate. When a crystal is attuned to the electromagnetic field of the body, it will resonate with its vibrations in harmony with the bodily energy centers. When those centers vary by too great a margin from the vibrational charge of the stone, the individual will respond to the difference in vibration rates as a sort of irritation. Inasmuch as the stone's vibration rate is inflexible, once the charge is set, the person who is using it will reflexively alter his or her own frequency to return to an alignment with the stone's energy to relieve the irritation. This is the same principle as wearing a brace to correct an injury or deformation of a limb of the body. This is the basic physical principle by which crystals and other crystalline substances work.

Although there are many different ways in which crystals and stones can be used, these uses generally fall into three categories, each of which will be discussed separately - Life Stones, Healing Charms, and Power Talismans.

LIFE STONES

The Life Stone is, in general, the talisman of the Spirit's evolutionary growth and the transmutation of its Karmic cycles. It is used to trigger an individual's belief in his or her own inherent abilities, which in turn may trigger the crystalline nature of the piece and cause access to whatever virtue its nature may offer. Life stones are generally worn for a long period, generally through a cycle in a person's life. They can be specific crystals or charms obtained with this purpose, or they may be pieces with an unusual shape, internal anomaly, or unique color that has particular significance to the individual. They may also be pieces with unique keepsake or curiosity value. In any case, they are the "luck charm" or companion stone that is constantly in the individual's possession regardless of what other stones he or she may be working with at any given time. Unlike healing charms or power talismans, life stones are generally not charged with any specific purpose or keyed to one specific energy center, but are charged to the pattern of the wearer as a general key, focus, companion or help. This is done either on purpose when the piece is obtained, or as a process of wear and possession over time. Its purpose is to guide a trait of personality or cycle of the individual Karma not apparent in the short-term perspective.

A form of Life Stone is a simple "Luck Stone". Luck stones give virtue either by their own nature or by virtue of an unconscious will or intention placed within them. These are the simplest of pieces and often have some unique characteristic of shape or internal anomaly that makes them distinctive.

HEALING STONES

Healing stones are used for a certain specific need or purpose, such as restoring and renewing energies which have suffered damage and depletion through shock, illness, or injury. They are chosen for their functional suitability according to the basic nature of the afflicted individual and the nature of that individual's affliction. These stones are cleansed of all previous charges and alignments, then charged and aligned to the spectrum pattern of the individual by the causative intention of the Healer. Healing Stones carry the signature charge of the Healer, not of the afflicted, and remain under the Healer's conscious direction for the span of their intent. Once the desired result is achieved, they should be removed and cleansed for reuse. Their purpose is solely remedial, that is, to restore balance whether to mind, spirit, or body.

Stones may be worn on the body to lend energy to the entire body or to a specific area, because they are a way to tap into specific energy patterns. When using stones to tap these energies in this manner, always remember that the desired result is balanced strength. The nature of crystals is so precise that they will supply what energies are needed, often bringing the rest into focus by resonances of their power, if their charge is properly set.

A person may seek self-healing by using stones with resonances that satisfy the inner needs should he or she attune the self to them. These stones should be worn until they no longer serve. Once its purpose is accomplished the healing stone should be removed, lest dependency result, just as braces and crutches are cast aside so that the muscles will not atrophy through disuse. In addition, as with therapeutic exercise in the physical, these newly balanced energies should be stabilized and reintegrated by harmonious surroundings and meditative exercise, after the stone has been set aside.

Stone Elixirs

There are a variety of ways to use the beneficial energy of crystals and stones. One is by placing them on the energy meridians of a body. This will be discussed in Chapter 6. There is also the ancient practice of making stone elixirs. Fill a glass bottle with spring water, distilled water, wine, herbal infusion, massage oil, aromatherapy oil or whatever is appropriate to the occasion. The bottle should be closed with a lid, cork or stopper to prevent the liquid from going bad or dust settling in it. Tap water that has been chemically treated with fluoride and other chemicals will greatly alter the way in which the water becomes charged. Place a crystal or combination of stones and crystals in the liquid and allow it to stand in a sunny window for at least 24 hours. This will allow the water to become energized with the particular vibrational energy of the stone and allow this energy to be taken internally. It is extremely effective when energizing oil for massage, anointing, and aromatherapy. Care should be taken, however, not to attempt to charge liquids that will spoil in this period of time (such as chicken soup). It is also wise to take care that the mineral used is not inherently toxic such as compounds of arsenic or mercury. To subtly enhance the energy of the charge, it is also helpful to use a colored glass container of the color that corresponds to the energy center you wish to affect or the energy quality you wish to focus. In the course of this work, certain particular vessels will be specified for particular purposes of the practice. It should also be noted that energized liquids should be made within 24 hours of the time they will be desired for use. Water loses its charge over time and will not store unless the crystal is stored in it.

STONE TALISMANS OF POWER

Stones and talismans of power are similar to healing stones in that they are often, but not always, intended to serve for a specific limited time span and their influence is intended to apply to certain specific workings. By "workings of power", we mean any undertaking in which the participant or participants intend to exert their will and focussed energy on a situation to cause a change in that situation. It is generally understood that in so doing the participants will be working through their own power structure and with the force of their own centers. These workings generally use more that the individual's given supply of life energy. It is therefore the purpose of these talismans to reinforce, support, and replenish the energy drawn from these centers as it is used.

In composing these pieces, take care that the stones chosen are equal to the task at hand. It is also advisable for each talisman of power to be composed and balanced for an individual wearer as well as for one specific task, even if that wearer is not going to wear it all the time. For the workings of power, chose a stone that will replenish the specific energy that will be diminished in the task. These stones are worn to replenish energy during times of working with intense ranges of energy and should not be worn constantly. Doing so is likely to make excess demands on the life force of the individual. It is understood that workings of power are those practices that are above the participants' normal range of energy usage. To ask those energies to operate at that level all the time would put a serious strain on the energy system as a whole and over time is likely to be unhealthy. There should be times of rest in which the life systems are restored and allowed to return to their natural unaltered levels. When the work is done, the stone should be put aside so that it can be recharged and renewed. The wearer of the talisman should also renew him or herself.

The Laws of Harmonic Resonance

When making talismans, practicing healing, or engaging in any other forms of power working, one must consider and take into account the basic laws that govern these arts. The cornerstone of all the principles is the Law of Harmonic Resonance. It says that since all creation came from the one Prime Source, each manifestation of that Creation holds within it all the elements of the Prime. All workings of healing and power are simply the action of one energy system or group of energy systems to amplify and magnify one particular energy or system of energies. Because all life forms are extensions of the Prime, they have the potential capability to reflect that Prime's wholeness and perfection. They can contain within themselves all that is, in the same way that a single raindrop contains within itself all that is in the nature of water.

It is the nature of this Universe that it is binary. It is bi-polar, and this holds true on all levels of energy. Therefore, any energy helix will have a center balanced between two opposite points. Even if those points are separate, when they are brought into proximity, they will join and form a resonant balanced whole. It is also true that, as all energies are a reflection of the Prime, they will seek to become whole and be like the Prime that is their source. When this is achieved, a bi-polar balance is formed that is a reflection of the perfect Prime.

An individual is signified by his or her frequency - vibration - and it follows that this frequency is a harmonic of the Prime. Also, these frequencies are harmonically resonant with other similar frequencies, and when these frequencies are combined, they form a resonant harmonic that is more powerful than either of the two separately, as they become more complete. This is demonstrated in all things whether on sub-atomic levels or in the interrelationships of beings or the attraction of planets. This also applies to individual beings.

In assembling a complex talisman, there are two points of frequency and harmonics to be considered. The first is that the elements of the talisman should be harmonically resonant with one another thereby forming a balanced whole. Secondly, this balanced talisman should be harmonically resonant with the being who wears it in order to bring about a larger balanced whole.

It should be noted that certain groups of stones are resonant with each other - such as tourmaline or beryl and quartz - for they may grow from the same mother rock and in the same environment. That is why one can find quartz formations with tourmaline or beryl crystals shot through it as inclusions. Although these are stones of different families, they are formed under similar conditions and share in the same birth matrix. They are, therefore, harmonious and compatible. However, within these groups there are individuals that are more compatible with one another than others. To determine this, it is necessary to closely examine the individual resonance of each stone and to examine the interactions of the various stones with one another to find which best aligns with which.

It is a basic principle that an energy matrix will draw, or attempt to draw, to itself whatever it lacks in order to become a whole frequency. This is best demonstrated in the interaction of atoms to form molecules. The atoms will bond to one another by virtue of what is extra in one supplying what is lacking in another. The atomic bond is formed when one that has a specific abundance fulfills the one that has the appropriate construct of acceptance.

This is true of stones and talismans as well. It is the nature of any energy matrix system to be whole in and of itself, as atoms are whole unto themselves. In the case of higher (complex) life forms it happens that, through misadventure and/or the workings of Karma, these energy systems become unbalanced, or less whole. When this occurs, external energy harmonics may be supplied temporarily until the individual achieves its own balance again. At times it may be necessary or desirable for an individual to take a higher level of responsibility or power than he or she ordinarily possesses in order to fulfill some specific task. This calls for some specific talisman to supply this energy form. In this case, the nature or intensity of the required energies that may be low or unstable in the individual should be carefully examined and the stones balanced in accordance with that specific desired resonance. Then when tuning the piece, the energy helixes should be joined together so that they work in concerted harmony.

THE LAW OF

PARALLEL RESONANCE

There is also a corollary to this law, the Law of Parallel Resonance. This states that those things that are similar to each other are attracted to each other and will effect one another. When considering whether two resonances are sufficiently similar for this law to be applicable them, the degree to which their harmonics are similar should be determined, whether they have the same or similar signature pattern, and if they are in proximity to one another. Then, if all these factors exist, their resonances can be directed to act and interact with one another. The more similar they are in nature, then the more thoroughly and quickly this interaction will be accomplished. This law explains the necessity of choosing the stones with the most compatible signature pattern for the one who requires the activity of this stone. This also explains the choosing of stones that are compatible with each other to work in concert together in a single piece. This has a direct bearing on the creation of thought forms and the process of fetching, both of which will be discussed later. This is the basis of all sympathetic magic - that is, the constructing of adequate parallel resonances.

These laws may be seen acting on many levels in this Universe in both the physical and the spiritual, for they are basic concepts of its construction. Let us explain how this concept applies to crystals and other stones. To heal a person, you may not simply inflict on that entity a resonance with which he or she is not compatible. The practitioner must consider both the unique resonance of the individual in question and that of the stone to be used. Then, the healer must consider what element in the individual is lacking or excessive, and choose the stone or stones carefully so that the resonance of the stones fulfills this lack or draws and balances the excess. Each element must harmoniously integrate with the other. This might not be a simple singular energy type or resonance, but a complex pattern made of two or more resonances that form a specific harmonic pattern. A pattern of stones should be considered that has the appropriate resonance with each other, and that will supply what is needed in the entity's energy pattern. Both the stone choice and the charging of the piece should be suited to the harmonic of that individual. In this way, they may easily fulfill their function while causing no imbalance. Keep in mind that these Laws do not only refer to stones or to healing alone. They are pivotal to all workings of power. They are also essential to the workings and balancing with the self.

CONFIGURATION OF CRYSTALS

When selecting a stone, each one should be examined singly and judged on its own merits and configuration. Just choosing a representative of one family and type or another is not generally enough. It is as though you were selecting a dog. Just as the purpose you wish it to serve in your life will somewhat determine the size and breed, so also you will select a particular individual based on the matching of your two temperaments. This is how you should select any stone. You will have an idea of the purpose it is intended to serve and this will determine the family and type in general, but after that, you must select the individual stone with just as much care.

Now, we have mentioned that the personality, that is, the essence of the quality of its powers and potential, is dictated by the way in which the internal axis structure is laid out. The seed of this structure is planted when the first molecule of the material is formed. Others of its kind are drawn to it in the way of atomic attraction and so, block by block and layer by layer, a crystal structure is formed. Ideally, the larger crystal is the image of its smallest element, and so it is an integral harmonic structure. In truth, nothing in nature conforms to the ideal. Stones and crystals are formed deep in the earth and are subject to many random stresses and stimuli such as pressure, temperature, gravity, and natural radiation. All these forces will have a bearing on the way that the molecules form and the crystals and stones grow. Many random things can happen to the growth medium of a crystal. It may be rich in some components and poor in others. From time to time, as the crystal grows, other elements may be added that change its structure or color. Sometimes some elements are used up and growth stops altogether, or it finds new ways in which to combine. Sometimes, there are elements and ideal conditions for more than one type of crystal or stone to form, and so they form simultaneously, joining with each other. Sometimes, there is more than one pattern that a given group of atoms can form. This will result in a crystal that, although a representative of its kind, its axis structure and shape are somewhat different from what might be termed the ideal. When this occurs, the way in which the stone behaves will differ slightly, having particular qualities unique to that configuration but nonetheless conforming to the energy and behavior pattern of its family and type.

We will point out and explain a few of these that pertain to crystals in general. The student should be aware, however, that, just as with people, every individual is different in its own particular way. We will try to give some general guidelines that will help in your studies.

AXES & TERMINATIONS

Generally, when we envision a crystal, we think of a naturally facetted transparent stone with one end either pointed or naturally facetted in some way and the other end either naturally secured to another stone, others of its kind, or broken sharply off. The termination of a crystal is the regularly shaped top. This termination forms naturally as the crystal grows. There are some crystals, such as garnets and certain formations of fluorites, that form "in the round" forming regular, three-dimensional geometric shapes in which the terminations are difficult to define in these general terms. Please understand that in this beginning we are speaking in generalities. The termination may be sharply pointed as in the case of quartz, or it may be flat with beveled edges as in the case of beryl. Whatever the specific the termination is the end of the crystal farthest away from the base rock. Now imagine a line from the center point of the termination going directly to the center of the base where the crystal is joined to the base rock on which it formed. This is the center axis. It is the resonance of this axis that gives the crystal its true character and nature. The sides of the crystal are sometimes flat and sometimes tapering toward the tip. The sides form angles where they join. Imagine a line joining the center axis to the angle formed by the juncture of two sides. This is called a secondary axis. The pattern formed by the center axis and all secondary axes is the signature configuration of the crystal. When this structure oscillates / vibrates, it gives the signature frequency of the crystal.

Each crystal family and type has its own unique pattern of termination, number of sides, angles, and axis patterns. This is a primary point of identification. Even a broken shard of a stone will exhibit this distinctive pattern under magnification. This is why a stone will exhibit the traits of its type even when it is cut and faceted. Its internal crystalline structure remains although its surface configuration is altered. This is also why even stones that have no external evidence of crystalline structure will still have a vibration pattern. Their internal structure is crystalline although their exterior is not.

Matrix & Base Rock

The termination of a crystal is its positive pole, as its base is its negative pole. Imagine the field pattern around a magnet. This is very similar to the way the energy pattern around a crystal would look if it were visible. A crystal grows attached to a base rock or matrix. You could call this its mother rock. Its energy field is interwoven with the larger energy field of the mother rock. When a crystal becomes detached from the base on which it has formed, its energy becomes temporarily less stable. When it is the intention to use the crystal as a talisman, it is often helpful to provide the stone with a substitute for this mother stone to provide this pole with a more consistent and linear flow of energy. This can be accomplished by flattening the irregular end of the crystal and applying a metal base or cap. This will be discussed in detail in the sections dealing with metals and talismans.

DOUBLE TERMINATION

A crystal that has formed with a termination on each end is a consistent whole in its energy field, for it forms its own complete helix 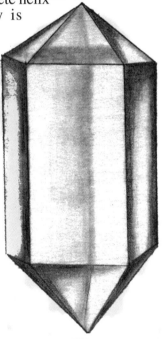 and is self-contained and its energy is self-generating. When using double terminated crystals for talismans and power tools, consider that its most centered energy is at the center point of the crystal. The point of energy amplification for double terminated stones is in the center rather than at either end, for this is the point at which the cyclical energies of each termination are most powerfully joined, assisting and amplifying one another. Imagine the field as you did above, but this time rather than singular, it looks more like a figure eight. Therefore, should it be desirable to qualify their energy, the qualifying stones should be placed in alignment with the center axis and centering on its center point.

TWINNING

Crystals are said to be twinned when two or more have grown together in such a way as to be always inseparable. This does not mean as a cluster on base rock, but two forms together which form one whole and complete crystal. They may be *contact twins* in which case each crystal has its own center axis, but shares a common axis lattice with the other. These form in many combinations that include multiple twinned terminations. They may be *penetration twins* in which case the two or more forms share the same space and complex axis lattice. In either case, they behave as a single structure and have amplified power according to their nature and the clarity and integrity of their structure and terminations.

There are also contact twins that have grown opposite from one another from a single source point on the base. At first glance, they may appear to be a double terminated single crystal. These are beautifully resonant pieces and are capable of great stability at high and sustained power levels. These may or may not be suitable to the use of the uninitiated or untrained depending on their power level and abilities. They could easily prove too strong and cause a serious overload. These stones may be tuned to fine levels of purpose and power by placing other stones for focus and intention on the pivot of the central axis. In general, the patterns and configurations of crystals as they grow together provide a virtually endless variety of energy patterns. It is for the practitioner to select the working stones carefully so that each stone is appropriate and adequate to the intended work.

INCLUSIONS

There are times in the growth cycles of stones and crystals that conditions are optimal for more than one type of stone or crystal to form simultaneously. At these times, a crystal or stone will form that contains one or more of these secondary formations. These formations are called *inclusions*. This behavior includes the formation of whole crystals within other crystals. Each crystal retains its own identity while growing in harmony with the other. Examples of this type of growth are seen in the formation of tourmaline or aquamarine in quartz crystals, rutilation (titanium oxide needles) within a crystal, as well random noncrystalline formations such a black matrix inclusions in emerald and chlorite in quartz. These are only a few of many examples of this growth behavior. These inclusions can form in a random way crossing and recrossing the lattice of the main crystal, or in regular geometric patterns precisely aligned with the axis pattern of the main crystal. This precise alignment often results in a phenomena called *asteration*, or starring such as the star patterns visible in rubies and sapphires.

Because inclusions form under the same conditions as the host rock, they grow in harmony with its resonance. Their structure grows along side the primary structure of the stone, adding the vibration of the secondary material to the primary signature of the host crystal. This is a powerful combination. Such stones must be judged for the whole of the combined resonance they produce. The presence of inclusions cannot be discounted. If the purpose of the work calls for a clear stone, then inclusions will cause a disruption in the desired energy pattern regardless of the degree of harmony in which the two materials were formed. Other types of inclusions will generate great intensity in the basic energies of the host stone. An example of this is any form of asteration, whether in quartz, corundum, or any other stone. The presence of such an extremely regular three-dimensional formation in concert with the signature pattern of the stone, amplifies the power range of the host stone as well as the range of focus of this energy. They become both very specific and very powerful, far more so than an example of the host stone without these inclusions.

GHOSTING

A specific form of inclusion known as "ghosting" or layering is caused by varying intensities of inclusions or color occurring in different layers of the crystal's growth pattern. This can be visible from one or more faces of the crystal and will appear as though one crystal has formed perfectly within another like the layers of an onion. Sometimes these are whole and sometimes they appear in part. This formation acts as though one crystal has formed perfectly within another aligning perfectly together and sharing the same axis structure.

Ghosting occurs in two ways. One is in intensity of color. This seems less like an inclusion than a variation of color in a single stone. In actuality, it could be considered as both. As an example, we will point out the layered amethyst. The violet coloration forms in layers in perfect harmony with the clear layers that can be considered pure quartz. This is due to variation in the chemical composition of the growth matrix as the crystal was formed. At times, there was more and less available material to form the violet coloration while the silicon dioxide of the quartz remained constant. They are unified by the central axis, even more so than a team of horses is unified to the purpose of pulling a wagon or plow by a single yoke. The pure quartz serves as focus and driver for the amethyst nature and magnifies its power to twice or more its singular strength. This is because a colored stone is, by its very definition, less pure to its basic kind. The color is an inclusion on the atomic level, while the clear stone has no inclusions and is therefore stronger. When both colored and clear are brought together on a single axis, they join their natures and each contributes to the other.

The second type of ghosting occurs as a secondary type of material included within the main structure of the host crystal. An example of this would be the formation of chlorite "ladders" or ghosts in quartz. The chlorite is definitely a secondary material but is included in the growth matrix in such a proportion that it forms according to the quartz axis structure. This produces a unique and powerful harmonic within the crystal. In either case, the layers amplify one another. Each boosts the other in clarity and power while all are unified to one purpose. A true perfect ghost is powerful to its purpose in color and may be considered in energy harmonics as two crystals formed perfectly one over the other with a singular in axis lattice frequency. Should it be necessary to use only one stone, then a ghost crystal is the best choice for its strength and balance and may stand in the place of several stones.

GENERAL GUIDELINES

A stone should be chosen for its initial vibration which is determined by the trueness and clarity of both its structure and color. These two elements give it its identity within the context of its type and its own individual identity. The proportion and placement of the structure, color and existing inclusions and other natural anomalies are fixed and unalterably give it its own unique character. It is up to the practitioner to judge and evaluate how all these elements work together within the context of the single stone, as well as how they work within the larger context of the intended talisman, the nature of the work intended for it, and the nature of the individual who will use the intended piece.

The power of a stone is directly proportional to its structural density and integrity and to the precision of its color. Energy is transferred through a crystal by means of its atomic lattice - that is, the way in which the atoms are bonded together. If their atomic bond is strong and complete, the greater the potential for a strong and consistent field. To the degree that their structure is weakened by incomplete or weak bonding, the potential of the energy field will be weakened and less reliable. A strongly bonded structure will reliably retain its charge for a long time (and when kept within a properly shielded container even longer), while a less strongly bonded structure will allow the charge to dissipate and become unstable. This may be a desired result in some applications and should be kept in mind. An example of such a stone is fluorite and calcite. Therefore, the scale of hardness in stones is a reasonably reliable guide to their working strength.

Precision of color is important, because the element that causes the coloration in the stone is an integral part of the crystal's signature vibration. To choose a crystal for working in multiple or intense power ranges, all aspects of a crystal's behavior must be carefully examined, but to begin the meditative work and learning process, any representative crystal of good quality will do.

Color is made in stones by the addition of particles to the basic crystalline formation of the stone and or the way in which the atoms arrange themselves. No matter how regularly the extra particle is distributed, this causes differences in the way the basic atomic structure joins. This will cause the energy to flow through the stone in a different fashion than it would in the same stone if it were clear. To the degree that the color, which is truly an atomic inclusion, is not bonded smoothly and completely with the basic atomic structure, it detracts from the strength of the bond of the energy lattice of the stone. Colored stones function as though a strong clear stone were joined with a colored qualifier that is less strong. As the practitioner drives power through the strong primary form, it will cause the weaker, secondary, qualifying form to become unstable unless he is aware of this phenomenon and adjusts his energies to accommodate it. This is why clarity of color is important. Muddiness and inconsistency of color indicate that the color-causing agent is not distributed evenly or consistently within the energy lattice of the stone and is not bonded well with the initial structure. This could indicate an energy anomaly or weakness in the structure of the stone. Sometimes color can be changed by external means (whether natural or intentionally induced) such as heat or radiation that changes the way in which the stone refracts light. Changes in color are an indication of changes in the internal molecular structure of the stone.

Archetype stones are those whose color and crystal structure most closely vibrate to the pure frequency of the archetype color. The colored inclusion is bonded with the utmost perfection to the basic crystalline structure. This makes them ideals of strength, smoothness, and versatility, and, consequently, uniquely adapted to a variety of tasks where this level of power is a key issue, provided that they are used within the context of their natures. In the workings of the trained adept for higher workings of power, it is always wisest to use the stone of highest working potential.

The color of a stone is part of its internal harmony and structure. The stone and its coloring addition have been fashioned of the same forces and come from the same base matrix. They are harmonious together as though they were brothers - one larger, older and stronger, and the other one younger and following in the elder's path. Therefore, it is wise to treat colored stones as though they were clear primary stones with colored qualifiers. Then work the talisman from the spectrum balance of the base and qualify through the color. This will greatly extend the power potential of a stone that would otherwise be considered a weak element. One must work in full spectrum and in full balance with regard to the piece.

In choosing a stone, consider its qualities and measure these against your perceptions in your objectives and goals. Its crystalline perfection is the first consideration - its center axis should be unbroken as it radiates to the other angles. Without a whole main axis, the stone is useless for general purpose and must be adapted according to its nature, although some of its virtue will be retained even in the most irregular fragments. A majority of the outer faces should be free from blemish and not impaired by other matter, inclusions, or matrix, although the natural separation marks of intersecting crystals of the same species is permissible. These faces and their adjoining angles should enter the termination without break or obstruction. Ideally, the termination should be perfect on a majority of its sides and angles and, especially at its point. This is the first consideration for its load capabilities. A talisman designed for constant heavy power transmission must necessarily have a clearer and more precise energy structure than one intended for low intensity general use. Recall the analogy of electrical resistance when considering this matter.

According to its use, the purity of the stone should also be considered. Inclusions of various foreign metals and matter must be judged in view of their proportion and position. They may add grace or virtue as long as the center axis is not greatly impaired or if they flow in accordance with the growth patterns of the piece. For example, smoke or gray ghosting or chlorides in quartz or layering in amethyst, may be most harmoniously joined with the basic crystalline form of the stone, and it may be desirable within the context of the work to have such included elements. They are often in harmony with the patterns of natural growth and they are in direct sympathy with its power directive and add their virtue according to color specification.

Rutile in quartz may be desired for its power transmission capabilities. However, excessive rutilation interferes with the base resonance of the crystal. Such stones are best judged by their own merits as composite stone, rather than as augmented examples of the base crystal family. This can be difficult to control. Inclusions may run unpleasantly counter to the axis structure, interfering with the primary purpose. Beryl structures in quartz are an ideal example of this. Choose carefully in this matter. The black tourmaline crystals inhabiting quartz may provide too great a ground even if their proportion in volume is small, especially if they interrupt the axis structure at too great an interval. While this type of piece may give an impression of great power, it is merely energy of an erratic nature and can never be focused truly as would be desired. However, if these imbedded crystals are rightly positioned this provides a piece of unparalleled grace, power, and balanced force. These pieces are most precious in their rarity and if one should ever come into your possession be sure to keep it.

PREPARATION & INTERACTION

CLEARING

When a stone comes from its natural environment, it has already been subjected to a variety of natural phenomena such as static electric discharge, heat, light, cold and the shock of separation from its natural ground. It also has been influenced to a greater or lesser degree by all hands that have touched it on its journey to the hands of the practitioner. Understandably, this will make its energies unfocussed and somewhat random. It will have parts of many patterns, but no whole focussed configuration to its vibrations. Also, a stone may have been previously owned and used by someone else and a portion of this charge remains. By clearing and charging a stone, we mean that before it is used for its intended purpose, its random and unfocussed vibrations as well as any previous charges need to be reset to a neutral configuration. This is much the same idea as erasing a blackboard at the beginning of a class or study. This does not mean that you wish to remove the entire personality and identity of the stone. It simply means that you need to clear away those things that would inevitably distract from the purpose you have in mind for it. The currents must flow in perfect alignment to accomplish its intended purpose.

The simplest way of realigning a stone is to allow it to remain in sunlight for a few days. Alternatively, place it in a plain wooden box with no metal fittings until the charge has dissipated. This method will be sufficient for simpler stones, but requires a minimum time allotment of one lunar cycle. This is the equivalent of letting them rest. It will not remove serious negative vibrations that have been programmed into the stone, nor will it remove any previous charge that is set into it by a competent practitioner. However, it will allow the vibrations to become less erratic so that whatever remaining charge there is on the piece is revealed. This method will never work on emerald, ruby, or sapphire crystals, and will take a minimum of thirteen lunar cycles for diamond crystals if the charge on the container remains entirely unaltered, that is, unentered by Spirit and thus uncharged.

A stone may be cleansed and charged by a process of meditation. This method may be used by those who are new to the study, because their own personal focus is not likely to be as disciplined. It is appropriate that they go through one complete meditative cycle in journey with the stone and cleanse its vibrations. A more experienced practitioner may cleanse a stone by intending it to purity by a surge of pure blue/white energy through the right (dominant) hand, via the heart. This requires simply a moment of pure focus.

A stone may be freed from excessive static charge but not totally cleared by placing it briefly on a large black tourmaline. This will not interfere with the basic nature of the intentional charge nor with the signature of the owner, but will calm and restore its purpose and balance when it has been subjected to excessive or erratic energy levels.

Salt and salt water are also commonly used as a clearing medium, but keep in mind what will occur. The interaction of the salt with the surface of the stone will nullify all surface ionization and thus all stimulation of the center axis. This is the equivalent of resetting the stone to absolute zero. It will retain no charge of its owner, its purpose, or its identity. This is a radical process and will remove much of the personality of the stone that the individual felt drawn to when he or she selected it. Therefore, this process is not generally recommended unless such an extreme result is desired. If such a strong procedure is desired, it would be advisable to use seawater. There are many minerals, ions and trace elements in sea water that are not present in water mixed with regular salt. The use of sea water in this process will definitely cleanse the crystal but will preserve its character and personal integrity. More commonly, it is sufficient to wash the stone in clear running water and leave it in the sunlight for a complete sun cycle. Then it may be recharged by the intention of the user and this recharging will remove whatever remains of the previous charge.

COLOR CHANGES

You may notice that when crystals and stones are cleared for the workings of power and meditation they often appear to become physically clearer and lose their color. This may also happen when a crystal or stone is consistently used for a certain length of time in deliberate power workings. This is the reason why this occurs: Stones are a product of Nature and are thus not perfect in their structure and makeup. They contain anomalous material in small quantities and their atomic/crystal structure is not always perfectly aligned in their process of growth. This is unavoidable and to be expected. As they are cleared, the flow of concentrated energy will cause the particles to reform on the atomic level and form a more precise bonding among them. In workings of power, this process is even more pronounced. In addition, since the nature of their structure is vibratory, the Spirit who clears them will sing them into harmony during this atomic realignment. This change of the basic structure will allow light to pass through them more directly and easily making them seem clearer or paler in color.

As a stone works and fulfills its purpose, it may seem to change color according to the degree of the intensity of the work from moment to moment. This indicates the passage of energy through the stone as from moment to moment the interactive level of the individual's energy level interacts with that of the crystal. This is an excellent way to monitor and measure the progress of any work the stone may be doing. Opals of all varieties and members of the Beryl family are particularly notable in this behavior. Should a stone suddenly become extremely cloudy or manifest a color that is not within the desired range of energies, that stone should be removed and exchanged for one of a stronger or more specific nature.

INTENTION & CLEARING

We will give an initial demonstration in the form of a deep meditation so that the mechanism of this process may be understood on all levels. However, as soon as you are familiar and comfortable with this process this lengthy procedure should not be necessary. You should practice this often until it becomes easy, comfortable and natural. Then, when you begin working with various stones and energy helixes the action of charging may be done smoothly and without effort or strain. We mean to show you by meditation, how a stone does clear and then become charged, so that you will know and understand the nature of this procedure.

For this exercise, choose for yourself a single terminated clear quartz point. It should be generally clear and free from unnecessary fractures, inclusions, or anomalies, whether internal or external. All sides and the terminations should be clear and free of chips or interruptions. For this initial learning process, it should have no secondary crystals formed with it but should be singular and alone. It should be totally clear having no color within it other than, perhaps, a light white frost close to the base. For this part of the work, it is necessary to have the actual stone at hand. The archetypal form is not suitable here, as the archetypes are, by their very nature, perfect within themselves needing no clearing. Also, let this particular stone belong entirely to the student, and not be borrowed or shared. It should be kept safely in a wooden box or cloth or leather bag close to his or her person or in the accustomed place of his meditative work. This is a personal learning tool and this learning will be confused if the stone is cluttered with intentions of more than one person. It should not yet be set in a metal base for this purpose.

It is well to state here that all things have a sort of archetypal existence that we will call the primal form. This is not a true archetype. We mean that all things exist on many levels, that anything can and does exist simultaneously in many universes. In this way, we will demonstrate to you what occurs in your stone, guiding you through its nature and form as it exists in this primal universe. You will see that its true form and nature are manifested and not limited to this physical plane. In addition, you will learn that, as something is manipulated on one level, so all reflections of it are manipulated and thereby changed on all levels of awareness. By these meditations and exercises we will show you how one may work on many levels of awareness at once, so that the process is uniformly done. As a change is manifested and then reflected to different levels, so these reflections are somewhat distorted as the reflection is, to some slight part, distorted from the reality of the original manifestation. Whenever a working is manifested, it changes into an energy form and thus is slightly different than in the original context of its manifestation or creation.

❀ - MEDITATION ON INTENTION & CLEARING

Lie down in the place where you practice your meditations, with your crystal in your hand. Begin with breathing as in the previous meditations. With the first slow breath, you feel yourself leaving your body and drifting outward. As you take the second breath, you are free and drifting. As you release this breath, you find yourself, once again, in the field of clouds. You see before you how they turn and change. This time they are pure white with complete purity and radiance. They are soft and are not fiery. They are cool and buoy you up gently, supporting your form in effortless flight. You move across them and through them rejoicing in their patterns and textures. --- You feel all cares drop from you as you touch them. Your focus becomes clear, detached, and pleasantly objective. You see all things and yet you are still apart from them, with a unique sense of identity and awareness. You know this is your privilege as spirit in form. This clean clear awareness of identity is yours and requires no thought, no effort. It is a fact of existence. --- All things in this universe are unique and special unto themselves as you are unique. All things are linked together in the universal brotherly union of life and within that shared life. You are at peace and aware of all of these things. You move forward on the winds, but you do not drift aimlessly. You are guiding and propelling yourself by your clear intention. It is an effortless process of decision from moment to moment. --- You move forward, supported by your own intention. Feel the body/form you have created for yourself here. Feel its unified energies flowing in perfect accord with themselves and with their surroundings. --- Pause now among the clouds. Examine this form. Extend your hands in front of you. Examine them and note their wholeness. See how they glow softly. They are luminescent, and they pulse with the healthy glow of energy and power. --- Now extend this energy out from your hands, feel it reach outward and encounter a tuft of cloud with this energy and make a shape with its substance. It is easy to shape this cloud form. You may make it thin as paper. --- You can make it swirl in spirals, or you can make it dense as a brick. --- Under your shaping energies it may become anything you choose. You are delighted with this whimsy. See how you can cause it to spin, thin, and coalesce. It becomes a bubble floating in a rainbow transparency. It grows larger and more radiant. --- Draw it closer now. You can hold it in your hands. You can feel how strong it is now, how resilient, and how feather light. It is delightful holding this glowing bubble. You play with these cloud forms for a while until you are comfortable with them and their changes. --- Now put the clouds back the way you found them, and watch how they melt and flow back into their own forms. They are one with themselves once again.

You move forward again now, and you know what you are seeking. You seek the primal form of your crystal, the one you held in your hand and studied just a short time ago. You see the clouds moving now, swirling slowly and softly. They fold back. Within them, they hold a shining form. You seek the crystal form. It shines before you now as you have seen all the others shining, but now you notice a difference. The crystal you see before you now is your own. Notice its distinct differences. See where it has been separated from its base rock, how it is rough and irregular. Now notice the sides and the termination, and see how they shine. --- See the striations on the sides where it has formed in the earth layer by layer. --- Regard the pattern of its sides and angles. It is unique and perfect in its own existence. It is like the archetype you have already seen, and yet it is uniquely itself. Its pattern exists only as itself. Even though it may be reflected many times, and there may be many stones that share its basic nature, none are identical. It is special.

You move within it now as you have done before to experience its matrices and its songs. These matrices are unique. Notice how subtly they are formed and observe the differences from the archetype. --- This crystal is not simply singular as you see it more closely. You notice that it is made up of countless tiny cells. Each is the same as the other. They are fitted together perfectly end to end, and each one sings its own energy note. You hear these notes all around you. --- They are the same, but each is different, just as different voices in a choir are different yet all sing the same note. They blend together in harmony and balance to form the one pure note of the crystal. It vibrates purely and gently as a single harp string in the wind and fills your whole form with radiance. --- Yet something here is not right. There is something slightly amiss in the harmony. You look around you with all your senses. Yes, over there, there is an anomaly. The harmony is not quite true, for in its growth it was not absolutely perfect. --- Extend your energy now as you have done before from your hands. Flow this energy to the spot where this anomaly occurs. Feel it, encounter it, and interact with it. Now, by the decision of your will, cause this anomaly to change and to flow. Yes, there it is. The note is now aligned. The harmony is straighter, purer, clearer. --- Move beyond the stone now. Move outward from it, but maintain your connection with its matrix until you can envision its entire form. --- Now reach out again. The harmony is still slightly untrue. Envelop the form of the stone entirely with your radiance, your power, and your energy. Now your intention and will interacts with the stone. --- The pattern of song becomes clear and clearer still. Yes. Now you feel it become true and clear, unique in its special song, but with all notes singing clearly and truly in balance and harmony with one another. ---

You see that what you have done is right and true. You examine the stone again inside and out, extending all your various senses to interact with it checking its lights and its clear pure song. Yes, you have done well and it is truly harmonic now. Now, for the last time in this clearing, extend yourself again to it. Intend through your energies that it shall remain like this, that it shall be so. It is finished for your purposes at this point.

Now you move away from it. You see it shining there within the flowing clouds of white and silver. It is safe and perfect. You move away from it and begin the return into your own body. Breathe deeply - let the breath release slowly. Once, twice, and again a third time, as the life and vigor flows through your form. You have returned. Now pick up the small stone you have beside you. It is almost surprising to see it in the palm of your hand, cool and solid. You feel again your pleasure in it. Now extend the energy from yourself through your hands and into the stone. Feel it interact as before. Intend the smooth cool structure to realign and to reform subtly. The song of the stone becomes clear, a pleasant pure note. Feel the note inside yourself. Know that your stone is now clear on many levels in many spaces and times. You are truly aware of its song within itself. It is waiting now to be filled with its purpose - the purpose you have designated for it.

CHARGING

By charging a stone or crystal, we mean the intentional programming of that stone to perform a specific function or task. It is a process of directing the personal energy field of the practitioner or wearer in a particular way so that the electromagnetic nature of the individual's energy fields will influence the surface ionization of the crystal and align, change and charge this surface in a particular and specific pattern consistent with the individuals goals regarding the stone. This sounds highly technical and difficult. It sounds as if we mean both stone and owner should glow in the dark when this process is successfully completed. Quite the contrary, it is a natural process that often happens spontaneously at low levels of intensity. It can happen in a moment or more slowly when a piece is in an individual's possession for a longer period of time. What we intend to show here is how this can be done intentionally to serve specific ends. Heed this well, for it is the pivot and center of this work and without it, all the rest has no use or functional meaning at all.

The simplest and most common means of using a healing stone (and also a Life Stone) is to cleanse the piece and then, in the wearing of it, causatively allow its virtue to interact with the wearer's aura. Choose the stone for its inherent nature and its attraction to the wearer. Remain aware of it and be at peace with its influence. This may be done if there is no practitioner available for its charging. It is highly inadvisable for a person who is ill to charge his or her own stone. In this case, it is likely that the imbalance of that individual's energies will be transferred in the charging to the stone and it will not heal the ill but will perpetuate the condition. A person who is ill may certainly use stones, but should use just the stones' own natural vibrations without charging them, if it is necessary for him to work alone.

The charge is set by the intention and will of the healer using the right hand and the heart pulse of white light to align the vibrational frequency of the stone within the parameters of the atomic structure to match as closely as possible the identity code vibration of the Spirit. This in turn aligns one with the other for whatever work is intended. Then the interactive vibration frequency of the color will bring the desired balance, as traction brings alignment of the bones, by constant gradual pressure/stress on the energy fields.

THE INITIAL CHARGE

To examine the process of charging a stone closely, we will proceed with a guided meditation using the crystal selected for the clearing process. Do this on a day when you have rested well, eaten well, and revitalized yourself in your physical form. Take small occasions during this time to examine your stone. Feeling pleasure in its clarity, stroke it as you would a small pet. Observe it as you would a flower and enjoy its new state. Feel its perfection and readiness. Do this for a day or two until you are once again restored and are ready to proceed. During this interval, do not neglect the exercises of breathing and balance, they are most important to maintain yourself in your studies.

In charging a stone, you must first know the purpose of the charge. Decide what task you wish to set it to perform. You must have this firmly and clearly in your mind, intention and will before you begin. For this initial lesson, we will set the purpose for you. It is also a purpose you will set for many stones during the course of your work with them. You need to consider the nature of the stone: it is quartz and clear. This presupposes certain things, certain qualities about its nature and capacity. Being quartz, it is suitable as a general purpose stone. It may manifest along a broad spectrum of energies all at once. You should now read the first part of the section on quartz and also the sections on clear stones and white stones.

The purpose we will set for the charging of the first stone is that it will contribute on all levels to the balance of the student. It will aid you in your endeavors by bringing the focus of energy most needed at the time. It will assist you in opening your path of awareness in the most harmonious and balanced processes. This stone will be the first tool you use. After this lesson on charging is completed, the student should carry this stone on your person in a small bag of leather or natural fiber cloth. It may be worn on a cord about the neck or carried in a pocket or pouch. Do not set it as jewelry yet until the time has come in these studies when you are instructed to do so. It should never be far from you, because it is your gateway into the wisdom of these things. It is also a private tool with special energies and should not be left lying about. At this stage of the work, the stone needs to be in close proximity to the student in order for it to manifest its intended virtue. This is the purpose of these endeavors.

✿ - *MEDITATION ON CHARGING*

Seek again the place of the primal stone as we have shown you. The clouds are yours in this, for your comfort and pleasure. Take some time in playing with the clouds. Notice their shapes and fires, how easily they change, notice that they contain all the colors and radiance of rainbows. Take one of these rainbows and magnify it. Feel how pliable it is in your hands and how easily responsive it is to your will. Now experience this magnificent rainbow one band at a time; see how each band shades into the next so that they only seem to be separate. Take one resonance at a time and feel it on your skin. Be aware of its texture, its smell, its song, and its temperature. Now experience it yet deeper. --- Blend it within yourself. Become this spectrum. Feel how each shade and resonance blends in with the shades and resonances of yourself. This is the true full potential. --- Now as it rests within you, stretch out your hand and, with your intention, a solid stream of color flows from your fingertips. Now change the color. Form it, change it, and play among the colors that are part of you. Now experience them as energy. --- Feel them vibrate down your arms, across your shoulders, up from your belly, tingling on your neck and scalp.

You are enfolded and permeated by the energies of the dancing colors and you begin to move in the dance with the colors. By your will and intention, see them change and unfold. Yours is the joyful dance in the rainbow clouds to the music of their ever-changing song. Yours is the will that plays this music. --- Now you begin to gather them in. You mold them inside you like wet soft clay. They are all within you now, held just below your heart. They are yours and ready to use at need. You can play with them or work with them for they are entirely under your control.

Now look about you. From within the swirling cloud you see your crystal rising. It is familiar in all its faces and facets. It flashes in the surrounding lights and glows with its own radiance as though in welcome. You reach out to touch its glowing sides. Now at your touch, you let flow from your fingertips the rainbow energy. It flows around your stone and fills it with all the various colors. --- See them flow along the axes, watch them swirl with the stone's energy matrix patterns. Now, with all true intention and will, say to the stone, "Mine. You are mine. This energy you hold is part of my own. You will release it to me at my need. As part of me you will know my need and fill me as you fill yourself with the limitless energy of the universe. We exist with each other in the flow of all things. You and I are together." --- You know that it is by your own intention and will that this is done and accomplished. It is right within the flow of all things. Now your stone begins to answer you with a true sweet note. You feel its singing, the song comes into you, and you resonate the song of the self. You feel your own song and the song of the stone in perfect balanced harmony. It weaves within you as the rainbow weaves, pure and balanced, synchronized with all the various needs that your balance manifests. All things are within you and your own will and intention. You may change this at any time, but only by your conscious will and intention. This may not be altered nor interfered with by any being, for this is the manifestation of your birthright energy. This is your place in the flow of the River of Life. This is the well of your strength and power channeled through the potential of the stone. It glows forth from you and around you like multicolored raiment. ---

Now you feel another pleasant change take place. The colors meet and join, they are truly blending one with another. They become one whole perfect blended resonant radiance. A pure clear light surrounds you now, as all colors and none. All energy and potential are within you, ready to show forth whatever color you desire at will. In addition, its strongest center lies at your heart held close yet radiating forth like a beacon. It is a bottomless reservoir of energy within you of pure clear light energy. ---

Now you are drawing back towards your body. You feel yourself re-entering your physical form. You feel your new energy and strength permeating the form. You are one with it. You begin to breathe deeply again. Your eyes open. Reach beside you and take your stone in your hand. Through your hand via your heart breathe into it all you have experienced. Feel it resonate on your palm, feel its answering song. It is charged to you and to you alone will it answer. You know this and take pleasure in the fact. Place it within its carrying bag, and place the bag on your person. Go forth and revitalize yourself. Know that you have done well.

SELECTING YOUR STONES

To select a stone for either yourself or another person, first consider that person's identity pattern, that is, the specific unique vibration pattern of the person in question who will wear or use the stone. This code is unique to each individual, just as fingerprints are unique. Then consider the nature of the purpose to be accomplished or the Chakra to be raised to balance within the framework of the identity code. Consider the strength of the being's energy. These are the considerations to have in mind when selecting the family, color, and particular stone or crystal. Match the stone first in strength and identity structure to the being, and then tune in color and location of wearing to the balance desired. Remember that all work with crystals is an exercise in interactive harmonics of vibration and must always be conducted with that in mind. A powerful stone may seem like a good choice at first, but is the energy field of the individual under consideration strong enough to integrate those powerful harmonics? Perhaps a stone of lesser magnitude would be more appropriate. Some stones are extremely specific and narrow in their band of energy interaction. These may be a good choice, but consider that by using such a specific stone you may be neglecting some of the secondary harmonics that also need attention. Perhaps a wider range stone would balance the whole field more effectively. It will take some time, meditation and experience to become personally familiar with the stones and how they will interact with different persons and energy types. It is always possible to choose a less powerful stone and then change the stone to a more powerful or specific one as the work progresses.

WEARING &

PLACEMENT OF STONES

Once a stone is charged with your purpose, it will probably work to its fullest potential if you carry it somewhere on your person. This is a large generality and has as many exceptions to it as rules, but this is a good place to start with your learning and experience. We have not yet discussed metal in connection with the stones you use. In the beginning, it is a good idea to wear your stones set in silver. This metal more than any of the others we will examine, encourages a consistent flow of energy throughout the system. As for the placement of these stones, their location over specific areas is mentioned within the text for each separate gem. If the stone is not set in metal, wear it in a soft bag of organic material such as leather or fabric, hanging around the neck so that it hangs generally over the heart area. This is the most central point of the energy fields of the body and the point of their greatest interaction. Therefore, a stone will have be most useful when hung at this central juncture.

Gems worn for healing should be worn aligned with the vertical axis only so that they will interact with the main course of the body's energy and influence its interactions directly. Gems worn on the hand are not specified for healing unless the defect is in the hands themselves. Gems worn on the hands should be used for the purpose of focussing power, and should be used as qualifiers for the body/spirit's intake and outflowing energies.

In the transmission of power or energy the stone will sometimes seem to glow as the structure channels and releases energy. In the way of the

Universe, energy is often manifested as light. It is a predictable physical effect that working stones will often slightly glow or manifest a sheen or luminosity. This is the most positive of signs and it is well to mark this.

OVERLOADING A STONE

It is possible to ask more of a stone's energy capacity than it is able to supply or to put more energy through it than its atomic structure is capable of accommodating without losing some of its stability. When a stone is burned out through overload, it will cease changing color and usually take on a dull or gray cast. It will feel dull in the hand and cease to respond in a way that is appropriate to its programmed function. This weakness may also cause the stone to fracture or chip. Only one who is experienced in this practice, or one who is an adept, should attempt to restore its power and balance, and even then, this will not always be possible. In any case, the stone should be put away in a quiet place to rest and restructure itself according to its own nature. It may be replaced in the work by a stronger one, or one that is more particular to the nature of the intended work.

WHEN THE WORK IS DONE

You may notice that when the intended work is accomplished, the stone is no longer noticed in the wearing. This is because awareness of a stone's presence is directly related to the differences between the existing balance pattern and the preset interactive harmonic of the stone. When synchronization is achieved, this difference is no longer present and so the stone may be forgotten and put aside or exchanged for a more powerful stone if further work is called for.

A RAINBOW OF EXPERIENCE

So far, we have worked most closely with clear quartz. At this point in your studies, it would be a good idea to broaden your perspective of energies by working with colored stones and stones of different families. This is the list of the colors that will be needed along with a suggested stone of that color range. At this point, tumbled or cut stones will not truly serve the purpose of experiencing the full magnitude of each energy potential. You should take your time and find appropriate examples of each crystal type.

For these beginning exercises, the crystals you use should be terminated on at least one end and this termination should be without breakage or flaw. The color of each stone should be a clear, even and true color rather than a mixed shade or tint. This should be a true, clear green rather than one tinted by blue or yellow. The red should be rich and vibrant, not washed out or cloudy. It should be explained that rose quartz is not suitable as rose for this study for it is most often pink, which is pale red not rose. In addition, rose quartz is not strong in its color bonding for wide range working. If you are color blind, have someone else choose for you, for physical sight only is a small part of the perceivable spectrum. We are speaking here of energy archetypes, not solely physical phenomena.

Once again, we urge you to take your time and choose the stones carefully because it is this collection that will form the nucleus of your working stones. It is not necessary that they be set at this time. You can work with them in small bags as we previously discussed, although it will be fine if they are set in silver.

WHITE	Quartz, Moonstone
RED	Garnet, Ruby
ROSE	Rubelite Tourmaline, Beryl (Morganite)
GOLDEN	Topaz
ORANGE	Citrine
YELLOW	Heliodor (Yellow Beryl)
GREEN	Peridot, Tourmaline, Emerald, Tsavorite Garnet
PALE BLUE	Aquamarine
BLUE	Iolite, Sapphire
VIOLET	Amethyst
PURPLE	Garnet, Ruby, Siberite Tourmaline
BLACK	Tourmaline (Schorl)

CHAPTER 5

JOURNEY OF THE SPIRIT

In every age there have been those who explored and practiced the crafts of power. They have called these crafts by many names and conceived of and explained them by as many different systems of philosophical and theological images and constructs. Among the many who have sought powers and knowledge along these paths, there have been some few who have realized that mastery is not the province of a single philosophy or theology, no matter how intricate or profound. Mastery is not limited to any one set of terminology, rather, it is the product of the inner person and that individual's dialogue with those higher inner voices of his or her own angelic spirit. This dialogue will lead that individual to an awareness of his or her higher nature and consequently to an awareness of that connection with the greater universe beyond. All philosophies and theologies that are based on true spiritual working will eventually lead the individual to the inner gateway - the personal and unique portal to the connection of the personal divine with the Universal Divine. All manifestations of power come because of this connection because it is by the recognition and acknowledgment of the Higher Self that the higher powers come within the range of the individual.

We want to assure you that this connection has always been there and will always be there. The portal is always available. Were it not, none of this would be possible or even conceivable. You are part of the Universal Divine, just as a single facet is part of the greater whole jewel. In addition, as such a facet, you have the potential to reflect all the Inner Light that is the radiance of that jewel.

In every Universe, there are laws that govern the channeling and use of these powers. These laws pertain to the nature of the Universe in which the powers are operant and also to the individuals who use these powers, for there are certain precepts that pertain to conscious life regardless of the Universe they dwell in. We will begin in this section to explore power as it pertains to the individual, to its direction, channeling, and use, and to the growth necessary to use it well and wisely.

It is written in the Ancient Books: There are basic principles by which the Mage may practice his art and the Wise may seek further wisdom from among the worlds and heavens. There are ways by which the Seer practices her Calling and by which all may seek relief and sanctuary. These are the disciplines and methods of power and working with energies. This is how they may aid all Humankind and Creation. Those who walk in the ways of power are like the Warrior and these disciplines and procedures will stand them in good stead should they choose to heed them. A great deal has been surmised, written and bantered about regarding these arts, but when any truth was told about them, it was cloaked in many mists so that only the few could penetrate and interpret it correctly. Let us now set the feet of the Apprentice upon the path so that those who seek wisdom may go forth in safely and in strength.

ETHICAL PRINCIPLES

The first principle of all crafts of power is that of *ethics*, for without an understanding of ethical conduct the work will proceed flawed and end in ruin. By ethics, we do not mean simply a set of arbitrary and judgmental rules and regulations of behavior. Ethical conduct rests on the premise that actions result in consequences. The practice of ethics deals with making choices about the results and consequences of, not only one's physical actions, but also one's attitudes and motivations. The purpose of this work is so that not only individuals, but Humankind as a whole can grow and expand, can return to a greater awareness of connection and kinship to the one Universal Divine. Those acts that defy the principles of ethics retard this process and will eventually cause the practitioner to lose those talents and powers that he or she had gained. This is because those acts that cause pain, coercion, and darkness inevitably darken the spirit of the individual. A practice or act that does not acknowledge and respect an individual as a creation and participant in the Universal light implies that the practitioner does not acknowledge his or her own identity as a part of the Universal Divine and denies him or herself respect as well. On a spiritual level, the practitioner will find this painful. In the deepest analysis, you see yourself as you see others.

Responding to the actions of the conscious self in its learning environment is a function of the Higher Self. The Higher Self will reject those things that inhibit the connection of the whole individual to the Universal light and will act to limit the conscious self's actions that contribute to this limitation. The Higher Self will reject those connections to powers and abilities that are contrary to the individual's basic good and the quality of light within. This process may not be instantly visible, but will accrue over time as Karma.

Ethical precepts concern all Callings and interactions, because ethical behavior and respect for all Life is necessary in any and all dealings within the scope of Life. It is necessary to recognize and respect the dignity, individual determinism and blessedness of all Life and Living Things on whatsoever a scale. Take care to proceed with good will and respect toward all things. The burden of responsibility of the work rests upon the shoulders of the worker that it should cause no harm. Also, take care to have respect for the self. It is neither wise nor permissible to allow one's self to be harmed should this be preventable.

This respect for the other individual begins with a respect for that individual's free self-determinism and right of choice. Unless the situation is life threatening, no act or practice should be undertaken upon an individual without that individual's informed consent. It is for an individual to choose whether or not he or she wishes assistance or intervention and to determine the degree of intervention or assistance by knowing what the process will entail.

Do not do any work with an individual without that individual's informed consent; except in those times where life or lives are threatened and no consent can be obtained. Then, let the intention of the practitioner be good will to all living things and a general respect for Life. If intervention is necessary and the individual cannot accept or reject of his or her own free will, as in the case of insanity, delirium, great injury or unconsciousness, then the process should only be done up to the point of dealing with the emergency. When the individual has returned to full sensibility, then the work can proceed according to his or her wishes. If a person is incapable of granting permission, the aid should be given only to the extent of dealing with the emergency. In general, only the act or procedure consented to should be done to the agreed level or degree of completion. Let the determinism of all creatures be respected, not only their right to grace and comfort, but their right of refusal of that comfort. No person may fully know another's Karma or destiny and no one has the right to interfere with that destiny or Karma or an individual's choices regarding it. If a person chooses to refuse assistance, that is their right, and this must be respected. This will sometimes be very difficult to watch or be party to. Objectivity must be maintained in such situations to avoid improper entanglements and high levels of empathetic emotional stress on the part of the practitioner.

Sometimes it will be necessary for you to work with animals or children below the age of true knowledge and self-discipline. Animals must be dealt with only to the point of their necessity but no farther, for theirs is the right to freedom and growth according to their kind. Let them be given safety and comfort according to the nature of their lives. As for children, it must be at the discretion of their protecting adult or guardian that treatment be given them if they are unwilling.

If any individual seeks aid, comfort, or healing in any form, let them only ask for it and it shall be granted to the full scope of the healer's ability and resources. All this must be considered, and these precepts are true of healing and of all workings of power and will. Knowledge and power come with the responsibility for their use, their affect on the individual involved, the practitioner, and those individuals involved in the situation.

SHIELDING

A shield is a layer or condition of energy projected by the practitioner so that his or her work does not disturb others and is not disturbed by others. It is like a curtain at a window or a wall or screen around a room. Shielding does not imply an adversarial, fearful or combative attitude. Rather, it is a matter or ensuring quiet for one's own space and respecting the space of others. If the energy work involves another person, as in the case of healing, the shielding should include that individual. In fact, it is important that this individual is included in the shields of the practitioner, because in the process of the work it will most probably be necessary for the individual to relax all personal shields in order for the work to be successful. The practitioner's shield should protect them from harm, interference, or any accidental occurrence from the outside, and insure that no undesired energy escapes outside of the accomplished work. This should be the first step of any work.

Shielding is also necessary in healing so that the resonance of illness and negativity will not affect others. It is important that those unhealthy and negative energies be contained until they are purged or cleaned and then returned to the pool of the Universal power to become again pure force without coloration or intention. It is also necessary to provide those receiving treatment with an energy environment that is free from the chaos and stress of the world around them. When one works toward the healing of another, it is necessary for the first level of that person's barriers and shielding to be taken down in order for the healing process to take effect and the beneficial energies to be received in full strength and intention. This will leave that person unguarded and vulnerable to all manner of ills and distractions unless the healer establishes some interim counter-measure while working, until the person's shields may be made whole and reset again after the process of the work is complete.

Shielding is also necessary for the practitioner's sake. His or her concentration should be directed solely on the work and he or she will have neither time nor scope to consider the surrounding energies and influences at this time. Therefore, automatic shields should be established to insulate the practitioner from the intrusions of the world and the negative energies of the one who is ailing so that he or she will not unintentionally carry away negative or harmful energies. Therefore, the practitioner should establish a place of quiet, harmony, and safety at the beginning of the procedure.

The degree and nature of the shielding and centering may vary according to the necessities of the procedure, the nature of the surrounding environment, and the abilities and experience of the practitioner. However, in doing energy work, it is far better to be overly cautious than to rush ahead prematurely or inadequately shielded and prepared. The shields should begin within the practitioner and from this protected core radiate outward for some distance beyond the physical body. In the case of group work, then the shields should extend for some certain distance beyond the physical boundaries of the area required for the work. They may take many varied forms according to the worker's discretion.

LEVELS OF SHIELDING

First, there is the basic personal shield that should have been being built through meditation from the outset of the first training. This shield secures any person of any sensitivity at all against any unwanted intrusion. Its basis is the center of the self and knowledge of the safety and strength of the willed intention of the individual. This is the level with which we began in the first chapter of this work. The strongest of the shields is that of the innermost self. This is known sometimes as the wall of the inner temple and it is the strength of the integrity of the inmost self. By integrity, we mean the strength and wholeness of the true spiritual identity. Only at greatest peril should this true shield be ignored or breached, for the risks are very great. It is the seat of the individual's power and dignity. It is also the shield of the unconscious self. It should only be broached in case of the most serious emergency, after all other methods of healing and communication have been tried and have failed. This shield should have been built from the beginning of training, and should never in any way or for any reason whatsoever be intentionally lowered by the practitioner, unless in the most protected of spaces and circumstances.

The second level of shielding is the mid-level shield of the practitioner that is the protection of the conscious aware self. It is a psychic layer, and should protect the practitioner from the mental/psychic vibrations that would ordinarily impinge on the sensitive awareness. It lies outside the inner shield but within the shield sometimes known as the social layer. It is more personal and intentional than the social layer, but not the intimate level of the inner shield. The practitioner accesses his or her subtle senses and intuitive knowledge behind this level. This inner shield is like a curtain, protecting the practitioner's resources of strength and meditation. This shield is cultivated in the process of the work and is for the maintenance of his personal privacy and the security of his resources. It functions as a filter for energies directed towards him or sometimes away from him. It is this secondary level of shielding that can be extended to include the individual or object of their work.

The last outer layer of the personal shield is sometimes called the social level and exists in all individuals and usually is active concurrent with the aura of the body. It is part of the knowledge of even the lowest self-aware creatures and dictates, on an unconscious level, the degree of physical space a person requires around the physical body.

HEALER'S SHIELDS

In the process of the work it is necessary, especially for the Healer, to establish safety and continuity for the person upon whom he or she works, so that alarm and shock to the individual will not result when his shields are broached during the healing process. Ideally, this should take place in a cleansed and protected space that the Healer has established for this purpose. However, sometimes a Healer will not be able to work in a place that has been previously cleansed, shielded, and secured for this purpose, for the nature of this Calling will take him or her to the places where the sick and injured have fallen. In these instances, the Healer may extend his or her personal exterior shield to encompass the person on whom he or she practices. In this way, the energy of this shield layer is extended by boosting its energy from the heart chakra and guiding its extent through the will energy of the brow chakra to overlap and encompass that person upon whom the Healer is practicing. In the meditation, this extending of shields may be envisioned as though the rainbow bubble grew to a size that it will comfortably include both the healer and his patient. First, it is laid over the person's shields extending beyond them. A harmonic resonance is established and integrated peacefully with them. This should be a procedure that the Healer has practiced and developed privately through meditation. This shield should stand in place of and not in addition to the patient's own exterior shield. The Healer then may strengthen and reinforce the patient's own energy fields, so that the patient may feel safe and protected within this enclosure. The Healer may go even deeper into the patient's personal levels and this will be made easier by the fact that the person is stabilized and relaxed and therefore does not feel this as an intrusion. Then, when the security of the person has been established, the Healer will sense within that person a relaxation and extension of trust to the Healer that will enable him to do the work in the fullest and deepest way possible. It is this perception of relaxation that gives the

Healer a tacit permission to complete the process of the shielding for this is the inner being allowing the work to proceed by its own determinism. Then the shields of the individual may be gently moved aside or augmented while the work is in progress. This will have some certain beneficial results.

In the case of injury or shock, the individual will have created for him or herself a certain level of pain block shield. This may have initial benefit, but if they are maintained too long, they become rigid and the essence of life withdraws from the area. This will cause the energy nodes to atrophy, and while it may have been necessary to inhibit the pain of a wound - whether physical, mental, emotional or spiritual - in order for life to continue. It is the nature of the Healer's work to deal with the true ramifications of the pain and its energy parameters. To begin the healing process, first remove the pain blocks. Then, the Healer should put his or her own energy shields in place of them, while reconstructing the area behind the blocks. When the work has been completed, the practitioner should reestablish the individual's own shields. This time the pain blocks should be put in place only to the degree that they will assist the healing process. Pain blocks should not be so intense that they cause the individual to withdraw from the injured area and deny access to beneficial and healthy energy flow and stimulation. They should also not be so strong that normal sensory input from the area is cut off or diminished so that the individual does not take proper care with the healing area. This should be done cleanly with gentle healing reinforcements on the areas of affliction which may be used in the ongoing healing process.

At each level that is manipulated, the Healer must first remove the person's shields and replace them with an extension of his own. Often these shields should not be removed altogether but merely pushed aside and parted as one would with a curtain. If it is done in this manner then, as the Healer withdraws upon completion of his purpose, these shields will replace themselves automatically and the Healer need only reinforce and secure them. In any case, when the work has been completed, regardless of what has been done or the necessity of monitoring the patient, all shields must be replaced before the work is concluded and the Healer withdraws. Neglect of this procedure will cause certain anomalous energy fluctuations and certainly a general weakness in the patient, as these shields are an extension of the person's energies and chakra system. A sick or injured person will not be able to replace those shields adequately. An attempt to do this will drain away the energies from the areas that truly need the healing. Remember that the first instinct of any living organism will be to reestablish the energy field of senses and shields surrounding it. This use of energy during the time of illness and recuperation will surely be at the cost of the true healing process. A person who is delirious in a fever may not realize that those shields are gone, and, unless they are replaced and strengthened, that person will be left prey to all manner of random energies that will disturb the healing sleep of that individual. This can considerably slow his recovery. Pain blocks may be reestablished to react automatically, but only if it is possible for the practitioner to monitor them and the afflicted person is informed of their existence and locality. This is so that he will not over strain the injured area until it has healed. It should be noted here that pain blocks may serve to reduce shock and inflammation of the area and may lessen the detrimental effects of high fevers and can be most effective. However, they should never be used as a license to ignore and injured or afflicted area. Therefore, they must be used with discretion and ideally only when outside monitoring is possible. These procedures are valid with both mental and physical healing, and require very few adaptations from one to the other.

SEER'S SHIELDS

The need for shielding also holds for the Seer and the Mage. The Seer leaves her body to seek the answers of the greater world. This leaves the body vulnerable to all manner of excess and unnecessary energies. The Seer's world is fragile as it must be guided and guarded by another when she is in the deeper intensities of her work. The lack of a place of safety created at the beginning where she may leave the body safely can result in a general weakening of the body's energy fields and of the security of its balance and strength. Seers work in two ways. One is by leaving the body and traveling in the spirit form to other planes and dimensions. The second is by opening the body/mind as a vessel for other plane vibrations to be translated into this physical world. In either case, it necessitates putting aside the ordinary framework of anchors and safeguards that the body and integrated personality have established. Safe space and shields are an integral part of allowing the Seer to freely release her holds upon the current dimensions of her reality without unnecessary distraction or worry concerning the safety of her physical body and personality construct. This assurance of safety will, in itself, strengthen and assure her in the outer world and reserve her strength and her wholeness of mind for the task at hand. Fear is the gate of evil in the outer worlds, because in those realms one may easily and unknowingly create what one fears merely by thinking on it. Fears regarding safety and assurance may certainly be reflected there and, at the least, shade and cast doubt and uncertainty upon the vision which she seeks.

MAGE'S SHIELDS

Those who work with Power are similar to the Seer and Healer in their need for shielding. Their position is at the juncture of many worlds. Their vision and power ranges are wide and their Calling is to manipulate all the layers and levels of energies by the assertion of their will and intention. The impact of this work on the energy complex of the body/mind/heart/spirit may be considerable and may lead to vulnerability on all these various levels of awareness. It is the nature of this craft that all those realities are brought together. These realities narrow and focus through the practitioners so that they are able to shape them as the potter does the clay and form them into renewed coherence. It is essential then that their centering be absolute and beyond doubt. They must be trained and sure in the disciplines of shielding and centering as much as in the disciplines of concentration and intention. This is essential so that no unexpected energies or occurrences will come upon them by chance and so that the result of the work will be pure and rightly completed according to their will.

It is also necessary, given the scope of his proceedings, that the Mage and all those with whom he works guard not only themselves from the outside influences of whatever nature, but also protect the outside environment from the influence of their work. Accidental or unrecognized energy leakage is not permissible in these matters. Therefore, the energies need to be coherently bound and focused. If these proceedings do not take place in protected space, then all things around them (all sympathetic and resonant energies) will be affected by them. Regardless of how benevolent the intention of the work is, this will be harmful to many. At the very least, it is an invasion of the privacy and peace of those who do not wish to participate. Therefore, the powers and energies need to be contained and limited to the space allotted for them until the final point of the work is accomplished when they are released according to the pattern and the presence of the work. Only then should the protective barrier be carefully removed. This careful and purposeful removal of the shields and wards after the full procedure should hold true for all activities of power and intention including those of the Seer and Healer.

WARDED SPACE

Depending on the nature of the work, the practitioner's shields may be all that are required in the way of safety precautions. However, he or she may consider it desirable to establish a permanent place of quiet and harmony that has its own shields and barriers existing even when the practitioner is not in residence or work is not in progress. This is called warding a space and may be temporary or permanent as the situation dictates. Any room, dwelling or outside area may be chosen for this process and in the creation of these wards, the grace of peace may be established in the place. Remember that to the degree that a place is shielded from the unwanted energies and vibrations of outside influences, a feeling of quiet and peace will exist in and around it. It should be remembered, however, that even if these wards are permanent, the activation of the extended healer's shield while within them is still a valid courtesy to the individuals involved and will aid greatly in the process of the work.

In a truly formal setting, the practitioner, whether Healer or Mage, should raise his energies, and, if possible or desired, his female counterpart should raise her energies with him. This operation is well suited to the use of balanced polarity. Then he (or they) goes through this chosen place to cleanse it from energy residuals of whatever nature. This should be done by grounding the energies and returning them to the Universal whole without regard to their content. This is like erasing and washing clean a chalkboard. When purging the space, they should move counterclockwise around the periphery if they are in the Northern Hemisphere and clockwise in the southern. They should be carrying incense (frankincense, sandalwood and myrrh are well suited to this purpose), ringing bells, and expressing the force of their will as they speak, declaring that the place is free from all which has previously been. Next, they should raise a shield around this place constructed from the energy drawn from the source of their power but not composed of their personal power. They should align this raised energy and extend it to the basic energy flow of the earth so that it will be self-maintaining and renewing. The direction of their work should be clockwise if they are in the Northern Hemisphere of the earth and counter clockwise if they are in the southern. By this action they will establish a sphere of energy. Make sure all windows, doors, and any physical means of ingress and egress no matter how small, are sealed with this shield and that the means of egress may be passed only by those of cleanliness and right intention. This may be renewed and built upon at regular intervals if so desired, but the only true maintenance it should require is the intention of the individuals who created it to remain. Various forms of intention as to its nature, strength, and permeability may be established when these shields are set, and these qualifications should not be appreciably changed unless the whole process is repeated. In this cloistered space, the more serious and delicate matters of healing and practice may be accomplished. These shields need only be reinforced at the beginning of any single procedure.

If an individual is engaged in a course of study and meditation, it is wise to employ a similar procedure for warding his or her living and working quarters, so that his or her studies will be easier and free from distraction and his or her sleep will be peaceful. Wards of this nature may also be established for the peace of those around them, and are especially effective around the living quarters of children so that they will grow well and in harmony. These shields should not be established in fear, for then they will be tainted by the nature of that fear and automatically draw unto themselves that thing which the fear has imaged. Rather they should be set with the intention of privacy and peace and a love for the order and flow of all things. Each individual should do this for themself so that each person's space will ideally suit his or her inner nature. However, these personal wards should exist within the perimeter of a greater system of wards around the entire property set to generally protect its inhabitants and act as an augmentation of the inner wards placed by the individuals who dwell within it. This system of greater wards should be created by the collective action of all persons who intend to dwell within them so that their personal wards will integrate well with the intention and fabric of the greater. However, this procedure which may be done by and made to serve many people, should be implemented and focused by one couple only so that it will have unity of focus and purpose.

These wards will be especially beneficial in the case of new comers to these studies and will help them develop in the work, because they will not have to contend with the added burden of filtering unneeded or undesired energies. They can feel free to see clearly and be at ease. This warded space will serve for the Mage and those around him. It will not only shield his or her neighbors from the energies of his craft, but it may also function like a crucible for building and refining those energies which he or she wishes to gather, manipulate, and send in whatever form. They will be contained, untainted, and will serve him better because of this.

In all, this shielding and warding of personal energies will contribute greatly to the focus and continuity of whatever power work and individual wishes to embark on. It establishes a base of power and energy for the practitioner and, as it is used and becomes more firmly established, it will act as a kind of center from which the practitioner can draw great energy and peace. It will also prevent the practitioner's energy work from encroaching on or disturbing the peace of his or her neighbor's space of energy. Now that these things have been established, a new level of practice and study can begin.

KARMA AND ENERGY WORK

In any area of spiritual activity, the question of Karma must be considered. Karma is a force of primary importance in this Universe and has great impact, particularly upon the ability of an individual to heal another person as well as himself. The basic mechanisms of Karma must be understood before any working of lasting value and effectiveness can take place. Karma is the basic mechanism of action/reaction by which any individual seeks to bring themself into alignment with the spiritual nature of this Universe. Many make the mistake of thinking that this is merely a system of punishments and rewards exterior to the individual, but nothing could be farther from the truth. Karma consists of decisions that an individual has made to keep from being harmed or to keep from harming others, and its primary operating formula consists of data regarding incidents as that individual has perceived them. Karma is directly connected to the individual's integral identity code, his direct nature as spirit, and, indivisible from the nature of the Prime. The current personality is only a transient manifestation of that greater essence which may vary greatly from life to life. Karma is the coil that binds any individual into the framework of this Universe by means of the chakra system. It is very important to see Karma as a form of energy manipulation on the part of the individual. By seeing it in this way, both the individual and the practitioner will gain the objectivity and reality perspective to deal effectivel Kwith karma and its manifested results.

The workings of Karma will surely come to bear upon any work or healing attempted; and therefore, it is necessary for the student to understand some of its basic principles. Karma is simply the presence of energy interactives within the scope of an individual's life. Many will not understand this, for they consider that Karma is something that occurs from outside the self. It is the nature of the entities in this Universe, due to its bipolar nature, to express relationships in terms of opposites, and to express situations in terms of adversarial relationships, as self versus objective. Inasmuch as this situation is an expression of the bipolar nature of this Universe and consequently of Individuals in this Universe, this means that the situation is part of the self, and is an expression of the self in its relationship to this universe. It is predictable that an individual will relate to karma in such an adversarial relationship - that is, as though this were an external situation force upon him without acknowledgment or agreement. In fact, karma is a creation of the individual and is part of the way that individual is grounded in this Universe and time frame. But in addressing these things it is imperative to bear in mind that nothing can be created by any individual that is larger or more powerful than the individual that created it. Therefore, it contains within it the seeds of its own solution/dissolution. To the degree that the individual has invested it with force, it contains all the force within it necessary for its undoing. This is the essence of this form of energy resolution. The individual that created it can access the intensity, the force, the power of its creation and maintenance, and will then have all the force that is necessary to manipulate the situation and the choice of releasing it. Note that the word "maintenance" was used here. This signifies that, not only is there inherent in the interactive all the power of the initial incident of its creation, but all the energy with which it has been maintained and centered and has captured the attention of its creator.

Karma represents a system of learning situations agreed upon by the individual intending to bring that individual into harmony with his or her own true nature as one with the ultimately serene Prime. The elements binding these operating decisions to that individual operate on a different level of reality than the mundane personality/self. They are the property of the Higher Self and as such they are carried in their own separate partition of memory accessed by the individual but existing outside this space/time continuum and operating in the physical universe through the deep subconscious of the individual. They work as the unseen energy template that directs events, interactions and behavior. Therefore, the individual's Karma may seem to be outside the realm of his or her control because it is activated by energy interactives set up between the individual and the object, energy, or situation he or she has agreed to deal with and learn from. These decisions take place prior to incarnating in the current physical body. As the individual is born into the body, its energy patterns are established to key him or her into the energy cycle of events and interactions that will enable him or her to most effectively meet the challenge.

Because of these created interactive energies, an individual will repeatedly create or bring himself into interaction with similar situations attempting to causatively and intentionally control and resolve them. Successful completion of these cycles will neutralize these energy interactives and the intensity of his attachment to that situation, and by the neutralization of this energy release the power of the interactive. This is very important to realize. But there is a level of reality about this that is often disregarded.

THE ENERGY PATTERNS

OF RELATIONSHIPS

When we fall in love with a person, is it because we sense in that person a link in the code of our Destiny? Does the combination of energies make a greater harmonic that in turn keys both lives into a desired karmic pattern? It is more than social expectations, this primal attraction that links two lives in tandem. And, contrary to our cultural expectations, it may not be permanent or even pleasant. A pattern is formed that remains valid until the energy cycle between the two parties is completed, then the bonding no longer holds or it may change to another form of agreed upon bonding. This works like two pieces of a jig-saw puzzle that fit together, then together the shape they form fits into a frame. The nature of the shape of the frame determines the energy nature of the relationship. The shape of the frame is the karmic purpose that the relationship occurs in order to fulfill. Unlike puzzle pieces that are inert, the two participants change because of their interaction. It is when two energy particles meet that heat and light are generated – then change results from the interaction.

It is much easier to understand this if you look at this interaction as a series of energy patterns. This visible physical universe is only a mask, a façade. By judging appearances and results, the observer misses its true nature and the true nature of interactions and relationships. The true nature of an individual is as an energy pattern as we have discussed at length. Physical structure is a phenomenon of energy. Relationships are interactions of energy patterns. Looking at life on the physical plane is like looking at a clock. You become accustomed to judging the position of the hands relative to each other and relative to their position on the face and draw certain assumptions about time when you do this. But you forget that behind this face and hands is a mechanism of gears and springs. That is the true nature of the clock, not the information it provides or the façade from which the information is derived.

Life in this universe is like the clock. The physical mechanism is so visible and obvious that it is easy to overlook what truly drives its activity – it is energy, states of energy. The states this energy assumes determine the interactions of the energy. Energy is the principle vehicle of this Universe and it is driven by the will and intention of Spirit. It is easy to see the endless shapes it takes and still easier to forget the essence of what generates these forms.

Relationships are manifestations of energy patterns that form harmonics. Purposes and goals are manifestations of energy also because they express event sequences that are complex combinations of energy activity. These combinations include but are not limited to relationships between people and objects. It should also be kept in mind that the individual's primary purpose in this or any other universe to learn, grow and develop through situations. This is done by manipulating energy in pursuit of goals and purposes. Relationships with people and objects only further that end. But the appearance also masks the truth of the activity. When the individual releases his or her attachment to the appearance of situations, that is, to the face of the clock, he or she can apply himself to the reality of the clock, the mathematical relationship of the gears and drive springs. In terms of life and relationships, this means that the focus of attention must go beyond the façade of personalities and events to address the true mechanism of energy patterns that exists as their formative and driving force. Only then can true understanding of patterns emerge and the individual make progress.

This is not to imply that the individual should adopt a mechanistic or cold attitude with regard to other individuals. The true nature of any spiritual being is joy and compassion. Respect for oneself and respect for all life should be implicit in all interactions. It simply means that the individual must expand his or her awareness to the true nature of situations without becoming mired in their circumstances. One should never mistake the clock face for time itself. The hands do not cause time to pass, they arbitrarily measure it. Just as physical manifestation reflects the energy of which it is formed and the spiritual intention that drives the energy.

Now that this is understood, we can return to the question of relationships and destiny. Once it is understood that the true nature of relationships is in the patterns of energy they provide, one can understand the resulting changes that are possible given this combination of energy acting on a goal or circumstance. Lovers come together and are changed by the interaction with each other and as a result of this change become different people in their ability to form other relationships on different levels and to interact with circumstances. This is equally true for intense friendships. It is observable in the relationship of a parents with children. In this case, these effects can also be observed in their reverse. When there is no bonding of energy patterns in infancy and childhood, the individual can fail to develop the ability to establish these vital connections throughout life. Lasting impairment can occur because of this. It is also seen in relationships in which passion and obsession turn to antipathy which deteriorates into destructive behavior, sometimes culminating in violence. It is important to remember that it is not the mental or emotional content that is a real concern. That is incidental, the stage dressing only. Again, these are conditions of energy and energy interaction. These are patterns of energy combinations that allow the participants to interact with their goal/purpose pattern. Altering behavior can sometimes alter the pattern, but it is more significant to alter awareness and intention. This is spiritual change reflected into physical manifestation. This changes lives, not just events. Change in action or physical circumstances is the indicator of change of energy states on a much deeper level. Once again the physical universe is like the hands of the clock, indicating the passage of time, but only hinting at the true movement that drives them.

A powerful relationship does not have to be lengthy to have a profound effect on its participants. It is the resulting energy of their interaction that is in question. Just so the case of children only living a short time. The nature of their lives interacting with their family creates many changes in the ability of the family members to relate to each other, their life purposes and other children. This is true for individuals who form friendships or intense working relationships even for brief periods of time. Any form of deep personal attraction is involved. This is all in pursuit of goals and purposes on a karmic level – on the level of life purpose. The combination of the patterns of the two parties involved creates a pattern that keys them both into the complex pattern of their desired purpose. It is not just the emotional or intellectual content of this relationship that is the question here but the actually nature of the energy combinations underlying the façade of mental, physical or emotional.

The unique energy patterns of each individual are specified by the combinations of energy harmonics represented by the chakras as displayed across the levels of awareness that result in the combined energy pattern of the individual referred to as the energy system complex. These are the linking patterns that locate the individual in time and space, that is, with the physical universe. They also key to the energy patterns of the energy patterns of endeavor and experience called karma. And it is these patterns that identify individuals to one another as part of completing these patterns. It is as though an individual were saying, "Oh, I need a triangular piece to accomplish this goal. Aha, here comes one now." And the energy field is identified and interacted with.

There is a temptation to see this analysis as dehumanizing or unfeeling. It does not lack compassion or joy to acknowledge a truth. It does not deny the wonder and beauty of seeing the stars in the Milky Way if one is also aware of the laws of astronomy and physics. In one sense of the word this viewpoint is "dehumanizing" because it is human to give great weight and validity to emotional conditions and intellectual activity. These functions are seen as necessary and treasured as the essence of the truth of a situation. It is feared that to lose them is to lose the value of the situation. It is common to mistake sentimentality and hysteria for true compassion and concern. Just as it is common to mistake mental activity for higher analysis. By recognizing each situation for what it is, it is possible to move beyond its appearance into its reality and regain control over its elements. When this occurs, the participants can come to terms on a vastly different basis than ever before. They can interact on a basis of shared interest and true partnership to pursue shared goals more effectively.

It is energy that is the true essence of life in this universe. It is also energy that is the true nature of goals and interaction. Karma and Destiny are terms that are often applied to this. These are misleading terms, however, because they imply special or unique conditions isolated from the flow of experience. Life itself is a manifestation of Karma/Destiny. Experience is its teacher and its implementation. Energy is its essence in this Universe because it is the true mechanism of learning and purpose.

NEUTRALIZING KARMA

No matter what else Karma may or may not be philosophically, it is a matter of energy mechanics. The energy of the attachment may be neutralized and this will free the individual from repeating the cycle of action or maintenance of a condition. It will also release all the energy that the individual was using to maintain the situation. It will release the basic cause of the limitations that the individual set up for him or her to deal with. This includes physical parameters as well as mental, emotional and perceptual ones. This neutralization of energy is possible by the activity of a trained healer, but is more effective for the individual to do it him or herself. Nonetheless, when it is accomplished it will only bring about a temporary release and freedom. Unless the individual gains knowledge and understanding of the situation, unless he or she sees the situation objectively and fully releases himself, he will continue to reconstruct the energy pattern of the interactive and no lasting healing will be accomplished.

The healer will see instances of this taking place in terms of recurrent injury to one specific body part, or chronic illness to one system of the body while the rest of the body remains in good health. This is also seen in social situations such as in the example of a woman who takes one mate after another who all eventually abuse her, or an individual who despite great resources and talent continually fails and brings to ruin his chosen enterprise. Recurrent incidents or situations defying all logic of chance are common examples of what the healer will have brought to him, and the healer must acknowledge the Karmic nature of these patterns before his work can begin on a truly effective level. It is important to realize, though, that in any case, relief of the current situation must be achieved before Karmic healing begins. A person must have relief of his or her pain and suffering, or disengage from a constantly restimulating and entrapping situation. Only then can work on a deeper level be done. In other words, bind up the wounds, and then seek their deeper source.

This can be further complicated by the fact that, more often than not, more than one individual has created and agreed upon a period of interaction to resolve a purpose shared between them. This level of Karma on the emotional level is often as illusive as it is complex. An individual may be unaware that an intense relationship - love, hatred, etc. - is founded on causes that began outside the scope of the present lifetime's incidents. In such cases it is important for the individual to see him or herself as a unique and separate entity, having a destiny apart from the other individual with whom they are involved. This does not necessarily mean abandoning the other person. It simply means that it is necessary to establish a relationship based on present time values and goals. Maintaining karmic energy interactives with others will only result in the continuation of hidden agendas in those relationships and obstruct the individuals involved from reaching their fullest present-time potential.

There are two means by which Karma may be neutralized and the cycles of purpose that have been agreed upon neutralized. The first is the causative completion of these intended cycles, with a positive result. Failure is never completion and this karma will remain to be activated until the circumstance or one sufficiently similar to it in all major respects is achieved to the proposed desired conclusion. The second way is by the disengagement of all interactive secondary modes. This complete disengagement must be in this plane of existence, and will free the individual completely until reengagements are interacted or until that individual translates causatively unto another causal plane. This is what you know as Ascension, that is, the total disengagement of time/matter/space interactives. This is the supreme acknowledgement of the Higher Self being the total self in union with the Prime source of all. At this time, the individual is no longer technically the individual, but united with all creation. As such, by uniting all elements of creation within himself, he is no longer a the mercy of its opposing forces but brings them all in harmony within one greater perspective.

KARMA & THE CHAKRAS

Deep healing work and full balancing of the Chakras by means of Akasha/Karma therapy is very powerful. It involves dealing with the energy of karmic interactives, as it is part of the integral fabric of the energy patterns of the chakras. We have previously explained that it is the energy harmonic of the chakra pattern - that is, the resonance of the individual's energy helix - that defines that individual's identity from lifetime to lifetime. This is how the individual remains as a personal identity when the physical body is disunited from it at death, and why that individual is not simply reabsorbed into the Universal consciousness. That individual's identity is written in this framework and it translates from lifetime to lifetime as it incarnates with each physical form. This energy fabric contains the memories of previous lives, and as this energy pattern integrates with a physical form, this pattern is impressed on that form. Then the growth and development of both the physical form and the levels of awareness in this universe are molded by this energy. This type of healing should only be attempted by those of long experience in the craft who are strong and firm in the disciplines of centering and meditation for the danger of mishandling or entrapment is very great. It should be emphasized that this type of healing is only truly effective when the healer deals with it as a form of energy mechanics.

The chakra centers carry the life energies of the body as well as its karmic codes and memories. Consequently, a great deal of the Karmic record entails damage, impairment or prejudice of the energies of these centers, and in order for healing to have its full effect, these centers must be unburdened of the energy constructs that hold the disability illness or weakness in place. The healer will often be called upon to clear one or another of these centers. If it is one of the peripheral ones, then the energy level of all other centers will rise to complement and compensate for the new energy load of the one previously impaired. The concept of Karmic injury needs to be clarified so that it will not be confused with injuries of the normal kind. Karmic injury contains not only pain to the individual, but also great power affecting the very individual itself, the spirit, the life essence. This almost always includes some form of content, that is, information perceived by the individual that involves a decision made by him or her containing elements affecting his or her destiny, karma, chosen means of life expression.

IMPLANTS

There may have even been implants, things done to an individual by another purposefully, using pain, drugs, electricity, light, et cetera, along with direct informational input to the base and/or heart chakra or to the energy system as a whole. These are artificially placed directives that can act powerfully to motivate the individual. Because they are connected with the functions of the base, heart or crown chakra, they have direct impact over the life functions of the individual when they are activated. In most cases, implants were placed in order to influence an individual's behavior regardless of the physical body or life situation. For example, if it was desired for an individual to avoid a certain group of individuals, the energy patterns of these individuals would be incorporated with that implant. This would result in pain, physical sickness or personal aversion when the individual came into contact with these people even after many generations of incarnating into different bodies. Implants can be deceptive, because quite often they are still active millenia after the circumstances dictating their inception have vanished into dust.

These behave in a similar fashion to present lifetime implants. These are of a far lesser magnitude than those existing over ages of time and connected with the karmic base patter, but they can be no less insidious in their influence. Current lifetime implants are nodes of interactive energy attached to the life pattern of the individual by another individual. They can prove difficult for the individual to detect because they are placed outside the sphere of that individual's conscious memory or personal activity. Very often a person will use a sexual and/or karmic connection with the recipient and place such an energy pattern for the purpose of possession and control of that person. This is often the key to diffusing long-term abusive relationships. By determining the implant and releasing it, the individual can be released from the base cause of the energy attachment of a toxic relationship or pattern of behavior. Energy implants can manifest in a variety of ways – as physical debilitation or illness, recurrent injury or chronic pain, or a pattern of self-harming behavior. Whatever their guise, their source must be determined, their effects diffused and then the energy void that they leave occupied with a healing energy until the individual is able to reconstruct his or her energy pattern completely. The practitioner must also deal with the fact that the individual who has received such an implant has agreed to it on one level or another. This will almost never be on a conscious level, but the treatment of such an injury must always include dealing with the reason that the individual feels the need for such a connection. This may take time and patience on the part of the individual to fully recover, but will bring lasting benefit and an improvement in a wide scope of life conditions that might have seems unconnected to the original energy pattern.

KARMIC INJURIES

There are accidental incidents of the same magnitude that have the same impact. These incidents have enormous significance to the individual and are carried very strongly as operating premises that will retain their impact long after others incidents of injury of a less stressful kind would have given way to regular healing procedures.

Karmic injuries have occurred on many more levels than just the physical energy system and they are not solely recorded on that individual's genetic survival chain, that is, the physical life force. They are integrated into the very fabric of the individual and become part of the integral personality. They are carried within the basic mnemonic framework of the individual, that is, the life structure, and reside there in exactly the same way as scars are recorded on the living tissue of the body to be borne until death destroys that form. They are impressed deeply within the life force structure itself that, in this Universe, translates itself to the chakra helix. We say helix here because we mean an entire self-contained energy structure in the same way that an atom is self-contained. If one part of it is damaged, then the other parts will seek to compensate for that damage. They will do this in a number of different ways, but they must do it so that the structure will not disintegrate or terminally overload. This must be kept firmly in mind while addressing these injuries. No healing on this level of energy can be accomplished or have any real effect on the individual without balancing the entire system to adjust to the new level of energy once the injury or weakness has been addressed.

The base chakra is the entry point of energy into this system; therefore, it is here that initial informational impulses are assimilated, giving data about the quality of the energy construct in which the individual is located. It therefore dictates how the individual will relate to that construct. It acts almost like the balance mechanism in the ear. The reaction to its perception is on an instinctual level and is not within the individual's control unless conscious efforts are imposed to override it. This is because information contained in the sphere of the base chakra is not integrated with the individual's perception of time and cause/effect. As the input of that chakra is dictated and qualified, so all the rest are dictated. The heart chakra is the natural means by which all internal energies are balanced, correlated, and finally expressed by the individual. The crown chakra is a source point of information from the seat of higher awareness and the energies of higher planes of consciousness. Therefore, there are two points of informational input and one point of energy expression/output. If one interferes with the way information about the individual's environment is received and assimilated, that is, if you interfere with the ability of the base chakra to assimilate information or transfer this information to the rest of the system, then that individual's ability to understand and survive becomes seriously altered. If you alter or harm any other energy node (chakra) within the system, this will cause backflow and recurring harm and confusion. For example, a karmic injury to the belly (Warrior) chakra will sometimes symptomatically express itself as impotence because the energy does not pass freely. When there is an injury, there will usually be a compensating reaction to the opposite harmonic center that will distort itself in an equal and opposite way to compensate and enforce a balance. For example on a much smaller scale, you will notice that when one hand is injured, the other will begin to stiffen up because the energies are attempting to balance.

This is the basic mechanism of action/counteraction. When there is a karmic injury to one of the centers along the vertical axis, the energy impulses of that event are recorded in that center. An image of the event is recorded there with all information or decisions regarding it, and this recording is given all the power of all the energy that was available at the time. This is an important point to consider. For example, it is as though an individual were struck with a lightning bolt. The event would then be recorded with, not only that individual's own full stock of power, but also the additional tremendous force of the lightning bolt. This is why "enforcements" have such enormous power over the individual, because they are recorded with a level of power outside his normal purview. And they are recorded on the basic life structure energy centers themselves along with that individual's own conclusions as to how to avoid further similar injury and how to counterbalance their force upon his integral energy structure. Then, all the other centers of the energy system will adjust themselves in an attempt to return to normal balanced levels, operating in harmony with one another.

As the healing process is begun, the practitioner will encounter a record of all the various injury incidents recorded on an energy center and should begin removing them one at a time. The effect on the rest of the system will be that all compensating dysfunctions will then be triggered. As each incident is removed, the healer will notice the reaction of the centers keying in their past responses and attempting to compensate. Even after everything on the track of the single chakra under scrutiny has been dealt with, the healer will have all the counterbalancing compensations to consider that will need to be brought into realignment. If this realignment is not done and then maintained until the energies stabilize, the force of these existing energies will simply cause a manifestation of the problem again as though it were still in place, or the healing process will take a very long time and will be only partially successful. This takes some serious work and considerable skill. If all contributing energies are not handled, there will be a reoccurrence of the problem. In addition, if the injury is centered in the heart chakra, this will restimulate other injuries to other areas. This is because, as the level of energy at the heart center raises, the other chakras will attempt to raise their energy level to come into equilibrium with it. This will cause other blockages and injuries to become visible. If the healer is aware and competent, this is a good result because with the renewed power of energy, the lesser blocks shock be freed very quickly since it is most likely that they are of lesser magnitude. This is because, once the center chakra is damaged, the whole power level of the individual drops, and the individual power level of each of the centers drops to compensate for it. In addition, as we have previously explained, an incident can only be recorded and/or manifested to the level of power that it was initially recorded.

We should point out here that no individual could be completely healed from all Karma. That is not the purpose of this Universe. The purpose of being in this place is to learn and to grow, and karma is one of the tools that enable this to happen. As injuries or other dysfunctions are addressed on this level, the individual should be guided to examine his or her life purpose and the impact that this dysfunction serves in his or her life. It will be through this personal examination, combined with the energy release effected by the healer that true relief in a situation will be accomplished.

TIME, PERCEPTION & EVENT WAVES

Linear time as you know it exists by virtue of your perception of it. Although time does exist as a factor necessary to the existence of the physical universe, it is not perceived the same either by different levels of beings or on different planes or levels of existence. The key to understanding this is to see individuals, places and events in terms of energy / vibrational interactives. It is the human energy system complex, known as the Chakras, that sets up the complex vibrational code that identifies us as unique individual entities. It aligns us with the vibrational harmonic of the physical universe so that we are able to function here. It also aligns us with our karma, which is what we are here to experience / deal with / learn from. This karma can be seen as an energy code that an individual is interacting with and perceives as a chain of events in linear time. In actuality, event complexes (such as karma) happen in waves like ripples in water.

Imagine a wave hitting a beach. One wave (energy force pattern) hits the sand at approximately the same time along a long line of shore. Our physical universe awareness is like one pebble on that shore. That one pebble does not perceive the event as happening anywhere else but in its particular location. It perceives its experience as unique rather than as a function of the beach as a whole. By virtue of the way our energy system complex anchors us in matter/space/time, we are like that pebble and tend to see things as individual occurrence rather than as energy patterns. Beings who inhabit physical bodies have therefore constructed the mental architecture of linear time in order to relate to such broad events seeing the "surf" as a line rather than as one generalized event. Karma is such an event waveform occurrence for individuals. All individuals are living more than one life at a time (depending on how you want to relate to it). Each karmic life lesson is being dealt with by all those "previous" or other lives concurrently. By shifting the vibrational pattern of energy complex, it is possible to see things from the point of view of those other identities that are experiencing the same problem but in different ways. This is the value of past life regression. Not that the individual can look back on the roots of an occurrence in his or her past, but that he or she can assume a different viewpoint from one of the other selves and, perhaps, from that point of view see the present situation more clearly and, hopefully, solve the problem, learn from it and move on in conscious awareness.

Karma exists outside the individual's physical sphere and may be the template directives of more than one personality occurrence in the event wave. It is also a point to consider, that when those "other" personalities are discovered, love, compassion and/or admiration for them can enable the individual to welcome them back within the spiritual self. In this way they can be healed and their experience/life essence reintegrated with the individual. This conscious reintegration often results in a feeling of health and wholeness in the individual because the conflicts are resolved and put at rest and the individual then has recourse to a wider and fuller range of life essence and experience through these other facets of him or her self.

We have pointed out here that the individual can adjust his or her perspective using the appropriate meditation, chakra work, and crystal work to broaden his or her awareness and alter the basic elements of the energy system complex. There is every possibility that an individual can reach a sufficiently expanded perspective that will put him or her into a different pattern. By virtue of this energy shift, the individual's identity codes are changed. Consequently, the anchors that place that individual in the physical universe would be released, an "escape velocity" achieved, and the individual able to translate into a broader plane of awareness/ existence.

This is one aspect of the nature of the coming changes. Such an event wave is coming that those who have the preparation will be able to make the shift. It is the nature of the changing of ages. Energy planes and conditions are not always aligned in such a way that such changes are possible. Sometimes it happens that an individual will achieve such a state but the energy states that differentiate the plane of existence are not aligned in such a way as to make a full translation possible. The changing of the ages indicates that such an alignment is taking place, and it is for this reason that many beings from other levels of existence are able to enter this plane and communicate with the spirits here.

These event waves are also relevant for various identity groups such as tribes and nations and, in a broader sense, this is true for Humankind as a whole. There was a time in the history of nearly every civilization that a supreme prophet or avatar was manifested. It was usually when that civilization was at a turning point in development - such as the legends of Isis and Osiris coming to Egypt to bring the hunter/gatherer tribes out of barbarism. Jesus came just as Rome was reaching her zenith and was already beginning to crumble from within. Quetzalcoatl arrived at just such a propitious moment in the cultural consciousness of Meso-America. Each of these individuals was part of a greater event wave that, from time to time, washes over Humankind enabling social and spiritual evolution.

MACROINTERACTIVES AND POWER

To the degree that an incident is complex and involves the life force and creative intent of many individuals, is of long duration and holds the attention of the individuals involved, then it achieves great force and power of its own, drawn from all the individuals that have and are constantly contributing to it. Such complex incidents are called Macrointeractives. These are event waves such as we have just mentioned that impact nations or peoples. To the degree that an individual was pivotal in the formation of an interactive, then that individual has access to all the power contained within it, constituting far greater energy and force than he himself alone has contributed to it. Therefore, he or she may release it and draw it to conclusion in his or her own life pattern by means of this mighty force. By its energy, we mean all these things combined that have far reaching consequences for peoples and cultures effected. This includes emotion, intention, physical sensation (particularly pain), and importance of attachment, degree of circumstantial magnitude such as the fall of nations and continents, the wholesale destruction of civilizations, great battles, the fate of races, and participation in natural disasters.

This accessing of power and its resultant release may take place on one or both of two levels and methods. The one is the conscious realization of a basic incident at the foot of a chain of similar incidents. These similar incidents were shadows of the initial created incident that an individual has caused, allowed, and maintained. Since he has created it into his existence, he will continue to have it in his existence until he has disassembled it. He may do this by the conscious realization of circumstances and events and their causes and motivations and their TRUE results, not assumed or lesser results. This process is extremely difficult and can be deeply traumatic. The incident has been created to the limit of this individual's skill and power and has the contributing force of other individuals. The individual must deal with the incident only in personal terms. He or she must limit his culpability and actions within the events to what they actually were not what he assumes or wishes. For instance, one individual cannot be responsible for the downfall of or overthrow of an entire people or culture regardless of his or her stature within the community. Such dissolution is the result of many forces coming together and developing over time. To attempt to take karmic responsibility for an entire people is to distort the true personal issue of feeling such a responsibility. No matter how traumatic or graphic the recollection of the individual's participation in the events, he or she must realize only his or her own participation in it - not his or her assumed interaction with all other participants. If the individual truly accomplishes this realization, he or she will confront and avail him or herself of all the energy with which he or she has invested it. At the point of this realization and dissolution, this energy is released. Then he or she may feel a tremendous rush of power that is the pent up force he or she has engaged in it. By the release of this force and the attention he or she has had to tie into it in order to maintain it, he or she gains the power and ability to rise above the previous state and propel himself farther forward into larger and freer realms. Note: Whether those realms are of this Universe or are of others it is not important, that option is there.

However, the action of consciously confronting these elements is extremely difficult and more often than not will only result in embroiling the individual more deeply into the circumstances. This process should only be attempted with the guidance of a qualified practitioner. The second option is the active analysis by the individual of his or her life purpose. This is a process of daily sequential intention. By the force of the individual's present time acknowledgment and will power, the purpose and goals of the lifetime will serve to bring the individual forward and will, of their own force, move the previous limiting circumstances aside. This is an example of energy confronting energy, of equal forces creating a new circumstance. It is an act of creation and is an actualization that will bring about a higher form of consciousness in the individual involved. For, in the process of creating a present time circumstance, the individual also releases those individuals surrounding him or herself from whatever interactives they may be engaged in regarding him. This also frees them and their energies. There will be times when these surrounding individuals resent this behavior and regard it as a disconnection or betrayal of a millennia-old game of interactions. However, in the greater scheme of things, that which frees an individual is healthiest for all.

This phenomenon may be observed often in Life, although it is more likely that by conscious effort of will that solution is brought forth by the impetus of growth in an individual. We often see those who rise in awareness beyond what may seem to be crippling circumstances. An individual throws off these shackles by great endeavor and righteous solutions and goes forth using the impetus of this releasing power. He or she then creates for him or herself a life of greater scope and power than anyone who knew him or her had imagined possible. This takes great strength and effort of will on both accounts.

Even at the unraveling of smaller interactives, the individual experiences a great surging of energy and strength, perhaps laughter, giddiness, unaccountable wisdom coupled with serene joy. This is partially due to the releasing of this pent up force that is then released within his purview. He or she now has access to conscious use of this power and may use it or allow what he or she is unable to reassimilate to disperse and return to the Universal energy pool. Regardless of what he or she does with it, he or she will be far more powerful in life than before because he or she will no longer be using his or her energy and intention to maintain this situation. Now he or she will be able to use this energy and intention to create a far more positive and conscious present time situation.

In the case of the giftedly powerful who are actively using their gifts for what is called "magic", the force of this released energy may even result in anomalous occurrences across the fabric of accepted space/time parameters, small localized warps in energy potential and perceptions and the like. The fabric of the physical universe elements becomes disoriented somewhat with the excess of these forces, while the bulk of their power remains in the individual.

To the degree that an interactive takes on a complex proportion and encompasses a great many wills and entities, great land masses and the like, then the single individual who disassembles these Macrointeractives is able to avail him or herself of the entire scope of the power engaged in the creation and maintenance of the incident. In the unraveling, he or she takes on great amounts of this stored potential.Even individuals who are involved in the initial source incident but are currently unaware of the release of it share in this benefit, for a great deal of the force of the maintenance will be released. They then become freer of it themselves and thus more powerful to overcome it in their own lives, both because some of this energy is released back to them, and because the incident then attains a condition of lesser force than before, because it is not maintained by so many. Great is the power of the individual or individuals who unlock a true macrointeractive, for then they will have the entire power of the race or national consciousness at their disposal to create and change time and space according to their intention and will. They may truly take into their hands great destinies for they have the power to achieve this change and refocus. All shall then benefit from their action and strength.

Let us not minimize the cost or the effort to the individual in the act of unraveling such an extreme condition. This will be difficult and will be potentially disorienting and likely painful to that individual. The greater the power contained within the incident, the more difficult it will be to release. The more complex and forceful it is, the greater the danger of becoming entangled in it. By entangled we mean that, as these incidents are connected to the individual, this individual continually recreates them for himself, remanifesting them again and again in whatever terms his environment will permit. Failing to grasp and release an incident only contributes to its force by adding the energy of the acknowledged failure onto it. Individuals who are joined together by events will be drawn together and, to the degree that the situation parallels the initial event they will seek to reenact it, trying to release it, that is, to succeed where previously there was failure and to be free of it.

This is the great game of this universe and the great source of entanglement with it. There is great danger here of allowing oneself to be dragged into the situation, and refusing to truly unravel or solve it. There is the fatal tendency to become involved in it and not rise above it in perspective that will automatically render the individual incapable of controlling it. In order to manipulate these circumstances to best advantage one must stay above apparent circumstances and observations. One must disregard one's own reaction save only as an observable indicator of force and reaction. One must, at all costs, maintain one's strength of stance from the absolute present moment and judge all realities from the present not the past. Should one lose this perspective then the incident will only gain more force through repetition of failure and, consequently, all parties involved will have less power over it.

It is most important that this purpose be achieved to beneficial and ethical conclusion. One must examine the elements of the situation for validity before continuing with its maintenance or its disassembly. As one comes closer to the solution of the interactive, things, forces and perceptions appear to both accelerate and to slow down. One may perceive oneself as helpless in the eye of a storm. However, this helplessness is only a manifestation of change and not reality. For as one approaches the center, one becomes increasingly aware of the interlock of power forces resident within the situation, and there are fewer options of interaction. A man running rapids in a small boat is far from helpless, but surely, his scope of activity is greatly limited to the demands of each moment at his task.

By this metaphor you surely see that it is imperative to remain aware and in control from moment to moment and not be swept away out of control. Interactives will never unravel or release of their own accord but must be intentionally manipulated to do so. This is the pivot and main consideration concerning this matter.

THOUGHT FORMS AND **PROJECTED INTENTION**	Inasmuch as this Universe is created and maintained by the combined intentions and beliefs of many individuals, so it is governed by the considerations of those resident individuals. Should an individual hold a consideration as truth, that

belief will become the truth for that individual. To the degree that he is sure and certain of the truth of that belief, it will become an operable governing law within that individual's life and surroundings. Thought forms are created by this principle, that is, by the conscious decision and knowledge that a thing is true and by this principle are they manifested and demonstrated. Nothing is concrete, permanent, or immutable; all things are subject to change.

To the degree that an individual has full knowledge in his mind and full intention and will in his or her heart that a thing is true, so it is true. As he or she determines that a thing has existence apart from himself and that it will go forth automatically as an extension of his or her conscious will, it will indeed become a thing that moves of its own power. That power is derived directly from its creator and is a part of its creator even as its passes from him. As a group of individuals agree together that a thing is so, it will have even greater life and force, for it will be part of a greater pool of life and will hav greater energy of intention and will. Therefore, their creation will have even greater force and duration than a creation that was done by only one. In this way and by this principle all things are governed in this Universe and continuum.

A thought form is a construction of energy, made by an individual or group of individuals to perform a specific task. This task may be communication with a distant individual or other action of energy that takes place on a closely parallel plane so that it is perceivable to individuals on this plane. On the other hand, it may take the form of an action on other planes with the intention of influencing those more fluid planes in order for that change to translate itself to this plane. Or it may take the form of an action on those other planes with the desired result being information gathered from those planes and brought back to the practitioner who created the thought form. It may take any form the practitioner chooses or no form at all other than the cohesion necessary to transmit its message or carry out its purpose. If its work is intended for this physical plane, it is a common practice to place this thought form into an image whose physical form conjures up feelings that will make it easier for the thought form to carry out its purpose. This is a common practice often called sympathetic magic.

To create a thought form, an individual has only to decide that such a thing is so and that it has an operable existence. As he or she does so, it becomes invested with part of his or her own life force that sets it in motion. According to the principles of its creation, it will, if so ordered, achieve what is a semblance of independent thought and life apart from its creator. As an example, an image is made and into that image is placed the thought form of loving, perhaps, with the initial intention to act as a balm of peace to a warring clan or people. And it is set up and the principle explained. The people then draw from it the energy of the initial charge, which is love and unity. Then as they sense that the image is indeed one of love, the resulting good fellowship is returned to that image along with the energy of gratitude. In this manner, a cycle is begun of giving and withdrawing and the principle takes on its own life in a manner of speaking. This may continue for many centuries and, even if copies of that image are made and carried away to far lands, they will retain the thought, for their makers retain that thought and belief and so in turn endow them with the quality similar to the initial charge. However, this charge will understandably differ slightly because the original maker is different from all subsequent makers.

This is also a true principal without any physical form to charge. A practitioner may create a form of his or her own will and mind. With the power of imagery, force, and will he or she can create a form constructed of pure energy that will go forth and act upon his or her will. As he or she works with the image, he or she reinforces it with his intentions. As he or she joins with others to create this being of energy, it will have added power and strength. As others contribute to it, it will grow in intensity and reality. Others who are knowledgeable may also contribute to this form whether they are the original creator or not, and in this manner generations of the wise and skilled may contribute to this single created form. This can happen even if those future individuals are not aware of how they are contributing to it. It should not be thought that this form is truly a living creature, for it is not. It is like a machine, tool, or automaton that may resemble life and may be composed of energy but is not truly alive. It does not grow, evolve, or have a destiny apart from the destiny of its creator or creators. It is bound to all those who have created it and all the acts it performs and effects that it causes will be bound into its creators' destiny and Karma. Remember this and do not create anything for which you would not wish to answer.

It is by this very principle that this reference work and all coexisting reference works were formulated - that is, by the construction of an interactive energy matrix of thought forms created in such a way as to exist without maintenance. It was constructed so that all things and events occurring within certain specified energy parameters would be recorded in their entirety within its retrieval framework. Initially, it was created as an experimental teaching device for novice access only in an attempt to make important information continuously available without having to be generated on a present time basis by a Teacher or Master. Later, when this proved to be successful, the lattice of codes was expanded to accommodate further specified access codes and information that was expansive in its nature. This included works on power processes, pivotal individuals, and events. As a safeguard, these references were placed within certain access parameters that precluded access by the unready, the untutored, or those with non-benevolent intent. Inasmuch as these references were created as an energy matrix - that is, without physical manifestation of form - they could be accessed directly into the learning process of the individual and, when tapped, become not merely information but usable knowledge in its truest sense. This is the most complex and highest manifestation of thought form construction that has yet been achieved on this plane in this continuum. One may see by studying its nature and construction what else may be achieved of lesser complexity concerning all manner of thought forms. It should be noted here, however, that although this information base may expand infinitely, it does not grow nor create on its own. It has neither power nor potential to draw independent conclusions from its resident information or to expand itself through extrapolation. It may be accessed with intent to add data, but it cannot generate this on its own, and this is the true nature of growth.

Racial consciousness is a variant on this thought form principal. Groups of people with genetic codes in common have basic energy patterns in common. As with all other karmic mechanics, these energy codes are affected by energy interactives that occur in the form of physical universe events. Therefore, groups of people with a consistent genetic heritage of at least seven generations (but most often 15 or greater) will hold certain traits, beliefs, and attitudes in common due to the operant energy interactives of those specific codes. This is also true of clans or family groups. This may be seen demonstrated in the Passive Guardian potential manifested clearly in your time in the Hopi Tribe of North American Indians. So great are their interactive imperatives that they will remain interlocked with the planetary destiny and with the land they physically occupy as a tribe until their final transition.

This racial consciousness is deeply ingrained with cultural awareness, that is, the integration and awareness of a cultural continuum. Taking this into consideration, whole nations, clans and individuals may be motivated by means of racial and cultural imperatives even if they have been raised to adulthood untouched by their own kind. This is true not only in matters of power and healing, but also of direct empathic and telepathic access.

THE PRACTICE OF CREATING

A THOUGHT FORM

As life has resonance with all other life, it follows that life may affect life by its own intention. It may conjure life, that is, call forth together that which is energy and vibration and intend it into a form and give this form a purpose. This procedure is merely the extending forth from the individual its own life force, differentiating it from itself so that, while it remains a part of that individual, yet it has mobility, direction, and purpose of its own. It is not a separate consciousness but an extension of it's creator's consciousness. Any number of individuals may gather together and contribute from their collective intention to create a form which has even more potency in that it has been created from the intentions of many. This is a complex act of directed will, and yet for some occasions more efficient in its work, for a thought form is created from the raw building blocks of energy and thus it has separate existence.

The process of this is meditative and may be accomplished by a single individual, or, in the case of a group, may be accomplished in one of two ways. The group may raise a quantity of raw and undirected power qualified only by the nature of the power (if that). This power is then shaped by the leader of the group according to the specifications previously agreed upon by the members of the group. In this case, it is the leader's singular consciousness that has the final say in the shape and directed purpose. In higher workings in which all participants are trained in the ways of power, this may take the form of a guided meditation throughout the group with the entire assemblage building the form systematically.

FETCHING

In either case, the procedure is fundamentally the same. The practitioner enters the meditative state and centers himself in the worlds. He or she achieves his unique position and is aware of his relationship to the many worlds. Then from the fabric of these worlds he or she begins to form and image. It does not matter whether this image is simple or complex, only that the form suits its desired function. The practitioner will see this form slowly coalesce until he or she sees with their inner eye its color, smells its smell, hears its breath and knows with certainty that it has life from his life and the raw power of the Universe. Then shall he or she speak unto it from their center, with the voice of their spirit, from himself to itself and inform it of its purpose, because it is the nature of all life to have purpose. He should never forget, however, that its life is his life and its purpose is his purpose and, any intelligence it may have is also his. When he or she has filled it with all these things, he may then send it forth to do as he wills.

However, let this be said of these workings, he or she must always set a limit on it, that when its work is accomplished all these energies shall return unto him for reassimilation or dispersal. If this limiting is neglected or insufficiently specific, the form will roam free, and having part of consciousness will likely think itself free, become confused, and do mischief. The practitioner is responsible for the acts and achievements of this thought form even as though it were his own hand that performed them. In addition, the practitioner should remember that this life energy is his and as long as it is apart from him he is no longer whole, therefore, this severance must be mended at last. Therefore, let there be a limit set in the initial creation, whether in time or result, or at least the length of the physical life span of the practitioner.

There is a similar process that is the reverse of thought form creation sometimes referred to as fetching. Fetching may be described as a calling or summoning a specified vibration of energy or life, generally that of a cognizant creature such as a person. One may fetch a non-incorporate spirit, or a thought form, or an animal that has some degree of self-awareness, or a group of animals or creatures if this awareness is centered in group consciousness rather in individuals. In this calling forth of this energy, effects may be created and acts accomplished upon its energy patterns that will effect it at all levels of life. These acts may cause it to perform physical acts in physical life, or change attitudes, or accelerate its regeneration (healing) or degeneration, all these by the manipulation of its energy.

The process is much the same and may be accomplished as before by one or many as the nature of the work dictates. An image is created by the practitioner causing it to seem as like the individual as may be within the practitioner's ability. Energy is malleable and, therefore, so is its vibration. By using this principle it is possible to take raw energy and shape and endow it with both a signature energy pattern and complex subsidiary energy patterns so that it will simulate an individual life form. The practitioner must take great care with this so that it will be as identical as possible. Then, by the Law of Harmonic Resonance, it will BE that life form in his reality. Moreover, since it was the practitioner that created this, it now within his power to manipulate this energy to his purposes. In this manner, the practitioner may accomplish healing from a distance. Also, those who have a bond together join with one another across space and time and even across the worlds, for the Law of Harmonic Resonance holds true in many dimensions of Universes.

When the practitioner is satisfied that his intention is worked upon this energy construct, he may return it to its source. This source will be the energy pattern it most closely resembles because, according to the Rule of Parallel Resonances, differentiated energy will be drawn to the most identical energy pattern and assimilated into it.

The Law of Parallel Resonance states that those resonances that are sufficiently similar to one another will draw to one another as they have similar base forms, and only the external harmonics may be lacking from them in likeness. To use the analogy of music, this is to say that two notes may be the same but separated by an octave. Alternatively, they may be only separated by part of an octave and yet their resonant harmonics may be so much alike that they will resonate with one another forming a greater whole. This is the mechanism by which these forms seek out and act according to their directives, for they are set to patterns that are like those things they act upon. However, nothing is perfectly identical to anything else. This would defy the basic principles of this continuum, for even the most perfect mirror is not the thing that it reflects. Therefore, thought forms will return at last to their creator unless that creator has become fundamentally changed during the interval of their separation.

This is the explanation for what is known to be the rebounding of spells and magic. If a thought form or fetch is made not in the likeness of the object of the process, but only reflects the practitioner's feelings about that object, then the form will be most similar to that part of the mage and seek to join with him, for this is the thing most like itself. Thought forms are not accurately created from emotions but from intelligent will as are all processes and workings of power. This should not be disregarded in even the slightest part for it is the key to the success of these workings and a strong and potent argument for the strength of the objective disciplines of the practitioner.

CHAPTER 6

ENERGY WORK WITH STONES & TALISMANS

Energy work is often referred to as healing in this day and time, because it is most often done to remedy some condition that has fallen out of harmony or adjustment within the individual. This may manifest on any of the levels of awareness as a dysfunction of that level, and result in discomfort or malfunction of that level. In a broader sense, however, the term healing can imply working to return an individual to an ideal state of harmony with himself and with the Universal whole. This includes a variety of energy work intended to expand the consciousness and identity of the individual, and it is in this sense that we mean healing. When we refer to a Healer, we refer to an individual whose purpose is to facilitate this process of expansion and renewal.

Until now, in this work, we have focussed most of our intention on preparing the student to undertake this work. We have presented guided meditations and techniques as well as the underlying metaphysical theory behind the basic elements of energy work, particularly with regard to working with crystals, stones, and metals. We will now expand on these principles with the intention of providing the student and practitioner with basic grounding in the specifics of crystal and stone work. We will guide the student and practitioner into the fundamentals of talisman construction and the ways in which complex talismans can be used for a variety of purposes.

HEALING BY PLACING STONES ON THE BODY

There are two basic forms of healing that involve direct interacting of the energy systems of the body with the energy fields of crystals and stones. The first is a process that takes place over an extensive length of time involving the use of talismans of various construction that will later be discussed and explained at length. The second is a process of placing stones at various points on the body for short periods of time. Under the guided energies of the healer's hand, these stones and crystals emit directed energy and energize the energy system complex by their interaction with each other. In this way, they act like a talisman interwoven with the body's energy matrix. The helix they form among themselves is coherent with and overlapping that of the body so they become intertwined, interlaced and thereby interactive. This is a good way to begin experimenting with the different ways crystals react with the body's energy fields. Because the placement of the stones is specific, their effects tend to be more immediate. This makes it possible to monitor their interaction with the centers and areas on which they are placed with a certain degree of precision. This can be developed into an intricate process whereby minute and specific qualities of energy are initialized and balanced against the existing bodily field.

This process is a very powerful healing technique in the specific sense of being an initial remedy for an illness, injury, or trauma from whatever source. It is also a good technique when dealing with an individual who has had a long debilitating fever or other condition that lowers the level of the entire body's energy complement. The individual may not be in a position to initialize his or her own recovery. Its effects are immediately felt because they are augmented by the Healer's own energy intention. It is also a powerful technique for lowering barriers and reducing or removing blockages to one or more of the chakras. A secondary benefit of using this method is that the effects can be closely monitored by the practitioner. This will allow any extreme or undesirable effect to be adjusted and brought into harmony with the desired result and the individual's energy limits.

The effects of this process are transient. Once the stones are removed the augmenting energy of the Healer's intention is no longer in place. It is therefore advisable to reinforce its effects with a talisman tuned to maintain the beneficial effect to be worn in the form of jewelry.

THE PROCEDURE OF PLACING

STONES ON THE BODY

This will give the student an idea of the basic layout of the stones. The procedure may be adjusted to accomodate the desired result and the Healer's preferences.

This procedure should always be done within a warded and protected space free from unnecessary noise and distraction, for it will be necessary to interact with the entire shielding and energy system of a body already weakened by physical trauma. The body should recline on a comfortable flat surface and, if the circumstances permit it, in alignment with the planetary magnetic field, the top of the head pointing in the direction of the closest magnetic pole. This is not crucial but may be of some benefit and aid to the Healer. It will align the body with the planet's energies and make them slightly easier for the healer to access, draw, and bind with the energies of the body. If possible, the body should be bare of clothing at least in the areas that will be treated so that the stones will contact the warmth and resonance of the skin as closely as possible.

Place a double terminated quartz crystal with a very clear single point at each end over the heart center of the body. While doing this, the healer should raise the earth power to align and join with the body's energy flow so that the body's fields draw in one complete current with the earth's field. This should not be a radical process that conflicts with the body's own field, but a gentle and natural procedure that strengthens and enhances it. Be careful that the intensities of the energies used are considered and monitored as the procedure continues. From this central stone place four terminated tourmalines - sea green or grass green but matching in color, size and strength - in rays pointing outward to the quarter axes of the body, that is, towards the shoulders and hips. This will form the central pivot of the work.

Then, beginning from the base chakra and working upward place stones corresponding to the energies of the individual chakras. The points of the lower ones pointing towards the feet and of the ones above the heart pointing upwards towards the crown. This should form a strong secondary helix over the first so that the body's field may be reconstructed thereby. It is entirely at the discretion of the healer, according to his wisdom and the circumstances, to choose which stone of what sovereign strength should be used for the chakras. This choice should be dictated by the nature and degree of severity of the illness and the basic nature of the afflicted person. Then place corresponding stones of virtue in the palms of the hands with the terminations pointing outward toward the fingertips. By this, we mean clear stones that correspond to the desired result. This can be stones that refer to the basic energy quality of the area under treatment - for example, if the heart chakra is being addressed, this stone might be a clear beryl. If a particular issue or attitude such as a phobia or trauma is being addressed then a stone that addresses that parameter should be used. Quartz may be used in general circumstances or when a more specific stone is not available. When all the stones are in place, the Healer should raise and balance the energies of the body. With his or her will and intention, he or she should superimpose a healing field to counteract the energies that are weak or out of balance, while reinforcing the energies that are whole.

Take care that the horizontal helix is also included in this and that both axes are balanced with respect to one another and the body's strength. This is the reason for the stones in the hands, and is very important in the success of this process. The circuit of the energy may be raised from the base or extended from the heart. However, in the case of this illness and injury it should not be brought from the crown, for this is the reversal of all nature. It is the nature of injury that it conflicts with the access of the affected area to the life giving survival energies of the base chakra. The base chakra controls access to the healing and renewing energies of the earth and the physical universe. The energy flow should be initialized from the base and, when this is flowing strongly, should be brought into union with the crown chakra energy. This should be the principle source of healing energy rather than the crown. Once the full pattern is established, the Healer should determine that the energy flow through the crown is clear, free, and complete within the energy system. To complete this procedure, the Healer should determine that the energy flow is clear in both directions. If it is not, then he or she should clear these channels according to the relative strength of the organism, keeping in mind that this is an entirely different matter than initializing the flow of healing from the crown. Then the energies should be raised, balanced, centered, and strengthened at the discretion, direction, and control of the healer. Remember that the stones should always remain within his sphere of control. Also, remember that the Healer should be using his or her own energies to guide and direct the individual's attachment to the energy field of this planet and of the Universal flow. At no time do we mean to imply that the Healer should use his or her own personal energy to sustain and augment the individual's fields. Energies that are lacking should be supplied and then bound within the whole from the Universal pool of energy.

After this has been completed to the satisfaction of the Healer, the stones should be removed in the reverse order of their placement. Generally, a stone or talisman is given the person to wear to reinforce and continue the healing process. This talisman should remain entirely in the healer's control and should be monitored by him and eventually returned to him when its function is complete.

For this procedure, the base ends of the stones should be cut or ground flat but not capped with metal to regulate and insure the extent of their energy inter-relationships. If a talisman is given for the individual's use following the procedure, it may be set in accordance with the procedures discussed elsewhere.

From this basic procedure, many others may be derived varying widely in their complexity and duration. The healer may hold a rod or wand of crystal and direct the body's energies with this rather than placing the stones upon the person should circumstances dictate or should this be the simplest way to accomplish the desired ends. Alternatively, he or she may use this wand to direct energy into the stones placed upon the individual. Should a complete set of perfect crystals be unavailable or in some cases too intense, then, apart from the heart star of quartz and tourmaline, this may be any rough or polished lump of stone. They may be cut in axial alignment or left merely as they are found, for their purpose is to join with and reinforce the strength of the center star and add their energies to it. However, in serious cases, the stone of the most afflicted Chakra should be a whole crystal so that its energy may be centered and best aligned.

In general, a healer should use best what comes to hand and what he feels is appropriate to the situation. He or she may use black tourmaline or amethyst, held rod-like in the hand to drawn out excessive charge or locked up negative force. He or she may use amethyst, clear quartz, or any tourmaline to direct specific energies into the body and to guide and direct the resident energies. These stones may be set in a wand with a metal shaft, suspended from a silver chain or wire, or held as a rod in the hand. He or she may place white quartz on the brow, along with or in place of a colored stone, to hold all other energies stable while he or she is working elsewhere on the form. This will also soothe and cool the afflicted area. If no white quartz is available, then a star or flower of chalcedony will work nicely in its place with only minimal differences. When using the white quartz in this manner, The stone should be wider than it is long and set butt downward upon the skin, pointing outward from the forehead. This will cause it to seek access to the mineral content of the skull bones as a ground and thus connect fully and efficiently to the specific energies of this center. It will be of undeniable benefit both as a temporary calmative to the injured or afflicted and will help reduce any lasting undesirable effects of shock from any illness or injury or from the necessary force of the procedure itself. At the practitioner's discretion, a black tourmaline may replace the clear quartz at the heart center once the procedure has been initialized to act as a calmative and to draw out imbalances and negativity. The joints of the feet and legs may have stones placed upon them should it be necessary to extend the reinforced helix thus far or should the nature of the injury center there. But take care that wherever the injury is located, place stones both above and below it with regard to the energy flow of the body so that the healing current will pass through the area and revitalize it in a complete and unified circuit of flow.

This matrix of stones is used to facilitate the transmissions of the healer's will and intention and to aid his assessment of the extent and nature of the ill and the effect his work is having on it. Remember that it is the practitioner's strength, intelligence and industry that determine its benefit, for the afflicted person has no discretion nor determinism of his own and will have given himself fully into the healer's care for this procedure. The healer is, therefore, responsible for the completion of all matters pertaining to the affliction, for the thoroughness of the procedure and for its monitoring afterwards so that it will proceed smoothly to its desired outcome.

After all steps of this procedure have been completed, should the situation permit, the energies of the afflicted should be wholly rebalanced and reinforced according to the strength and needs of that person. A full balancing should be done and maintained afterwards until the healing process is complete so that the organism will not heal imperfectly or be impaired or confused.

The healer should remember to refresh and revitalize him or herself. Let him or her take care not to retain any unbalanced or harmful energy but to release these forces to return to the universal energy pool. He or she should eat well according to their needs, join in grace with his or her partner if that is possible, and have access to the necessary quiet or recreation of peace to which he or she is entitled. In this way, care be taken in the maintenance of both the afflicted and practitioners alike so that their work shall flourish and be effective.

SIMPLE HEALING WITH CARVED IMAGES

We will now discuss the process of healing sometimes referred to as sympathetic magic and its relative effectiveness in certain instances. This may be defined as the act of engaging another individual in the process of agreement with a practice and, therefore, of assisting in the active use of power. This may be done with or without the individual's overt consent depending upon the necessities of the procedure. In essence, it is a process by which the practitioner creates an energy matrix field stronger than that created by the individual being healed. This field is superimposed over the one of lesser strength so that the field of lesser strength will modify itself and reach a harmonic of the stronger field. This is the essence of all the works of healing.

Carved charms are a means of circumventing what might be the unhealthy intention or ignorant consideration of the individual to remain in an ill, mad, or injured state. The healer may induce belief in a form whose essence carries the desired cultural or personal connotation of the energy that the practitioner wishes to impose upon the individual. The individual can often be helped more easily because of his or her identification with whatever symbology is used. They also represent one way to implement one's desired procedure without undue use of force, which could, by its intensity, negate the value of the work desired. Such charms are but one instance of the power of created thought forms. They are constructions formed from the collected and concentrated energy and intention of one or more individuals to serve a certain purpose for any specified or non-specified duration. The formation of thought forms is fully discussed in its own section. The charms are simply some physically manifested form of the energy in a symbolic frame of reference.

Sympathetic magic and healing relies on the use of physical objects shaped to resemble a known or unknown thing. These are often charms and images constructed of metal and stones, but may be any object whose form conveys some type of recognizable subject matter with the desired meaning. This might be a recognizable resident of the physical world such as a plant or tree, or an unknown thing such as a mythical creature, dragon, or benevolent spirits referred to at times as gods. It has been thought by some that the forms themselves have certain virtues, but this is not so. They provoke in the owner/wearer a certain response that may be favorable or sympathetic to the use and intention of the working talisman. Generally, these are used for children who, having no conscious understanding or tutored knowledge of the process, can be shown by the analogy of the represented figure the mental attitude to assume to allow the energies to work more efficiently. They are used to heal anyone who is untutored and most especially those who have lost any type of purposeful recall of their faculties. Then the shapes are chosen to represent images within the unconscious mind, which stimulate those buried processes. In those who are just beginning to learn the power resident in the stones, these carvings and markings may serve as an aid to memory before the full process is keyed within them at initiation.

The shapes of the charms should be recognizable to the wearer, and should evoke some predictable response. The represented force should be common in the mythos of the people and accepted as at least somewhat valid by the wearer. It is not as wise to use the images of gods and demons unless those images are entirely benevolent ones. Even then, this is not wholly desirable lest the wearer credit all the power of the healing to a supernatural agency rather than the constructive use of his own energies. It is better to use images of legendary characters and animal archetypes so that they might stimulate desirable and effective internal personal responses according to the intention of the healer. This perceived information is important in the choosing of the image most suited to the purpose and the specific individual's balance potential. It may be gathered from private conversation with the individual, telepathic information, and/or familiarity with the specific cultural mythos of the individual in question.

This technique is extremely beneficial when as individual has no knowledge of the techniques of healing by using stones directly. A charm carved from a sample of the stone or crystal that will be effective in dealing with the individual's difficulty can be greatly effective if that individual agrees with the subject and content of the charm. This links the individual to the energy matrix of the stone on an unconscious level and activates its benefit even if he or she is not versed in working with subtle levels of personal energy.

CHAPTER 7

THE ENERGIES OF METAL

Metals exist in nature as elements; that is, they are some of the fundamental building blocks of this physical universe. As elements, they form part of the atomic structure of stones and crystals but are bonded in a different way than when they exist in their elemental metallic form. Examining the nature of the individual elements in a crystal's atomic structure can often give you some interesting insights into the nature of its energy properties. This also explains why some metals are extremely compatible with certain stones and crystals and why others seem to work in direct opposition.

The atomic structure of metals is different in character from the majority of crystals, although metals may be found in their own natural crystalline forms. When metal is combined with stones and crystals it can complement and amplify their natures. Because of their atomic structure, when crystals are put in line with an electrical current they oscillate, that is, they vibrate at a particular frequency that is determined by the way those atoms are put together. Metals, however, conduct electricity. Their atomic natures dictate this property. This complementary nature of crystals and metals allow them to serve together in talismanic energy work. Metals also help transfer the electrical current of the body's energy field evenly across the basis of the axis structure so that the vibrational energies of the talisman's components are compatibly and coherently integrated with one another. They also help the individual in integrating the resulting talisman with his or her own energy field.

Just as each crystal family has its own signature vibrational pattern that distinguishes the nature and quality of its energies and function, each different metal has its own signature nature of conductivity and harmonic resonance. Metals can be combined into alloys that unite their capacities just as stones can be combined into talismans. Nevertheless, because of the nature of the process of alloying, the energy of the resultant metal can sometimes differ from the nature of its original components.

IRON & STEEL

Iron and steel are analogous to the color red and the corresponding base chakra. The energy of iron activates the basic life force drive, especially on the physical level, partially because it resonates with the base chakra, and partially because one of the significant components of human blood is iron. It will take on a magnetic field and, as such, is an element in generating an electro-magnetic field. This magnetism interacts with the iron in the blood as well as the electro-magnetic fields around the body, and to some extent, the electro-magnetic impulses that activate the nerve channels, nerve centers, and brain synapse activity. Healing with this magnetic energy is a new field of study for this day and age and will be greatly more developed in the coming century as general scientific knowledge about the body's energy field grows. It is not a new science, however, and much was known and developed in this line of study by the Ancient Healers before the Fall. A person who does not have a sufficient iron level in their blood will not only feel physically weakened, but will also have inhibited brain activity. Iron will focus and drive any field to which it is attuned and once this tuning takes place, this function will be virtually automatic.

Iron is the metal of control and physical creation. Culturally, in ancient times, the smelting of iron from its ore was the first step of higher technology. This represented a far more powerful process than the alloying of bronze. The smelting of iron and forging of implements from it represented a great technological achievement. These implements, whether tools for war or peace, were significantly harder and more durable than any previously known. This knowledge greatly extended Humankind's control over the environment and, consequently, heightened its survival potential. Those who worked in such a craft were held in highest regard because they were as midwives to the birth of a new age of strength and achievement.

Iron is dense and firmly integrated with its own structure, but it is brittle. However, its particles can be made to integrate with one another and their density compounded so that the brittle nature is changed. The ancients tell us that, in the case of certain forging techniques, steel can take on a vibrational property that behaves in the same way a crystal would. This produces a harmonic field and amplifies its energy as part of the individual's energy field complex. Carbon added through this working process, will provide the interlink that is needed to make crystal structure whole and, in the process, the properties of iron are amplified and magnified to a substance of the highest power of this nature. Remember that a diamond is the crystal of carbon. The properties of iron, alloyed with the properties of carbon and worked together become a combination of the greatest strength of energy and power.

It is important to pay close attention to the working parameters of setting crystals and stones with iron and steel, because their field generating properties are so strong that it will significantly interact with any stone set in them. This may cause basic changes in the way certain stones function and resonate. In some instances, these changes will be permanent or semi-permanent and extremely difficult to alter or clear.

This property will also be true for individuals. An individual who carries a significant amount of steel for a long period will become integrated with the nature of this metal and changed by it for a time. Be sure to decide whether this is desirable. For example, the natures of the Warrior and steel are compatible and in harmony with each other. It is in the interest of the Warrior's development to wear some object of iron or steel somewhere on his body constantly, unless he needs to be healed of a wound. Wearing steel while healing from a wound or serious illness will change the energy patterns of the body in the process of regeneration. Nevertheless, in other times, it will help the Warrior find his strength and develop his own nature. He should keep his blade near him, for if its is well made, it will become as his heart and the driving focus of all his energy. He should use it with his dominant hand and all the power drawn upward from his lower Chakras will center in his heart and be poured forth through the blade. This will also have a significant effect on the energy property of the heart chakra. A shield bound with iron can also draw energy from his enemies' blows and transmute this force into his own strength.

As another example: A woman who is pregnant should not carry steel armaments about her person for the child's nature will be adjusted according to the intensity and duration of its wearing. Although the raising of power by this means, occasionally, will cause no harm, but likely strengthen the child when the energy is truly channeled and directed and the work cleanly accomplished.

Both iron and steel have great potential and strength to raise and channel power. They can be used to tap even the life energy potential of the Great River of Life. The individual who holds the blade that raises this force can then become its catalyst and driver to his own purposes. However, this places a considerable demand on the energy potential of that individual. He or she must not only be highly trained and disciplined but also in good physical health. This level of power use can put a tremendous strain on all the energy systems and it is not without reason that we make this prohibition. A weak or untrained individual could face significant energy overload of some or all energy systems if he or she works with iron or steel too much or too intensely. However, with training and practice it is an invaluable asset to the practitioner.

Crystals of iron include Hematite (Fe_2O_3 Iron Oxide), Pyrite and Marcasite (FeS_2 Iron Sulfide).

=============================
COPPER
=============================

Copper is the metal of the Analogy of the Rose. It is the power union symbolized by the King/Queen balance.

It is the metal specific to the combined resonance of base and heart chakras and resonates on the dual ray of rose/green. It easily conducts both electricity and heat while remaining flexible during this process. It's energy has a balanced fluidity and will easily adapt to many forms of energy work. However, it does not retain the charges its conducts for any great period. This is ideal if it is going to need to fulfill a variety of functions and many different resonances of energies are to be used. An exception to this characteristic is a charm or talisman worn close to the body of an individual for many years. It integrates to the fabric of the being who possesses it, growing towards a union with its wearer. That is, as it interacts consistently with the basic energy fields of the wearer, it will gradually and subtly conform in its own energies - its own conductive nature shaping its energy lattice to respond completely to the wearer. Such talismans are very personal and strong. However, such a charm cannot be created by a simple cleansing and charging; it is the product of years, use, and familiarity.

Due to the open structure of its pure form, copper interacts easily with other elements and compounds causing it to corrode and tarnish easily. It is generally soft and malleable unless intentionally hardened by hammering and vibration. This is the so-called Egyptian secret of hardening copper tools. The more they are worked, the harder they become. However, this process is not always practical when making talismans and other regalia. It also reacts with the skin chemistry of the wearer.

When combined with other metals into alloys, its vibration is a most agreeable and accommodating harmonic and adds smoothness to otherwise harsh resonances, along with physical structural flexibility. This is its purpose in the structure of bronze. When set with garnets it encourages the rose side of its nature and makes a good talisman for an individual drained of energy. This may translate as warmth or strength, but in any case is most effective in cases of physical debility and weakness.

Copper works well when set with green stones of any nature (particularly those that have copper as part of their structure such as malachite, turquoise, and chrysocolla). It is also compatible with emeralds and strongly green crystalline opals (although there are many contradictions against this and much care must be taken in the balance). Peridot makes a most joyful companion here in company with strongly white stones.

The Ancient texts describe an example of copper regalia being used to balance and augment the spirit: "The Queen wears a wide copper belt to balance her passions with the wisdom of her heart. This leads to a condition of great health. It also powerfully centers the her ability to draw power from the Earth itself. Set with glowing crystals (quartz or any true, clear driver) she dances before her Lord for their mutual joy. Let her sandals be set with copper discs that her strength be further raised in the Morning of Beginnings. She will walk upon the Land beside him that it be healed. And so the green ray of her love and dedication is fulfilled in his company. And upon her breast shall be the rose stone of her love. She is the True Mother of the Land and her power is great over it."

Yet copper is easily misused, because of its changeable and malleable nature. If you make tools of copper for your own use, they should be stored in a separate sealed container away from other charged implements. They should not be handled at all by any other person until the work they are intended for is completed. This is because the energy parameters of copper are so easily affected and another person's energy, however benign or well-meaning, will alter their charge. Copper is often chosen for healing when the talisman is left with the one who is sick or injured, for it will release its charge over a short space of time. This will allow that the individual does not become dependent on the healing charge after his or her recovery. Instead, it will gradually grow into a close harmony with its wearer as a reminder of its healing function.

A copper charm may be worn by the elderly whose life energies burn low. Copper will help stabilize and reinforce a low physical level vibration because of its balancing qualities between the heart and the base chakras. Such a charm may also be worn by pregnant women in order to help them balance their energies from day to day. Copper charms may be worn by young girls coming into womanhood to help them balance their vibrations, find peace with their changing bodies, and grow into their fullness with grace. However, a bride should refrain from wearing a copper charm until after her wedding night because will interfere with the communion of their two natures striving to keep hers alone in congruity.

It is unwise to make bells of it in its pure form, for they will not strike consistently pure notes. Reserve this function for finer metals that will hold their temper and continuity when making bells for dancing or ritual use.

In all things, generally, copper serves as the hearth fire of the spirit especially in things mundane and raises the chi to its proper levels in the untrained where this is needed. Two crystalline forms of copper are covelite (CuS Copper Sulfide) and chalcocite (Cu_2S Copper Sulfide).

BRONZE

When we refer to bronze in this work, we are speaking particularly of an alloy that is approximately, but not limited to, 90% copper and 10% tin with a trace addition of zinc. An alloy is a mixture of two or more metals under heat that results in a metal that has different properties than any of its components. In current days, phosphorous is also added as well as a variety of other trace minerals to give the metal particular properties. The practitioner and student may wish to experiment with other alloys of various compositions to determine their specific and unique characteristics.

The combined resonances of the materials in bronze corresponds to the belly chakra. The predominance of copper in this alloy engages the interaction of the combined heart / base channel. The addition of tin to the copper energizes the solar plexus chakra and the addition of zinc serves to center it with the belly center. The combined resonance of the alloy is centered to a full balance potential of the lower chakras without the magnetic nature of iron or steel.

Bronze resonates easily with most orange stones such as citrine and carnelian and harmonizes well with certain yellow stones such as jacinth (yellow zircon). This gives strength to the muscles and skin of the body because it encourages the circulation of blood by the stimulation of the energy in the outer portion of the body's energy helix. However, this does not intrinsically contain the higher vibrations of spirit. It stimulates spontaneous action and reflex capabilities but does not stimulate the higher reasoning faculties with it. The ancient texts tell us that "when it is worn upon the Warrior's breast, he will manifest the heart of the ancient Tiger that is extinct upon the Earth."

The Ancient Texts also tell the tale of a sword of great power: The ancient sword of the Master Smith was called GyrLyon after this energy and was lost under the waves in the Fall. This was the blade with the perfect carbon content, and potential force could be transferred into it almost without limit, and by the power of the Warrior this force could be unleashed, but by his hand alone. Long was the answer sought again to the making of this blade that its force should be renewed to the True People. But as the Smith perished, so did this process, the truth of the blade was not only in this most perfect forging and alloying but in the song of his spirit that he did sing into it. Let the sandals of the Warrior be bound with bronze, and discs of it attached to them as well so that he might draw this current from the earth and upward through the basal center to be modified by his will and then unleashed through the blade in his hand.

Statues and sculptures of all kinds are well done with this alloy for they will hold any form of charge well. The metal does not flow with the lightning power of steel, but holds energy firmly with great potential so that this power may be stored for future use or sudden unleashing. It is possible to charge a bronze object and have it retain the charge because, the presence of copper allows it to take a charge with great specificity and the addition of trace materials will moderate the copper's tendency to dissipate the energy. These additional materials cause the bronze to hold any charge until it is specifically called upon to release the energy. It is not only the metal of warriors but also of sculptors, for figures made from it will hold the energies and intentions of the artisan longer and with greater detail than any other will. For this reason, it is an excellent choice for sympathetic charms.

GOLD

The vibrational energy of Gold is analogous in energy harmonic to the color yellow. It is known as the Metal of Dominion. Its nature is dominant and it will drive and focus any stone set in it, and translate its energies to the fullest potential, magnifying them to their optimal level. Gold is an ideal conductor. It will easily channel and transmit the intention and energies of an individual with very little distortion. It is very useful when doing power work with dominant stones such as diamond and members of the corundum family. It will guide and control their intense energies to keep them aligned with the intention and purpose of the work.

Its energy is like the all-pervading energy and power of the Sun that extends its influence even to the places that are shadowed from it. It is the metal of kingship, because it enables the individual using it to focus and direct his or her intention through stones set in it. Gold extends its blessing throughout the energy system, encouraging those channels that are already strengthened, and giving them constant reinforcement. It draws energy and restores those systems placed within its dominion. When used in settings in company with silver, it provides the active balance to the silver's subtlety, for their helixes will join to form one harmonious union of energy.

When keyed to or bound around a chakra, it will both concentrate and magnify those energies. Its nature is warm and shall be sovereign in those cases where that nature would provide healing.

Its dominant nature is best demonstrated when it is set with stones of the corundum family and also with diamond for their natures are well attuned and will construct most potent tools for all intentions.

Pure gold is very soft and it is consequently alloyed with a variety of materials to give it hardness and flexibility. However, care should be taken in the choice of these additions because, as these materials are added to increase physical hardness, so they alter the grain structure making it denser and less conductive. There are processes of power work that even a small degree of baser metal will mar or obstruct. Therefore, the complete composition of any alloy should be carefully considered. This is not to say that any alloy is undesirable. There are times when a good deal of fine-tuning of energy and power can be done by adjusting the subtle elements in a metal's alloy. However, it is necessary to know what the components of an alloy are and their proportion so that its true nature can be understood before the work begins.

As a general guideline, gold is best alloyed with silver and copper for this focus of its work. Let the alloys of gold be no less than three-quarters pure (18-karat), for in lower proportion its nature loses its potency to a great degree. However, this may be compensated for to some extent with the addition of copper if the intended work is not of too great a significance, or if the nature of the work is such that the influence of pure copper is intentional and desired.

The ancient texts tell us: "This is the metal of the True King and shall be bound about his brow accordingly. This is the wrist cuff of the true Adept Healer. This is the signet ring and force of dominion of the True Queen when she speaks and wields power in the name of her Lord. Let this as well as his be set with an emerald when healing is at hand."

Stones set in gold and worn at the heart have the pervasive effect of their power, and this will not be counteracted by any when the power is used rightly. Gold may be inlaid into any other substance both of other metals and also natural substance such as wood and bone, so that it may have channels of power like running rivers to accomplish any purpose, and this most potent if rightly done. Any runes of characters set in this manner will form glowing nodes of their significance and act as capacitors in the focus of the energy of the work.

SILVER

Silver could be called the Metal of the Moon, for its nature is of a subtle and flowing kind and allows for changeable fluctuations of energy. In terms of color translation, its energy vibration is analogous to all shades of the color blue. It aids in the general flow and dissemination of energies throughout any talisman with which it is constructed and then with any individual's energy system into which the talisman is placed. It also allows for these energies to adjust to one another without one overriding the other and without unnecessary force or direction so that the individual wearing it can receive the greatest benefit from the use of such a talisman. Its nature is of a peaceful and passive sort. It is the least intrusive of all metals and will only minimally "color" the piece with its signature pattern, leaving the stones free to interact without addition or opposition to their combination of energies.

This property makes it ideal for setting stones for beginner's in crystal work. It will allow them intimate access to the stone while providing the stone with a coherent and consistent energy intake structure, but it will not interfere with the vibrational qualities of the stone itself. This will allow the student to wear and use the stone or crystal and to focus on its unique properties without interference or complication from the vibrations of its accompanying metal.

This particular quality makes is a good choice for any talisman or regalia related to scrying or any other practice of the Seer. It allows the stones of such a piece to be interactive both with each other and the individual using them but does not interfere with these energies or interpose any focus or direction of its own. The Seer's work often requires multi-plane subtle shifts of consciousness and energy, and this is a good quality to consider when building talismans for her. It also provides a subtle connection throughout the many planes of travel providing a kind of energy trace that will allow the Seer's conscious awareness to follow it back to the physical plane. This will not interfere with the Seer's perception or ability to translate what has been seen and must be mentally retained.

When worn as a circlet around the forehead, it will help greatly in the translation of power from modulations into useful knowledge and translated forms of power. When worn as a bracelet around the recessive hand or wrist, silver aids in perception, drawing, and channeling all manner of energy forms and vibrations, whether of the nature of physical ills, power intake sources, or sources of information. Its nature may even be said to be neutral, although this is not literally correct, for it marks nothing with its specifics, but subtly assists by clarifying what it does transmit.

The ancient texts tell us: "It is the metal of the Priestess and is specific to her that her work should be eased in all its aspects. When set solely with moonstones of the perfect white/blue ray shall mark her diadem of power throughout the ages. In times of war and attack upon her from many sources, this will act so strongly even unto the saving of her life and reason, for all energies directed at her will be translated by its virtue to her own translation and usage."

Electrum is an alloy of varying proportions of gold and silver. In Ancient Days, the ideal proportions were equal of each. Electrum combines the fluidity of silver with the focus and direction of gold, making it an ideal setting for talismans and regalia dedicated to high intensity power work and making it prized above all other metals except platinum. This is because it represents the interlocking power of the active and passive principles, and as such is analogous to the color purple/violet. Electrum has both the power to draw and to send forth creating most beautifully the desirable double helix of metal. It is the King and Queen together in their union and may be used of itself or inlaid on any substance to provide the most potent channel of power.

On rare occasions, electrum occurs naturally in a combined formation of silver and gold lying side by side within the Earth, so compatible and harmonious are their natures together. The process of alloying and working this metal should be done carefully so that there is a perfect union of its content and proportion and so that the resulting color is the most delicate yellow/white.

This may bind the brow and wrists of the Adept whether male or female and their energies shall be unified accordingly. Moonstones and any stone of the beryl family are very harmonious with its nature as well as Iolites and lavender sapphires.

Platinum is the most potent of the noble metals. Its nature is to focus and drive in the same way gold does but with a single-mindedness that has caused its energy to be compared with lightning. For this reason, it is an excellent choice for setting diamond and any member of the corundum family. It will add structure to their charge as well as being able to easily supply their energy construct demands. It will easily and agreeably pattern itself with the energy field of the wearer over a period of time and become a strong and vital element of any talisman of power. However, its intense nature makes it generally unsuitable for any lower power range of stones below the hardness of seven unless there is a specific purpose in mind.

Its structure is very dense and tightly aligned while still being an excellent conductor. Its retains its integrity regardless of any but the most extreme circumstances and even then returns very quickly to normal once the incident is past. It is difficult to work because of its high melting temperature and care must be taken with the crucible so that the metal does not oxidize. The ancients say of it: "This metal will remove all obstacles placed within the purview of its dominion and shall move all energies forward and through as though obstacles did not exist. Its nature is of the pure white light and ray and its crystalline structure so dense, pure and well aligned that no more need be said of it for all that can be imagined may be accomplished within its dominion."

❀ - *MEDITATION ON METALS*

We begin the journey into the nature of metals by examining the most crystalline of all metallic structures - tempered steel. Extend yourself once again towards the field of clouds. Once again, you fly above their folding and changing masses. They churn and flow beneath and around you. You see a shining form gleaming out from the heart center of the clouds. They turn and roll, and then they draw back from the center. --- The shining form grows larger and ever larger until it fills your entire field of vision and you see that it is a shining cylinder of steel rising before you. As it grows ever larger, you see that it is becoming thinner. Its inner structure is expanding so that it seems almost transparent. You move closer and closer until you pass within it. You are now surrounded by its delicate intricate structure. ---   Look around you — see how the delicate fibers of metal arch and curve around you like strangely beautiful and symmetrical lacework. Listen. There is a song. The breeze is blowing through its archway, and you hear the high thin music of its natural vibrations. It is sweeter and clearer than the purest flute or most sensitive harp string. ---

The breeze blows again, this time it carries a strange and pungent scent like that of oil. Feel its texture, let its music carry upward and upward, and as you soar through its beautiful resonant structure you begin to notice a regularity, a balance. You notice also that some of the fibers are not like all the rest. Some are dark gray and dull looking; some are very, very fine; more delicate than the finest silk thread. Now you recognize the darker ones as carbon. See how they balance the regular shiny threads of the structure. Notice how there are various trace elements bound in with the other predicable parts - slight anomalies in the overall whole formation. Yet, they join harmoniously, their various notes blending in the thin high breeze like the voices of a chorus. Each one is unique. Each has its unique note to add to the endless song on the wind. Some of them add strength, some flexibility, while others withstand erosion and lock the structure against the incursion of other elements. Some glisten and shine, others are dull, and some have colors as dull red or bright yellow. Yet, each is part of the harmonious structure of the metallic unit. By touching each one you know what function each separate element serves; you are part of it and you know its nature and are in tune with this harmony. ---

Now you begin to expand. You permeate the structure. It is part of you and you are part of it. You resonate with its song, and it answers to your song in return. You fill one another. As your songs merge you, reach out to it with your heart. The glowing white light of your intention blazes forth. It resonates anew with a new energy and strength. Now you fill it with your intensity, and your desire. Your will infuses it as you make it truly your own. It is answerable to you always in your heart. Your songs will never again be entirely separate, for you are both part of the great song of the Universe. You know that anytime you wish you may enter the structure of any metal with your thought and intuition to know its structure and its song. Never again shall the nature of metal be closed to you. Know also that as you have filled this steel with your intention and will, so you may fill any metal object with your intention. This is the true nature of charging any metal or part metallic talisman. ---

Now you move back. You move away from and out of the steel cylinder. You move away to the distance where it seems small. No longer than the length of your arm. But look again, you are not distant at all. You have merely changed your size with respect to it. It is a bar now that you may easily hold in your hand. You reach forth and grasp it. It is pleasingly warm in your hand and through your palm, you can still feel its vibration and song tingling against your skin. Now you grasp it firmly in your dominant hand. Your feet are firmly planted beneath you. Your back is straight. You raise the rod of steel and point it before you. Now raise the Great River of Life as you have so often. It pulses up through the soles of your feet. It runs up your back like clear pure rippling water, and then down your outstretched arm in the form of pure energy. Feel how it ripples through the rod as well with no effort at all. The rod is truly an extension of your arm, and thus truly an extension of your intentional will. You may do anything you like with it, and it responds easily. Push just a little, see how easily the energy becomes lightning. It flashes harmlessly about in the fleecy clouds, but know for certain that this force can burn and blast. --- Change the energy modulation just a little now, just a very little, and the lightning fire turns to gentle radiant warmth. It flows gently forth and you know that it can warm and heal anything at which you wish to direct it. --- Now change it again and the current turns an icy blue. It may freeze at a touch or it may flow gentle cooling energy to calm the fever of a wound or ill temper of anger. All these currents of energy you may manifest through the conductive properties of any metal. ---Now feel the metal again, and know by its very nature it is creating a conductive channel through you. Anytime you raise the energy of the metal it will intensify the drawing force of whatever energy you wish to manifest. In the current it generates by its own inherent nature, you are able to partake readily of this property to raise your own energies when there is a need for this function. Remember that in the physical universe the steel you use to this purpose will retain the nature of the charge to which you set it. It will take on more and more of this quality, just as a crystal becomes clearer and more responsive to the purpose of your will. This is the nature of all crystalline structures. Remember this in order that you may optimize the potential of this capability. ---

Now you release the rod you have been holding, and you watch as it returns to the field of clouds from which it came. --- You are withdrawing now, and the field of clouds flows beneath you, folding and turning to hide the metallic cylinder. It is pleasant to know the knowledge of steel is part of you and will never leave you. You have gained access to a powerful tool - this key that is truly part of you now. — As you continue to journey through the cloudy reaches, you see yet another cylinder rising to meet you, shining and graceful, from the rainbow clouds. It is different from the first one. It is long and slender and gracefully formed, and its silvery gray. It almost seems to glow in the radiant light. You reach out to it now, and your hand encounters it. How silken it feels, how agreeably malleable. This is the metal you call silver and you recognize it by the gentle fluidity of its nature. Now it grows larger and larger in the manner of the first cylinder. It towers above you and fills your field of vision. --- Now it has grown so large that you can pass into it and you do so. Look around you, the slender arching threads of its structure are so much longer than those of steel. They are wider and more open leaving great vaulting reaches of airy space between where you may fly at will. --- The breeze blows gently here, stirring the long soaring fibers. The breeze lifts and carries you as you hear how the wind sings in the shining metal archways. Hear how pure and clear the sweet notes blend together. As you pass through the structure, note that there are very few different fibers to be seen. Their colors are pastel and muted. They seem tucked away and laying close by the true silver ones. They cling gently like a shy ivy. There are very few of them and they do not hinder the clear song of its vibration.

Draw back from it now, and look where you have been. See how the fibers form a pattern like a long graceful spiral of vinework going ever upward along the length. They condense as the rod grows smaller and smaller. Now the rod seems smaller still and very solid - it is no bigger around than your finger and about the length of your forearm. You reach out for it once again. You take it in your hand. Now you begin to sing to it, softly humming as though to yourself. --- Feel it resonate in your hand, as though in answer to your song. As you continue, notice that the answering song continues to build until it is no longer a whisper but a clear true tone. It becomes a harmonic in tune both to its song and your own. Hold the rod parallel to your body, and feel how it vibrates in tune with your energy field. Feel the resonant harmony between your vibrations and its own. Feel how gently the energies flow in accord. --- Now you release the rod. You know that its song is now yours and that it will be always be attuned to answer you along with all metals like it. ---

Now withdraw altogether and let the rod sink back below the surface of the clouds. You withdraw away from it farther and farther. --- Now it is time to return to your body. You feel yourself slowly becoming aware of your body, and you feel yourself re-enter it. Now you feel your breathing, your blood flowing, coursing beneath your skin, your heart beating and you are pleasantly aware of how relaxed and refreshed you feel. --- You breathe again as before; once, --- twice, letting power and energy return. You breathe again and your journey is done. At any time you wish, you may examine the structure of any metallic substance in this manner. You may, and should, partake of their essential qualities for the purpose of your studies, work, and enjoyment.

CHAPTER 8

COMPLEX TALISMANS

A single stone or crystal can be of great benefit to any individual who chooses to work with its energy. When set in an appropriate metal, the stones benefit is enhanced and amplified for specific uses. However, in the works of power and healing, there are occasions when even more specific resonances of energy patterns are desirable or necessary. Just like in music, where a single note would do, a chord might more fully serve the context of the piece. At such times, the combining harmonic patterns of more than one stone or crystal can be very powerful in focussing their spectrum energies for a specific purpose. Once the nature of the families of stone, their colors, and the metals in which they are held are known and understood, then the practitioner can begin to combine these energies to attune them to a wide range of powerful specific energy values.

A complex group of two or more stones can be assembled and tuned to work together, as a group of singers in harmony may each sing a different note, but the chord produced serves but a single note of the melody. Such pieces must be carefully designed so that the natures of the elements are harmoniously tuned and suited to one another and are joined and directed by the intelligent will of the practitioner. We will examine how these combinations may be chosen according to their function and purpose.

ELEMENTS OF COMPLEX TALISMANS

These are the general guidelines of technical construction used in assembling complex talismans. These guidelines are stated here to give the student practitioner a familiarity with basic principles. We have also described several classic constructions so that the student and practitioner can experience how the energies of stones and metals can be combined. This is a complex field full of virtually endless possibilities and can form the basis of a lifetime's work in energy manipulation. In a practice of this nature, there are always as many exceptions as there are rules. This is a list of principles and guidelines. We encourage the student and practitioner to use them as a baseline and departure point for assembling his or her own collection of working tools. Each individual is different in his or her patterns of energy and in the way they implement these energies in their choice of work. Therefore, while the basic talismans will remain unchanged and will function consistently for all practitioners, each practitioner will eventually assemble his or her own specialized collection of talismanic constructions to facilitate his or her unique work.

Complex talismans can be described as having three basic elements. There is the **primary** or centerpiece that gives it its basic character and defines the energy center or level of field from which it will work. Added to this, one or more **qualifiers** that refine and define the scope of this energy. The **driver** provides the final focus and unites all the other elements into a cohesive unit. A complex talisman will always have a primary and either a driver or qualifier. It may be as simple as a construction of a crystal mounted with another stone. Alternatively, it may have many stones set in a complex arrangement of harmonic energies where it is difficult to specifically define just which stones are the qualifiers and which are the drivers. Talismans may be intricate assemblages containing many different stones, but regardless of number of stones, the individual stones will fall into one of these three categories. For the initial purpose of study, we would suggest that the student begin with simple arrangements before engaging in complicated groupings and constructions. It is a good idea to consider that the simple solution to a question is the best answer. However, we also encourage the student to gradually expand his or her range of associations.

PRIMARY

The **primary** is the center of the talisman that determines the way the piece will act on the energy complex. For instance, a quartz primary indicates that the energy configuration of the talisman would center itself across the broad spectrum of body's energy complex, while using a beryl would indicate that it would center itself primarily from the heart chakra. It will be the cornerstone of the talisman from which the other stones will derive their basic energy impulse. The practitioner should be very selective when choosing a primary crystal. Flaws along the central axis will disturb the entire function of the piece. This is generally but not always, a clear crystal. This is because clear crystals embody all the various characteristics of the family they represent, as does the head of a clan embody the spirit of that clan or house. In addition, clear stones have the potential to disperse their energies across the full spectrum of energies, thus enhancing all centers. It is not always necessary to use clear stones as primaries, for it may be that, for particular focussed workings, a narrower band of energies may be desired.

Crystals are generally considered more powerful as primaries in power talismans because of the strong fields they generate in harmony with the body's energy complex. Their energies are more aligned to this than stones of an amorphous or microcrystalline structure. We strongly suggest that the student make a full study of the activity of crystals as primaries before branching out into the use of noncrystalline stones in order to become fully familiarized with this element. However, amorphous and microcrystalline stones can make unique and special primaries. Their pervasive energy fields can provide a unique base point from which to construct a wide range of personal working pieces. When such a stone is chosen, it is wise, if possible within the parameters of its structure, to make sure that it is cut in harmony with the prevailing grain structure of the stone. Even though no crystalline structure may be visible to the naked eye, it is often possible to discern such a structure, either physically under close examination, or metaphysically, by exploring the nature of its field with meditation and the practitioners energy sensitivity.

QUALIFIER

Imagine the talisman as a picture you are drawing. The primary would be the line drawing that dictated the subject matter and composition. The qualifier stones would be the colors and shading. They can make the leaves on the tree green for spring or orange for autumn and thereby determine the mood and feeling of the work. The *qualifier* takes the energy of the primary and translates it to a specific purpose by defining and shaping the way in which they express themselves. This may be all that is desired of the piece, for it may be complete to serve the intended purpose using only these two elements. These two alone allow for a specified energy of the general focus or nature and much may be done with these combinations. There may be more than one qualifier to give the piece further scope and specificity, since it is the qualifiers that refine and diversify the energy harmonic.

Qualifiers can be either a cabochon or faceted stone or another crystal. Opalescent or dark qualifiers, such as onyx or obsidian, have a strong steadying quality as qualifier that will stabilize both the talisman field and the general field of the wearer. However, obsidian is not ideal because it is volcanic glass and has no crystalline structure. It should only be used when no other is available.

DRIVER

For talismans that will be used in power work or any piece that is intended for higher intensity work, a third element is added. It is through this *driver* stone that the combined energies of the primary and qualifier are gathered, condensed and intensified through a stone of true clear focus. The driver stone must be one of great clarity capable of taking a constant high intensity load of energy. When we say that the energies of the talisman are qualified through the driver, we mean that the energy complex that has been set up through the combination of the energies of the primary and one or more qualifiers will not only be directed by the driver, but the way in which these energies are presented to the individual's energy system complex will be specified by the type of driver used. The choice of a driver stone is critical in your tuning of the piece. You should choose a stone that is in harmony both with the other stones of the piece and with the wearer and function intended. For example, if you are composing a talisman for healing and balancing, you may wish to choose a driver whose energies are gentle, general, and pervasive such as a moonstone. If, on the other hand, you intend to use the piece for constant high energy power work, you might wish to consider a diamond or white sapphire whose energies are piercing, strong and direct. If you wish the talisman to direct its energies on a specific wave band rather than a full spectrum one, you should consider a colored driver.

Clear stones make efficient drivers, because although their family nature dictates the final focus of the talisman's energy, their lack of a specific color allows them to guide and drive the purpose of the piece across a full spectrum of energy. Take great care in using a colored stone for a specified driver, for it is extremely important that the energy properties of the stone are reliable and true. It should be free from internal structural anomalies and inclusions that are large enough to be visible to the naked eye. It should be without visible grain or pattern because a grain, pattern, or shading in itself indicates an internal structural variance that will interfere with the stone's function as a driver. Such a variegated stone may be used as a qualifier if it is desirable for its particular energies to be present, but the driver must be free from such anomalies. Diamond is the most powerful of all driver stones. Its nature may run slightly to blue as that is the channel of pure will, but not greatly so. Any member of the corundum family may be used as a driver, also, as well as certain members of the beryl family, that is, emerald, heliodor, and clear.

Asterated stones make particularly powerful driver stones. The way they are cut assures that, if they are showing a clear and centered star, they are cut in alignment with the crystal structure of the native rock. Also, the fact that asteration is caused by the geometric arrangement of rutillations gives them a sharply defined focus and centered identity pattern that will serve very well in this function. It may even be convenient to allow an asterated stone to stand in the combined position of qualifier and driver

Both driver and qualifier may be either cut stones or whole crystals. However, if a cut stone is chosen, especially for the driver, it should be cut to maximize the spectrum potential and light refraction. The driver need not be facetted, but, if a cabochon is chosen, it should be carefully cut. Ideally it should be cut in alignment with the crystal structure of the native stone either running vertically along its length or perpendicular to it (that is, front to back). Its surface should be highly polished and not carved or engraved, because in such a precisely cut stone, such a carving would interrupt the external lattice of the structure. Exceptions to this ideal are moonstones and other feldspars as well as kyanite.

Sceptered stones are unique cases, because their energy patterns are so particularly distinctive. In almost all cases, they require a driver stone to be functional as talismans on any level. Their formation gives a closed energy helix, rather than open and cycling, and they tend to cycle energy in a closed loop. A driver stone is most often required to complete their energy cycle and draw the energy through. When this is done, they are tools of surpassing virtue, for their charge and power may be generated and held within, condensed, and then released by the will of the wearer to great effect. However, let the wearer be aware that this is its nature and govern its power level and usage. When the charge has reached its maximum load for the nature of the stone, its wearer should discharge it in some harmless manner or clear the stone entirely. Otherwise, the stone may overload itself and thus spoil its nature or harm the wearer. This does not apply to second growth (phoenix) stones that should be considered as a single crystal of enhanced nature.

Drivers may also be used very effectively on stones that are aligned twins, that is, two crystals growing opposite from each other on either side of the common mother stone. The interaction of their shared helixes is perfectly balanced and all that is required for power utilization is a driver added at the point where they intersect the ground rock or pivot point.

On stones that have double terminations, the driver and qualifier may be placed at the center axis pivot or center point so that they may most easily draw from the energy complex of the stone. This is not vitally necessary, and the drivers may be placed beside the stone or at one or another of the terminations but within the visible sphere of its energy construct. Care should be taken to observe how far this field extends beyond the physical boundaries of the stone.

SETTING THE TALISMAN

The final element of a talisman is the way the stones are bound together. The selection of the material is just as important as the selection of the stones themselves. This material will define the way in which the elements communicate with each other and the way in which the resulting combined energy is made available to the practitioner's energy complex. In some cases the practitioner may decide to place the stones in a bag of a non-reactive material such as cloth or leather to examine how they will interact without the additional energy of metal being considered. In some exceptional cases, the addition of any metal will interfere with the activity of the stone. However, it is more common for a metal to be selected that will contribute to the completed energy and activity of the talisman in consideration. The metal acts as an interface between the elements that gathers and disperses their complex energies, allowing them to communicate with each other. It acts like the wiring on a string of electrical lights, but in a much more general and complex fashion.

Observe the currents of energy generated by these multiple elements. It is necessary to construct the setting so that the energies of the components circulate well between and around the body of the piece. Before permanently securing the components, take a moment to move them around and on one another to experience and experiment with the subtleties of their placement. Any embellishments should be carefully chosen so that the artistic intent of the piece does not conflict with the energy helix of the combinations. Elements such as studs, extending pieces, wirework and grain work must be placed not only to suit the pleasure of the eye, but also to contribute to the interaction of the stones.

It is important to consider aesthetic considerations, for it is the nature of the spirit to love harmony and beauty, and this affinity will greatly contribute to the charging and use of the piece. It is through the heart that the charging is generated and, by this means, the heart chakra will naturally resonate with the perceived beauty of the object, making it more easily integrated with the energy flow of the individual.

SPECIFIC CONSTRUCTION

Again, these are general guidelines. The patterns and techniques described here are efficient and work well with a variety of stones and energy configurations. However, we are certain that as the practitioner develops with knowledge and skill in this practice, each individual will develop his or her own unique methods of combining the energy elements.

Begin with the primary crystal. If it is has a single termination, it should be flat and regular. An irregular or jagged base will cause anomalies in the axis energies. This flattened area should then be capped with an appropriate metal. The choice of this metal will set the tone for the entire piece.

If the crystal is double terminated, a band of metal should be secured around the pivot point of the energy axis. The base plate is the agent of the translation and integration of the energy field of the primary with all other stones that will interact with it. The action of the qualifier is to draw through the interposing metal plate from the primary and qualify those energies of the entire spectrum to a particular end or function. The qualifier stones should be attached in some way to this base. This will give them direct access to the energy center of the primary crystal. The driver stone should be placed closest to the center where all the energies meet and communicate so that it will have equal access to all the stones and can easily moderate their exchange.

Finally, in the case of jewelry such as rings or bracelets, the piece should be attached to the body by the metal that forms the greatest part of the setting. This will allow its energies to be translated more easily throughout the energy system complex of the wearer.

STONE CHOICE SPECIFICS

Clear quartz is a good choice to use as a primary for talismans that need to both draw and broadcast their influence throughout the full spectrum of the wearer's energy field complex. This is because prime vibration frequency is closer than all other crystals to the human frequency and will be the most sensitive and adaptable to the wearer's personal vibrations both in charging and in use. It is also harmoniously compatible to many different combinations of secondary stones. The only drawback is that, in extreme circumstances, it may be overdriven if the other components are not well balanced. When worked to intensely specific ends, especially when its components are not of its own family, it may not have sufficiently specific focus to accommodate the specific energy demands of the other components. Ideally, the primary, qualifier, and driver should be each harder than the next in that order, for then the powers will be sequentially boosted and focussed. The heaviest load should be on the driver in tuning and working with the piece.

When using clear quartz as the primary, it should be physically larger than the other two combined so that it will have the greatest draw from the metal ground. Quartz will pull from any key on the spectrum of tonalities. It will charge from and drive to all colors of the spectrum, thus its influence is distributed overall and there is no unbalanced drain on one vital system over any other. Also, as the wearer becomes accustomed to the energy field of the talisman, he or she may work from only parts of that spectrum rather than the full spectrum of energies offered by the piece. The full spectrum potential provided by the primary will harmonically resonate with the other elements to steady the field produced by the talisman. This is not only true of clear quartz, but of other clear stones to one degree or another, and this is the quality that makes them most optimal for use as primary stones.

In the case of simple talismans, they may contain only a primary with a qualifier. In this case, it is considered that the primary is the driver element as well.

The ancient texts give the following examples and suggestions for combinations of working energies:

As the student begins working with complex talismans, for talismans with only a quartz primary, a qualifier and no driver, it would be wise to choose a qualifier that is of the quartz family or that of chalcedony. This will not overdrive it nor ask of it any energy which it cannot provide. This is a harmonious combination and may be used to many great and varied purposes. It is the qualifier that describes and defines which part of the spectrum energy will be drawn to use. If it is not to the purpose at hand to use one of the quartz families, then a stone with an earth-spectrum resonance, such as garnet, is the next best choice so that a partial resonant ground is provided.

Should the primary not be of a most general nature, such as clear quartz, then let the qualifier be of a similar nature. For example, should it be of a stone such as green quartz, whose nature is primal and earthy, then it is well accompanied by garnet whose nature is also earthy. Then, these two may be driven by an element that unifies and strengthens to full band that is their equal in strength or greater such as moonstone or clear Mexican opal. Mexican opal is also known as Earth Opal and works well with the other two. Chalcedonies work well as qualifiers for quartz, because they are a form of quartz. Jade works well with smoky stones as long as their color harmonies are matched with respect to their natures and purpose, for both are peace bringers. Corundums and diamond are known as Stones of Majesty and are as close akin in nature of resonance as may be, and easily stand as primaries and drivers for each other. Thus is clear sapphire most exquisitely driven by colored diamond.

THE DREAMER'S TALISMAN

A specific example of a complex talisman using all three elements is a Dreamer's Talisman that can be used by Seers with any level of experience from beginner to advanced. The stress of maintaining cognizant awareness is great when it is done on multiple levels, and the crossing of barriers can cause a drain on the vital centers of the body when the energy is not boosted and cycled correctly. Use of this talisman can make the channeling of wisdom and power easier. Care should be taken to monitor the Dreamer to be sure that a drain does not occur before the operant is aware of its nature. This could cause undue stress on the life systems of the body due to the intensity of the energies received. This can easily manifest in a general weakening of the body's energies and cause illness, dizziness, and disorientation. Use of this talisman can help the Seer's life energies maintain their personal balance without becoming compromised by lengthy out-of-body practices.

Take an amethyst and place it with a clear quartz so that their energy accesses (non-terminated ends) transfer through a common ground or base (interposing plate) so that it behaves in the manner of twinned crystals that have grown from opposite sides of the base matrix. This juxtaposition will form a helix through a base whose purpose is specified by the type of metal it is, that allows their energies to intermingle. The healing properties of amethyst draw from the spectrum potential of energies from all centers directing them towards healing ends, and so is this power cycle completed.

A driver is needed to provide focus and strength, so that the energies will not be too scattered or generalized. The energies must be united into a tighter range than would otherwise be formed by the combination of the two stones by themselves. This driver should be placed where it intersects the plate between them and charged to tight focus according to its nature. This driver should be white or clear so that it will draw the energies of the highest and purest order and boost them into the highest ranges. Stones of the corundum family are too strong for this particular piece, because the color agent in the amethyst will not tolerate its intensity. Moonstone is a good choice in this case, because it will unite the energies without over driving either of the stones. The very structure of the moonstone that gives it its clarity and focus will also disseminate these energies gently and without harshness. Thus, the talisman will not over stress the wearer's life systems when it is used with proper consideration and common sense. Opal would also be a good choice of driver for this piece. Its multi-spectrum nature will allow it to function across the full band of the wearer's energy complex, while its amorphous quartz-like structure is generally compatible with the energy level and helix character of the primary and qualifier. Care should be taken to select an opal that displays the fullest range of the color spectrum. Take care when using opals as drivers, for they are not specifically drivers in the purest sense. Their nature is to disseminate the energies generated throughout their spectrum range, rather than focus and drive them. Australian opals are not structurally strong and should not be used where a heavy charge or extended intensity of energy will be concentrated. They do not have the strength to gather and focus a piece under severe or extended intense loads. It remains for the practitioner to choose which of the two suggested driver stones would particularly suit the intended wearer.

A similar talisman for a Seer with some experience uses aquamarine as the primary with an opal qualifier and onyx for the driver at the juncture between them. Because this Seer has more experience, he or she should be better grounded and able to translate his or her visions into physical communication. The aquamarine primary will encourage the smooth and even flow of energies throughout the energy complex while the opal will provide a wide spectrum of color energies to be available for any center that might need them. This will help the life energies to remain balanced through the shifting levels and energy demands from moment to moment. The onyx will add great clarity and stability so that the Seer can more easily clarify the visions on a conscious level. Also, added flanking quartz points extend energy across the spectrum lines and have an extra strengthening force upon the practitioner.

For healing serious traumas that impact the entire energy system complex, such as extreme grief or severe systemic injury incurred by a physical attack or accident, use black onyx at the base of the primary quartz. Then place a blue and green tourmaline, one on each side of the primary. These two cases are remarkable for this difference in construction, the black stone is the driver, and the flanking hanging crystals are qualifiers.

BALANCING THE

STONE COMBINATIONS

When combining stones with a particular purpose in mind, it is important to remember that no center works by itself. The body's energy complex should be in harmonious balance throughout its many parts and levels. Earlier we discussed in detail how the centers offset and compliment one another's energy properties. It is all well to decide to influence the intensity or clarity of one or another of them, but its counterpart must also be taken into account, as well as the impact such changes will have on the system as a whole. At this point, you should begin to work with the individual as a complex of energies rather than simply one center at a time. The first way you look at stones for this purpose is to examine their color. Color is caused by the addition of one or more different atoms to the basic atomic structure of the crystal. These atoms cause its energy to combine differently with other atomic units and this changes the way the crystal transmits light. Color is a vibration in and of itself, as well as being an indication of the vibration type of the crystal.

So here are a few examples and guidelines to begin your thinking about these patterns. These are by no means the only combinations available, nor are these hard and fast rules that brook no exceptions.

Purple stones (crown) should be accompanied with green (heart) often and conversely green with violet (brow), rose (heart/base), or purple. This will encourage a balance between the crown and heart chakras. This combination may be driven with diamond or moonstone or occasionally white or clear quartz when cut in cabochon. When using purple stones it is important to consider that working solely through the crown chakra for enlightenment is just as unbalanced as pulling solely though the base chakra for strength. Both energies are vital to the health of the individual but need to be balanced and integrated through the system as a whole. Adding a green stone to either one will encourage this balance and energize the heart chakra to activate a balancing energy. Rose stones work well in combination with green and blue. The driver should be of a soft white or clear resonance.

The ancient texts give an example of balanced energies: In the case of war, the ruby or carbuncle should have as its qualifier, chrysoprase or, perhaps, peridot, but never emerald. Their driver should either be a white, clear or, occasionally, black. In the case of the Practitioner where specific need dictates the emerald and ruby together, neither one nor the other should drive but they should be charged to interact with equal strength in harmony. By using this construction, the preparation for war or aggressive activity will not overtax the practitioner. It will assist him gently and with subtle purpose, and place all the forces of war at his disposal but not overriding and destroying his basic nature to seek peace and harmony.

Yellow is pleasantly qualified with blue and driven with green or orange, and in the odd instance, with violet. This is because the solar plexus and throat centers are the balances for each other with the heart center between them. If you need to put a purple driver with a yellow stone, the yellow color should be more golden than green. Combined with a green qualifier, this can make a good restorative talisman.

Brown and black primaries may be heightened in intensity and purpose by the clearest drivers available in harmony with the desired purpose. In other words, whatever qualifiers or drivers are used, regardless of color, they should be as clear and flawless as possible. You may also place green here as a qualifier to modulate the effects of the darker primary. This makes a good restorative talisman for someone sorely taxed by intense emotional or physical demands. This may also be well used in long term manipulations of "Earth Magic" and may be worn by either male or female practitioner. This charm may be used by those of the Priestly Calling who wish to heal the earth and its inhabitants from strife and injury of war by restoring and balancing them in the course of their work. It may also be given to an individual who is resting and recovering from strenuous uses of power or coping with environmental discord of any sort.

White stones may also be used effectively and widely as both driver and focus stones. They function like a lens fitted to the energy of the prime stone of a talisman. As the white driver is tuned and charged, the energy of the entire piece is fine-tuned and radiates powerful energy to the particular function of the piece. This is especially true of moonstone. The nature of its crystalline structure is layered in multiple fine sheets. This directs the power of whatever other stones it is set with to great force and purpose.

TALISMANS OF SINGULAR POWER

The following are some examples of stone combinations that work particularly well together and whichhave been used very effectively. They also make good examples for the student practitioner to examine because of the way the stones are selected and arranged. However, as the pieces are described and explained, the student should remember that these are pieces designed for use by individuals with specific training. They can present powerful harmonics of energy and, should the student choose to work with them, he or she should go carefully to observe their effects. In addition, unless otherwise stated, they are not meant to be worn all the time. They are intended to be used on specific occasions and then put aside in an appropriate storage container.

THE SEER'S TALISMAN

The Seer's Talisman amplifies the ability for clairvoyance and clairaudience and any similar psychic ability such as telepathy. It opens the channels within the Seer so that he or she can more easily perceive the currents of energy moving on planes adjacent to the physical. This will include those who do work in healing that see into physical structures for healing work and those who see into the currents of events and interrelationships for counseling work. It will ease the effort of having to keep those channels open so that the Seer can concentrate on examining and evaluating the information gathered.

This is a compound construction using the opaque, noncrystalline stone, Lapis Lazuli, as its primary. As such, it is the exception to many rules. Take a cabochon of lapis lazuli of any size and shape, being certain that the inclusions of pyrite are not excessive. They should appear as a faint powdering appearing as stars in the night sky rather than in large veins or pockets. Place six points of absolutely clear quartz around this cabochon, mounted base end inwards on the same plate that holds the cabochon and arranged around it like the pattern of the petals of a flower. This base plate should be of silver and never of any other metal.

When charging it, first charge the lapis lazuli and allow this charge to be distributed through the plate and thereby charging the quartz points by natural flow of power through the base plate. As the power is emitted through the axis terminations of the quartz, a matrix of interactive power will form across the lapis. This talisman should only be worn while the work is in progress and removed when the work is done.

TALISMAN OF THE

PLANET'S ENERGY

The second charm of this type is of the same force and configuration. The center stone should be a mixture of malachite and azurite with clear veins of each intertwining to make an integrated whole. This is so that each element should be strong unto itself and yet joined in strength and power with each other. This center stone should be surrounded with at least six quartz points as before. Should it be necessary or desirable to further qualify the piece, then the qualifier may be the purest and clearest golden yellow quartz, but not any other yellow or golden stone. This would render the energy matrix field anomalous and unbalanced. The qualifier should be placed in the center of the talisman and above the malachite/azurite for centralized and uniform qualification of the initial energy. This talisman will carry the force and power of the green earth and almighty sky, blue waters and the backbone of the earth. The points will drive this energy from the will of the practitioner and will unify them as lightning from his or her Dominion, so that his or her Will may be made plain within their sphere and purpose. A charm of lesser overt force may be constructed by using this same center stone and hanging at least three quartz points from it. The silver base on which the malachite/azurite stone is placed should be heavy and strong so that the intensity of energies will be gathered and dispersed smoothly across the energy fields of the practitioner.

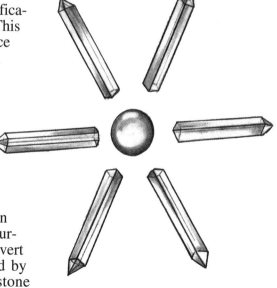

It should be noted that this charm and the lapis one have no preference according to the gender of the practitioner. They may be used to great effect by priest and priestess alike. These are pieces of the High Temple and of the Concourse of the Ancients and either may be used as a tap on the energy field reserves and wells of the Ancient Days. They are Atlantean in configuration and should be taken up with great care. They are taps to the consciousness of the Temple of Life and it is unlikely that anyone that did not study there can realize their fullest potential. However, in this New Age there are many who may come to this level of power and awareness, and, where this growth of power has taken place, many things are possible. However, let this be taken into consideration before these talismans are used.

CHAKRA TALISMAN

Sometimes an individual will need a talisman that will tune and balance his or her full chakra system. This may be because he or she is being called upon to use large amounts of energy in one specific area while not having the opportunity to fully rebalance the energy system complex. It may be that the individual is undergoing some healing process or personal growth cycle that requires consistent balancing from moment to moment.

The basic talisman uses a single quartz crystal that is either single or double terminated. This should be carefully selected both for its own internal clarity and consistency of axis structure and for its individual compatibility with the individual who will be using and wearing the talisman. Then, along its length, spaced evenly from one another, there should be a suite of seven qualifier stones representing the seven chakras of the body. The choice of these stones rests primarily with the practitioner with certain guidelines in mind. They should be of equal size and clarity because they must balance one another and work in unison. It is not the purpose of this piece to have one stone marshal or drive all the others. Rather, this is a model of the individual in his or her optimally balanced and healthy energy state in which all energies centers work together to present a unified harmonious field. As an example, it would not be suitable or balanced to use a ruby for the base chakra and a purple fluorite for the crown. Their energy parameters are so far apart from each other that the red stone would completely override the purple one. An ideal case would be using all stones from the same family. Tourmalines make a good choice for this collection because tourmalines come in a complete spectrum of colors and shades. They also work well for this because it is their nature to be automatically activated. They will work naturally together with the primary and with the wearer, with very little monitoring or adjustment by the practitioner. Alternatively, the practitioner may select each stone separately from different but compatible families to correspond to the optimal level of each of the wearer's centers.

The chakra stones should be within the comfortable energy parameters of the individual for whom the talisman is being made. A good guideline for this is to match the energy level potential of the stones to a level halfway between the individual's strongest and weakest energy centers. An individual who has been ill or under an intense amount of stress can rarely take the kind of energy demands that a suite of colored diamonds would have on his or her energy complex. On the other hand, a suite of fluorites or colored chalcedonies may not be sufficient for the energy demands of an individual who has been doing meditation and energy work and has a naturally powerful field.

Finally, when the practitioner charges the talisman, he or she should work through the quartz that, in this case, will be standing as both the primary and the driver. This stone should be keyed to the individual's optimal energy range. This will allow that, as levels within his or her energy system complex fluctuate, the quartz will draw on and activate one or more of the chakra stones to maintain the balance of the energy field from moment to moment.

This configuration need not be used solely for healing and rebalancing. There are a number of interesting variations possible with this type of talisman that make excellent working or learning tools. This configuration can be used to explore and experience the way in which the color members of a stone family react with each other and with the individual's energy system complex. The practitioner can select the qualifier stone from any stone family that presents a sufficient variety of colors to fulfill the basic energy specifics of the seven chakras.

The primary stone does not always have to be a quartz or even a crystal. It can also be a noncrystalline stone.

If the wearer is of a particular Calling or has a
specific purpose in mind, a primary stone
may be chosen to correspond to that demand. The chakra stones will balance
the wearer's energy field complex with
respect to the activity or energy engaged through the primary stone. As
an example: We discussed a Seer's Talisman using lapis lazuli as the primary.
Lapis lazuli could be used in the
Chakra Talisman configuration to resonate the wearer's field harmonic
through it as a Seer's stone and balance his or her energy centers with respect to that particular energy activity. Using a large aquamarine crystal
as the primary would extend the energy of the chakra stone element
evenly into the upper ranges of the
wearer's field level capacity. This can
assist an individual in bringing together many different aspects of personality so that the capabilities of each
are unified and available to him or her.

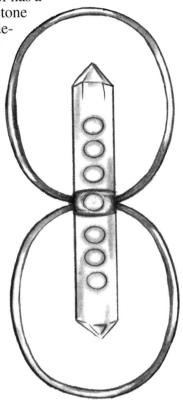

CHAKRA	CALLING	POLARITY	STONE
Crown	Priest	M	Purple Ruby
	Priestess	F	Siberite Tourmaline
Brow	Monarch	M	Amethyst
		F	Iolite
Throat	Seer / Teacher	M	Blue Sapphire
		F	Indicolite Tourmaline
Heart	Healer	M	Emerald
		F	Green Garnet
Solar Plexus	Dancer	M	Topaz
		F	Heliodore
Belly	Warrior	M	Pad Parajah
		F	Citrine or Zincite
Base	Smith	M	Ruby
	Artisan	F	Garnet

==
THE GRAND TALISMAN
==

There is a further variation of the Chakra Talisman called the Grand Talisman.

This talisman can be used for many levels and purposes because it simulates the specific pattern of chakra resonances of a particular individual. It is of particular value to the practitioner who is called on to summon and channel a variety of high intensity energies in the course of his or her work. It provides the practitioner with a wide spectrum of energy harmonics upon which to draw, while reinforcing his or her or personal energy base so that this does not become over driven, drained or compromised.

The principle difference in the two Talismans is that the Grand Talisman uses a clear stone as a driver in the heart chakra position. Because they have been charged as one unit, when one stone is activated, the other stones will react harmoniously with it, giving the entire talisman a resonant balance with both the activated stone and the practitioner using it. After they are completely assembled, they should be charged and aligned with the individual. This is done by using a mantra of the Chakras, beginning with the lowest and raising the energy upon matching each stone in balanced resonance with each of individual's chakras, until the whole piece forms one whole collected harmonic interaction with the individual.

For the base of this Talisman, choose a perfectly clear, regular, symmetrical and unbroken double terminated quartz point having no secondary formations upon it. The chakra stones should be flawless, of identical cut, size, and weight each to the other without variation in the smallest degree. Let them be of a size that, laid side by side in their settings, they do not overlap to the smallest degree the length or width of the base quartz point. It may even be possible to procure them all from the same geographic region of the planet and this is best of all, but not essential. The settings must also be identical and not differenced from one another in any way. The entire setting must be symmetrical and not weighted or embellished more on one side than the other.

As for the specific choice of stones, any may be chosen from the listings of archetype resonance stones. The primary consideration in this choice is the necessity to match the individual resonances of the practitioner's chakras and the overall general power level at which he or she will be operating. The final choice of stones is particularly personal in this case. This will be a personal tool that can be used throughout the individual's growth and development. It will generally not be outgrown in the course of study and discipline. For instance, a particular male may not have a complete sympathy or resonance with the emerald, but according to his nature and training may be more aligned with the nature of the tsavorite garnet. The use of this stone in this case is perfectly permissible because it matches the specific resonance of that practitioner's chakras. They should be chosen with the highest and most intense power load level of that person kept firmly in mind. Otherwise, if a stone is used that is not strong enough in times of greatest stress it will falter and fail. This may cause all the other stones in alignment with it to fail, because their energies are linked with its weaker ones. It must be noted that the original stones may well need to be replaced as growth and development takes place in the practitioner. These changes must be made consistent with the physical structure of the piece and the resonant relationship with the other stones.

The energy balance potential of the concept of a primary, a driver and a spectrum of stones united for a single harmonic is an interesting one to explore. The practitioner can also use the six colors of the standard color wheel around a single clear driver. An opal can be used in the center of a rainbow suite of stones. The base stone can be changed to a solid piece of metal. The metal of the settings can be changed. The principle that must remain constant in this is the idea of balance of energies, so that no one element overrides the others. These talismans are intended to synchronize with the wearer's personal energy system complex, and to the degree that the talisman is unbalanced, it will cause that field to become unbalanced.

THE VAJRA TALISMAN

In certain instances, it may be necessary for a practitioner to use a talisman that holds the force and balance of the full energy complex pattern; one with a complete working potential tuned to his energy pattern alone. This is not a chakra talisman that is his truest image of energy potential, rather, it is a talisman containing its own full potential helix tuned to focus in tandem with this practitioner's will force. Such a talisman is not often needed or used but can be effective when the practitioner is under great stress from many different things at once and he wishes to delegate the manifestation of force to an agent. This piece, when properly tuned to the practitioner, will function automatically without conscious direction. In tuning it, the practitioner should address it as though explaining his or her drives and desires, so that this piece can anticipate his will in its own. When focused in this manner, it will greatly aid and reinforce the practitioner's strength, cycling its own energies while restoring the practitioner in the natural course of its cycle of use. Let it be known, however, that this is the charm of a true practitioner. Because it is so finely tuned, it can become so sensitive to his or her intention that it will act without conscious thought to direct it.

It should be configured as follows: the base should be a double-terminated clear quartz, although it need not be perfect in its dimensions. Rather should it be uniquely pleasing to the practitioner who plans to use it. It may even be quite curious in its configuration, bearing in mind that the terminations and center axis must be clear and straight. It must have neither internal fractures nor internal nor external anomalies that would interfere with the pure flow of its power. Let this stone be bound around with silver or platinum according to the energy balance of the base stone. Then, upon its face set a diamond as the pure driver at the pivot. At the center of the upper energy lobe set an earth opal, that is, a fire agate or an opal from Mexico or Brazil, or a very hard black opal from Australia (although these are rarely found), and in the lower lobe set a pure white opal of all fire.

Now there are countless variations in the choice of stones to be set on either side of the diamond and should be considered accordingly. A red ruby and an emerald may be used together in such a combination, or a peridot with a red garnet. This choice may be left up to the practitioner keeping in mind the stones' characteristics and the purpose and individual for which the piece is intended. For occasions of lower power output or where the full spectrum helix is not desired or required, one may use a balance of a blue sapphire and a topaz. This is thus a very specific vajra and will manifest itself through mental intelligence and great force of will. Consider however, that in the mechanics of these stones, none of the drivers and/or qualifiers, should be of the same family or cousin family as the base stones. They must always be a higher power range stone than the base.

CHAPTER 9

THE CALLINGS & THEIR TALISMANS

There is one Prime Cause at the beginning of things and throughout the multiverse. This is the source of all Creation, and all things that exist are reflections of this one Prime. We have discussed these reflections as ideal forms and in this plane of existence, we may experience these ideals as energy resonances. These energy resonances manifest in many ways, and in our work with them, we have addressed those manifestations that are the most available and convenient in the Human experience. We presented them first as pure color and the color spectrum. We have worked with these resonances as they are physically expressed through crystals and stones. We explored the internal example of this spectrum that we can observe as the energy resonances in life forms known as the chakra system, and now we will expand on this idea. These energies also show themselves on a larger ideal scale as Callings, that is, the templates of personality types that Humankind uses to express and pursue its life goals.

As you live your life, you are constantly expressing yourself through one or more of your chakras. Your life is a harmonic resonance of balanced vibrations of the seven chakras as a whole. Ideally, to be a healthy individual all of your energy centers should balance in their power and flow with one another. However, as you go about your daily life, sometimes the energy of one or another center will be more expressive than the others will. For example, an athlete may work from the lower two centers, particularly if he or she is involved in a confrontational sport, in order to achieve very powerfully physical goals. This does not mean, however, that this individual is not a compassionate or highly spiritual person. It simply means that to achieve the desired purpose, the assertive and aggressive nature of the lower two chakras is the most appropriate and will show as dominant. Alternatively, a person with a particularly strong spiritual nature will resonate from the crown chakra. This does not mean that he or she is not personally strong and assertive, joyful or loving of life. It simply means that the way this individual addresses life is through a spiritual context rather than a primarily physical one.

This is very similar to singing a song. That song is in a particular key signature of music. As you sing that song you may change from one key to another, singing the first verse in the key of C major and the next verse in the key of G major. For variations you may shift the melody slightly and change to a minor of C or G. Much in this same way, you go about your life manifesting the energy of a particular chakra or pair of chakras to deal with specific tasks or goals. You may be about a long-term goal, but you use different centers and combinations of those centers to achieve that goal and to deal with the issues that come to you along the way.

The chakra energies are the internal example of the living resonance of the spectrum of energy in this universe. On a larger scale, these energies are expressed within the scope of Humankind as the personality types known as the Callings. They correspond to the colors of the spectrum and the chakras of the body, as they are the personification of the energy frequencies of Humankind as an ideal. They are the categories of ideals as are represented by Human personality/soul energy types. The Callings are the way in which an individual expresses his or her life purpose or karma. An individual's Calling will permeate and find expression throughout that individual's lifetime regardless of his or her social situation or profession. It is analogous to the base harmonic or key frequency of an individual's signature pattern. To continue the comparison with music: it is as though a person's life were a symphony. A symphony is written in one particular key signature that is consistent throughout, but there are many changes and shifts within it - modulations of that key signature so that the key seems greatly varied and changing.

Callings are also a good way to describe and expand on the chakra system and its relationship to the individual's conscious awareness. The concept of Callings is a good way to generalize and specify particular qualities of energy as they pertain to the human condition, experience, and consciousness. There are seven basic Callings just as there are seven chakras. There are also stones and crystal families that correspond to them.

An individual expresses the nature of his or her calling in many different ways, regardless of the physical work or profession in which he or she may be involved. For example, a woman whose physical work may be that of a housewife and mother may use this as a vehicle for her calling as an Artisan - making food, gifts and clothing not only for her family and friends, but for neighbors and charity functions. Her life will be expressed in terms of her physical creativity. A man's work may be that of a Priest. However, he may be using this position of authority to serve his true Calling of Teacher or Healer. Not all individuals express their lives in terms of Callings. Many have not come to the point in their development where they are clear enough about their own spiritual / karmic purpose to be able to have such a specific focus. It may also happen that an individual's early life may have a variety of influences and only after a significant incident such as a great revelation, physical or emotional upheaval will the evidence of the true Calling make itself known. These energy expressions are like a kaleidoscope in the way they express themselves in life just as the human organism is a constantly changing system of energy balances. The system of Callings is not meant to categorize or limit the way in which an individual can be understood, but to clarify and describe the way in which he or she achieves the goals and purposes of life.

As an individual comes closer to realizing the full potential energy spectrum of the Universe in which he or she dwells, the distinctions of Callings become blurred and insignificant, and the individual manifests many or all of them as the situation dictates or allows. This is the awakening process. As one Chakra of the body after the other becomes energized, one after the other of these energies could be described as being dominant in that person and the point from which that individual's energies are directed. But as the individual comes closer to being fully energized as a complete energy complex, and the pattern of harmonies comes closer into completion and balance, then he or she focuses from the center of his or her combined helixes and manifests from the energy system complex as a whole. When taken as a whole, the energy that is expressed may be perceived as undifferentiated clear or white, modified only by the nature of the specified quality that the individual is expressing from moment to moment.

There are seven Callings that correspond to the individual chakras and one high Calling that has the duty and power to unify the others within it.Each one has both a male and female polarity, as this is the expression of the basic energy configuration of this Universe. There is also an androgynous aspect of each one that combines elements of each polarity but is by nature neutral. This does not mean to imply specifics of physical sexual gender, but of universal energy polarity. This is just as atomic particles may be negative, positive, or neutral. Each chakra has a dominant energy polarity regardless of the gender of the individual. An individual may express a Calling regardless of his or her gender and each Calling will have an expression in each of the three polarities. Taken together, they stand as the fullest spectrum potential of the development of the human entity. It also follows that a crystal and a corresponding metal may be attributed to each one, because their energy patterns correspond to the signature charge of that Calling. They also correspond to the dominant strain of the harmonic of the individual's signature pattern. These elements can be combined to make a talisman to channel the energies and focus these specific energy vibrations. By using such a talisman, an individual can more fully and easily express his or her Calling through his or her life, and through that work realize the purpose for which he or she has incarnated. Stones and crystals have specific signature patterns that are first differentiated according to type within families, second as to color, and then according to specific individual stones.

PURPOSE & CONFIGURATION OF THE TALISMANS

For each of the great Callings there are specific talisman combinations of stones and crystals that can ease the burden of the individual's work. As we have said, not every person will manifest a Calling. This is part of the process of growth on this plane. Those who do manifest a Calling have a specific Karmic purpose in the physical life that is not the result of one specific incident, but of a larger identity or purpose of the Higher Self. Those who manifest the Callings have particular demands on their lives that are over and above what would be called for ordinarily. They inhabit a form that was derived through the demands of evolution on this planet and has only partially configured to adapt to the demands made upon its systems by those of the higher orders. Thus, they may need or desire support for the survival mechanisms of the physical form, as well as for the awakening higher awareness. As they grow and progress, these limitations will no longer be a problem. As the race develops, the form that houses it will evolve according to the new demands placed on it. Indeed, this change is already at hand within the sphere of reality. However, the days have not yet come when the mages may live at will with their Callings and walk as other men. Therefore, we shall call forth ancient knowledge to aid them. Among them are a few that have the strength to bring this knowledge forth and make it known. It is our intention that these individuals flourish, and, through their work, all people. It is no longer a time for these people to conceal their work in shadows. The time has come when this work should be done in the light and for the benefit of all. The Age of Darkness is at an end and a new age of strength and purpose is at hand, when the children of men shall stand in the glory of the Sun of their Beginnings.

In an individual's journeys through the physical life, he or she may have an overriding purpose that exhibits itself as his or her Calling. Each individual, in his or her own unique way, approaches and exhibits his or her Karma in the pattern and means dictated by a Calling, regardless of what that Karma may be. His or her energies can be identified with this key signature pattern as well as the individual pattern. When this purpose and Calling is recognized and acknowledged by this individual and when these studies and efforts have borne fruit, the individual will come into the awareness of his life on a fulfilled and higher level. A person may have great potential in a Calling and a strong desire to pursue it. However, that person will still need study and discipline in order to actually follow it to the fullest potential in his or her life. Note that the term Calling indicates abilities and potential rather than knowledge and experience.

At this point in his or her development, it is well that he or she wear someplace on the body, preferably upon his breast, the stone of this Calling to help sensitize him or her more fully to that universal energy resonance. Its power can open the channel to his or her inner power by helping him to find its resonance within himself and acknowledge his or her connection to it. This is the individual's first acknowledgment of reunion with the greater universal whole and connection with the archetypal wellspring of this vibration. By acknowledging and reinforcing this connection, the individual can gain access to the gateway of power within him or her self. This work will also be restorative to his or her energies and a source of higher knowledge. It will help the individual form the conscious bridge to the Higher Self. It will provide a link to the Universal knowledge and record of that Calling so that his wisdom and understanding can increase and his skill will be greater than it was before.

When an individual first begins to feel and express a particular Calling, he or she may wish to work with a novice stone. This is a stone or crystal of the same color as the archetype but of lesser intensity so that he or she can become accustomed to this particular frequency access and working. Another variation of this is a talisman of clear quartz that has as the qualifier stone of the Calling. This piece can most gently but effectively integrate the individual with the necessary energies until he or she becomes ready for the stronger stone. As the individual comes into the full range of his or her abilities, he or she may choose to wear the stone of that Calling set in the metal of that calling. If, as in the case of steel, iron, or platinum, the metals are unsuitable, unavailable, or unworkable for the binding of this talisman, a substitute is chosen from the list below.

Use the following metallic substitutes:

For the Artisan and Smith, rather than iron and steel, copper can be chosen and charged to its reddest resonance rather than its green prime resonance. Let this also be bound in with silver, so that the resonance of the metal permeates the energy field of the individual to simulate the active permeation of the Calling's natural metal. Also, in place of platinum, silver may be used and charged to its white resonance rather than the blue. In either case it would be helpful, but not essential, that a small piece of the natural ores of the principle metal be put in the setting as though it were a qualifier stone so that it will set up a harmonic with the metals of the setting and keep the tuning true. Mount the qualifier stone directly on top of the primary quartz with the metal interface between.

This will make a full resonance and give the primary the most complete access to those qualifying energies. Another configuration on this theme is two crystals, flattened on the base end and set end to end with a metal plate between and a driver with the disseminating qualities of moonstone set to unify and direct their potential. In this case, both crystals should be chosen with the utmost care not only for quality and compatibility with the wearer but also for compatibility with each other.

In all cases, however, the stones chosen should be of singular clarity, all sides being whole and unmarred and the termination being clean and unbroken. The primary stones should be crystals, not cut, except flattened on the base to make it suitable for setting and to bring it into optimal harmony with the metal as we have previously discussed. Cut stones are not sufficient in this matter although they may stand as substitutes. This crystal will work with the full resonance of the individual who wears it. It will therefore need to have a full axis structure and complete sides. In the case of a novice talisman, the quartz should be in crystal form, but the stone of the Calling can be cut or fashioned. The choice of this quartz crystal may take some time. This is a very personal choice of stone. The individual should make this choice with the heart because this crystal is intended to resonate with the full complexity of his or her personality and the Karma linked to it. It should be a single crystal rather than a cluster. However, in this singularity it can express great individuality. It may be a phoenix crystal, parallel twins, a sceptered crystal, or one with interesting angles and faces. The only prohibition is that the central axis should be straight, not offset or bent.

We should also point out that an individual need not be devoted in a life-long pursuit of a Calling to wear and benefit from the Talisman representing it. Many individuals take on these qualities and characteristics from time to time in their life journey, sometimes so much so that it absorbs their whole focus of living. As an individual becomes aware of this, it is often helpful for him or her to wear such a piece to help fully understand the nature of the part of the life path that they are experiencing. Such a talisman can bring about strength and insight to enhance this growing experience. It can also help the individual balance this manifestation with other aspects of life so that he or she can keep it in perspective with the wider range of his or her experience. These talismans may also be used as focal points of meditation to bring a certain energy or essence into the energy system's vibration that the individual may feel is desirable. For example: a person who is shy and lacks assertive force may chose to wear a type of warrior talisman in order to enhance his or her inner strength and presence. But in all these cases, let those who would do the work demonstrate these Callings with grace, and let them know that this is the means by which their spirit will find itself and its unity with the Prime. This is the path of power and of peace in their strivings and greatly noble is this gift.

The talismans may be worn constantly, if so chosen, or they may be unnecessary if the individual has centered the energy in such a way that wearing the stone would be excessive to the system. This would seem to be the case with the Talismans of the Callings (those also used in the Great Gathering), as they are that individual's nature expressed. However, this is not always so for the Talismans of the Callings, those in which quartz is the primary and the qualifier is the Calling stone, are the Talismans of the expressed energy signature rather than the inherent one. This allows the individual to center the energy of his Calling and direct it with great focus and specificity across any spectrum and from any specific center. It provides a way to avoid overload or excessive draining of personal energies. In addition, by its primary, it provides a way for each separate Talisman to be linked with the others in the Gathering and, at last, with the Master Talisman. This will result in a strong and unified focus to powerfully project the energies, for in the Master's Talisman, also, are the separate stones as qualifiers matched to their harmonic and, by these stones all are drawn together.

The pattern of the Calling Talismans is a generally beneficial one. It may be used for any individual who needs the virtue of the qualifier dispersed throughout the general system where the singular stone of the qualifier would stand as too narrow or intense an energy. This use depends on the way the stone is charged and intended by the user or practitioner. This is also true with any of the other Talismans, that their direction of energy, whether internal or expressed, is determined according to their use by the Practitioner. The energy may be directed inward through the qualifier and, by the nature of the primary, generously and graciously distributed across the full scope of the individual's energy system. This will neither drain nor overtax any one center. Or, if the flow is directed outward from the wearer, the energy will be drawn in a balanced way from the energy system complex as a whole and have a broad and selectable range of power.

DUAL RESONANCES

There is a second series of Talismans that relate to the Callings. These are composed of primaries that represent that particular Calling of the individual and a qualifier/driver that represents the way in which that individual expresses that Calling in life. This expression manifests itself in the individual's energy system complex as the activation of a particular path between two chakras. These configurations can be used by specific individuals to deepen their identity within their awareness of their Calling. Alternatively, these may be used by any individual who wishes to develop his or her awareness of the energy represented by the composition of stones. As we have explained, these combinations may be used when an individual feels a particular energy quality is lacking in life or when he feels that an energy quality he already has in abundance needs to be balanced. The explanations provided for each combination may be taken literally for awareness in the Calling or as an allegory for the energies presented in cases of more general use.

They are composed of a primary that represents the dominant polarity of the Calling combined with the qualifier of the recessive polarity of the secondary characteristic. The chart at the end of this chapter will list the specific stones for each combination in detail.

ARTISAN & SMITH

CHAKRA: BASE

IMPLEMENT: TURNING WHEEL

STONE: RED GARNET / RUBY

METAL: IRON & STEEL

The Artisans correspond to the Base Chakra and the prime polarity resonance of this Calling is female. The Smith is the male polarity resonance of this Calling. The Artisan is the Initialization and the Smith is the Execution or Manifestation of this energy, but in all other respects, they are the balanced polarities of each other as sibling twins. The Artisan's metal is ferrous iron and that of the Smith is blue tempered steel. They correspond to the base chakra, because it is there that the life force energy of the physical universe first enters physical manifestation. It is the function of that chakra to shape energy and determine the way it manifests in the individual. This is the energy of shaping and creating, from raw energy into form and reality. Theirs is the resonance of Primal Creation; theirs is the manipulation of the physical world. Theirs is the unification of heaven and earth, singing unto it the lowest frequency of the harmonic as the Crown Priest sings the highest. Under their purview is the development of potentials and beginnings. Therefore, their color and resonance is that of the blood and power of birth. They bring forth into reality from within themselves and of the fabric of their own Spirit what was begun in the darkness of conception, and this is their prime function. They are like children in that they recognize no limitations to potentials. They are like those who have given birth, for their natures are fulfilled when their creations go forth from them and achieve their own place apart from their creators.

The Artisan is the maker of change. She is the one who initiates it, who generates it, and who by her will and force brings it forth; and by her side is her brother, the Smith, who manifests the mechanisms of that change. Their implement is the Turning Wheel, for Karma is known as the Turning Wheel, and Time and, likewise, Change. This may be seen as literal truth or as analogy to all things both greater and smaller.

The Artisan/Warrior conceives and builds the implements and engines of defense. This is the expressed harmonic of the base chakra with the belly. The Artisan/Dancer expresses the energy of rhythm and flow into tangible manifestation. This is the expressed harmonic of the base chakra with the solar plexus. The Artisan/Healer brings forth from others what they need but cannot realize for themselves. This is the expressed harmonic of the base chakra with the heart. The Artisan/Seer translates the dreams and visions of others into tangible objects. She also translates her own visions into this world. This is the expressed harmonic of the base chakra with the throat. The Artisan/Monarch is the hand of creation through order and reason. Hers is the overview of the potential. She draws order from chaos. The Artisan/Priest focuses and charges his creations through the act of that creation. This is the expressed harmonic of the base chakra with the crown

WARRIOR

CHAKRA: BELLY

IMPLEMENT: SWORD

STONE: CITRINE / ZINCITE / PAD PARAJAH

METAL: BRONZE

Warriors correspond with the chakra of the Belly, and the dominant polarity of this Calling is Male. At first impression, the Warrior seems to present the diametric opposite of the Artisan, for it is the Warrior who destroys. However, once the nature of this center is understood, it becomes clear that destruction is not the primary focus of this Calling. His purpose is to assert and to defend what the Artisan has created. Bronze is his metal for it is by Bronze that the children of the New Age first established sovereignty. It was by the power of the Warrior's arm that safety was established that others might live and create. He is the one who stands forth to establish his will among others, and by his song, all that the Artisan creates is established, protected, and enabled to grow and flourish. His is the first manifestation of individual consciousness, of the ego in the sense of realized identity, along with the will and strength to assert that identity. His implement is the Sword and in this may be seen the key to his nature. It is by the sword that the Warrior brings forth destruction. However, it is by his sword that the right of justice is established and the peace of nations is held, that all who dwell there may live in safety and harmony.

This Calling corresponds to the belly chakra, for it is through this center that the first unique identity of the individual is asserted. It is also by this chakra energy that the individual establishes his own kingdom and purview whether great or small. It is reflexive and instinctive as are all of the lower centers, yet in its heritage are the keys to the future and the establishment of all higher resonances. Neither Mage nor Adept may rise without having first established his own Warrior principle and understood it fully. Its balance is discipline and there can be no understanding or true power without discipline. As the Artisan represents birth, the Warrior represents survival in all its necessities. Only through this may one at last come to recognize true identity.

The stone of the Belly Chakra is Orange and its archetype is the orange sapphire called the Pad Parajah, and its metal is bronze.

The stones of the Warrior/Artisan bring the directed passion of his heart to the task of creation, thereby transmuting pain to beauty and bringing about harmonious realignment. They remove the barriers of self-doubt and self-consciousness from the flow of creativity. This is the expressed harmonic of the belly with the base chakra. The Warrior/Dancer brings these energies forth through discipline and control. This is the expressed harmonic of the belly with the solar plexus. The Warrior/Healer asserts the force of balance and defense for the sake of those whose strength is lost, that they may come again to their own balance of life in a place of safety. This is the expressed harmonic of the belly with the heart chakra. The Warrior/Seer transmutes his aggressive force into tone and sound. He is the Singer who not only purges and balances his own nature, but also allows others to share this force of energy. Thus, they share in this cleansing and raising of energy. This is the expressed harmonic of the belly with the throat chakra.

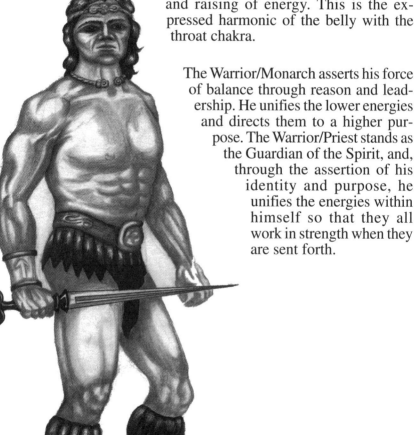

The Warrior/Monarch asserts his force of balance through reason and leadership. He unifies the lower energies and directs them to a higher purpose. The Warrior/Priest stands as the Guardian of the Spirit, and, through the assertion of his identity and purpose, he unifies the energies within himself so that they all work in strength when they are sent forth.

DANCER

CHAKRA: SOLAR PLEXUS

IMPLEMENT: BELL

STONE: TOPAZ

METAL: GOLD

The Dancers correspond to the chakra of the solar plexus and the dominant polarity of this Calling is Female. It is the Dancer who establishes and communicates through feelings and brings instincts and emotions to the fore, manifesting them in disciplined and expressive fashion. She turns prime urges and energies into expression through a basal understanding of the physical principle. This is the establishment not only of expression but also of grace through the physical medium. This is the apex of instinct that was begun by birth, established by survival, and now is understood and expressed through discipline and guided action. Her's are the feelings and emotions both received and expressed, the communication of and through instinct. It is through this chakra that the highest of the physical animal urges becomes at last joined to the higher forces of spirit reaching through the heart chakra above. It is she who brings up from the Earth that which is at once the lowest and the highest the Primal Force and expresses it. By her energy are emotions received and acted upon and the establishment of identity is made complete. The metal of this calling is Gold for it is the energy of focus through true passion.

The Dancer's place is one of change and balance through change. She does not cause or bring this change but institutes the balance by which this change is used for productive growth. Her implement is the Bell with which the rhythms are set and by these rhythms, the pattern is established. The sound of the bell is the carrier of her expression, as are the carrier for all basis of thought. This sound is permeating, penetrating and resonates with all within its range as are the emotions that she utilizes and personifies. By the superimposition of rhythm, order, discipline and control are established

The stone of the Dancer is the Sunbright Topaz. Its color is purest yellow, and its metal is gold. The talismans of the Dancer are those in which the Primary is yellow/golden and they express their energy through the solar plexus. When qualified by secondary stones, they express their energy through that center according to her necessity or desire. The Dancer/Artisan is she who, through understanding of rhythm and movement, translates these to physical manifestation whether through objects, regalia, or patterned dance. This is the expressed harmonic of the solar plexus with the base.

The Dancer/Warrior draws forth great power from the earth and sends it forth according to focused and disciplined intention. This is the expressed harmonic of the solar plexus with the belly. The Dancer/Healer leads the others through the patterned course that they might come again into alignment with the flow of the River and into balance with their natures. This is the expressed harmonic of the solar plexus with the heart. The Dancer/ Seer, through the joining of rhythms, causes others to see their own visions. This is the expressed harmonic of the solar plexus with the heart chakra. The Dancer/Monarch perceives patterns in cause and effect and uses this as the basis to unify action with reason. The Dancer/Priestess leads the rites and draws the assembled company together with her paces that the Priest may gather then the energies of all. In addition, she leads the assembled company in the dance of the Gathering that their energies shall be whole and joined for their purpose. This is the expressed harmonic of the solar plexus center with the brow.

HEALER

CHAKRA: HEART

IMPLEMENT: CUP

STONE: EMERALD

METAL: COPPER

The Healer corresponds to the Heart center and the Prime Polarity of this resonance is Male. This is the Calling of the mid-point. This Calling represents and personifies the joining of all those energies that may be considered primal and basal, that are those of the Animal Man, with those energies that are of the higher resonance that are of the Spirit Man. This is the uniting of the Beast with the Angel. This is the bridge between them and by it the human attains the Godhead and is made whole. Humankind is both animal and spirit, that is, the physical body is the evolved genetic form that arose from the first seas and contains within it all instinctual and basal reactionary codes that enabled physical survival on this world. These codes are necessary for the maintenance of this form and are the basis of the first learning processes. They provide the interface mechanisms necessary to function with the human form on this plane. Yet, Humankind is also Spirit that has its roots, not in the oceans' depths, but in the depths and infinity of the Prime. Thus, the individual contains all those means necessary to manifest the whole spectrum range of the Prime. In order to continue survival while inhabiting this form, the individual must inevitably find a bridge between these two elements of his nature. First, it was necessary on a racial scale, to rise from the bestiality of his physical beginnings, and establish law that Humankind should come together in an ordered of whatever sort. It is the imperative of all growth that individuals learn discipline through patterned behavior. Rhythm is the key to conscious intelligence. In the passage of time, this integration became manifested on an individual scale and singular individuals discovered the balance of God and Beast within themselves. In the fullness of time, this will again become translated into a racial order that all humanity may assume a higher awareness.

The Healer manifests the balance and enforces it on an individual basis. His is the union of the Spirit with the flesh in which neither should rise above the other, and neither should be strained or starved from the union, but should exist in harmony. This is the nature of all healing, to establish accord and balance so that spirit and flesh will contribute beneficially to each other and both should survive well together on this plane.

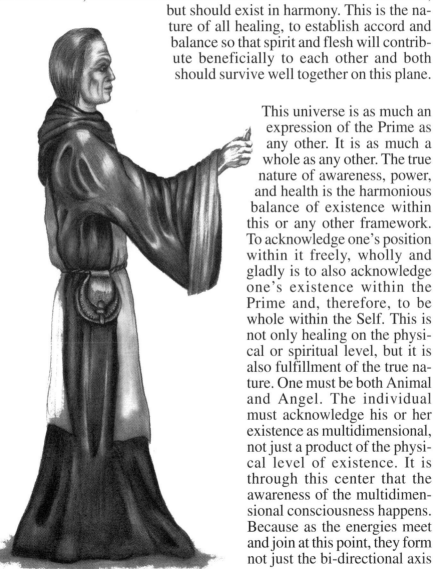

This universe is as much an expression of the Prime as any other. It is as much a whole as any other. The true nature of awareness, power, and health is the harmonious balance of existence within this or any other framework. To acknowledge one's position within it freely, wholly and gladly is to also acknowledge one's existence within the Prime and, therefore, to be whole within the Self. This is not only healing on the physical or spiritual level, but it is also fulfillment of the true nature. One must be both Animal and Angel. The individual must acknowledge his or her existence as multidimensional, not just a product of the physical level of existence. It is through this center that the awareness of the multidimensional consciousness happens. Because as the energies meet and join at this point, they form not just the bi-directional axis of the physical orientation but also the seven-rayed axis structure of the multi-dimensional being.

Therefore, the Healer's implement is the Cup, for it represents spirit held within flesh. Without the cup, the contents have no framework and are lost. Without form in this universe, Spirit is dispersed and has no true focal point, and therefore no true power for evolution, growth, or manifestation. Also, without its contents the cup is empty and serves no purpose. Form is void and empty without the Spirit that animates and directs. The Healer's stone is emerald of pure green and this color may also stand as an analogy. His is the point of the spectrum of life where the yellow of the Dancer's emotions is poised in perfect balance with the pure higher will and vision of the Seer's blue and neither outweighs the other.

The Healer/Artisan forms images in this world that will draw pain and unease out of others and stimulate energies that begin the healing process. This is the expressed harmonic of the Heart with the Base. The Healer/Warrior discovers the ills of the spirit. He guides others to know and revere their true selves and to heal with the power of self-knowledge and inner strength. This is the expressed harmonic of the heart with the belly. The Healer/Dancer heals through the attunement of the spirit by aligning the energies of the physical form with the Great River of Life. This is the expressed harmonic of the heart with the solar plexus. The Healer/Seer brings visions for others that they may know the truth that is revealed. This is the expressed harmonic of the heart with the throat. The Healer/Monarch is one who by his power stands as physician to a nation, having both the vision and power to set trends on a positive and healing course. The Healer/Priest brings mind, body, and spirit into accord and alignment. This is the expressed harmonic of the heart with the crown.

SEER / TEACHER

CHAKRA: THROAT

IMPLEMENT: MIRROR

STONE: SAPPHIRE

METAL: SILVER

The Seer/Teacher corresponds to the throat chakra and the dominant polarity of this Calling is female. This is the lowest signature of the higher resonance chakras and is directly linked with the power of speech. Before there was the power of speech there was, by necessity, the power of imagination, the power to symbolize, and the power to reach outward and hypothesize. This is the beginning of the path beyond the self and the inward path to find the true self. These paths are one and the same. As the Seer is empowered to see beyond this world, she also sees the truth of this world and thus the nature of many worlds and brings this knowledge forth into conscious usefulness and awareness.

Her implement is the Mirror, for by it Man has seen through countless ages both the images of the self and the universe beyond the self. In this she is also the Teacher, because by holding this mirror, she shows relation to other realms. By this perspective all consciousness can grow and develop. This is the Gate to Time and Space. This is the stepping stone of Infinity. Hers also is the blue of the late evening sky and the silver of fluidity. Hers is the point of creation in the spiritual range, for it is by her vision that power is conceptualized and all elements perceived.

The stones of the Seer are those in which the Primary is blue. The Seer/Artisan calls forth her vision and makes them into physical reality. She brings forth her visions from the otherworld into this one and by doing this, she demonstrates this understanding to those who have not her gift. This is the expressed harmonic of the Throat with the Base. The Seer/Warrior travels across the worlds seeking knowledge that she brings back for others to profit by. Hers is the Warrior's strength and integrity of spirit. This is the expressed harmonic of the throat with the belly. The Seer/Dancer is she who uses the alignment of her spirit through the rhythms of her physical form to follow the Great River and to gain her vision of the binding force of the worlds. This is the expressed harmonic of the throat with the solar plexus. The Seer/Healer draws aside the veils with her visions and sees the true cause of the ills of the body and the spirit. Then she opens this vision to those in need so that they can heal by self-knowledge and knowledge of the true cause and mechanism of the imbalance. This is the expressed harmonic of the throat with the heart. The Seer/Queen uses her insight to instruct her people with the knowledge of their destiny as a people so that their heighest potential can be realized. This is the expressed harmonic of the throat with the brow. The Seer/Priestess lays her hand within the priest's at the Gathering so that his perception of the joined energies may be complete. She also uses the power of her voice to lead the energies of those assembled with her upon her journey that they may share in her visions. This is the expressed harmonic of the throat with the crown.

MONARCH

CHAKRA: BROW

IMPLEMENT: SCEPTER

STONE: AMETHYST

METAL: ELECTRUM

The Monarchs - King and Queen - correspond to the chakra of the brow, and to the energy of sovereignty and manifested will. The Prime Polarity of this Calling is Male. The sovereignty of the Monarch manifests through the power of intelligent will, and of power directed and controlled through disciplined understanding. This power pulls together all awarenesses and yokes them to harness. This is the pure understanding and control of the self that allows no distractions. This is the counterbalance to the Warrior force and it is by the harmonic resonance to the King that the Warrior perceives the administration of his justice. The King sees beyond the self, and conceives in terms of wholes and patterns and by this ability to conceive attains majestic control over that which he has envisioned. His is true compassion, and he manifests his lordship through the harmonic counterbalance of the Warrior's might.

His implement is the Scepter with which he guides and directs his control and by it, this force is channeled through the pure will of intelligence. His is the strength of wisdom, the duty of maintenance, and the initiation of change. His is the seat of benevolence. In his understanding and strength he perceives the Universal abundance and its malleability and dispenses from it so that there will be order, discipline and controlled strength as well as abundance and plenty for all within his jurisdiction. His color is purple, that is, red and blue mixed together in equal proportions, for his is the sovereignty of both the basal world and primal nature unified by pure will uncompromised by irrationality. Thus, his understanding is based on clear perception. He brings forth the manifestation of his intention on the full resonance of worlds, for he knows their nature and purpose. He knows the sovereignty of spirit over matter, as he is aware of the essence of the Prime permeating and manifesting in all things. Spirit is always sovereign over that which it has created, and with this knowledge comes true sovereignty over all creation.

The stones of the Monarchs are those in which the Primary stone is the Archetype stone of the Calling. When qualified through the use of pure white driving stones of the same degree of intensity or greater than the primary stone, they express their energy through the pure focused harmonic and embody all aspects and the purest essence of that Calling.

The King/Priest gathers the combined energies of his people and is a bridge for that people through himself to the Infinite. This is the expressed harmonic of the brow with the crown chakra. The Queen/Seer focuses the vision of that nation, sees to its translation into this world, and communicates that vision into the other worlds that it may be manifested there, as well. This is the expressed harmonic of the throat with the crown chakra. The King/Healer may walk abroad across the land and stretch forth his power that both land and people may be healed and that all shall be fruitful and in bounty. This is the expressed harmonic of the heart chakra with the Crown. The Queen/Dancer weaves the rhythms of life through herself for the expression and fulfillment. This is the expressed harmonic of the solar plexus with the crown chakra. The King/Warrior stands as surest defense and justice on the part of his people. He both leads armies and dispenses mercy as he is moved according to his wisdom. This is the expressed harmonic of the belly with the crown chakra. The Artisan/Queen brings into physical creation that which is the need of her Lord and her people. She holds the shaping of their lives. This is the expressed harmonic of the base with the crown chakra.

PRIEST

CHAKRA: CROWN

IMPLEMENT: LIGHTED LAMP

STONE: DIAMOND

METAL: PLATINUM

The Priest and Priestess correspond to the crown chakra, and the Prime Polarity resonance of this Calling is female. However, this chakra, like that of the Artisan/Smith, manifests as both male and female, and will manifest the opposite polarity resonance of the base chakra whichever is most dominant. This is a function of the balanced helix of the individual's energies. The color correspondence of this Calling is pure blue/white, for in this are all others brought together and unified in balance. Through this Calling, all the other energies are focused and transmuted into power through intelligence and sent forth into manifestation. This chakra and Calling are the link with the Godhead and the intelligent and comprehending connection and awareness to the Prime. It is through this energy that all others are brought to balance and their powers and potentials made manifest. Through it all other natures assume their right perspective and are brought into alignment with the evolutionary process of Humankind. The Priestly implement is the burning flame, as may be illustrated by the Lighted Lamp, for it contains all lights and all colors. It is pure energy and is transformative by the nature of its action and function.

The stones of the Priest are those in which the Primary is violet or purple. The Priest/Artisan is a maker of icons, a designer of those objects that are intended to raise or energize centers of awareness in others. It is the expressed harmonic of the crown with the base. The Priest/Warrior calls forth his power from the center of the self and expresses it for the protection and defense of others with the focus through the heart center that all may be done in compassion. He teaches this defense to others so that they may become stronger. It is the expressed harmonic of the crown with the belly. The Priest/Dancer is he who conceives and designs those rituals of power that may bring together all others to raise and energize the centers of awareness and expression. It is the expressed harmonic of the crown with the solar plexus. The Priest/ Healer heals others by raising the energy level of their centers and connecting them to the higher energies. This enables them to be balanced and whole, and through their raised awareness, to come again unto health. It is the expressed harmonic of the crown with the heart. The Priest/Seer is the caller of visions who directs the power of those visions to their appropriate end. It is the expressed harmonic of the crown with the throat. The Priest/Monarch brings knowledge of spirit through reason and objective awareness to elevate the waking consciousness of the individual.

Similar Properties

Once the practitioner has a basic knowledge of the stones and the principles involved in combining them for energy work, many more possibilities for such combinations become clear. Many things can be done with the sympathetic harmonics of stone combinations as well as with single. We should remind the student that not only do talismans work on a singular energy system, but they are also connected to one another by the Laws of Resonance as well as by the general behavior of vibration and harmonics. After some study, the practitioner will see that by using such stones, he or she can expand on the possibilities for combining them into any pattern or combinations of patterns that will suit the needs of the situation.

There are many varieties of stones that may be chosen for each primary and qualifier and the choice should be determined by the individual's preference and need. They may be selected for their color, their crystal shape and energy qualities. Their uses are broad, aside from the obvious intent to addressing specific symptoms or conditions. They may be used to reinforce and regenerate energies and talents that begin to manifest in the course of development. They may also be used to balance an individual's energy. This is done by determining the nature of the individual's primary Calling, then choosing a qualifying element intended to bring about a balance and harmony that may be lacking in a nature too integrated toward one specific energy. They may also be chosen to help awaken some hidden or sleeping gift of that individual, whether for pleasure or need, that will make life richer for all. They may be used in healing the mind, heart and spirit and, consequently, relationships between individuals.

==
TALISMANS OF TOGETHERNESS
==

Certain individuals have a special resonance with a particular crystal type and color. This may be by personal preference, but more deeply, this may be their life stone or stone of their Calling. When it is desirable for this individual to forge a deeper relationship with another individual or to heal a relationship and increase understanding and communication across the energy system complex, talismans can be made for both parties to suit this purpose. A bonding charm that has the wearer's primary and the mate's qualifier can encourage gracious harmony in natures discordant with each other through either separation or disagreement. Should each of the parties wear such a charm, with honest openness and loving intention on the part of both parties, this can help to heal a rift between them and bring about greater understanding. Such a pair of charms will help to build a sympathetic resonance between them that could be referred to as an energy bridge so that it will make it easier for them to resolve their difficulties. Such charms may also be made for a love token that would give both parties access to communication over great distances. This does not only apply to lovers and mates, but also to friends who are parted for a long period of time, or come to a difficult disagreement. From this, one may also derive a mother's charm that can be worn during pregnancy so that, as the pregnancy develops, the mother and child will be harmonized and balanced.

Such charms may be chosen for members of various groups. This is done by choosing one special type of crystal, particularly crystals that have grown closely beside one another in the same pocket or cluster and have been taken from the mother rock all at the same time. This would be designated as the primary of the group or clan and then each qualified by the Calling stone or personal stone of each individual member; the strongest known example of the principle of the Talismans of the Great Gathering.

CHAPTER 10

GROUP WORK & THE GREAT GATHERING

We have talked at length about developing the skills and disciplines that the individual needs in order to proceed with this work successfully. Solitary study is of great importance because it is by personal work that the individual begins to see him or herself as a powerful individual. It is by working alone, when there is no other person around to rely upon for support, that the individual comes in contact with a true perspective on his or her own strengths and limitations. However, after the initial period of learning has been successfully completed, it is helpful to the student to work with a group of others of a similar skill level.

A group can only function to the level of its weakest member regardless of the strength of the others or the skill of its leaders. However, at all levels of study, group work can be extremely beneficial and enlightening to the participants. There is no better venue for practicing the arts of cooperative power use and experiencing complex energy interactions on this intensified level. Each individual will have gained his or her own personal perspective and insight into the work, and it can be very profitable for all involved to share these insights and techniques.

The results of group work can be very strong. It often happens that the level of strength achieved by the group is far more than the sum of the energies of its assembled members. This is always so, for it is a universal principle that the agreement of many individuals can create a far stronger reality than the will of one or a few. This is the way this universe was formed, that is, by the agreement and creative intention of many spiritual beings, and it is also this agreement that keeps this universe in place and consistent. It may, therefore, be desirable that a group of students who are still in the process of learning the basic levels should come together to pool their energies under the direction of a more experienced leader. This can be most effective and can also be a learning experience. It is necessary for each of the participants to have successfully practiced the basic disciplines and skills of meditation and energy work, and that all participants are ethical in practice and strong in body, will, and mind. Discipline is central to these practices, for the practitioner of power must have the will and strength of intention of a Warrior in all ways.

We will, therefore, discuss the principles and preparations involved in group work. It should be understood that we do not intend to specify dogmatic procedures. This is unnecessary as well as being unduly restrictive to the student's growth in these matters. Through time and observance, certain forms have grown in effectiveness. These practices should be observed and will be explained. However, specific wording and procedure should be unnecessary if the basic underlying principles are properly understood and respected. Many dogmatic procedures or rituals are available and will function well. Whatever the case, these procedures should be agreed upon and understood by all members of the group before the actual practice takes place.

This Universe was created by the collective intention of a group of individuals. It is also continually being created from moment to moment by the beliefs and intentions of all the individuals who reside within it. This is a pivotal point to understand. Life force and intention are the basic fabric of this place. Therefore, the fabric of reality can be manipulated by the degree of intention and belief construct manifested within it. The student must realize that this place is not solid and concrete, but malleable. It is only the student's belief system and background that makes this seem not to be so. It therefore follows that, by discipline, intention, and agreement, any group may come together and act upon this reality to alter its construct and move within its fabric. Group work within a ritual circle provides the ideal format for this activity. This is because a ritual circle provides a warded and protected space that will maintain the work free from the distraction and possible contamination of other energies. This allows the participants to relax in certain aspects and devote the majority of their attention to the work. This gives each member (and therefore the work at hand) far greater focus and power. It also provides the leaders of the group with a controlled and purified pool of energy with which to work. The members of the group may be monitored and guided within a controlled environment. This is important not only to the result of the work but to the health, balance, and general well-being of all the participants. Finally, the nature of the wards provides an enclosure that contains the projected energies. This allows them to be accelerated and intensified before being sent forth, as well as keeps them from interfering with the privacy and harmony of individuals outside the space.

The basic purpose of any power work should first be considered and agreed upon by the assembled group. This knowledge and agreement are the basic elements of the success of the work. The group may agree to join their energies to work for the healing of one of their number or one who is elsewhere. They may agree to raise their strength and commit it to the individual who leads the group for it to be shaped and set to some certain intention whether intense communication, creation, and shaping of thought forms, etc. It may also be that one among them is a Seer or training Seer and then they may unify their strength to shield and strengthen her. The leader of the group should serve as her guide and guard so that she may go safely and strongly forth into the many worlds to seek the answers or visions that the group requires. Surely, she will go far stronger with all the energy and intention of the unified assembly there for her to draw upon at her need. Whatever their mission is, it should be consciously agreed upon before beginning the work.

When forming a group, a leader should always be chosen. Each procedure must absolutely have one individual who collects, directs, focuses, and sends the energy. This leader may be chosen only for the duration of the work involved in the one procedure. On the other hand, if it is by the group's unanimous consent, the leader may remain in charge and take responsibility for all work of that particular group. In any instance, it is important that the leader is knowledgeable about the procedure being used and the principles involved in it. It is best, if it is a group of students, that he or she be somewhat stronger or farther advanced that the others participating. This is because, if one or more of the group begins to waver or if the energies inside or outside the circle become unstable, the leader is responsible for rectifying and restabilizing these energies before they are integrated and sent forth. This leader may be a single individual or a couple who works in such accord that they work as one. Even then, they should agree between them beforehand which of them will gather the energy, unify, and pass it to the other and which of them will give it its final shaping and send it forth.

A working group should be understood as a single unit composed of many parts, just as any individual is a whole energy system composed of separate chakras. These energies are various in their natures and are integrated and expressed by the action of the intelligent will of the individual. The members of the group should be understood in this context as the separate chakras of the group entity. They each understand and express their energies in many ways depending upon their understanding, their level of discipline, and their separate and distinct personalities. These energies are then directed, guided, integrated, and expressed by the leader of the group. This leader serves the function of the individual spirit, who, having these energies at his disposal then balances and uses them according to the desired purpose at hand. Ideally, this group should be sexually balanced by pairs of male and female, but this is not always necessary unless it is for the truly higher work of concerted strength.

When the group assembles, the shields and wards should be either initially raised or strengthened by the leader or leading pair drawing from the initial strength of the assembled gathering. The group may dance, chant, or assume whatever meditative state is appropriate and suitable so that their energies will be available and united in this manner. During this process and immediately afterward, the leaders should make sure that each member is comfortably linked to their mate (should those mates be present), and to the energy of the earth so that their strength will be sure. This will avoid any undue drain or harm by the function of the group purpose. Last of all, they should make sure that all energies are unified and joined in purpose so that the group works as a body, like a chakra system with the Mage(s) as the crown and will and the others aligned in concert with them.

When the members are aligned and their well being and unity are assured, when the shielding is reinforced by the concerted will of those assembled at the intention of the leaders, then the work may proceed when the leaders deem it proper. It is often a good idea to have one member of the group outside the central working area of strength to aid and assist the leaders and monitor all activities to assure that all remain stable and rightly done. He should be equal in power and strength to the leaders or perhaps even stronger. This member is referred to as the Solitary One. Some modern groups refer to this member as a Black Man because his function like the color black is to retain all energies within himself.

If crystals are to be used as the primary instrument for the group work, each individual should wear over the heart chakra the talisman of his or her Calling. The Callings and their respective talismans are discussed in detail in another part of this work. This section should be read and thoroughly understood before proceeding. This talisman may be a quartz crystal with the Calling stone placed as a qualifier, or it may be a single crystal of the archetype stone of that Calling. Whichever is chosen, it should be decided beforehand which pattern the talismans are to be. The group should all wear talismans of the same configuration, whether single or compound. Each talisman stone should be carefully chosen to suit the individual who is to wear it. Then the Highest One, the one chosen as leader, should wear a talisman based on the pattern of the Grand Talisman over his or her heart chakra. Each chakra stone set in it should have been chosen to specifically resonate with each of the smaller separate talismans to be worn by the group members. The quartz crystal upon which the chakra stones are set should be chosen to specifically resonate with the one who is to wear the talisman as well as to the other talisman stones. This talisman is the analogy, not only of the individual, but also the group, for the quartz crystal signifies the spiritual being, the entity as a whole, and the whole configuration of that individual's energy system. The individual stones signify the chakra energies that make up the component energies of that system. The individual Calling stones of the group members are used to gather energy through the quartz primary and focus it through the qualifier to purify and focus the powers given to the leader. The leader then uses his or her Grand Talisman in the reverse manner by gathering the various energies through the individual chakra stones and unifying them through the quartz crystal base.

The following discourse describes the pattern used in Ancient Days for the component members of the group, their singular stones and the expression of the work at hand.

FULL GATHERING

OF THE CALLINGS

During work of great power, chakra stones are worn singly and in this instance they are known as the Stones of Majesty that are similar in function to the Stones of the Callings. The term Stones of Majesty should not be confused with the stone group of that same designation, for in this context the meaning is different altogether. These may be worn in the Great Gathering of Power as singular amulets over the heart chakras, hung by chains around the necks of the participants or attached over the heart chakra in brooches fastened to the clothing. The Highest One should wear the full Chakra Talisman and each of the stones should be perfectly matched in resonance with the stone over the heart of each of the participants. It is by this talisman that the Highest One may unify the members of the group and gather their varied power to him or herself. Each of the participants, by virtue of his Calling, stands as a single Chakra of a Greater Whole Entity and the Highest One stands as the unifying center - he or she shall be as the Diamond that blazes forth. By this talisman, the power and strength of the Gathering is formed and its will is made manifest.

These are the stones that each member should wear. Take heed of this for they are differentiated according to the sex of the participant to account for the balance of polarities. This is most important for the quality of this special resonance should be well understood and taken into account.

The High Priestess should wear the purple tourmaline so that she is the balance for the strength of the High Priest. Let them work together in union, for this is the true nature of the Stone of Dominion.

The Siberite (Purple) Tourmaline is the stone of the Queen and of the Highest Priestess. It draws together and binds all energies. This is the summary of all worldly force and requires only the pure white force of the fully developed Crown to make its nature complete. It is the female nature that binds, collects, and nurtures life in its richest bounty. It is the color of the Womb and thus of all potential and requires only the whitest of lights in the higher realms of consciousness or the richest amethyst violet in the secular to be expressed. One force without the other, even at its most powerful, is incomplete and requires the other to make the perfect union. Let the Highest Priest and Priestess then achieve the balance of the Dancers poised perfectly outside of themselves at the merging point with each other for the Gathering of Power is surely their Dance.

If the ritual is hers to command rather than his, he should wear a perfectly transparent carbuncle ruby of the identical hue of purple as the purple tourmaline and she should wear a white sapphire instead of the diamond. Let them thus work as one within their natures. He shall gather in the power by the balance and she shall guide and direct its flow. Neither Priest nor Priestess should be set higher than one another, but let them be consorts and mates as equals, for neither rules the other. They are joined in dual balanced purpose.

These are the delineations of the positions of the group members with respect to one another, as they should stand within the group:

First, standing alone and apart should be the Solitary One. He stands alone and upon his breast he should wear onyx, obsidian, or, sometimes, black tourmaline. This should not be a composite talisman, but a single stone set in any metal of his choosing, but preferably silver, electrum or white gold. It is through him that the power is drawn within. It is through the Solitary One that the energy is monitored as it enters their purview and then into the circle as a whole. He is the Gate of Force and the Guardian of the Place. His place is outside of the Gathering of Callings and he is one unto himself alone. It is through him and by his power that whatever is being done is guarded and kept secret unto itself.

To the left hand of the Highest Priest shall stand his Mate the Highest Priestess and to his right hand shall stand the Queen wearing a violet garnet; then the King shall stand beside her wearing the amethyst of his enlightened wisdom.

To the right of the King shall stand the female Seer with deepest royal blue tourmaline and beside her right hand shall stand the Male Seer with darkest blue sapphire.

Then shall stand in line the Healer and his Mate wearing green emerald and tsavorite (green) garnet respectively.

To their right shall stand the Dancers, female and male, and their stones shall be golden garnet and sunbright topaz.

The Warriors then shall stand and she shall wear carnelian and he citrine.

Then at last the Artisan and her mate, the Smith, in deepest red. To her the garnet and him the ruby, although, should the ritual be directed by the Priestess and the Priest wearing ruby, the Smith should wear a rubelite tourmaline instead of the ruby, although this is not essential.

GATHERING OF

SINGLE REPRESENTATIVES

If a full Gathering of perfectly mated pairs is not possible, then such members of a full group as may be assembled should wear the talismans from the list of androgyne stones. However, all those present should be capable of whole grounded balance within themselves. The order of the group should be as follows: They should stand aligned from the Highest Priestess' right hand and she in purple tourmaline and beside her the King in Amethyst, the female Seer in royal blue sapphire, the male Healer in Emerald, the female Dancer in Topaz, the male Warrior in Citrine, the female Artisan in blood red Garnet. The Priest should stand outside the circle wearing both diamond and obsidian or onyx. In this instance, it is the Priest who should monitor the group for the balancing of energy as it is channeled for the use of the Priestess. Each member of the group should manifest and generate energy according to their gifts and nature. The leaders should gather this unto themselves and direct it according to the reason and purpose of the Gathering.

Should there be an altar, it should be in the center of the circle and all activities of this Gathering should circle around it. This is because the center of the circle is where the natural power flow of the gathering is at its strongest and most balanced. However, this is not absolute law. If it is desirable and appropriate, the altar may be at the point closest to the magnetic or geographic pole depending on the power needs of the purpose at hand. The movement of the members of the group within the circle should be clockwise in the Northern Hemisphere and counterclockwise in the Southern. The Solitary One shall stand outside the circle facing the nearest magnetic pole with the Highest Priest and Priestess facing him from across the circle. The other members of the group should align themselves as has been delineated. The Highest Priestess should stand in the center apart from all or directly in front of the altar, when not in alignment to the left of her Mate. If she is the director of the circle and wearing the white sapphire, then all the others shall circle to her left except her Mate who should stand to her right.

Let the room in which these arts are developed be enclosed and enveloped in true shielding according to the will of the practitioner. It should be the individual practitioner who sets these shields after purging the place by his own intention, for only then will he be certain that no one will be harmed in his path of study and working. It is true that no Mage may set a shield for someone else better than that individual may set it for himself. At the beginning of each working session, these shields should be renewed and reinforced, although a complete purging and resetting is not necessary. Use this reinforcement as an opportunity to build these shields stronger and more precisely each time.

Raise the shields, binding them first with each of the Earth's elemental forces, that is, air, fire, water, and earth as has been previously discussed. This is done by achieving a meditative state by dancing and breathing that should already have been practiced, developed and understood. Then contact each element and form it by intention into the shield, as a potter molds clay into his pattern. With each step, the worker should make the shields more tangible. After this is done to the certainty and satisfaction of the worker, the entire thought form shielding is bound in with the energy of the earth and the universe, as it were, the dragon force. This should be done in such a way that the entire working space is encased in a powerful sphere of protection and energy of will drawn and sustained from the basic forces of this Universe's life. In no way should this shield be constructed of the Mage's own energy, for then it will be subject to the anomalies and fluctuations of that personal energy. It should be shaped by the Mage's will and be of his signature and specific unto him and specified by him, but linked to a greater and more stable force that will sustain itself in accordance with the laws and continuity of all things. This space and shield should be reinforced at the beginning of each procedure, whether that procedure is merely meditation or power work to whatever degree. In this way, it becomes stronger and more specific, more responsive to the will of that Mage. In the process of shaping it he may set its permeability level by dictating how much it may admit of the outside world and in what fashion it should admit or absorb or reflect that energy. Its interior permeability, that is, the degree to which the energies may leave that space, should always be kept within his personal conscious control and tightly monitored by him. They should not be set on automatic unless the shield itself is set to emit energies. However, this is the emission of energy from the shield itself because it was made to do so and not the leakage of energy from the enclosed space within the shield. Energy should be released from inside the shield only after it has been raised, fashioned, and specified. At this point, the energy is sent through the shield by the will of the Mage. This is another good reason for keeping the shield proper under the conscious control of the practitioner, because he needs to be able to determine precisely the intensity, direction, speed, and content of whatever sendings are released through his shield.

This practice of shielding is suitable in all degrees of power work whether the Mage works alone or with others. Those others the Mage works with for raising power should either be his or his mate's direct apprentices or the Mage's equals in power. Otherwise, there is a risk that the weaker members of this group will become unduly strained. The intensity of the work should be only as strong as the weakest member of the group can bear, otherwise, harm will understandably result. This should be taken into consideration any time that the arts are practiced.

There is also a current convention known as raising Watch Towers. The Watch Towers may be defined as the alignment of the circle with the energy specifics attributed to each of the geographic poles. These energy specifics have been attributed to the elements of the Universe and represent the stages of the coalescence of essence into form. They have also been called by a great variety of names and external attributes such as angels, demons, winds, creatures and the like, and have been discussed at great length in numerous works. These should be set when the leaders make the first circuit of the group once the power circle has been initially established. However, it should be understood that these names and compass points are arbitrary and a later convention altogether. Each member of the gathering should be as a Watch Tower and there is no need for external raisings unless the power balance is incomplete and consequently disorderly. In a circle of Novices, it is necessary to establish these and then let them be under the guidance of the Solitary One after the leaders have set them.

It should be explained at this point that, just as the participants representing the energy centers comprise one greater whole individual, so do the Watch Towers represents the four Levels of Conscious Awareness of that group entity. Each one is a complete layer or level. One by one they represent the bringing into physical manifestation that which was begun as thought and energy. They transform into nested energy layers around the group just as they would around an individual person. To set them properly is to have a full series of conscious levels through which and by which energy and intention may manifest through the group's endeavors.

* When the priest leads the circle, He takes the diamond and she takes the purple tourmaline.

** When the Priestess leads the circle, she takes the White sapphire and the Priest takes the Purple Ruby

CALLING	MALE	FEMALE	ANDROGYNE
Priest *	Diamond	Purple Ruby	Purple Garnet
Priestess **	White Sapphire	Purple Tourmaline	
King / Queen	Amethyst	Violet Garnet	Amethyst
Seer	Blue Tourmaline	Blue Sapphire	Blue Tourmaline
Healer	Emerald	Green Garnet	Green Tourmaline
Dancer	Yellow Topaz	Golden Garnet	Yellow Topaz
Warrior	Citrine	Carnelian	Citrine
Artisan / Smith	Red Ruby	Red Garnet	Rubelite Tourmaline
Solitary One	Onyx, Obsidian, Black Tourmaline		

When working in the Gathering, only one of each of these stones should be represented, otherwise, they will interfere with each other. This is because the slight variable in resonance between the stones and their owners will take issue with one another. They should be set in gold inter-twined with the metal of their Calling. Other stones may be worn about the body to suit the qualifications of the work in progress, but none at the same chakra level. In this, the binding with gold is most specific because it will act as their common ground and key to their central and concerted focus.

APPRENTICE CALLING STONES These practitioners may have apprentices, that may wear stones congruent with the nature of their future Callings but that are of lesser intensity than those of individuals full developed in their Calling and craft.

CALLING	APPRENTICE
Priest	Clear Crystalline Moonstone / Amethyst
Priestess	Clear Quartz / Amethyst
Prince & Princess	White Quartz
Seer	Sodalite or Siderite
Healer	Peridot
Dancer	Heliodor
Warrior	Carnelian
Artisan	Rose Garnet
Smith	Red Garnet

It is by this basic structure and in this way that the initial base level of all higher work is achieved. This would include preferred and accepted dogmatic and ritual practices. Everything else is no more than a refinement upon these principles.

COMPLETING THE PROCESS

When the work is completed, the energy built up should be released by the group or individual involved. This is because the members of the group should not retain any undesired linkages or effects beyond what is already natural to them in their daily lives. This will also free their life energies to take their normal course. Their grounding should be separated from that of the shielding of the place. They should be released from the linkage and control of the Highest One. Then the shield reinforcement that was put up at the beginning of the work should be grounded away through the Leaders in the reverse order it was set and their personal energy unbound from it. Then the group may disperse, or as is more commonly done, they may eat good food that will strengthen their physical energies that may have been strained by the heavier load of the chakra energies and the extension of the group consciousness. Then they should rest and share fellowship until they feel strengthened and revitalized before departing. This will also help them reestablish their individual grounding so that they can return to their daily lives with relaxed and renewed spirit.

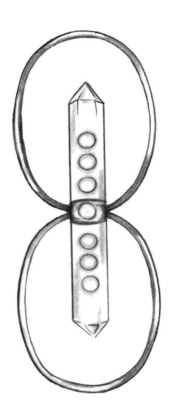

CHAPTER 11

TALISMANIC REGALIA

As there are many uses for talismans, so there are innumerable ways in which they can be brought into contact with the Human energy field complex in order to influence and amplify certain aspects of it. When we discussed healing by placing crystals and stones on the body, this introduced a basic principle: that by placing specific crystals at specific energy points on the body, the quality of those points can be redefined and altered in predictable ways. However, simply placing crystals on the body has its limitations in terms of duration and effectiveness. In many instances, combining the crystals with metal increases the scope of their effect and renders their energy more accessible to the individual. Forming that metal into a shape that encompasses the energy center in question and anchors the crystal not only in a specific location but in a particular orientation with respect to it makes the work that much more effective.

Fashioning regalia of any sort is the final step in the personal use of crystals for energy work. By regalia, we mean any sort of wearable or portable crystal talisman piece intended for the use of a single individual. This is as opposed to the great crystal work done with large stones used in group work or those permanently place in rooms or furniture for healing purposes and other types of energy work. Regalia can be as small and simple as a piece of personal jewelry using a single stone. Alternatively, it may be large and complex consisting of multiple stones in complex interaction with one another in a large piece of apparel intended for ritual or ceremony. Whatever its relative size and complexity, by the nature of its construction, these articles interact directly with the wearer's energy fields, for they are of sensitively charged material and they are constantly influenced and influencing the individual's energy helixes.

JEWELRY

The first of these is jewelry, that is, pieces of metal set with various gems and worn close to the person. Generally, jewelry is understood to be any piece or pieces made of either metal alone or stone and metal in combination intended to come directly in contact with the body of the wearer. We differentiate jewelry here from larger pieces such as armor, crowns, or masks, because jewelry is generally thought to be the personal possession of an individual. This is because larger, more complex regalia is generally considered to belong to a group or institution and used by individuals acting as that institution's representatives. The distinction is, however, a slight one and there is no clear dividing line.

When considering these pieces, first take into account the use to which they will be put and at which center they are to be placed. Those pieces placed on the hands qualify the temper of the energy drawn inward or flowing outward depending on which hand - whether dominant or recessive - they are placed. Bracelets and arm bands qualify the raw energy as it is cycled along this axis. A stone worn on the hands will have a noticeably different effect on the practice than that same stone in an identical setting worn on the brow or over the heart or in the naval. This is important to consider. For best effect, a stone must be placed as close as possible to the energy center it is intended to effect. Also, consider that matching stones worn at different centers may be tuned to one another in harmony so that they will interact together to create their own field within and surrounding the body. Stones of opposite but complementary natures should be tuned to contribute to and offset one another's purposes, and placed at different points to construct a complex interactive pattern.

Conversely, a single perfect gem, worn on the recessive hand may qualify all the horizontal perceptive intake of the individual, and be a subtle but most potent tool. A single perfect gem worn on the dominant hand of the body may be set to qualify all the energy outflowing from the body and be a very effective tool of power. A single talisman worn at the heart center may interact with the general field of the body (as the heart center is the Hub of the Wheel). It will serve as a talisman of defense, healing, and true potential energy that qualifies all energy incoming and outflowing from that center. Indeed, the placing of pieces about the body should be as carefully considered and specifically done as the choosing of the stones themselves and the setting of the charges. The wearing and placement is the completion of the process. The placing of gems and the sensitizing of the specific centers is as much an art/science as the construction of the actual talismans themselves. This should be practiced by meditation and circumspect experimentation until this is understood fully on a practical as well as a theoretical basis. It is important to remember that when using multiple pieces in different locations, you are creating a field between their energies. They are not inclined to work independently of each other, but rather to make a complex interactive field. A good analogy to this is the theme of multiple drug interactions when an individual is taking pharmaceuticals for a physical health condition. These drugs will not only behave in the manner they were individually intended, they will also create complex interactions within the body that may or may not be beneficial to the body's health. This is also true of crystal work, and we would urge the practitioner to regard the various pieces of jewelry worn as a system as a whole rather than as disassociated elements.

To demonstrate how jewelry may influence the wearer's energy, consider the copper or gold belt set with emeralds and topaz worn by the Dancer, and the disks and chains of her sandals. As she moves in the Dance, she draws up energy from the Earth beneath her feet. As the energy passes upward, it must pass through the field caused by the sandals and be qualified by the charged metal and stones. It then moves upward in this qualified form, upwards to her hips and waist (depending on the level at which the belt rides) and causes that center to be charged by this qualified energy. Again, it rises upwards through the pendant and pectoral collar, at the heart and throat levels respectively, to the headdress she wears of the same material, again charging the centers through the stones and metal. Energy passes downwards through her, also, following the same path, becoming charged and recharged, cycling the flow of potential power, qualifying it to her desired usage. So all of her accouterments charge and are charged within the specified field putting this qualified energy for use at her discretion.

Consider the rings, bracelets, and armbands placed along the horizontal axis. They effect and are affected by energy flowing outward from the heart center. Consider also the effect of the bangles hanging at the temples of her headdress, and the height, circumference and complexity of the headdress. Also, consider the earrings and how they connect and channel power. These are all in direct connection to the field potential of the body and interact with it as long as the pieces are worn, altering it and qualifying it.

WANDS, ORBS, BLADES & STAFFS

The next classification of talismans are those designed to be carried in the hand such as is blades, staffs, scepters, orbs of power, wands and the like. They are charged to their purpose in the process of their construction that may or may not be the case with pieces of jewelry. They are carried about the person and sometimes are intended for use in larger groups of objects to which they are harmonically tuned and joined. On the other hand, they may be constructed and charged as unique personal tools of power amplification and direction specific to an individual. When they are intended to be used by more than one person, their charge is more general. They are intended to serve many purposes for many years. Jewelry is usually extremely specific in its charge whether it is intended for personal use of for general use as a talisman of office or ritual.

WANDS

The same principles of construction apply to wands as would to talismans based on a double terminated crystal. In theory, a well-made wand behaves like a crystal composed of several different parts each having different energy qualities. The shaft and fittings of the wand create the bridge or circuitry that allows the elements to work together; binding them together in an energy complex that is whole and consistent. This shaft with its fittings also provides the physical interface for the holder of the wand to directly interact with the field created by the wand.

Wands are stones that, singularly by virtue of the size to which they have grown in nature, or combined with metals and other stones are intended to provide a directing, stabilizing, and/or amplifying function for projected energies. They may have a metal rod interposing between two stones for their length. Also, instead of a solid metal rod, a metal tube can also be used and filled with a material or series of materials that will enhance the energy properties of the piece. Crystals can be stacked end to end or with stones in between. Stones and crystals may be placed along its length and separated by spacers of inert material such as wood, animal hair or vegetable fiber. This will allow them to be positioned properly to rest under or beside the palm in which the wand is held. In some instances, it may be desirable to use wood for the shaft with stones inset along its length. Be advised that wood is a non-conductive material and this will greatly alter the way in which energy moves in and around such a wand. The practitioner would be well advised to work and experiment with many particular types of wood before choosing one over another and then use it with a particular purpose in mind rather than a general one. Oak is a good choice of wood because of its dense cellular structure, but this is up to the practitioner's discretion.

Wands may be single ended, having a single stone and the rest to the end metal. They may also be double ended, having two identical stones with interposing metal forming a metallically amplified channel that will behave like a double terminated crystal with metallic internal resonance with which the practitioner may make direct connection. Also, the primary of the rod may rest at one end and whatever qualifiers are wished may be set at the other so that the hand rests on their communicative energy path.

Some stones have grown long enough to be used as a wand in and of themselves. These can be bound with metal and set with secondary stones in the manner of the complex talismans. However, the practitioner should bear in mind that the purpose of a wand is different than that of a talisman. It is used to generate, amplify, collect, qualify and direct energy. It is an amplified extension of the practitioner's own energy field powered by his or her will and intention, rather than a personal talisman worn with the intention of tuning and adjusting the energy field complex of the body. Single stones that are used for wands should generally be longer than the palm of the active hand and should have a band of metal around the mid-point regardless of whether they are singly or doubly terminated. This allows for more complete contact through the skin and the palm of the hand.

Rods and wands are effective in circumstances where absolute specificity of direction is required for the working energy. They are good channels of focus for directing energy when setting shielded space and charging non-solid objects such as powders and liquids. It is not recommended that rods and wands be constantly handled, but rather used for a specific purposes then put aside in shielded space until needed again. The nature of their function is such that they should be fine-tuned and their balance considered delicate. Overuse or excessive handling will naturally cause them to take on too much of the signature charge of the handler that will override the purpose charge of their function. This is because they are generally intended to serve as boosted channels of pure power, changing the nature of this power according to the nature of their construction. They are direct channels of force and retain from each usage the nature of whatever energy they have channeled. For example, if a blade is used to shed blood, that blood charge will stay on it, along with the pain and death charge of the creature that is injured or slain and the emotional/mental charge of the wielder. In another example, a green crystal wand used by a Healer will become charged with a general aura of peace and healing. This will permeate it s structure to such a degree that it will retain this charge for a long time even if it passes out of continuous use and is laid aside. Scepters and staffs will rarely have this form of charge, but will take on the nature of whatever workings of power or intention the keyed user channels through it.

ORBS

By orbs, we mean those objects of ceremonial regalia that are carried by royalty. We do not mean scrying orbs - that is something entirely different. Orbs were initially intended as residing places for stored energy, of whatever nature. In Ancient Days, they were used as receptacles of information and keys of the genetic code directive. They are trappings of power and might according to Lore of the Ages. Nonetheless, care should be taken as to their tuning and use, for, whenever they are taken up, their potency is great.

BLADES

When blades are forged by the Master Smith, he puts their initial charge into them as part of the process of their making. This is the first layer of charge and it may be neither changed nor altered unless the whole blade is reforged and reformed. The second layer of the charge is done by the one who receives the blade from the smith, the one who has bought or commissioned it. This charge is more specific in nature and purpose, but it may be removed or changed as will be discussed later. The piece itself takes on a highly potent charge by virtue of its structure. When the charges are complete, the blade will sing of its own nature and resonate with the hand that wields it. It will prove to be heart of the wielder's heart and part of him or herself and will answer his or her intention even without his or her conscious will. This creation and charging process holds true in the forming of any hand held implement of power.

CLEANSING & CHARGING BLADES & OTHER METAL OBJECTS

As is discussed in their own separate section, metals, when properly tempered, are capable of taking a charge from any proper source and maintaining it to whatever certain degree it is within their separate natures to retain. When a blade or any piece of jewelry or talismanic regalia is new from the forge or has been transferred from one owner to another, it is advisable to cleanse the metal from previous charges, so that the new work will not be prejudiced to any degree. New metal, however well worked, requires this process to become initially aligned and then to take a charge properly. For this reason, the metal should be cleansed, as a crystal would be with the initial intentional heart pulse of energy that will align the fabric to a receptive state so that the initial signature charge may be placed. As the practitioner works, so specific is the cleansing charge that his own signature will be placed within it at this very same moment. The piece will then answer to his hand and calling immediately.

When stones are set within the metal, charge and cleanse the piece as one single piece - one entity - first and then proceed with the individual directives for the stones. With the softer metals - copper, bronze, silver electrum and gold - this is an easy process and the charge will quickly set for they are of a malleable nature. In the case of iron, platinum, and steel objects, cleansing may be accomplished in two ways and possibly a third depending on the intended future disposition of the blade or object. The first is as seen above with the heart pulse, while being careful to allow no other charge on the carrier wave. This will leave the piece primed and set; ready to take a charge from whomever receives it - as in the case of Warrior blades that are house talismans, but of the Lesser Class. Those intended as of the Greater Class should not have this attempted on them, for their charge is great and usually annealed within them by the Smith's song and thus their charging is part of their initial fabric and fiber. To change the charge on a Greater Talisman, the blade should be removed from all accouterments, fittings, and embellishments, retempered. The plain blade should be completely reshaped, with a new song by a smith of high and great ability to this task, so that it becomes a new thing, a further reincarnation of its entity pattern and will. Nonetheless, unless true and mightily worked, it will retain the essence of its initial charge slightly but not in any detail.

Now, there is a third way a practitioner who placed the initial charge can accomplish this. Then may he, and only he, receive the blade into his hands and draw forth from it to himself in one great breath all that which he has placed into it. This is possible for some to do who are aware of the nature of the blade's charge, for this is in the nature of the steel to pour forth its power to its master. This process will almost surely result in some degree of shock to the practitioner unless he has prepared himself with the greatest discipline and care beforehand. He must take the weight of the full force of the charge all at once, no matter how benign its nature or intent. This he must immediately ground fully and without retention of any part, and he must pour forth this charge into another object whether large stone, place, dwelling or body of water but NEVER into another person.

When the energy has been taken and then discharged, the participants should rebalance and center themselves so that all possible residuals be taken and distributively balanced. However, if this is not possible, the master should immediately pass the blade out of his keeping sheathed in leather or, preferably, silk. In this way, it will remain in this nullified and receptive state until recharged by the one destined to receive it.

Nothing whatsoever can be done to alter the fact that the blade has been charged at one time. The crystalline structure will remain in readied alignment and will immediately become recharged by whatever or whomever it next encounters. The master should then, after this procedure is complete, not attempt further work until the residual charge has become balanced and his system has renewed itself to its accustomed health as he was before this operation was done.

CHARGING A MASTER BLADE

We will speak now concerning the process of singing the charge. The true sword of a Master must be made by a Master. His hand alone shall be on the blade. Every lace and fitment must be crafted by that one hand alone. Let him chose the metal himself from the foundry and let the forge be kindled by him alone, first from the Earth's fire and from the fire of his spirit. The bellows should be turned by one who is not only of his blood, but of his spirit as well. If his assistant is his child, this assistant should be of the same sex, whether the Master is male or female. Otherwise, both Master and assistant shall be two who dance together as one - male and female together a pair of the true union. If the Master is childless, a woman of his heart may turn the bellows, or one who is the son of his true spirit. Father and daughter or mother and son should not work together as one in this endeavor, for they are too close kin and the polarity and nature of the bond between them will nullify the charge.

They should know that the blade they forge will be that of a Master or a Great House. They should prepare their will and intention to this resonance and their spirits to this enterprise. As the metal of the blade is formed, the Blade Smith should sing the song of this purpose. In this way, he will he pour forth his spirit to this blade. Let the energy flow forth from his hand into his hammer and into the blade itself. Let him send this along its full dimension with the song of its purpose and the song of its truth and strength. Thus, the first charge is placed into its fiber that no one will deny or transgress against in its use.

The second charge is placed as it is first honed and shaped before it is fitted, so that it will carry its charge to the very edge. This should be a song of love and blessing of the settling to its true purpose and balance and of the one who is to receive it, but let that one neither see nor touch it yet.

Then the fittings should be cast or formed, both pommel and crossguard, in the same pouring from the same crucible along with whatever pins and rivets are necessary. They should be tuned and sung to in the finishing with the song of trust and virtue for the blade to stay in the grasp of its wielder and transfer its strength to him smoothly and surely. Let the charge also be sung to these fittings that, although they are of different metal, they will be in harmony and contributive to the song of the blade itself. When they are finished and fitted to the blade they will all sing one song.

The third charge should be done when the fittings are placed. Hilt, pommel, guards and the like, and all those embellishments that are fitted after the blade is placed in the handle such as stones, chasing, and the wrappings of the handle itself, if this is appropriate. The fashioning of the sheath and its fittings as well should be charged in this same manner at this time. (Unless the mate of the one who wields it is to make this sheath.) All these should be done by the hand of the Smith himself or of his apprentice or assistant as has been previously explained above. Each element should be chosen to enhance the true purpose of the blade and be in balance with its specific charge and nature. Then the final song of its making should be sung into it. That is the song of its completion, the song of the Smith's love for it and his pride. It is the song of its going from him as a child goes from its home at last to seek its destiny in the greater world. He should sing of those things that are to come, of the one who has commissioned it to be made, and of its purpose in serving him and his line. He should also sing of the genetic code of the line into which it passes and of the deeds done by this house and line.

After these things are accomplished, its intended owner should be notified and sent for. When he comes, the last of the Smith's charges will be accomplished. The Smith alone should do this. Only he can release this blade of power, for up until this time it has been his alone as a child is its mother's charge and under her guidance until the child comes of age. Then the Smith should, place the blade into the hand of the new owner, and with one surge of the heart chakra through his hands, bind all these previous charges to the hand of the receiver. Then the blade's purpose and virtue will pass entirely to the man who is to wield it.

The new owner will then take up the blade. As he does so he should lower all shielding around his spirit and person for this moment and receive into his deepest heart all that which the Smith passes over to him. Then he will echo and sound forth this new song within him with the heart pulse of his love and acceptance for it and his recognition that it will be his companion and defender in many worlds for the course of his days. In addition, should it be so desired, this charge may also be passed on to whoever inherits the sword should this owner leave his body. This may be done in the same way as the Smith has passed it over. Alternatively, it may be that this passage is not possible should death come by misadventure. Then the charge may be discovered by the deep reading of the blade by a Seer or by the one that finds or receives it. The blade's complete charge and history should be accepted and assimilated by the new owner.

WEARING BLADES

It is the nature of the human structural form and the function the blades are intended to serve that large blades are generally worn from a belt around the hips or across the shoulders. This causes them to intersect the fields of either the basal or heart chakra. Bear this closely in mind. Metal blades have the ability to take, sustain, and conduct a charge. This occurs because of the nature of the metal and the way they were charged when they were forged. The charged implement will strongly influence the energy of the base chakra that is the source of the life energy or the heart chakra that is the hub of the expression of the energy of the body. The charge nature of steel is very strong and more so depending on the quality of that steel and the energy of whatever fittings are on the piece. It is important for the Warrior to rest and pursue more gentle arts, so that the power of the blade will not consume him. Read well the listing regarding steel and iron so that full understanding can be achieved before working with blades as implements of power.

In the case of scepters and similar artifacts, this is not so very crucial, for they are not worn on the body nor generally carried for extended periods. Staffs, although they may be carried for extended periods, do not continually intersect the major energy centers but extend outwards from the hands. They are usually carried for ritual purposes only and thus their placement about the person is not significant except in the specific instance of their use. Consider, though, that in their initial construction there is usually one gem that is set to carry one specific charge that is different from all the others.

CUPS, VESSELS, & LAMPS

The third classification of talismans is that of ritually charged objects such as cups, vessels, boxes, and lamps, made of metal, stone, or a combination of both. They are intended to contain substances or other objects either for the purpose of charging their contents or for protecting and shielding the charge that is already on those contents. In the case of cups (or any container intended to hold and serve food or drink), the charge on the vessel is transferred to the contents to enhance the nature of what is intended to be ingested. This may prove a potent additive and great help in the course of healing as with water or medication for cooling fevers or washing wounds. This principle can be extended to massage oil containers, or as with water or oil in the ritual preparation, anointing and bathing of seers, participants, and initiates.

The principles involved in making and charging containers is fundamentally the same as those involved with any article capable of taking a charged energy field. The energy fields generated by the atomic structure of matter, particularly stones, have already been discussed. We know that, although a complete crystal is optimal for workings of power, even the smallest piece or shard may serve in a similar capacity. Even a small piece of a stone has the same atomic structure, and therefore, energy characteristics, if not the intensity and focus of a complete crystal. At times, it may be necessary or desirable to use these properties to influence things other than the human energy system complex. Objects of all kinds may be fashioned to serve these functions. As an example, one may wish to transfer this energy to food or drink so that the virtue of the charged stone imparts or enhances a specific virtue of the food. A stone container may be made to hold this food. Then the stone is charged which will then act as a focus or driver that will then charge the contents. Examples of this process can be seen in two particular cups used for ritual purposes.

THE DREAMER'S CUP

The Dreamer's Cup is a standing cup of dark blue chalcedony (siderite) or, less preferably, sodalite with veins of white running through it. On one side or on the stem, if it is desired, shall be the form of a woman so that its function will be known. The female figure has long been used as the symbol of the soul of man, being symbolic of the intuitive aspect of his nature. She is also symbolic of the Mother Goddess who guards all the dark reaches of the otherworld, for in many cultures these other realms and levels were thought to be within the womb of the Great Mother. In addition, the individuals who have used this vessel have most often been female and the presiding Priest male so that the polarity balance would be maintained. As a further note on this procedure, if the Seer should be male, then the presiding official should be female to maintain the whole helix of the action. This will allow the Seer to have his or her energies balanced and renewed in the most harmonious manner.

The priest should cleanse the cup, drawing from the united energy of the company, and then fill it with wine. He should then charge both cup and wine with his intention and the intonation of his voice to the purpose of the Dreamer's Quest. He should then hold it for the Dreamer to drink, the Dreamer touching it only with her lips. This will allow her to go forth from her body to her purpose, and return unharmed with clear recollection of her experience and vision. When she has returned, the Dreamer should drink from it again. This time it should contain a mixture of honey and herbs to invigorate her body and clarify her mind. This mixture should be charged in the same manner as before, but this time to the purpose of her clarity and health.

This cup may be used by many Dreamers, but should only be charged by one Priest as his signature charge is on it. Should another wish to use it, it must be fully discharged and made void or it will not answer rightly and the desired purpose not be accomplished.

THE CUP OF JOINING

The Cup of Joining is used when individuals come together to swear the bond of their union. The priest should take a standing cup carved from white alabaster or chalcedony and into it pour red wine. Then, saying no words, he should place the cup into the hands of the couple for them to charge together. They should charge the cups and its contents with nothing else but the nature of their love and bond at that moment. Then first one then the other should drink from it, both having their hands still on it, until the last drop is drained from it. Thus, they shall be joined inseparably. They should keep the cup and use it to no other purpose than to pledge and renew this bond when needed or desired.

BOXES & STORAGE CONTAINERS

The same principle that applies to charging food and liquids can also be applied to solids objects. Any object placed in a charged container can be infused with the energy of that charge if the atomic/molecular structure of the object is such that it is capable of taking a charge. There is also the practice of storing articles of power in special containers that will preserve the charge on an object or defend it against casual or intentional interference from outside energies. To accomplish this, a box or container of some appropriate stone can be charged while empty. The practitioner may then place within it whatever is desirable in keeping with the function of the piece.

The charge of boxes and containers should be refreshed and reinforced from time to time. They do not have the specific personal contact as vessels do and may therefore, especially when they are new, dissipate or generalize their charge. This should be monitored until the charge is satisfactorily stabilized.

LAMPS & BRAZIERS

The great and subtle benefit of using stone lamps or candleholders is often ignored. Lamps may burn with perfumed oil that dissipate their fragrance in the course of burning. Lamps also produce heat and light that cause vibrational effects to the oil contained in them. The vibrational field of many types of stone is enhanced when the stone is heated. It is, therefore, possible to place a charge on the objects that is only operant when heat and light activate it. The charge in the oil will be dispersed throughout the area along with their light and the scent of their oil. Because of this virtue, in ancient times, healing lamps were lit in the resting-places of the sick. This allowed their subtle virtue to permeate the air and add their energies to strengthen the weakened spirit and body. The same principle may be applied to censors and braziers, that is, vessels for the burning of incense. Braziers for incense may also be used in this fashion, although in this instance the charge is placed on the metal, most stone being unsuitable for the heavy load of intense heat from burning charcoal. Candles can work in much the same manner if made and used properly. This can be a great enhancement to aromatherapy techniques.

SCRYING MIRRORS & BOWLS

The making and function of scrying mirrors and bowls are similar. These are objects with highly polished reflective surfaces often intended also to contain a small amount of liquid such as water or wine. These objects are generally designed to be held in the hands or to be in contact with the body during the process of the work. The general principle behind their function is that the hands of the Seer will activate the charge on the bowl or mirror and in turn charge the liquid. The reflective nature of the surface will assist the Seer in attaining a trance state that will enable her or him to view things at a distance in either time or space. Such objects are generally understood to be the property and tool of one particular person and it is not recommended that they be shared by more than one Seer at a time. When not in use, they should be kept in a box or container designed for the protection and enhancement of their charge. In this way, the power and nature of their charge will grow and be consistently reinforced.

ARMOR

Let us now discuss those objects referred to as Armor. They may serve a dual purpose: first, that of shielding the body from physical harm, and, second, that of channeling and directing energy and the flow of the raised Warrior Chi as armor of a psychic nature. A derivative of armor is manifested in the form of the accoutrements of the male Dancer whether he dances alone or in the company of the female and should be the key to his own energy of the Great Dance. They should be formed of iron, steel, brass, bronze, or copper in that order of preference. The terms brass and bronze are used interchangeably in this context. The most optimal metal for Dancing regalia is bronze inlaid with copper, silver or copper and silver combined. This inlay should take the form of tracing the currents of the body's energy. It should serve as a connection between and among the various stones set thereon. It acts as wires in a current of electricity to distribute and blend the variant energy forms from the stones, centering on the various energy nodes of the Dancer's body.

The following is a description of the Warrior's ceremonial armor derived from ancient sources. It is an excellent example of the way in which armor can serve the energy system complex:

The various elements for the arming are as follows: The breast and back plates should be solid and connected to each other by means of pins and hinges at the shoulders and adjustable metal buckles and straps at the sides, thus forming one single piece without break. They should have the tracing of the inlaid metals on the front rising from the solar plexus center and upwards to the heart, outward from the heart and flowing towards the shoulders in spirals. In the major spirals, stones should be set in the following groupings: ruby balanced by green garnets, brilliant orange citrine above the heart surrounded with topaz, droplets of citrine and carnelian proceeding towards the belly point down, flanked with rubies and topaz alternately. Over this piece, the gorget should be formed as a wide collar across both back and front and with a high collar. Just below the throat kill point, a ruby surrounded by emeralds or green garnets should be placed with the pattern proceeding outward with topaz drops toward the shoulder points and all traced with inlaid patterns of silver and copper. The shoulder paldrens should be of the type that flare high above the shoulders and are attached to the breast plate by means of pins and small chains. These should be connected to the upper arm vambraces by rings and pins. These upper arm vambraces should be traced with silver and copper, and the medallion of rubies, topaz, and citrine repeated. This should be done on the lower arm vambraces as well. However, those on the lower arms should be hinged and pinned to form one solid piece. They need not be connected to the upper arm pieces except by small chains at the elbows to keep the upper arms from flopping about.

On his brow should be a band of bronze set with a single large citrine and flanked with a smaller topaz on each side. The helm should be of the common conical variety with a hinged section across the neck and several sections of small plates ringed together across the throat. Be certain that these are medallions of stone at the brow and on the pieces that cover the temples. This is very important.

The plates that cover the lower legs should match the upper arm vambraces with medallions to correspond, and should connect to the tops of the foot plates that cover the sandals. There should also be a leather skirt that covers the buttocks and upper legs. This skirt should be split as shown and each split tipped with a metal medallion of the same metal and design as the breastplate but without stones. Thus attired shall he go forth to war, and in each point of the placing and usage of stones this shall correspond to the regalia of his female counterpart.

When dancing the Dance of Great Power, the Warrior should be attired in the gorget and shoulder paldrens, in the brow band, but not the helm, and from the band his temples should be covered with medallions set with stones of citrine, topaz, and green garnets. About his waist should be a hinged metal belt with inlaid medallions of stones front and back. His dancing sandals should be set with medallions across. Medallions on the knees should be connected to the sandal tops by fine chains. He should dance with his talisman sword in his dominant (right) hand and a bowl of fire in the recessive (left) hand.

MASKS	The Dancers' masks correspond to the faceplate for the Warrior's helm. These are later additions to the regalia and are unnecessary when the proper headdresses are

worn. They serve in the energy flow around the head. They should be inlaid with metal, set with stones at the brow, and attached to the head by means of a metal band. The only purpose of power they are known to serve is that of taking on a Primal Aspect as has been done since Ancient Times to take on the characteristics or raise the internal image of the Gods. In truth, this procedure is intended to raise one primal chakra center above all others to manifest the aspects of this energy above all others in a ritual situation, and personify it through the archetype of its resonant energy form. Let this not be done overmuch or without circumspection or true ritual preparation of the celebrant participants. This is the greatest talent of the Temple Dancers and a greatly varied range and intensity of power may be raised by this. It should not be attempted by the uninitiated or the Unchosen.

Masks are usually accompanied by elaborate headdresses and pectoral collars, because they help raise and distribute this power into manifestation through them. They also physically counterbalance one another so that they may be worn comfortably throughout a wide range of movements. Pectoral collars serve the same function as the gorget in armor but do not need to have a high collar and may therefore be used interchangeably as the comfort of the Dancers and the situation warrants. Their function is to distribute the power from the heart and throat in a concentrated flow outward to the shoulders where it is manifested as wings of fire. The counterpoise of a pectoral collar should center on the back at the heart level. These collars act as the counterbalance to the girdle worn about the hips. If they are set with harmoniously chosen and tuned stone combinations, this can work extremely well.

In the present time, masks can channel a great deal of power, particularly when they are charged to assist the wearer to take on an aspect of personality or energy. This can be of a person, animal, or energy archetype that the group wishes to include in the energy manifestations of a ritual or ceremony of power. The individual or individuals doing such work in the masks should be closely watched and supervised to make certain that they are not overtaken altogether by the force of the alternative identity energy. This can be a function of the Leader of the group or of the Solitary One, whichever is decided to be suitable given the larger context of the work. The preparation is very much like that for a Seer, and once the wearer of the mask has completed the ritual function, he, she or they should go through grounding and centering meditations before continuing with further work. It can be extremely taxing on many levels to take on such an aspect and care should be taken that this does not compromise the individuality of the participants.

TALISMANS OF NOBLE HOUSES

We have mentioned Noble Houses, their artifacts and heirlooms, but to fully understand these objects and their charging, it is necessary to digress somewhat and discuss the energy constructs involved. A noble or royal house can be defined as: the vibration of a group of individuals who only reincarnate for certain Karmic purposes within certain vibrational parameters resident in the energy helix of the DNA. The key point here is that this includes only a limited number of particular individuals. The energy helix that includes them is wide enough in band wave to permit a certain amount of variance, but is specifically limited to admit only these few.

There are times when individuals are incarnated many times into one genetic lineage because they have a specific purpose within that framework, a specific job to do concerning the people they rule or the landmass they govern. Long ago, they were taught and trained that the focus of this guardianship was resident in certain artifacts of various natures that may have now been forgotten and may not even still exist on this plane. Objects such as signet rings have stones that are the focus of specific active power of the leaders of these lines. These stones are set to aid, enhance, and balance the interactive energies of these individuals in their activity of shepherding the destinies of groups, peoples, and nations.

Occasionally, individuals may be born into a line of inheritance that are there for other karmic reasons and do not know of these talismans nor can they use them. The talismans are tuned to certain individual frequencies that are now out of the range of the inheritors, and thus these objects are lost or forgotten until another individual arises that has the ability to key the energy in them.

This may also be keyed to time cycles or keyed to respond when levels of energy are intensified or altered in some way. This is the origin of legends in many nations of certain talismans becoming known only in times when the destiny of a people is in contest. Note the tales of the Grail and the Sword Excalibur linked to legends concerning the return of Arthur or Bran the Blessed - the avatars of the Cup of Life and the Sword of Will and the Defender. Minor noble houses may also have such talismans of greater or lesser antiquity and power, such as rings, pendants, and badges of hereditary office.

Let us clarify and expand on the interactive energy helixes of the body and how they interact to causal purpose. This is the actual mechanism by which Karma is implemented and is a principle of great importance in the mastery of its effect. Each physical body, being generated from the Life of All Things, creates its own field and this is codified in its signature pattern by the genetic structure. In addition, each Spirit is known in this plane by its signature energy construct. When Spirit enters Matter, these two energy patterns interact with one another forming a vibration that is a harmonic of both, and becomes unique and distinct. As either Spirit or Flesh is affected by events, the vibratory pattern is directly affected. The pattern is changed accordingly as the harmonic is altered. In this way, memory codes are built up and transferred from one lifetime to the next. This is because incidents of sufficient intensity are strong enough to alter in some ways the energy patterns of the Spirit in its peripheral modes. First, Spirit is recognized by the unique key signature patterns and then by its secondary or peripheral manifestations and modulations of that key pattern. These interact and are affected by the patterns of the physical body. These code alterations may occur by happenstance or by causal determinism; and it is this later case that is of issue here.

Vibration may be altered for this purpose by pain or desire, whether an individual places this on itself or it is placed on him by another. Individuals may use this mechanism to suit their own desired ends by causatively conforming their patterns within specific genetic codes, or interactionary vibrational codes. Therefore, it is with noble hereditary houses, that knowing that memory may not always serve, to decide that their purposes must be accomplished perpetually. To accomplish this they can causally link their personal patterns to genetic patterns so that their intentions will be fulfilled and that part of their consciousness will be triggered by this planned interaction only when it is time. Even unwittingly after centuries, part of that spirit will be resident in genetic codes, so that these spirits will hunger to be reunited with that resonance that is most pleasing. The resonance brings about the strongest feeling of wholeness and strength. So it is with royal houses, and with kindred kind who, not wishing to abandon one another, join in this manner by their own desire to accomplish a mutual purpose, so that one or another should not be left behind. They bind themselves purposely to one another and only by their intentional conscious union do certain peripheral patterns form and develop that are the "Memories" of their purpose and intent along with the tools for its accomplishment. Stones as well, when set in artifacts, may cause this interaction with spirit, as with the crown of a king, or his regalia of estate, so that when he attains this office he will take

them up under certain special conditions. This occurs in coronation proceedings, when their qualities trigger in his spirit the knowledge of his
ancient purpose that otherwise he may not have the capacity to consciously
recall.

This is the stone keyed to a specific wave band class of a noble house,
ruling, or a priestly line.

It is said by the ignorant that, should heirlooms of a noble house or artifacts of priests be stolen or attempted to be used to purposes contrary to
their initial charge then they shall bring "bad luck" to the thief. These
pieces are intended to have their final key charge transferred by means
of specific ritual or initiation, and if this is not rightly done then the piece
will function wrongly in unready hands. However, this technique has
gone out of practice and contemporary ritual objects rarely have this
quality built in unless, by some twist of accident or fate or destiny, an
ancient gem is set in the piece, and then this charge continues. In their
construction, these objects follow the same rules as all other lesser talisman types and are used accordingly.

PART 2

STONE FAMILIES AND TYPES

The next step in our study is to examine the great gemstone crystal families as they pertain to the energy centers of the body. We have previously mentioned that each of the chakra centers has a corresponding crystal family whose energy lattice structure parallels the vibration harmonic of the chakra center. We are speaking here of the key signature pattern of the crystal family. Each great crystal family is typified by a characteristic axis pattern in its structure. The vibrational pattern of this lattice is unique to that family and it is what gives the crystal and all stones cut from the crystal its distinctive nature. As we also explained in the section on colored stones, the color of the stone is produced by the addition of certain atoms or molecules of different material that are introduced in a regular way into the crystal lattice itself. They become part of the crystalline structure itself and have a direct bearing on the vibrational frequency pattern of the crystal but not to the degree that they change its basic nature. To a great degree, the exterior shape of the crystal is the shape of the atomic *lattice* from which it is built. As atoms are added to produce color they change the refraction of the crystal, that is, the way in which light is changed as it passes through it, but they do not change the basic structure of the crystal. In each family there is one above all others whose color harmonizes ideally with the harmonic nature of that family. We will call this the principle of the family.

Many different atoms and groups of atoms may be able to bond to form a crystalline structure. This results in crystal families that may have members of many different colors. Some of the crystals may even have more than one color present. Then the crystal will have the basic nature of the family while applying to the specific energy resonance of the center corresponding to the color vibration. As with families of animals and plants, many crystal families have a variety of branches and sub-branches leading to members that bear small resemblance to the principle crystal structure at the top of the tree. Beneath their structure, however, their basic atomic structure will be that of the principle. You should keep this in mind when dealing with the properties of all stones. It is necessary to understand the nature of the family to understand the nature of the individual members.

Some crystals grow under the same combination of circumstances as others. One growth medium containing many different elements can produce several different kinds of stones and crystals. This will result in the crystals and minerals being found together either, mixed together like the colors in agates or as inclusions and rutilations. Because they are formed together and under the same geologic conditions, they are harmoniously compatible with one another and when their energies are brought together, they make uniquely powerful combinations. As for the activities of the stones, as we have stated elsewhere, it is not our purpose here to discuss the activity of every stone possible within the Earth's geology. We intend to give guidelines to the major stone families so that the practitioner can have a working basis of information to then increase his or her experience with a variety of crystals and stones. We would also like to point out that the stones behave in characteristic ways because of the nature of the elements of which they are composed. It is possible to draw basic generalities about the behavior of a stone by examining the behavior characteristics of its elements. These elements act not simply on one chakra or another, but on the pathways that connect the chakras. They also act in a multidimensional way by reacting with the four levels of energy bodies of which any sentient individual on Earth is composed. The crystals and stones will act to connect and resonate with one or more of these bodies to encourage a three-dimensional harmony within the person's energy field complex. This is always very important to consider when working with stones. It is misleading to say that, while one stone will raise an individual's higher awareness, another will help sexual energy. This is too limiting a viewpoint. The individual is a complex harmonic of all four levels of awareness working together. Each level of awareness - physical, emotional, mental, and spiritual - has a manifestation in one or more of the chakras. It is the balancing of this multi-level harmonic that is the true basis of healing.

ARTIFICIALLY COLORED AND SYNTHETIC STONES

Before beginning with a description of the major stone types, we should mention those crystals that are grown by man. There is no true harm in these stones, unlike those altered by force. But we should point out that these copies do not hold the range of power specifics resident in their natural counterparts. They have not had the benefit of the variety of forces and stresses and information resident in the way of nature and, therefore, are not complete. The strength of a stone's nature rests in its subtle diversity. Just as people are not all alike, not all crystals are alike although they are superficially similar. Therefore, in the process of growth those things that bond best together seed each other and the bonding, while varied, is stronger for this fact. Those stones that are artificially grown do not have this strength, having been formed with unnatural speed without regard to natural combinations and selections. They may be used in workings of power, but only in those positions that do not require the full spectrum strength of a stone. They may be used as tokens as all facsimiles may serve as tokens but they are not "real" as they are not naturally formed and are not truly formed integrally within the Earth's energy field nor according to its laws.

Artificial stones can be pleasant to own and useful as mnemonic devices. They may add accents of subtle energy to whatever piece they are placed upon, but they should not be given the full weight of a charge. They have less strength and dimension than a natural stone of the same kind. For as it is a human being who is a natural product of this planet who charges the stone, then the stone should also be a product of that system. In this way, the basic energy currents will be compatible. Their energies, when well matched, will be harmonious together.

This may be held true of all stones that have been altered from their true nature by artificial processes. Stones that have been subjected to radiation, excessive heat, and electricity sufficient to markedly alter their coloration have been altered from their natures to such a degree that their power value is negligible except in the hands of those barely aware. Their emanations may serve in some small level, but not for any great or intense work. Care should be taken in the examination of these stones, for on the surface they will appear to have some specific virtue, but their depths are destroyed and will hold for a short time then fail, giving forth unpleasant and sometimes harmful feedback. To the students who are unfamiliar with the work, this feedback may even be mistaken for some form of energy output, but it will be of no use and will serve to ultimately harm the user.

QUARTZ
SILICON DIOXIDE (SiO_2)
CHAKRA: FULL HELIX
CALLING: ALL
ARCHETYPE COLOR: CLEAR AND VIOLET

One of the largest and most diverse crystal families is Quartz. The name quartz is often used as a synonym for crystal in many cases and with some reason, for this is the most common of crystalline formations and the one most closely attuned in signature to the Earth's vibration. This stone may be considered the "work horse" of all stones because its energies can be easily attuned to virtually any energy pattern and level, along with being able to maintain that tuning and load level reliably until causatively altered, regardless of length of time usage and load level. Its energies are readily and equably qualified by any of the range of opalescents (silicon based) and work in harmony with any other stone to provide not only a focus driver, but also a white/rainbow energy booster regardless of combination.

This family includes both macrocrystalline and microcrystalline varieties and sub-families. Macrocrystalline is defined as those stones formed as a whole crystal, and microcrystalline as microscopic crystals fitted together to form a larger piece that to the naked eye exhibit the characteristic crystal shape.

Quartz will focus, boost, and drive naturally according to its nature. It is in this function that one should be aware of the wearer's disciplines. When anyone takes up a tool of this flexibility, that individual should practice discipline and clarity of focus in all levels of his or her awareness. It will manifest a full spectrum radiance in its focus to distribute from and across the full band resonance, energizing and driving wherever the intention is placed. It is, in this respect, a teaching stone and will open the perceptions of self-awareness. This is a great tool to help in the journey for those who are reaching outward to expand their spirits and return to the Universal Whole.

Wear it in any position; set it in any metal to intensify the work intended. It is especially compatible with tourmaline and aquamarine and any other stone found in nature within its matrix.

Quartz in colors, save for the brown or smoky, is unsteady for higher power working as the colored inclusions do not hold as well as the clear base that carries them. Children may use all the colors and also the clear, for it amplifies their brightness and charms them greatly to their great benefit. Quartz is also compatible with the nature of their energy field being not too specific, and will allow them the space and flexibility of growth and awareness.

WHITE

White Quartz is often underestimated. Its structure is greatly variable in its continuity because the white color is caused by anomalies in the structure prevent it from appearing clear. As is the nature of white, it holds the qualities of all colors within itself and, with certain intentions, releases these energies gradually and gently, acting as a stabilizer in long-term working. White quartz may generally be regarded as the interim form between crystalline quartz and chalcedony, for it has the energy and power focus potential of quartz having a crystalline structure and the dispersive energizing/grounding function of chalcedony.

It may be used well as an altar stone. It is extremely beneficial for children who have been born with the Gift but have not yet come consciously into the knowledge of its working. It will mediate their energies and act as both focus and strong calmative. It integrates the power centers gently and allows them to grow straight in quiet harmony with one another until the Gift wakens to its fullest potential. It may also be worn by those sorely tried and, thus, fatigued or harmed in the workings of power, because it assists in their convalescence and brings them slowly into balance again while soothing their pain. It is well placed in herb gardens and at the feet of trees in Sacred Grove that their systems will be graciously energized.

Do not rely on it for courses of great power, for this is not its nature nor virtue. The anomalies that dictate its slow and patient nature will greatly impair and, at last, destroy it if too great a load is placed on it for too long. Yet, where it is found as the base of other crystals that are clear at their termination, it provides a good measured release of energy from the base plate and greatly augments their functions. However, consider carefully its nature and limitations in this. White quartz should not be used for any major works of power unless its part in that work is a minor or subsidiary one, and the majority of the power load is assumed by other stones or a more appropriate nature. Used outside of its sphere it will prove of great detriment to the purpose of the piece, but used within its scope it will be of greatest virtue indeed.

SMOKY & BLACK (MORION)

Smoky quartz gives peace by its grounding nature, for it acts as a filter to all vibrations. Should the piece be clear at the base, it focuses and draws in the nature of clear stones throughout the spectrum and then projects these many energies through the smoky termination, filtering and grounding them. Should the stone be smoky at the base and clearing toward the tip, it projects only those energies that have been filtered and cleared through the spectrum focus and acts as a piece with a clear driver built in to it and acts with great strength. All smoky, brown and naturally black stones act in this manner automatically once this charge is set.

Remember that for any true virtue to come of the piece, it must be activated to the wearer's signature pattern alone. It should not be keyed, as with other healing stones, first to the patterns of the practitioner and then to the wearer's under his guidance. It should be tuned to the wearer's pattern alone, for in these activities it is of the greatest importance that it act in response to the wearer's needs specifically. It may be charged by the healer first, but only energized and not patterned, it will then take on the pattern of the one who wears it and has need of its virtue.

It is of great virtue as a qualifier to all clear stones, particularly when used by beginners because it can filter out inconsistencies of their work and stabilize their intent. Do not give this stone to children for extended periods of time, for their true patterns are, as yet, unformed and for them to wear this at so early an age will unnaturally force their patterns into lower levels than are healthy for them to bear. It may be used briefly to soothe transient conditions such as the agitation accompanying fever and the like, but in extended cases, it is not the best choice for a child's healing or calmative stone.

As with anything that is powerful, it should be used circumspectly and with respect for its strength and nature. It may be a great help to the healer to automatically filter and soothe vibrations that surround him or her in the process of the work. It will act automatically, once set and tuned, and will free the healer's attention and energies to the immediate demands of the work. It may be used by the Seer to remove all personal signature traces from what would be seen and translated, but use it only for this specific work. Remember that the Seer must be reinforced in general life with the pattern of his or her own personality. His or her Gift is a treasure, but also is his or her identity and must be cultivated as a tender plant. In this activity, refer also to the section on Talisman of the Seer and also to those Talismans specifically described to other Callings.

RED

Red quartz is rarely found but may be used in place of ruby in women and children who require its virtue, but have not yet found the warrior's heart in themselves. Be advised its nature is subtle and easily mistaken for being less powerful than it truly is. In this place and time, this type of quartz is often called "Pecos Diamond" for the location where it is most often found.

In recent years certain crystals have been found that are being called Red Phantoms. It is important to mention these at this time because they have come into the sphere of humankind as a particular tool to help on many levels. Their influence will first be noticed on a physical level, because they will stimulate the physical energy system in a general way, resulting in a feeling of increasing vitality and endurance. This can be extremely helpful to persons doing a great deal of psychic work or healing on a psychic level. It will regenerate and strengthen their personal energy systems within the physical body. But more importantly, the red phantom will assist the individual on a cellular level, strengthening the energy capsules that surround the cells themselves. This will strengthen the individual's immune system and resistance to physical degeneration.

The farther reaching ramification of this is that this energy field will be strengthened to integrate with the other energy levels of the body so that they will be encouraged to work in unison, vitalizing the individual on all levels of awareness. Once this strength has been established, it is far easier for other, more subtle work to come in behind it and make the desired changes. It will help the individual relate on a more positive instinctual level by sensitizing the energy fields so that they are more responsive to interaction with other energy complexes.

It will help the individual in communication on many levels because it will energize the energy connections that unify the subtle bodies. This stone can be used by the practitioner to restore energies and strengths expended in the course of the work. The practitioner can also use this on those who are being worked with to strengthen all energy fields in the process of the work. This stone draws from the earth energy and consequently corresponds to the vibration of the lower chakra. We do not advise that it be worn constantly, but rather be used as a healing tool or focus for meditation, or kept near an individual in the course of the work rather than worn. Meditation with it - whether by conscious journeying within it or by holding it in the course of other meditation work - can be extremely effective and beneficial.

ROSE

Rose quartz may be known as the raiser of passions of a primal nature and a soothing and healing influence on the heart. Its color is often caused by the inclusion of manganese. Manganese is an element that stimulates the resonance of the heart chakra. Wherever it is found, you will find that, although the color of the stone may indicate connection with another center, the energy of the stone will be closely linked with the warmth and healing of the heart resonance. It rarely occurs in distinctly formed crystals but is more often found in microcrystalline formations.

This is a stone of a primal nature and is most strong in its beneficent life force. It is beneficial as a restorative for the individual's sexuality because it helps revitalize the channels between the base chakra and the heart, and by doing so encourages a balance in feelings and perspective. This is an activity that takes place also between the physical body energy complex and that of the emotional body. This activity should be closely observed. This may be used to call the base energy and raise those from sorrow who no longer have any need for that sorrow. It encourages an individual toward self-esteem and helps reforge the links with life and joy that have been damaged by emotional neglect or abuse.

Its activity will be distributed generally across the complete energy field, because it is quartz. In its furthest extrapolations, the rose quartz can be used as a key to the Great Flow and can tap this energy into the entire being or simply the base channel, however the practitioner may seek to guide it.

Take care that its color is rich if true spectrum rose is desired, for as the color is faded or pale, its influence is diluted and narrowed. This is often overlooked and thus the stone is often thought weak, or merely a love stone. It may, indeed, be such a token and, given between lovers in token of their pledge, it can serve as a vibrant bond between them. It may be well used as a marriage stone, for often this is the nature of their bond. Remember, however, that its sovereignty is far greater and that when rightly used it may enliven even the saddest of creatures. Let this also be noted that the practitioner should be aware that the working of this stone entails a bond of great energy and the unwary practitioner has been known to become entrapped in his own workings through this power and chakra.

Set this in silver that it should work subtly or in gold that it should work joyfully. Set it in copper that it should honor the Lady but then only let it be accompanied by green stones that its influence be mollified, for the copper drives it too strongly when left alone to itself.

ORANGE (CITRINE)

Citrine carries the gladness of the Primal Sun in which the earliest men rejoiced. This is laughter from the heart; this is safety from the troubles of the darkness. This is the torch in the hand for safety and light on a dark journey. This is the fierce brave heart of the lion and will be on the breast of the Warrior for his true courage. Citrine is the spirit twin of carnelian, the sun-bright chalcedony, but has the more powerful nature in that it is one whole crystal and has always a white or clear base.

If a small child should be troubled by nightmares and fears of the darkness, let him be given a citrine. It should be white at the base then some clear then golden bright orange. Let it be hung around his neck at such a level that he may easily look upon it should he so desire that the gladness of the stone will fill him. And at the giving let this tale be told:

The Tale of the Golden Lion

In the earliest of times and most ancient of days, when the world first began there lived within the sun a great golden lion with wings of fire. Each day the lion flew above the earth and with his bright passage he drove away the demons of darkness that troubled the children of men. But as the earth was round the darkness followed behind him, and the demons troubled the children in the darkness. When the great lion heard their cries he saw their need and from his heart took pieces of his light and fire and placed them in the earth. These became the citrine and they dwell beneath the earth. Now, even in the darkness when the lion flies to the other side of the earth his fire may be seen to drive away the demons and their evil. And around our necks and within our hands we may hold his light and have his bright courage always with us.

GREEN

The ancient texts speak of two types of Green Quartz that occur commonly as crystals. The first is quartz with chlorite inclusions and the second is green citrine

Chlorite inclusions in quartz render the crystal singularly powerful for drawing energies from the immediate currents of energy most closely allied with the physical plane. This is not to imply that they are limited to physical earth energy. Rather, they embody a combination of energies that are available through the medium of the quartz that surrounds them to be accessed by the wearer. This combination of subtle energies provides an easily accessible field for use as restoration, balancing, and protecting the individual. It is as though the wearer was drawing around his or her space all the surrounding energy for his or her assistance. Because the energies are part of the continuity of the wearer's immediate envi-

ronment, they are not only easily accessed but constantly and automatically renewed - both these qualities making the process feel virtually
weightless and effortless.

Such a crystal can integrate with the life energies of the wearer and provide a talisman of singular value on many levels of that individual's life
and work. These crystals can provide an extremely powerful buffer against
negativity in the environment because they are tuned to the prevailing
harmony and balance of the Earth systems energy complex. They are
effective whether this negativity comes in the form of intentional destructive intent sent at the wearer, or general ill will and negativity generated in the wearer's vicinity. This buffer is active on all levels to which
the wearer may travel. This means that the wearer's dreams will not be
troubled by random or intentional negativity unless it is self-generated
or unless there is a message for the wearer that is important to be heard
and understood.

There is an important concept here to remember. Self-generated negativity is not at issue here. If an individual is creating his or her own darkness, this is something to be dealt with by other means. If he or she is
intentionally opening the door to externally generated negativity, then
the behavior of any crystal will not prevent the individual from being
influenced by it. All individuals must ultimately be responsible for what
they allow to influence them. The influence of any crystal can be overridden. It is, however, a good method by which to discover what comes
from one's own inner darkness and what comes from outside. When one
eliminates the impact of external forces, what remains must be evaluated
to find its origin.

Green citrine is a strong protective stone drawing together the strength
of the earth energy with the power of the belly chakra's warrior nature. It
reinforces the individual's sense of identity, while also allowing that individual to banish any eternally generated negativity that may be hinder-
ing or clouding his or her energy system complex. Its nature is active and
assertive and has been used very effectively in dislodging energy implants and their lingering effects. Once they are dislodged, it provides
for the space left behind to be protected while the energy system's natural regenerative power takes hold to heal it.

VIOLET (AMETHYST)

Since long ages ago, amethyst has been known as a holy stone and much regarded for its healing properties. When set with jade, it is most soothing to the spirit and mind and should be worn in this combination by those seeking healing for mental derangement caused by excessive and/or prolonged stress. Amethyst embodies the violet ray of the Transcendent Spirit and is activated at the brow chakra. It is often associated with the crown chakra because it is at the brow center that the highest light of universal consciousness first becomes manifested in objection realization and experience. It becomes the property of reason and individual awareness. Let the wearer be aware that the true nature of the light of the crown chakra is truly white and admitting all rays. This is but one of its higher resonances and connection to it, and for this energizing all other centers and energies should otherwise be in balance. This is the Opener of Ways that its wearer may freely be aware of higher voices, both his own and those of the Guardians.

As a Healer's stone, it aids the practitioner in accessing this energy and intelligence so that he may be a channel for Universal light energy into the physical world. It gives access to the crown chakra in that it helps open the gateways to the spirit. This stone is often worn by the Initiate Priestesses before the taking of their final passage so that they may accustom themselves to those voices that are the nature of their work. Therefore, those who would seek enlightenment and wisdom, and those who would act as seekers and seers might do well to partake of this virtue. For this purpose it is well worn beside the white focus stones such as cats-eye and moonstone. Diamond will drive the energy too strongly except in rare instances. Let it be bound with silver and placed upon the brow that the visions will be clearest. Let it also be placed above the heart, set in silver with aquamarine, so that its benefits will permeate the body and what is gained may be translated as there is need.

Be warned, however, that there may be difficulty in wearing this stone in actions of extreme power and duration. It will become fatigued and thus pale, muddy, or dark. Then let the piece be put aside for a while. This bleaching or muddiness is a certain specific indication that another type of stone should be chosen for the work in progress and that the wearer is not in full balance with the violet potential. Chose another stone better suited to the wearer and his needs or the result will have no virtue but a dead stone.

Amethyst is most fortuitously worn in either gold or silver when worn upon the hand that the precious healing of spirit may flow both in and out and be extended to those in need. This is often to be seen as a gesture of blessing.

Do not mistake violet for purple as purple is an entirely different matter. Most gracious of all those stones are those who have pure blue also in them as well, for then all manner of these things may be achieved. For blue magnifies the pure intelligence and render these voices most useful and reasonable to the wearer in all matters.

AMETHYST QUARTZ (AMETHYST BANDED WITH WHITE QUARTZ)

Amethyst quartz is a formation where layers of amethyst are found side by side with both white and clear quartz. This is sometimes found in amorphous microcrystalline structures and also in the form of crystals. These stones are generally found to be easy to work with since the nature of the white quartz constantly moderates and smoothes the energy flowing through the amethyst. This configures an energy field that is easily integrated with the energy system complex as well as being strong within its own elements. Although it does not have the direct focus of pure amethyst, it is able to take a higher energy load because of the mediating effects of the white quartz and consequently makes a powerful charm for meditation and higher vibrational healing work. It can also be effective in helping an individual connect and work with energies directed from his or her own Higher Self as well as the directing consciousness of his or her soul group.

BLACK AMETHYST

Most sovereign of all healing stones is the Black Amethyst. It interacts with the helixes of both body and spirit healing by drawing forth whatever is ill or unbalanced. It should be set in silver in combination with stones of the purest white nature such as moonstone or diamond and its sovereignty is thereby focused and specified according to whatever nature of ill it is guided to draw forth. Remember that its healing nature is that of a purgative and that before grief and trouble of the mind are comforted, it will first bring tears. Its nature is to bring the problem to a focus so that it may be examined by the spirit. Therefore it is said to heal both of its own power and by the understanding and perception of the wearer.

Place this stone over the heart or brow chakra that its rays be most beneficial. Never place it upon the throat chakra for it will stop speech, although this condition may be rectified by its removal. It should not be worn on the hands because it will cause an imbalance in the lateral axis energies. If worn at the crown it will cause the energies to be blocked and flow back against themselves. This will bring about headaches and, sometimes, ocular dysfunction that will endure for some short time after its removal.

RUTILATED QUARTZ

Rutilated quartz may be, in the basic crystal, smoky or clear and, in the rare instances, rose and amethyst, and these should be considered as per their colors. The rutilations are metallic fibers of titanium oxide that conduct strong flows of energy with little resistance, amplifying it in this process. This trait, combined with the spectrum energy of quartz, makes these extremely powerful generating stones where large amounts of raw energy are required. The practitioner must be aware of this trait and rule this nature with disciplined intention, because these fibers most often form in a chaotic and random pattern across the axis structure of the main crystal. These should not be regarded as interruptions to the energy axis lattice but rather as amplifications of it. When these stones are cut in facets or cabochons, the fibers themselves should be regarded as the energy structure lattice and power channeled according to its structure. The practitioner should closely observe the thickness of the fibers, the color and their relative density as well as their pattern (if any) through the stone.

It has a tendency to override any stone set as its qualifier unless this relationship is constantly monitored and disciplined. However, tourmaline is a notable exception to this. This is because it is the nature of the aluminum base of tourmaline to activate such a stone or crystal without the conscious intent of a practitioner. Tourmaline is also formed under the same conditions of heat and pressure as is rutilated quartz and as such makes it a companion stone with much the same energy and capacity.

Gold or electrum will give rutillated quartz a focus that copper and silver have insufficient strength to impose upon it. In this way the stone can be ruled through its setting if this should be desired. Metallic crystals such as hematite make qualifiers for it being in harmony with the metallic nature of the rutillations. This strengthens the power drive potential of the stone many times over. But let the bearer be aware that this will greatly enhance its metallic behavior and care must be taken as to how it is used and the well being of the bearer.

STAR QUARTZ

There are two types of stars in quartz. In most stones, the asterism is caused by a rutile inclusion resulting in a single star whose legs wrap from the front of the stone to the back of the stone, thereby making two stars, if the back of the cab were domed and polished. This is because rutile orients to the center axis of the crystal, only. In this case it behaves in the way of rutillated quartz but with a much higher degree of focus, because the rutile is in a regular geometric configuration with respect to the central axis. Its energy is very strong and, when placed with stones to give it focus and direction, it makes a strong talisman, particularly in working of power or focus of will. Singly this typed of stone can be used to help in focus and concentration when dealing with a specific problem that requires attention to small details and acute memory for patterns and flow. We do not generally recommend that this be worn on a constant basis, as this intensity of focus will eventually cause fatigue and burn out. The stone should be put aside to rest when the wearer becomes aware of changes in temperament, particularly, fatigue, snappishness and impatience. It goes without saying that as the stone may need to be rested, so, also, may the wearer.

The "higher order" of stars, or a multi-star, is caused by a silimanite inclusion (aluminum silicate dioxide) giving it many properties that are akin to sapphire. This will orient itself to the center axis as well as the other six crystal faces, causing seven stars on the front of the cab, and another seven on the back. This form of truly multi-starred quartz is extraordinary in its properties to focus and direct energy on all levels of the spectrum and to all levels of the energy system complex. It operates across all bandwidths of the human range of consciousness and connects to the guiding and directing Higher Mind energy. It stimulates the individual's connection to this higher group awareness and will encourage his or her linkage to the access of information resting in higher order plane data arrays. In the ancient days of Atlantis, this was a stone often used by the higher adepts of power and allowed them to link their various energies without loss of personal determinism, and without loss of power in the exchange. It is recommended that, if qualifying stones are used in connection with multi-star quartz that they be also clear or a rainbow suite of stones. This is so that the energy range of the star quartz will not be limited in its ability to draw the many levels of consciousness and identity together.

MICROCRYSTALLINE QUARTZ (CHALCEDONY)

Chalcedony is a sub-family to quartz, for its structure is as quartz particles linked together to form a solid formation referred to as *microcrystalline*. It is seen in a great variety of colors and patterns and mixtures of those colors being formed of inclusions of various sorts. The wide variety of chalcedony includes agate, chalcedony, chrysoprase, heliotrope (bloodstone), jasper, carnelian, moss agate, onyx and sardonyx (banded agate). Its colors and patterns come as much from intrusions and inclusions of other material as they do from the crystal matrix itself. Its variety of color and pattern are almost endless and can be used for any task for which colored quartz would answer with a few considerations that will be discussed. In all its forms it may be carved or shaped into any vessel or object desired and thus this object may be truly charged with the nature of any work desired according to the principles of color and form. Attention should be given to the pattern of the grain that the power structure will flow smoothly and according to the function of the piece.

Do not think less of its power because it is only found in block form. Its potential manifests as though it were a cluster of points, densely joined and aligned so that, whatever its shape, its multitude of points resonate to one purpose and pattern. In Ancient Days, vessels of chalcedony were set upon the tables of the High to magnify their potency and strength. Lamps of it were lit to resonate their energy by heat/light interaction to permeate the councils of the Wise and subtly invigorate them. Artisans sought after it that, as they worked - it being a most agreeable medium - they might sing according to their craft and by their song infuse their work with the truth of their visions, for it is most easily charged in the working.

Its colors are as varied as the hues of the rainbow and their intermixtures even more so. Nonetheless, we will describe here a few of its basic and most common colors so that the student may know its properties and judge their patterns rightly according to his purposes and powers. It is for the student and practitioner to experiment and experience the qualities of whatever stone of this group they would put to use because it would be impossible in any space to describe in complete detail the varieties and combinations of energy potentials in these stones.

WHITE

We have spoken elsewhere of the Cup of Joining and its nature and all other vessels that can be formed of this substance. White chalcedony is closest to crystalline quartz and, along with the black, is the quickest and truest to take a charge of power and retain it whole and unmodified. Boxes of all sizes may be worked of it and, when bound or inlaid with metals, make most potent guardian depositories. Mark well that this will take most fixedly the signature pattern of the worker and, once done, this pattern will endure firmly until the piece is cleansed and discharged.

The white is the significator of pure, undifferentiated power and may potently take any charge of nature placed within it. It has also unique conductivity in that energy passes through it easily and is altered by the nature of the charge, but the charge itself neither dissipates nor magnifies. This is most beneficial in the case of a box wherein any working charm is placed. Chalcedony also can be used for rods or wands intended to direct and facilitate the flow of energy. In this case the stone should be unflawed (uncracked and unmarred by variations due to anomalous inclusions) and its grain should be aligned with the desired direction of the energy flow.

It is also common that charms are carved from it. These may be charged in the same way as any pure crystal. It is well to remark here upon the effectiveness of charms. In the untutored it is wise to use some pleasing shape with, perhaps, some symbolic meaning to the healing stone. This will trigger a willingness or agreement, that is, some sympathetic reaction to the power of the working. Such charms may be the image of benevolent gods according to the religion of the people or the shape of a natural creature that denotes to the person some healing or strengthening spirit. Such a shape will remind and reinforce the nature of the work at the most basic and instinctual levels and so cause the wearer go into agreement of their own volition with the work of their own healing. Such charms are greatly effective when used with children and also with the ignorant or untutored.

BLACK (ONYX)

This is a stone of marvelous virtue in that it will draw energies into itself and hold them undissipated for great lengths of time. Thus the power of the piece may be added to over the space of many workings and this stone will hold the energies of many workers. Many individuals may contribute to the stored energy. They will come together in one harmonious vibration stored as pure energy.

Then a single Adept may, by the power of his Will alone, use and direct this stored power as he desires.

A box made of this will act to cleanse the pieces stored within it, but be minded that it must be discharged from time to time. A rod made from it may draw forth bound-up charges such as pain from injuries and, used prudently, may speed the healing. But do this gently and with discretion that not too much energy be thus withdrawn lest an equal and opposite negative charge be created in the energy field. Any object made from it may be filled with energy and set to key at a certain specific pattern, but be aware of this, lest it do harm to the unprepared.

Black chalcedony makes a most potent blade when fashioned to the songs of a Master as he forms it, for he will sing his heart into its working and thereafter it will be his alone. The power that it draws will serve the maker as he desires. As with smoky quartz, it has the power to clarify the mind and energies by removing all tracings of anomaly in the waveform pattern. By this, it clarifies any working for all energies drawn into the piece become raw potential and will be held there until they are called forth.

ORANGE (CARNELIAN)

Orange Chalcedony is also called Carnelian or Sard and behaves as though it were a form of citrine condensed and magnified. In all ways, it encourages the strength of the heart, courage and firmness of intent. It may be used in place of citrine. But the practitioner should be aware that its radiance tends to a redder nature than citrine. Carnelian has been known and prized since ancient times for the richness of its color and the strength of its energy. It carries with it the warming and strengthening energy of the summer sun and has been credited with dispelling all forms of negativity directed at the individual who carries it. In truth, carnelian strengthens the inner sense of identity, and well-being through self-esteem. It does not so much dispel negativity as encourage and brighten the wearer though the agency of the belly chakra, so that negativity is less likely to find a foothold or have so strong an impact. For this reason the Ancient Text often credit carnelian with warding off and expelling demons and other forms of malevolence.

As it is mixed with white it has a warming and calming effect, and when it is banded or mixed with white it is called Sardonyx. It is well used in healing, as it lightens the heart and brings forth the positive force of the

spirit. Worn at the throat it strengthens the voice of the body and all force
of command of speech. Placed upon the wrists or fingers it enforces the
energies proceeding from the hands. In these and all other uses, pay heed
to the grain in the working.

It is not generally advisable to use it in the workings of peace, especially
that of scrying and in all things wherein the nature of the moon is manifest, because it is truly a stone of the sun and has no subtlety in these
matters. Its nature is overt and joyful. In the redder ranges it is aggressive and assertive, and it will conflict with and override these subtle
pursuits. Within this stone lies the true courage and heart of the Lion; his
rage and his pride, also. It may be well worn by both warrior and maiden
alike, that its joyful strength will contribute to their natures. There is no
metal in which it cannot be placed for right working according to these
principles.

GREEN

Moss Agate is a translucent chalcedony of much
virtue and may be used with pleasing effect in
those applications where a true green quartz crystal would be too strong or dominant. As the
Green Quartz is called the Stone of the Mother, so is this one known as
the Mother's Daughter and embodies the strength and peace of the growing earth and the green life that flourished beneath the waters of ponds.
Its mossy structure is caused by the inclusion of hornblende. Its red and
brown coloration is due to oxidation of the hornblende as the stone was
formed. The hornblende is a complex silicate containing a variety of
metallic elements that combined give it a balanced, earthy and cooling
quality. It is well used to sooth fevers and calm individuals under stress
and anxiety, while giving also of the green regenerative qualities. It is
not as quick to take a charge as the green quartz, but, when rightly done,
will hold such a charge for many years. It is well worn in company with
amber and this makes a most virtuous combination for women heavy
with child, and those nursing, because it strengthens the courage of the
bearing woman and provides a greater link for her with those powers
that are natural and gracious. It is well made into blessing charms for
babes at their Consecration although these should be put aside when the
child is well into the age of speech (approx. 5 years of age). It is pleasingly carved into the likeness of birds and fishes and any living creature
that is not basically considered as a predator. It may be worn and utilized
by any person of any power level, so general and generous is its virtue.

Moss agate is not to be confused with dendritic agate whose fern-like
inclusion patterns are formed of iron or manganese. Dendritic agate acts

quietly to strengthen the heart / base chakra connection and encouraged the wearer to draw strength from the beauty and stability of the earth matrix. It will encourage an attachment to the Gaia consciousness - Mother Earth spirit. This can be very healing and strengthening for those who have dysfunctions or illnesses caused by excessive exposure to the environmental stressors of cities and urban pollution and overcrowding. It should be remembered, however, that for such effects to be effectively treated, the individual must be removed from the source of the negative stimuli.

Chrysoprase - The virtue of chrysoprase is to encourage sensitivity to the peace of the fruitful earth and all things that dwell therein. Its properties display similar effects to that of jade. However, because of its membership in the quartz family, chrysoprase has a wider spectrum of activity and distributes its influence across a broader range of the human energy complex than do any of the jades. Because its coloring is due the presence of nickel in the atomic structure, it keys this healing peaceful activity through the mental process of the brow, bringing with it, not only peace and healing from shock and trauma, but a clarity and healing of mind. Another way of saying this is that it works to heal the heart chakra through the mental body.

This is highly beneficial when an individual must work through old difficulties and griefs. This can help those who have suffered abuse as children as well as those who have suffered early traumatic loss or conflict. It may be that in adulthood much of the trauma has been resolved or put aside but the scarring remains. It is through the activity of chrysoprase that these scars are dealt with and a new peace and clarity are found.

In certain instances cabochons of chrysoprase may be used in place of peridot and epidote where the general quartz nature is more preferred that those more specific bands. Its nature is restorative and regenerative and it possesses a strength that is unexpected, but intensely gracious. Its nature is to work generally throughout the system, but have its basic charge nourish the heart chakra and from this center its benefits spread outward throughout the body, giving forth peace and restoration. When placed in tandem with a fine crystal of quartz or beryl, its force and power are greatly magnified and enhanced and it acts very powerfully to promote growth and healing. It is not a Talisman of the Healer but rather of the Healed and may strengthen and reinforce all those things that the Healer has balanced and set again in motion. It may be given by the practitioner without reservation to those who require his assistance even to children. It is unique among the truly green noncrystalline stones as it has no sexual polarity bias and can be worn by males as effectively as by females with no bias as to its virtue and no lessening of its potency.

Green Aventurine has the particular virtue of being closest to the primal energies of the growing earth. It is useful in the practice of nature magic and may be helpful in drawing the primal power of the earth itself; known otherwise as the Breath of the Dragon. Its focus may be of virtue in the restoration of the living earth. Trees may be planted by its virtue. This is sometimes called the Stone of the Mother and holds some of the energies of Spring and its vitality. If it is found in true crystal form, it should be guarded and treasured for this energy.

It is a regenerative and restorative to the entire physical system working through the heart chakra. When its inner sparkles are caused by inclusions of mica (Hydrous potassium aluminum silicate) that energize and activate the heart center's own regenerative system. It also has a soothing and cooling nature, similar to jade, and makes a good stone to help in the treatment of depression or low self-esteem. It helps integrate the positive aspects of meditation and contemplation into the stream of conscious awareness.

When the inner lights are caused by inclusions of goethite, Iron hydroxide, it strengthens the vital systems of the physical and emotional bodies and supports the vital life force in the process of gentle healing. It is very well suited to be used with rose quartz in balancing and healing charms because their two natures will help and support each other.

BLUE (SIDERITE)

Sometimes called blue aventurine, the color in blue quartz comes from the inclusion of micro crystals of blue crocidolite (blue hornblende), rutile or zoisite. We may call this the Journey Stone because of its ability to help in out-of-body journeys to other levels and planes of reality. It will make the journey easier as it will facilitate exit and entry of the body through the brow chakra while allowing the clarity and focus to bring information back from these planes with clarity and calm. The blue zoisite is particularly remarkable for this function. It will also help reinforce the traveler's connection with the body and sense of personal identity so that neither the vital systems nor the personal identity of the traveler is in question. Many look to this stone for inner guidance and the ability to find the certainty to act on the strength of inner knowing. It helps the wearer attune him or her self to the sense of mission or purpose in this life and will help the individual follow that sense. In this it will also help those individuals integrate this sense of mission with their daily realities and personal health so that all levels of awareness are served.

Cat's Eye Quartz
Hawk's Eye
Tiger's Eye

Cat's-Eye Quartz is of similar structure and nature to star quartz. Its appearance is due to the inclusion of quartz in parallel fibrous formation with hornblende. This results in a moveable line that follows light across the surface, giving it the appearance of a vertical pupil of a cat's eye. Hornblende is a complex silicate and is also seen in moss agate. Cat's eye quartz gives a focus for the mind and spirit along with a relaxing and cooling effect that, when worn as a pendant over the heart chakra, will be of great benefit in workings of scrying and spirit travel. It helps clarify visions and the sending of energies over distance. It makes a good focus stone for the eyes of the body and the eyes of the mind, as well, and may prove effective in inducing light trance states. This is because the quartz has been shaped into fibrous crystals that are very sensitive to the vibratory rate of the energy system complex as a whole, and are quick to respond to amplify the energies that are called up and focussed.

Hawk's eye forms in a similar fashion to cat's eye quartz forming fibrous parallel inclusions with a blue variety of hornblende call crocidolite. This is also what gives blue siderite its color and the properties of the two stones are very similar. However, due to the parallel and densely fibrous nature of the microcrystalline structure, the nature and behavior hawk's eye is intensified and it will act to clarify and strengthen the individual's belief in what they have seen on other planes and levels of consciousness. This significantly aids the self-confidence that a Seer or Traveler needs to move with clarity. In a general way it leads to removing of self-doubt on any level giving the wearer a confidence and resulting clarity both of vision and of expression. In this way, it helps with focus and the mental process in general.

Tiger's Eye - As the hornblende in Hawk's Eye oxidizes, its colors become increasingly red, brown and golden which results in Tiger's Eye. This is a strong stone for giving an individual balance and confidence. This leads the individual to a general feeling of well being in the ability to see his or her own abilities honestly and to trust them. By extending the resonance through the lower chakras it encourages a balance of energies within the wearer between mental exertion and physical health - between the inner life of the mind and the outer life of the body. It can be very useful for both visionaries and those who spend a great deal of time in mental pursuits to keep the energies of the physical body active and healthy. Conversely it encourages those with extremely physical lives to extend their awareness and understanding into more mental and contemplative areas.

It has been highly prized by the Wise to be used as signets and seals, for these signets will transfer in the impression the signature charge of the possessor and prove as surely an identification as the pattern incised upon the seal itself. Worn closely about the brow and temples, these stones prove a sure and certain aid in the workings of the Will in terms of the Earth Magic. This is because they have a similar charge to the earth's nature, although this should not be confused with the far more powerful signature conductivity of the green quartz.

JASPER & OPAQUE CHALCEDONIES

The term jaspers and opaque chalcedonies covers a wide range from within the quartz family. Some within this group are microcrystalline; others are not strictly so, being formed in a multitude of ways over time. Their beauty comes in their nearly limitless variety of color and atomic content, while having a hardness that makes them suitable for cutting in any sort of fashion from small pieces to be set in jewelry and personal regalia, to larger works carving whole pieces such as cups and boxes.

Densely opaque chalcedonies are the result of a great deal of coloring element combined with an extremely irregular internal structure. They still have the nature of the quartz family (silicon dioxide), but in such a form that they are slow in response and require great force of intention to utilize. Their virtue lies in the fact that they may be shaped and worked in accordance with desired function, and also in their property that, when properly initialized, they may store great amounts of power to be used for many purposes. Despite their tendency to inertia with regards to energy charges, once they have taken a charge they will integrate it throughout their intricate and irregular structure making them strong personal talisman charms. This is especially so, when they are used for a long length of time. We would not advise that they be used for workings of power, but rather for personal meditative work or to give a particular qualification to a complex talisman with a quartz primary stone. It is not generally recommended to use them as qualifiers with other families of stones. This is because, when their primary is quartz, this will further activate the quartz nature of their composition and provide them with the strength and focus their irregular formation would otherwise lack. In this way the two stones can go hand in hand assisting each other. If it is necessary to use a primary stone from another family, it should be chosen for its kinship and similarity to the element that gives the jasper or opaque stone its dominant color.

JASPER

In general, we will explain that it is appropriate to chose jasper according to its color. If it is desirable to have a particular color resonance about an individual, jasper can be used without overriding the signature of other stone. This makes it an excellent choice for children and students who are just beginning their exploration of color energy. It also makes a convenient touch stone to trigger a reminder of desired energies to be concentrated on.

RED

This is the chalcedony of martial energy, the Fire of the Sun. In choosing this piece it should be uniform in color, for its color is based upon a high concentration of inclusions, and, as they appear uniform, so they are in conformity to the energy flow of the stone.

Red Jasper conforms to all the principles of carnelian, although in greater measure, for this is the stone of controlled and directed passions. It is subtler than carnelian and this is the nature of its force - to draw for the energies of the body to their fulfillment and channel them into useful force. Its nature is not active in that this must be done by intention of the possessor and will not be accomplished without active intention. This is indeed the nature of all opaque chalcedonies - to perform effectively by active intention only.

This is not a sovereign stone in that other stones serve better to these uses. But as one requires a shaped object, this is well used for that service, and in considering its properties combined with other stones, these principles are well to consider.

YELLOW

Yellow jasper is of the same nature as red but of a more actively mental nature and may serve as a key to mental agility and wit. It assists the individual in restoring his or her natural optimism and balanced outlook on life.

GREEN (HELIOTROPE)

Green jasper is known as Bloodstone when spots of red jasper are distributed in its pattern. Without the red it is known as Heliotrope. It is well-formed to a blade for the cutting of herbs, for it will not detract from their true energies in any measure. It will also aid in the renewal of energies because it gently enhances the strength and clarity of the wearer by its restorative nature. Sometimes it seems to have a calming effect by removing some of the harshness of fatigue of mind and especially of emotion. The Healer may partake of its virtue, and the novice also, if it is carried as a personal charm.

In choosing this stone let it be for the greater part green and dense, with the red in small measure and the yellow in like part to the red to aid its function. It also subtly aids the balance of polarities in the wearer and makes a strong practitioner's charm when worn during the workings of earth magic and the summoning of the forces of the physical and astral levels.

BLUE

This a royal blue stone sometimes streaked with white and lavender. Its nature is similar to lapis lazuli, sodalite, and dark blue tourmaline in that it can help to clarify visions in scrying and intensifying the will. Yet its nature is inert in that it requires great intensity of force to initialize its function. When rightly charged it is powerful in clarifying both dreams and visions alike, so that the information gained thereby may be made intelligible and useful. Remember that lapis lazuli and sodalite are put to much better use in this. The Dreamer's Cup may be made of this or of the White inlaid with Blue (See also Dreamer's Cup).

OPALS

When speaking of opalescence and opals, there are two separate principles involved that must be understood. First of all, opalescence is a quality, a behavior of light showing in ripples and sheets of various colors within the stone. Second, the stone called Opal is a form of hydrous silicon dioxide occurring in different forms and levels of hardness that sometimes, but not always, exhibits this rainbowing quality. The rainbow color is given to the stone by microspheroids of cristobalite within the structure and the play of color is determined by their density and configuration. Opals can be considered in three categories: **precious opals** that are either white or black as a basis for the opalescent color behavior, **fire opals** that occur in transparent or translucent golden, orange and red-orange, and **common opal** that can be either of the first two types but has no sheets of interior color rainbow quality. The rainbowing behavior of crystals with healed interior fractures should not be confused with the properties of natural opals whose color sheeting is a behavior of its basic structure and composition.

Precious opals result as a combination of influences when the basic opal matrix stone contain pockets and layers of microspheroids of cristobalite. The color is activated by the presence of water within these layers of the stone. Because they are so harmoniously interwoven, they operate as though of one force. The first essential characteristic that underlies all other manifestations, is the natural character of the base stone. This basic stone is akin to quartz and is considered within the quartz family. Water is a large makeup of these stones and consequently they are easily charged to resonate with the Being's temperament and energy. As water makes up a large portion of the human body, this gives the stone an even greater resonance to the human organism. But, because the layers of color interrupt the layers of matrix, these pieces are naturally fragile. Too great a charge of energy can harm or damage their physical structure and be as harmful to the stone as excessive heat. They are fine reflectors of personality and may often be used as Monitor stones, but in this the Mexican is more optimal because of its greater structural stability. Because of their kinship with both the body through their aqueous content and the subtle bodies through their quartz nature they are highly responsive to changing mood and intention of the wearer and can be extremely powerful tools when used in balance across the full spectrum of their nature.

To the degree that these stones manifest color and depending on what these colors are, they may be used as a focus driver on any piece. The water in their makeup will take a constant varying charge from the energies of the stone and focus it through the ever-changing color structure of the opalescence. In this way, the energy of the stone may be keyed across the color spectrum, through the constant of its crystalline basic nature. Chose the opal wisely with this in mind, for they should emit those energies most strongly that are most needed and add the other colors as a secondary effect to help provide an internal balancing effect as the stone combination is in motion to its purpose.

Remember that opals may be over-driven or unintentionally stuck on one form of emanation when used by an individual who is untuned or untrained in the working of the entire spectrum of power, or one very

powerful who is sick or damaged of body and therefore manifesting one
ray too strongly for the stone's structure. The water in them will charge
to the overload and the stone may become permanently damaged with
this misuse.

FIRE AGATE

Fire agate is a form of opalized chalcedony
and is the most powerful of the opal stones
for its microcrystalline composition makes
it physically stronger in its structure than ei-
ther of the other two. Nonetheless, the nature of trace materials that give
it its opalescence are heavily biased with iron oxides which lend this
stone a heavy earthy nature and respond strongly to the base earth energies. However, when these properties are taken into account, this will
make it an excellent adept stone not only as an intake qualifier, but as a
personal healing stone, and as a stone of expression as well, giving the
energies of the wearer any of its color virtue manifestations that may be
commanded at will. Notice should be taken that its nature is extremely
strong and this stone should only be used by those individuals who have
a basically strong earthy nature, or whose training has brought them to
such a point that these natures are well integrated into their system of
energies and balances. This stone is well set in gold, platinum, electrum,
bronze and silver, but among these gold and electrum will bring out its
best and strongest qualities, refining its nature and giving it a focussed
strength that is unparalleled. Fire agate is a natural companion to quartz
and makes an excellent qualifier for its nature. Talismans of this composition are so flexible and multispectrum based that they are able to replace many others with their strength and precision. However, care should
be taken that the Fire Agate will manifest easily all of the colored ranges
desired and not be limited to only a few, for it should be understood that
it will not give of a resonance that it neither possesses nor manifests.

OPALS AND IRON

Let none of the opals and most particularly the white Australian opals be set with
iron, for this will warp their nature to such
a degree that their virtue will be rendered
useless. Set them, instead, with silver or with gold to a most fortuitous
end. They are content with any stone with which they are in company
and will magnify and enhance its influence as far as their natures and
structural limitations will permit.

GARNET

CHAKRA: BASE
CALLING: ARTISAN/SMITH
ARCHETYPE COLOR: RED

Garnet is a family of crystals called Nesosilicates. They are related in structure in that the crystals do not exhibit the linear central axis structure often associated with crystal formation. Rather they are polygonal, often dodecahedron shapes. Their atomic structure varies within the general group. Each variant can exhibit one or more of the colors and it is important to remember that, while there may be more than one representative of a color, each of those representatives will manifest its characteristics according to the elements in its structure.

GROSSULAR	calcium aluminum silicate $Ca_3Al_2(SiO_4)_3$	Pale Milky Green Emerald Green (containing chromium) – Tsavorite Yellow Reddish brown to Orange (containing iron) – hessonite
PYROPE	magnesium aluminum silicate $Mg_3Al_2(SiO_4)_3$	Red
ALMANDINE	iron aluminum silicate $Fe_3Al_2(SiO_4)_3$	Red to Violet-Purple
UVAROVITE	calcium chromium silicate $Ca_3Cr_2(SiO_4)_3$	Emerald Green
SPESSARTITE	manganese aluminum silicate $Mn_3Al_2(SiO_4)_3$	Orange to red-brown (cinnamon)
ANDRADITE	Calcium iron silicate $Ca_3Fe_2(SiO_4)_3$	Red, brown or black - Melanite Yellow Topazolite Emerald Green - Demantoid

Garnet is the stone of the Earth and all its many and various resonances. It draws energy through itself and transmutes it, giving it a distinctive energy pattern as it emits the flow. Garnets of any color have no center axis as is generally understood, instead, the radiations of the energy grid form a three dimensional star pattern with a singular pulse pattern rather than a true helix configuration. The only way known to encourage them to conform to a regular pattern generally found in other crystals is to cut them along specific grain lines within them taking only the segment that conforms along a radion and considering that radion as an artificial center axis. For this reason they are more ideally suited to use if cut either as cabochons or facetted. They are not adversely affected by this cutting and work as well cut as whole.

Their workings are virtually automatic and easily manipulated by any practitioner as they respond truly to the primal base chakra and are its harmonic reflex when properly tuned. Because of this natural resonance with the base chakra, garnets are naturally active in energizing the vital energies of all four levels of the energy system complex. They encourage and stimulate the development of the kundalini through the spinal column. Each of the colors and configurations of garnets corresponds to a center of connection between centers that will allow this activation to occur. All colors are wonderfully suited for constructing complex talismans for the untrained or for children. The more dense their color, that is, to the degree that they are dark or opaque, they will pull strongly inward unto themselves and act as a reservoir of energy to be called forth at need, and in this they are powerful in every sense of the word. When worn as crystals, they should be used for this natural reservoir capacity, the wearer attuning himself to the signature pulse pattern of the stone and drawing from it in harmony at need. They are as fiery and resonant as rubies in all the red/rose/purple range. They are as strong in the green and virtually identical in nature as green quartz with certain exceptions stated in later references. Take heed when they are worn.

Their energies are best bound with gold to give them a more specific nature of direction that otherwise it is not of their nature to possess. Silver will truly disperse their properties both from intake and outflow directions and will make them more difficult to handle for the unwary. They are well situated in iron and steel and integrate well with these purposes. However, for those it suits, setting them in silver will, in a general sense, render their workings quite similar to rubies. They are not as durable as rubies for long term intensive workings of high nature, but are more specifically so than rubelite tourmalines so that one may use them easily as a channel of primal energy and they will serve nicely. Their nature is joyful, purposeful, passionate, friendly and warm. Let care be taken in their use with the specified limitations and particulars held firmly in mind.

Colors of garnets often occur in more than one of its subgroups and care should be taken to examine the composition of each.

BLACK & BROWN **GARNET (MELANITE)**	There is no truly black garnet as such, but only those that are so intense in their specific color that they appear to be black as they appear to give forth no light whatsoever and are completely opaque to the

eye. As is the case with any stone with this configuration, they do not behave in the manner of truly black stones. They do draw energy within themselves, but in the manner of giving forth they are known to give it forth intensely altered according to their colored inclusions. Those of this type are generally red and brown and must be considered solely as the ultimately intense member of their color group.

Brown garnets act in the manner of truly brown stones although its specific point of resonance is the base chakra as with all garnets. They draw in energy through this center and reduce these vibrations to their truest common level. Its action is strongly calmative and strengthening to the nerve centers from the base upwards and gives the effect of a strong purifier by allowing no anomaly to remain in the energy system complex. In this way, they will leave the path clear for other and higher workings when their pattern in complete. Do not attempt to use them in conjunction with other stones, for their activity will prevent the dominance of all others and render the work useless in the extreme. They may be used very well with stones of their own family to great effect when healing one who requires the energy of the rose/red/violet running through the system along with the calming brown. This red energy will be to no avail for the use of overtly outreaching power in this case, but will serve most beautifully to re-energize the entire system as the brown does its work. Brown garnet may indeed prove a stronger calmative than any other brown stone and may be used reliably in place of dravite tourmaline in all respects with the consideration that it is slightly less self-activating and should be initially cleansed and charged by a practitioner. It will continue with its intended function unhindered by any until its work is done. See, however, that its progress is monitored and that it is cleared from time to time as a matter of course so that it does not overload. Also be aware that some sensitives are adversely affected by its action. The indication of this is that the skin beneath it will be sensitive and prolonged use may result in sulkiness and irritability. If this occurs, it should be replaced, for this is a sign of the system rejecting these activities due to a general lack of sympathy with the basic vibration pattern of the stone.

RED	

Red garnet directly addresses the primal energies of the base chakra and is particularly suitable to the female polarity. In general, it will bring up the earth fire energy in a vibration structure that the entire energy system complex can easily assimilate and enable the system's natural balancing capabilities to use that energy where it is most needed so that a balanced vitality and strength is easily achieved. Other red stones may have a tendency to over tax centers that are weak or debilitated by physical injury, impairment, or those that are blocked through shock and trauma. To use a red stone in such instances is to encounter a certain risk of aggravating those blockages by applying too much force behind them. The garnet, however, can provide an admirable bridge through those unbalanced energies, as the energy system complex will link to its energy naturally and in ways that are most suitable and compatible.

It may be used in place of ruby when that resonance is considered too strong or narrowly focussed and can be worn by young people as well as those who are new to power work. It can strengthen a child's vital forces on all four levels of the energy system complex without fearing that it will overtax those systems. Consequently, it can be useful in the treating lasting or debilitating illnesses as it has a direct benefit to the vital life forces. In women who have bled excessively in childbirth, garnet will serve the same function and will help them recover their natural energy level quickly. For individuals who engage in work that requires a focus on the higher energy levels of the energy system complex to a certain exclusion of the lower levels, red garnet will be a great help in balancing the life force energies, re-centering, and energizing them when their work is completed. When used by priestesses, who have no skill in the moving of aggressive force, it will focus this most graciously without harming them.

This is truly the female polarity of the ruby as the rubelite tourmaline may be considered to be without sexual bias, that is androgynous, and its color should be clear and without inclusions. The maximum percentage of inclusions to volume should be no more than 3% total volume. Flaws may be disregarded except those that shatter the very center of the piece and then this stone should be taken for cutting, as a center fracture will render it valueless in crystalline form.

Red garnet may also be used to raise and reinforce the life energies of a female harmed in usage of power. Take heed of this that a priestess severely harmed in the course of her service may be greatly healed by using this stone when its healing charge is set by an adept and, most desirably, her mate. Then she can be virtually raised from the dead in the terms of her power. This may be also charged by the Priestess for her Lord should she wish to give him the heartening gift of her strength in an hour of trial.

Garnets may be exchanged in love between any two and will then act as a tandem link for nurturing and strength. The reserving capabilities of garnets provide an ideal matrix setting for the placement of signature patterns for the purpose of connections and linkages. For this they should be generally set in gold or copper, but silver will do where the others are not available. In tandem usage they should be of the identical color or ideally cut from the same raw stone. When they are cut from the same crystal, the linkage that may be achieved by such a coupling should be greatly remarked upon. For this last use, rose has insufficient strength to bear this load well. In the case of working with energy implants, red and rose garnets will greatly help the individual regain vitality and clarity of personal purpose after the implant has been removed.

Should this stone be overworked, you may recognize it at once for it will darken and soon show all the signs of having been physically burned. It is then useless and should be discarded. Otherwise, it is greatly potent in such cases as of weakness in childhood.

ROSE

This is a gentle but powerful stone of the rose primal energy and may be understood in this capacity as a strong link of vitality and love connecting the base and heart chakras. It may be freely given as a love token or a token of healing with good will from a loving friend. Its basic nature allows it to be given to virgins and children without harm or fear of unduly awakening latent abillities, unless it is specifically charged to do so. It may be simply defined in all terms as the red garnet in gentler form with the additional resonance of the heart chakra connection. Because of this linkage between the two energy centers, rose garnets make an excellent choice when working to restore the vital energies both of physical health and emotional self-confidence. It can be effective for use both in cases where traumas are external in nature as well as those that are internal and self-induced. Rose garnet may be accompanied with green crystalline stones such as emerald, peridot, and tourmaline to magnify and enhance the heart/base communication and accentuate its nature to balance the energy system helix. They may be set in copper when the red energy of copper needs to be enhanced

ORANGE (CINNAMON)

Orange and red-orange (cinnamon) garnets encourage the connection of the base chakra to the belly chakra. They are particularly effective in treating dysfunctions of the identity, that is, those cases where an individual is moved from his or her own sense of life purpose and determinism by circumstances and events that seem out of their control. Such instances go beyond the expected examples of those who are driven from their homes in time of war or disaster. They can be extended to those individuals who, because of their infancy and childhood, have not been able to bond with a place or family, and to those who have not been allowed to exercise their need to form emotional bonds. This can also include those persons who have been forced against their will to submit to emotional abuse or to the loss of persons they have loved. This may even include a beloved animal if that attachment was deep and the loss traumatic.

Orange garnets will encourage such persons to develop an optimism that life has denied them. They will strengthen the individual's courage to form attachments that are emotionally healthy and meaningful. It will allow them to leave the scars of their past behind and build a present and future in their own pattern and design. We encourage the use of this stone where an individual desires to leave one way of life for another as it will strengthen the bridge of self-confidence during the transition and allow that person to have the strength to be guided to a fulfillment of their dreams.

GOLDEN & YELLOW

The yellow garnet falls under the classification of golden rather than yellow stones. Its nature is restorative from the nature of the sun, and it typifies this regeneration as in the golden topaz but to a lesser degree in that its nature is more subtle and earth-centered. Its nature is of the filtering action in the way of all garnets as it will draw energies from the life force, from the base of the current of the flow and by filtering them, then release only what is in its nature to provide. In that case, it will revitalize the energy with the rejuvenation of the sun's ray, with the essential assimilation and activity of the "ray of heaven," pouring the power that awakens and stimulates into the system.

This may be truly called the Stone of the Dancer. It is not the stone that is worn while dancing, but rather with this stone the Dancer prepares to go forth. It is by this energy that the Dancer raises up her energies and pours them forth and is ever renewed with the process. Do not mistake this resonance in any way for that of green. Green will encourage the system to re-energize itself. The golden ray in this stone will regenerate of its own action; it will renew any energy it finds with the golden light of heaven. It will reform the wave pattern rather than adding a harmonic to it and this is its greatest virtue. It does not function its best when given to those who recuperate from illnesses, because they have not sufficient strength and drive of their own and the re-editing of the life pattern may inhibit in some part their ability to heal themselves. In the use of this stone, do not neglect to consider that there might be a reason for this drain of power that might be masked by its usage. Use this rather for those who must perform with great vigor, or those who must endure much over great spans of time. In this case, let the wearer set the stone himself to its purpose to invigorate him according to his anticipated needs. In this way, dependence on this stone may be avoided. He should do this by his own intention, that he may be aware of its actions and capabilities, and in this it will serve him well, set in any metal he desires. It may improve the intelligence by raising the strength of the system and thus brighter and stronger.

GREEN

Green garnets are stones of the living Earth, as is green quartz, and the results of their actions are similar in appearance although different in actual execution. The green quartz typifies the primal force of the earth and is diffused through the heart channel, whereas this green power and focus is centered, as with all garnets, with the base chakra. It is not easily used in workings of true power, but in raising these energies for use within the Spirit's energy system, for the purpose of personal absorption, green garnet is very powerful and operates throughout the system virtually without the conscious knowledge of the holder of the stone. For this activity, it is best to find a whole crystal and leave it uncut, simply allowing the piece to do its work after cleansing and charging. Its activity is typical of garnets in that is pervades the system and bridges gaps and imbalances. When encountering a center or energy channel that is damaged or defective, green garnets will seek to energize channels connections, in a behavior that is, metaphorically speaking, like that of encouraging damaged nerves to heal and regenerate. This will allow for healing energies to then fill the area and restore it to a more functional level.

The polarity preference of all garnets is not at all to be ignored or discounted and when used according to this principal is a most potent energy focus. The action of all of them will be in a passive way. That is, they will interact with existing systems to allow them to expand to their fullest potential. Green garnets set singly in silver then worn at the heart chakra level encourage the raising of the pure green Earth force. Do not, in these workings, set it with any other stone and most specifically with moonstone, for it does not need the extra focus and drive of moonstones and will become too strong and linear for the general welfare. If it is necessary to place a driver with it, choose the female polarity white drivers; the white sapphire is preferable. Set it in platinum or electrum and it will serve as no other for the power of the Earth Priestess in all her primitive and blatant power.

For a talisman of great power, set green and purple garnets together. This will serve as a balance talisman of primal resonance and act as a gathering focus of great power when raising of the female dragon principle. This talisman is extremely powerful in its healing and restorative properties, especially in the hands of the priestess whose sovereignty lies within the purview of the earth itself from the soil to the deep stone beneath. This is a variant on the Talisman of Dominion that may be used accordingly. It may be bound with copper, silver or electrum, but electrum would be the best choice and when done correctly will be truly hers and hers alone. It may also be worn by the Earth Priest when he has no Priestess to balance with him in his Rites. In this instance, for it will exert the balancing female polarity in his nature.

Green garnets may also be used to stimulate the healing processes of individuals suffering from the inhalation of toxic gases due to volcanic activity and should be worn about the chest area while remedies of herbs are administered.

PURPLE

Purple Garnet operates from the same power level as the purple ruby or the purple tourmaline, acting through the brow and crown energy centers. Its vibration in this area of the spectrum balances between the highest chakra and the lowest more strongly than do any other violet stones, because of its ruby identity and its purple coloration. This may be of considerable interest to those who wish to channel the higher wisdom without neglecting or over-driving the balance of their energy system complex. When used in this fashion, they help alleviate or avoid headaches that so often accompany this stage of power development. This may also be charged when in pure crystal form to enhance the flow of the serpent power (kundalini) and aid in removing blockages in energy that occur along the spinal column and which will cause inflammatory degenerative maladies if not corrected early in development. Do not believe that because this stone is colored with the energy of the higher resonance that it will focus those powers only, for like all garnets it drives a primal pattern signature from the base chakra and may be used well to purposes of this nature. It is not ideal to set this stone in copper but this may be done if properly considered. It is unwise to set this in iron, but in steel it may take a potent charge when used for specific healings within this combined sovereignty. Gold, electrum or silver make ideal choices for setting because they integrate well with both the nature of the stone and the general combined vibration of the energy system complex.

THE ZINC GROUP

CHAKRA: BELLY
CALLING: WARRIOR
ARCHETYPE COLOR: ORANGE (ZINCITE)

The presence of zinc as a dominant element in a stone connects that stone with the belly chakra through all four levels of the subtle bodies of the energy system complex. The other elements that are found present in the structure of the stone indicate the specific nature of the channel or subtle body it will work through. Wherever it is found, zinc allows for the healthy establishment of identity while minimizing ego-centeredness. It allows the individual to reach forward from the present time self with renewed optimism and energy.

ZINCITE
ZINC MANGANESE OXIDE
(Zn,Mn)O

The presence of manganese with zinc in zincite establishes the connection between the belly chakra and the heart. It allows for courage brought on by the increased ability to lay aside fears and phobias due to early childhood abuse or abandonment, or through past life connections to similar damage. In general, zincite promotes action and intelligence based on present time considerations. The advantage of such a viewpoint is that the individual is more flexible and more aware not only of surroundings but of things as they are rather than seeing them painted by fears or self-deceptions.

Its colors range from deep red to pale yellow, indicating that its activity stimulates creativity and spontaneity. It stimulates the development of personal power based on personal clarity and strength. When an individual can see beyond self-doubt and perceived limitations, many things are possible. This is an excellent choice of stone for those who choose to pursue a karmic destiny.

HEMIMORPHITE

HYDROUS BASIC ZINC SILICATE

$$Zn_4((OH)_2/Si_2O_7).H_2O$$

Blue-green to colorless and white, often formed in lustrous globular layers, hemimorphite assists the linkage through the energy system complex, so that the individual can put aside egotism and personal agendas and reunite with the Higher Self. It releases the individual from the shadows of nightmares. It assists the individual to reassert control in his or her life. It reaches past the ego concerns to reveal whatever self-limiting mechanisms the individual may have in place that may not be on a conscious level. Its works to release self-doubt. It has a cooling and healing effect on the sense of self and personal identity. This can greatly help the individual rise above limitations placed upon him/her by others who seek to control through intimidation and emotional abuse.

Hemimorphite is a stone of Awakening, for by removing self-imposed limitations, false ego, and limitations imposed by others, the individual can begin to recognize and open to the possibilities presented by his or her inner beauty and potential. It further facilitates personal awakening by working through all subtle bodies as a whole without limiting its activity to one particular chakra. Its activity is healing and clarifying and can provide an invaluable bridge between the past and the desired future.

SMITHSONITE

ZINC CARBONATE

$$ZnCO_3$$

Smithsonite completes the spectrum of the zinc-related stones. Its colors range from white when pure, to pale blue to green when copper is present (appearing very similar to hemimorphite), bright yellow with cadmium traces, pink or violet with cobalt or manganese, and brown with iron hydroxide. Because smithsonite is a carbonate, its internal structure is not as hard or strong as other members of this family. Its energy field presents an "open" feeling that makes it a good choice to use with other stones to give an identity and qualification to a talisman, while the other stones carry the load of the energy signature.

Smithsonite helps the individual through transitions. It helps alleviate the individual's fear of change by acting through the belly chakra to build self-confidence and self-knowledge without the restriction of ego agendas. The trace elements that give it its color indicate the center through which it will primarily operate to exert its influence throughout the subtle bodies. Its carbonate base will key it through the emotional body, but this will easily translate through the other energy structures.

When used for an extended period of time as a single talisman piece, smithsonite will assist the individual to become aware of his or her communication and connection with higher plane guides and guardians. These may be perceived as gentle internal voices of help and comfort or may be more generally perceived as beings of light or angels. It works in this way because it helps reveal the ego centered agendas as self-limiting and a hindrance to the desired self-realization and growth. This opens the way for the individual to establish a greater peace with his or her spiritual nature and be more willing and open to accepting guidance from other beings and from the Higher Self. All variations of the zinc family will work in this fashion to some extent, but the smithsonite is best of all because its structure resonates with the emotional need in all individuals to relate to the higher consciousness/godhead energy from which the human spirit sprang.

TOPAZ

HYDROUS ALUMINUM SILICATE
$Al_2SiO_4(F,OH)$
CHAKRA: SOLAR PLEXUS
CALLING: DANCER
ARCHETYPE COLOR: GOLDEN/YELLOW

Topaz is sometimes known as the stone of the Sun Children of Atlantis, for it is by these highly intellectual and optimistic vibrations that those children built their empire and Temple, and it was also by these vibrations that this sad land fell at last beneath the sea. Topaz is the stone of the mind, and it energizes it through all those faculties known as wit and cleverness. Its colors range from blue, yellow and smoky brown, that are commonly worn as gems, and also green, that is rare and highly valued, and also pink and rose and golden. All these colors bring to the mind those resonances that are characteristic of that color resonance and energize the thoughts accordingly. It may be of great benefit to those who seek a means by which to manifest their creativity into reality, for it initializes those functions that in turn will find means and ends.

Topaz acts through the mental body via the solar plexus chakra. This is not the mind force of the Will Chakra, but rather that of the adaptability and sensitivity to rhythm and vibration of the solar plexus. It is the cleverness of brain usage and may be used to energize and engage those functions that are mental in nature. It is the direct harmonic of the solar plexus center that is known as the chakra of change. Indeed, it is through the mental intelligence that change is manifested from moment to moment. Intelligence provides adaptability so that an individual may deal with change and use it to advantage rather than allowing change to become chaos and be overwhelmed by it.

This is the activity identified with the planet Mercury in all its various manifestations. Take care not to allow this force to over-drive other functions that may not be yet raised to this quickness.

TOPAZ AS A PRIMARY

Topaz is very strong as a primary and will dominate the entire piece with its intense nature. Because of its connection to the instinct and sensitivity to natural rhythms, it can lead to impulsiveness when not used by the disciplined mind. However, the benefit of its nature is to raise awareness and counteract an excessively introspective nature. Take care that this piece is not too strong for its intended purpose. Its natural tendencies to override both its wearer and its qualifying stones should be monitored closely. In making and charging this piece, it is important to charge the qualifier and driver to their purposes well and in harmony, both with each other and the wearer.

CLEAR

Topaz may be either sparkling or clear. The clear without fractures will give a more general radiance, and a more smoothly energized flow. It may also be considered more intense by virtue of its purity, for its energy helix will run straight and be able to bear a great load without breaking. The sparkling kind will bring forth the dancing lights and bring out brilliance to its strength that can be highly desirable. It will bring forth flashes of insight and cause the pivot center of the axis to modulate well. In general, topaz can help an individual who is apprehensive of changes in their life or environment by helping them become more sure of themselves as they move within the flow of event currents in their life. Topaz, when clear, is the undifferentiated light of life. As it takes on those elements that give it color, so it takes on the qualities of those colors and the planetary influences that they symbolize.

In the crystal formations of topaz where the termination is flat rather than pointed, it may be considered as to have no central axis, but rather a solid formation in which the entire grain of the stone is aligned unto a straight flow of energy. This flat termination may be used to great advantage when the flat termination is used as the base of a cabochon stone. Topaz can be set in all metals to its greatest virtue as it will draw most strongly from the base ground of the metal and send forth this qualified radiance and this can be a great and remarkable piece for the workings of power indeed.

Pure clear topaz encourages creativity and individuality in the wearer, because it enhances the wearer's ability to sense and move with the subtle currents of his or her own life flow and the life purposes that move them. This is the stone of pure mental force and will energize the mind with no other qualifications. So great is its virtue that it may awaken that which would otherwise have slept in them. It will bring forth any gift, however latent, of whatsoever nature, when it is appropriately charged. It can serve as the key to their very foundation and, in cases where this is desirable and their body's health is strong and well monitored, it may be their key to the gates of their own paradise and strength of nature. Many are those who unwittingly have worn it and, even they have not recognized that they were then able to lead lives of greater virtue and strength.

Set in gold, it is purest to its purpose. When bound with copper its influence is interfered with in terms of general use and should only be set so for a particular purpose. When this purpose is accomplished, the setting should be discarded and the stone completely cleared and then reset before recharging to a different task. When set in iron use only when the ray of purity and of noble purpose is desired for the blade and its wielder. Combine with other stones to modify and invigorate their energies. This is the light that dispels death and darkness. Silver aids it in achieving balance with its companions and its wearer.

SMOKY

Smoky topaz has a calmative effect, very similar to that of smoky quartz and great care should be taken to be certain that its color is even throughout and not blotched. If it is necessary or desirable for the color of the stone to be variegated, the color should shade evenly from one intensity to another without breaks or striations. Interruptions in the evenness of the color indicate inconsistencies in the energy properties of the stone. A striated smoky topaz should be evenly striped and may be beneficial where its nature is known and understood, for its energy will flow and have the characteristic of internally boosted capacitance, that may or may not be healthful depending on the nature of the work.

ROSE

Rose topaz is the stone of the Temple Dancer, for it brings the true passions up from the base chakra and through to the head. It unifies these principals so that the true passionate power can be brought into the force of the work, and so that it may change from moment to moment in the ever-changing balance of the Dance of Power and Passion. It encourages and triggers the active sensitivity to rhythm through motion, translating the currents of music, feeling and the natural energy rhythm of all things through into motion and expression. Rose topaz is an excellent stone to stimulate spontaneous creativity and to encourage the artist to release the power of passion into his or her art. It is an excellent aid to breaking down blocks to creativity and expression.

This stone admirably translates through the mental body bridging from the solar plexus to both the heart and the base, creating one smooth flow of instinctive awareness. If it is worn by a Dancer in a ritual situation for drawing this particular resonance of power, it should be worn about the hips and even the feet. This will allow it to energize and direct the power at its point of entrance through the primal earth. It should not be set in iron or bronze, for this will inhibit its force. Rather, let it be set with copper or gold, let it be placed on the caps of bells made of silver, let it be cut and placed in platinum that its purpose will flourish. Gold will resonate with its purpose and enrich its vibrations. Though it may be worn in company with all other rose stones, its most pleasant companions are the rose and white tourmaline, for the white will act with it in the same manner as a moonstone, and magnify its influence.

YELLOW & GOLDEN

Topaz in its yellow hues may be most aptly worn by the Priest engaged in guiding and directing many various aspects of energies and powers, for it encourages the quickness to adapt to this ever changing situation as with a man dancing on fire with great joy. It is also excellent for any person seeking to overcome pessimism and reluctance to change and adapt. It makes a very usable talisman stone for those who would renew their lives after some great change of fortune whether for good or ill.

Golden topaz carries the vibration of the Sun Children of Atlantis. This is the vibration of the Archetypal Sun, for as the planet's sun gives life and energy by its light, so does its archetype give radiant life and invigoration. This is the stone of the Spirit in Action in pure form. The more the stone is yellow, the more the energy is qualified through it, energizing and invigorating the mind and intellect. As the stone is filled with those structural anomalies that refract the light, so it attains and gives action to this energy.

Let those of the Ancient Race have this about them according to their need, for it strengthens and maintains the linkage to the light of their beginnings and clarifies this purpose in the heart. It is most blessed to this use when bound about the brow and, in this placement, will bring peace and just pride of freedom and purpose in their knowledge and work. It may be worn with most other stones according to desire and purpose or where specified otherwise.

It may be worn by any who seek the energy and vitality of the Sun in its glory, particularly those who seek regeneration of mental faculties lost by injury or emotional shock, and those who wish its assistance in mentally creative endeavors. In this use, let it be monitored and watched lest the sun burn too brightly and the systems that it serves be too far accelerated.

The golden shades of topaz tending towards the orange nature make a pleasing talisman for the Warrior who sings. This will enable his songs to be powerful and purge from him the grief of his craft. Though it is the Warrior fate to be a Destroyer, it is not the nature of any spiritual being to destroy. These varying natures will disagree within him and cause, at last, his destruction if he does not also create Beauty, and the most healing of all Beauties for the Warrior is his Song.

In ancient days some told a tale of pure golden topaz that is both instructive and charming in its virtue.

THE TALE OF THE WARRIOR'S TORCH

In the ancient days the sun strode proudly and shone its light
upon the earth and always the children of men lived in its
virtue. Never did winter freeze them, nor the cold trouble them
for all was well within the earth. Then an evil demon rose in
smoke from within the earth and hated the children of men for
their gladness and laughter. "Thus will I destroy them," he
cried, "and I will eat away the sun that they will freeze forever
in darkness and their tears will gladden my way." So he flew
into the air and began to eat away the sun. But the greatest of
warriors saw the demon fly into the sky and he rose up to
defend the children of men. Long they battled in the sky and
raised great smoke and dust and noise. But the warrior was
only mortal and began to tire and the sun grew dimmer and the
days grew shorter and all the people were afraid that the war-
rior should fail and they would live in darkness forever. Then
did the woman of the warrior cry out to them, "Let us build
fires and torches, let us help the warrior with his struggle."
And on the darkest day they did so, shouting and singing out to
him to encourage his heart and drive the demon away. And the

demon began to grow weak and the warrior began to triumph
and thus the days grow longer. But the demon is immortal, born
of the trouble in the earth and he may not be overcome. Thus we
carry the golden clear topaz, that it should hearten us at our
times of deepest darkness for it is the torch in the hand of the
warrior and by its light our hearts may prevail. And in the Fall
and Winter months the stars they call the Warrior appear in the
night sky with his torch raised up that we may know that this is
true.

GREEN

In its rare green hue it is well-worn by the Healer who is engaged in research on a long-term basis, for it will re-energize his or her mind lest it become entangled in complex reasoning and hearten him or her so that he will retain a fresh perspective regarding his craft. This should not be confused with or intended to replace the Emerald, which is for the restoration of all his deepest energies, but rather for his or her mind alone.

However, consider carefully whether its wearer has strength and maturity so that this mental process will have a fertile ground in which to work, for topaz, without the basis of stability, will only over-drive the senses and energies and bring about less benefit than it should. Never give it to those who are mentally unbalanced or delusional, for it will only encourage their madness and give it more fuel to manifest its potential. Carefully watch after the diet of those on whom it is placed, so that their systems will adjust to its brilliance without becoming overtaxed in the process of initial contact personalization.

BLUE

Blue topaz is not often recommended for use by visionaries who work in a state of deep trance. Its active nature makes in unsuitable for a Journey Stone. But for those who wish to attune themselves to their own intuition and become more sensitive to the subtle energy rhythms of their surroundings, blue topaz makes an excellent choice. It not only operates on the topaz vibration, encouraging instinctive sensitivity, it opens the solar plexus energies to flexibility and adaptability to what is received through that channel. Its blue color resonance links it with the throat center allowing what is received to be articulated and processed through the rational mind so that it helps translate instinct into information and then information into teaching. To the degree it is blue, the more the spirit, mind and body are unified, flowing together smoothly in one purpose.

Blue topaz reinforces the power of will by bringing confidence in the intuitive faculties. It can also assist in the flow of energies and aid the balance of the nature of the Seer by helping to bring the Seer's visions into rational consciousness. It can serve as a cooling force for those of most passionate natures, mediating their anger and passions by rational thought. Blue topaz is a well chosen life stone for the warrior to enable him to balance himself throughout, for topaz agrees well in strength with those other strengths of his nature and passions. As his body and other forces are strong by the nature of his craft, so the stone will not contend against his other forces for precedence, but assist and aid them.

BERYL

ALUMINUM BERYLLIUM SILICATE

$Al_2Be_3(Si_6O_{18})$

CHAKRA: HEART

CALLING: HEALER

ARCHETYPE COLOR: GREEN (EMERALD)

The Beryl family includes emerald as its archetype, and also aquamarine as blue, yellow as heliodore, and red beryl as morganite. The beryls are stones of peace and the enlightenment that comes from within when one is at peace with one's own nature and circumstances. They act through the spiritual body, via the heart chakra, to bring together all the levels of the human energy system complex. They also act to extend this balanced energy outward through the horizontal axis. This, along with their regenerative abilities, is why they are often ascribed to the calling of the Healer. They are unifiers of the energies of the spirit, qualified to specific purposes by virtue of their colors. In all dealings with its qualities remember that the keyword of this family is *"reweaving."* Its nature restores all systems by knitting up what has become undone. It fills in gaps and tears in the energy system complex as a whole, centering its activity on the chakra that corresponds to its color. But its activity is not limited to that chakra. It is as though it used that center for a base note and then wrote a piece of music from the rest of the complex based on its harmonics.

To understand their basic nature, one may consider them as female, that is, passive and receptive in their functions rather than active stones of aggressive power. They are stones of modulation and flow that encourage balance and order in the energy systems. None of them should be set in any metal containing iron even to the least degree, for this will nullify their function. This also extends to combining it with stones that have a predominance of iron in their structure such as hematite. They are best worn in silver or copper, for this will amplify their functions and will be explained in accordance with the natures of the individual stones. Gold also makes a good choice of metal for the setting, but only if they are to be set to a specific task such as specific power workings, rather than charged to a general talismanic or healing purpose.

Beryls make good additions to complex talismans of power because their nature allows them to not only join with the separate elements of the talisman itself, but also to unify the combined vibrational pattern of the talisman with the wearer. This allows the talisman to operate smoothly within the basic energy parameters of the spirit's vehicle. It is unadvisable to incorporate beryls into talismans of war or any aggression with intent to harm or cause destruction for its own sake, for these intentions are contrary to its nature and will harm the stone. Also, this will cause the energies of negative aggression to be dispersed throughout a spirit's resonant energy system and cause a wide variety of ills that are not easily purged, and may cause injury due to over-driving of certain channels.

For all their receptive and passive qualities, beryl should not be thought to be a weak family, for their strength is in their subtlety. They work steadily throughout the system without disruption to any channel and will bring about great changes when worn with patience and charged correctly within the scope of their natures.

BERYL AS A PRIMARY

Clear Beryl (Goshenite) makes a good choice as the primary in talismans intended for long term usage involving healing or restoring of the energy system. Their nature is literally to reweave energy patterns that have become fragmented or disconnected. This makes it a good choice for talismans dealing with energy blockages and imbalances because it draws from the entire energy system complex to complete a healthy and desirable pattern. This distributes the energy throughout the system causing less chance of damage through overload or backlash. Beryl may be qualified by any stone of a green or blue nature, and also, but less commonly, the yellow of its own kind called Heliodore. In this combination will be great joy and potency. For a blue qualifier, sapphire is most sovereign and powerful even to the farthest range of the spectrum, for it acts as a most perfect triad harmonic in all the ranges of its color hues. When in this combination, it naturally attunes itself to the energy signatures of the Initiates and is most sensitive to the subtle energy modulations of the individual. Blue tourmaline may substitute for the sapphire in some cases but will not serve as well because its nature is not as directly focussed. The combination of clear beryl with a blue qualifier may be driven with green or red or purple. An opal here is well chosen, but not a moonstone, for moonstone does not have a sufficiently tight focus to govern the dispersive nature of the Beryl. Diamonds of any color may be used in times of necessity but may prove too strong unless their influence is intentionally desired. Emeralds may be used to great effect in talismans incorporating the violet ray and, to some special degree, the purple for its nature is such that it will work in harmony with other stones charged in accordance to its natural purposes.

RED AND ROSE (MORGANITE)

Red and rose beryls are stones of subtle virtue as they distribute the life force of the base chakra throughout the life system of the individual. These stones add a stronger, more forceful vibration to individuals whose nature is not to be forceful and aid them in tasks to which they might not otherwise be suited. They may also raise the nature of sexuality throughout the body giving it life and color. They may aid in the increase of blood flow throughout the body and increase the circulation of life-giving energies of whatever nature. Red and rose beryls may be of great aid in healing, particularly in women who have been greatly drained and/or physically injured in the course of childbirth, also, in the case of rape or other sexually violent injury that manifests on many levels of consciousness. In as much as the life force raises from the base chakra, traumas to this area can seriously effect the general system and especially to the mind, godhead and will that are its resonant centers. Violation of this area by force should be treated with great solemnity and consolation, for, especially in those who deal in the forces of power, traumas to this area may cause lasting effect of harm of the greatest kind. In these matters this stone may prove of true and gentle virtue, for it will aid in the process of the energies reasserting themselves gently and in health, after those areas are physically healed.

Morganite may be worn safely by many who may not bear the stronger and more intense radiance of other rose and red stones and may, indeed, prove as a stepping stone for them to rise to higher and more potent realms of force. This should be done wisely and in peace, for the nature of the beryl is peace and restoration and may be most potently used for healing and strengthening on many levels. This may be done with novices especially, for its nature is malleable and agreeable and can be used without harm in most cases.

YELLOW (HELIODORE)

Yellow beryl, heliodore, is most closely akin to wit and its color should be as the flower Jonquil. It promotes cleverness and a sense of inner joy combined with pride in ones own accomplishments. Its nature is creative and individualistic encouraging laughter and physical creativity. This is the brightness of Spring translated to the mental nature. It may be worn by children whose lives are aggrieved by loss of friend for it will bring back their inherent nature to joy and optimism. It does not have the lightening bright flash of the topaz nor the heavier resonance of quartz in these matters but will aid the spirit to find its own bright nature of wit most pleasantly in harmony with the balance of the other centers. Its color is caused by uranium oxide that encourages a slight distancing from the physical level of the body, allowing the wearer to release grosser or impacted energies that have interlocked with the physical body vibration. This will help the wearer release unwanted states of mental, emotional, or physical nature, to be replaced with a broader and more expansive overview.

Silver is its most beneficial companion, but gold is not ill-chosen to bring forth a richer resonance from its virtue. Copper is not generally recommended except in work where its virtue has a special purpose. This stone can be a gentle balm on the heart and spirit. It is most notably used in recuperation from sad shocks to the heart, for it helps the wearer to rediscover that optimism, seemingly lost, and to soothe the nature with its most gracious virtue.

GREEN (EMERALD)

The emerald exemplifies the highest quality of the beryl family. Its color is caused by the addition of chromium (and sometimes, vanadium) that links it directly to the emotional body acting through the heart center. It is the talisman of the master healer and is indispensable in this work. The emerald will allow the Healer's energies to be ever renewed regardless of what must be achieved in this vocation. It constantly restores balance to his system causing those powers of restoration to flow from him with focus and precision. This stone is greatly discussed in the reference to green stones, for the emerald is the highest among them. This is the unifier of peaceful power and a restorative of great power when the life systems are drained through shock or overwork. By its virtue, it allows the individual to draw upon great sources of energy for the restoration of his vital systems. It will, when tuned to this task, automatically supply what is spent in the course of any labor, especially those labors that involve selfless healing or creation. It is considered especially sovereign in healing the heart center. Then, by reenergizing this hub of the individual's energy wheel, the source point of unification and expression of the energy system complex, then all the rest of the wheel, that is, the body's centers and expression of energy, are likewise healed by its resonant harmonics.

This stone may heal the Warrior in his darkest hour, provided that his hurts were obtained in righteous purpose, and provided that his channels are otherwise clear, according to his disciplines. In this working, the Healer should be female so that she may bring healing to him by her nature and strength and he should open himself to its virtue.

This is the stone of the Healer Priest and of the High Kings who are no longer of this plane and of all sovereigns who would heal their people after strife of war. It is this that will sustain him in his labors. By its energy, a new blossom can be brought forth, provided that this sovereign is its willing Guardian. No healing thing is beyond his will, should its virtue be maintained within him, for no matter the magnitude of what he must pour forth, this will be safely and harmoniously returned to him.

The Healer should wear it set in silver, copper and gold and wear it upon the brow or over the heart that it may sustain him. The King may do likewise and carry it upon his crown or staff or worked within his chain of office. It should not be set in weapons of iron or steel for this will sicken both Spirit and Stone. If a blade is necessary for the chosen work, use bronze heavy with copper and devoid of iron, with but a little tin added for hardness. This will serve where the power of the emerald is needed and the focus of the blade is proper in all respects. However, the worker should prepare himself carefully in this, for the power of the stone may draw forth from him all his life and should he block or disallow the restoration of its virtue, the work will not succeed and his life will be endangered.

PALE BLUE (AQUAMARINE)

This is the stone of the Moon's virtue and the most sovereign of flow/reweaving stones. It is similar to the emerald in that its energies are restorative in nature. It integrates easily into the energies of the wearer, allowing them to flow easily and seek balance among themselves. Its pigment is iron, and the wearer may find balance where he needs it in the intake of life giving energies and the dispelling of those forces negative to his nature. It clarifies sight and workings in that, in its highest function, it allows no chakra to over-drive any other and, thus, balance is maintained. Incoming energies are dispersed evenly throughout and are more easily sorted; outflowing energies are sustained from the concerted energy matrix of the Whole and thus modified to balanced flow. As this balance is maintained, the Spirit is more easily restored from the Great Source, for channels are less likely to block when there is no internal imbalance.

However, when it is necessary or desirable to work from one center specifically, and especially when this is in a great degree, aquamarine may become overloaded and fatigued, for this spirit of work is contrary to its basic nature. Yet, in this case, it will aid the effort of the work by its restorative qualities and will do so to the limits of its capacity.

Set this stone with silver and wear it as comfort suits along the vertical axis. Give this freely in its paler shades to any novice troubled by inner conflict and his work and studies will be aided and his trouble calmed from within. Worn in silver upon the left hand it will aid in intake energies and healing perceptions. It may be bound with gold for more palpable activity, but in this take care to choose a perfect stone, for the focus of the gold will drive it hardly. It may be most beautifully bound with copper and it is thus set in the headdress of the younger female priestess, and upon the brow of the Seeress also. In this activity most sacred in the lunar rites, the copper will lend it strength and virtue beyond its normal limit, and keep the stone and its wearer safe. In this function alone, the aquamarine is considered in its own right to be a stone of power. Do not set it into any iron, for iron will interfere with its basic elements and render the stone useless, yet when removed from this metal its virtue is easily restored and it remains unharmed.

CORUNDUM GROUP

ALUMINUM OXIDE (Al$_2$O$_3$)
CHAKRA: THROAT
CALLING: SEER / TEACHER
ARCHETYPE: BLUE SAPPHIRE

Corundum in general corresponds to the throat chakra, that center that translates higher mind and visionary concepts and articulates them into useful communication. This is the center of both the Seer and the Teacher. It is the center of will and intention, of reaching outward from the inner world and the cosmic self into the physical Universe. This center addresses focus and expression and the stones that correspond to it are directly linked with those functions. Corundum aligns the higher vibrational energies with the slower moving physical ones – that is, it works through the mental body, via the throat chakra, to link the spirit and mind with physical reality. The color of the stone determines the way in which this focus will manifest and direct itself. The corundum family includes a wide rainbow of colors caused by the presence, in varying degrees, of iron (yellow and green), chrome (pink and red), vanadium (violet), and iron with titanium (blue). The pure red corundum is called Ruby. These stones behave according to the individual nature of the color resonance. The practitioner should remember that the nature of sapphire is in the point of the Will, and, therefore, their natures are direct and without inhibition. These stones work from the most integral point of the Being's personality center and manifest the truth of that nature, expressing it outward into manifestation and development.

Sapphire is known in all color ranges as the Stone of Fidelity and draws forth strength of purpose ever unto death and beyond. It is regarded as a stone of nobility and should be held in great honor. It may be used where diamond holds too broad a spectrum of activity when a narrower focus of should be added.

WHITE SAPPHIRE

White sapphire is the term used for clear or white translucent sapphire. It makes a strong driver whether in its crystal form, or cut faceted or cabochon. This is a stone of great virtue in the implementation of the will, and answers the consciousness of the one to whom it is tuned as would the finest horse or hound respond to its master's wishes. Care should be taken to chose a stone with clear, uniform color. The cutting of the piece be should be with regard to the grain of the stone, that is, the center axis of the crystal should remain as the horizontal or vertical axis of whatever stone is cut from it. To have this axis at a random angle to the shape of the stone will add confusion to the energies of the pieces particularly if it is used with other stones.

RUBY

Ruby is the name of the true deep red corundum and its properties are so distinctive that it is often regarded in a classification all to its own. Its coloration is caused by chromium in the structure and it is, therefore, linked through the emotional body, as is emerald. This stone encourages the expression of great passion by linking the emotional body with the means of its expression and articulation. In the instance of aggression, this is the stone of the Warrior Nature and unrepressed power. It allows for the expression of the purest force of energy whether for war or peace, to kill or to heal in all its manifestations, for it focuses the primal energy of the base chakra through the center of the expressions of the Will. Its colors vary from pale rose through orange, true red and purple, and in each of these aspects the nature of its color radiance should be taken carefully into account, for these color ranges are critical in a stone of this magnitude of drive and power potential.

As with all this family, it is the precision and density of the atomic structure that dictates its virtually limitless load/energy potential. This should not be underestimated, for the ruby, in particularly in the purple color resonance, will drive multiple ranges through red and even blue and will, therefore, over-drive nearly any other stone with which it is placed. To the degree that it is tuned to the wearer it will react automatically to the unconscious intention of that wearer and thus may be used safely only by those trained in the Disciplines lest harm result to either the wearer or his surroundings.

The ruby may also be a gently healing stone, for it answers to the chakra of warmth and life, and by using this stone that power may be raised to enliven all systems throughout the body. The stone should be charged to raise this current slowly and with circumspection, and will prove to be most sovereign in this respect.

This stone is known as the sign and stone of the King as he rides to war in righteous cause. This stone is the signet of the enforcement of his just wrath and none will stand against it. But once his cause is won, let it be put aside with honor lest it continue in its actions and overrule him by its energies. This stone may be thus used with impunity according to its nature as long as constant vigilance is kept over its functions and power.

ORANGE (PAD PARAJAH)

Pad Parajah is a pinkish orange sapphire whose coloration is caused by the addition of small amounts of chrome. The nature of its corundum/sapphire structure combined with the element that causes its color make it the most potent in virtue of this energy and archetype of the belly chakra. It is known as the Stone of Princes and is most virtuously set in their diadems. It establishes the right of the Warrior Prince as the Sun Bringer in time of greatest darkness. It is the most potent agent of the Healer's strength and by its virtue may he impose and establish his will and intention.

Well is it set in gold or platinum. Well is it borne into war in bronze or steel alike. Well is it worn by either sex, for so great is its virtue that it answers either polarity right well in harmony and strength.

YELLOW

Yellow sapphire enhances the activity of the solar plexus chakra in its intuitive and intelligent functions. It also allows for rational expression of this center's creative and individualistic aspect. It helps overcome the barriers an individual may feel with regards to the right to survival and participation in the universal abundance by bringing for that person's expression of identity, personality and an awareness of the right to exist fully. This can be of powerful assistance in overcoming the effects of emotional abuse as a child, and other issues of abandonment or betrayal. It helps restore faith in oneself that will translate into confidence in one's ability to move on all levels of awareness.

When in general use, it gives the gift of verbal agility – the ability to think on one's feet and express oneself well even in demanding circumstances, because it is always connected to the clarity of higher mind.

GREEN

The color agent in green sapphire is iron that strongly connects this stone to the lower energy centers making it a powerful restorative of the life-giving energies. It is a stone of both nurturing and awakening. It is particularly useful when restoring energies that have been expended through the mental and physical bodies. It provides this restorative power by balancing the flow of earth energy with the flow of universal energy as it enters the crown. Green sapphire makes a viable alternative to emerald when used as a Healer's personal talisman.

BLUE

The pure blue sapphire is the Stone of the Will, Focus and the unification of the Spirit. Its keywords would be Clarifying Focus. As with all other members of its family, it will cleanse the mind and will of the lingering effects of shock or illness. It can encourage a reference point through which all other elements of the energy system complex can be drawn into alignment both with each other and with time/space reality. It helps greatly with this alignment because it asserts a viewpoint and focus through which all other centers and levels can orient. The titanium in its structure links it directly to the energy source of the throat chakra drawing all other awarenesses through it so that whatever expression is predominant in the individual will be clarified and articulated in the clearest way possible. It will have a relaxing effect on some individuals because, to the degree they feel their thoughts and actions clarified and focussed, they lose the nervousness associated with being scattered. Seers and mediums can also benefit from its influence because it will help them focus on their vision and bring it through clearly in terms that their listeners can understand and accept.

This is a strong stone and will bring all other channels to bear along its charged line of focus while aligning either the being or the talisman piece well and truly to its appointed purpose. Its color should be a very clear and yet very deep royal blue and contain no more than 10% of its mass in inclusions, because any greater percentage will affect the axis structure and basic nature of its vibration pattern. In applications where this is not so critical and it is only the general nature of the stone that is desired and not a focussed power talisman, the percentage of inclusions may be slightly higher but to no more than 12% of the stone. The color should be clear so that the resonance of its color agent is not impaired. Should such a muddy and imperfect stone be implemented to a cause, particularly that of healing, it is likely to lead to confusion and headache. To the degree the stone is clear and pure, so is the degree of its strength. It is very well matched with diamond especially when set in silver or platinum and as with diamonds let the percentage of nickel in the metal be as small as is possible for it to be.

VIOLET

Violet sapphire is separate and distinct from purple ruby. Violet sapphire provides a clear and simple bridge from the higher chakras' functions of spirit and reason, allowing them to be expressed and directed into time/space reality. Its activity, while very strong and directed, will usually feel discreet and unobtrusive to the wearer. This is because it operates on such a direct level that it does not affect or interfere with any other levels of the energy system complex. This makes an excellent bridge to higher spiritual levels and gently allows for the clearing of the whole channel of energy so that the universal light energy can enter the energy system complex and be recognized and acknowledged. This opening also helps the lower vibrational energies to flow upward in a clear pattern through the spiritual subtle body.

BLACK

Black sapphire protects as it centers the individuality of will and expression. It removes unrelated waveform anomalies from the energy system harmonic. Its clarifies the individual's vibration and helps him or her to center his or her energies. By doing this, black sapphire clears all wave forms from the individual that do not belong to that individual, relieving that person of unwanted attachments whether intentional or unintentional, whether caused by another individual or by circumstances. When worn at the throat or heart chakra it provides this level of protection from moment to moment and allows whatever other stones are set with it to function without interference of any kind. This is an important stone and is of great value to anyone working in large groups of people or in controversial situations.

STAR SAPPHIRE

In sapphires and rubies, six-rayed star patterns are caused by tiny rutillations oriented to the crystal's axis structure. The star in any color of sapphire or ruby will greatly enhance its capabilities and range of focus according to the nature of the particular color. It is a natural augmentation and amplification of the stone's nature.

These have great virtue in the practice of scrying, for the star may be a focus for the mind while the blue radiance will clear the vision seen for all overcast of emotion and uncertainty and will focus this sight by the purest intentional force of will. Black will calm the sight of the seer and allow the vision to slow and thus appear clearer and in greater detail. This will also filter out unwarranted emotions of the seer as well as agitation, that the vision be purely itself uncolored by that which is superfluous and not needed.

TOURMALINE

ALUMINUM BORATE SILICATE

$(NaLiCa)(Fe_{11}Mg\ Mn\ Al_3((OH)_4(BO_3)_3Si_6O_{18})$

COMPLICATED AND CHANGEABLE COMPOSITION

CHAKRA: BROW

CALLING: MONARCH

ARCHETYPE COLOR: PURPLE (SIBERITE)

Tourmaline is a large family of closely related stones having similar basic properties. Each is defined as a tourmaline because of the basic aluminum borate silicate structure, but the agents that combine with this to give it its color define each as a separate but related crystal, having related properties but a unique nature. The strength of their nature is that their basic structure is closely bonded and joined and yet they accommodate a variety of other elements that give them a unique color and behavior. The bonding of the basic structure is such that, although it is extremely strong, it is also formed is such a way as to be able to incorporate many different elements and not lose its nature or strength. Therefore, the variety of colors it can exhibit are virtually endless in their shades and composition, often exhibiting several colors in a single crystal. The structure is also bonded in such a way that energy moves through it freely. This creates a strong field that retains its identity regardless of the strengths of other stones with which it is placed. These properties make the tourmaline family an excellent choice for general workings of healing, personal talisman work and focussed power work. It is the only stone that manifests every shade of the spectrum from true black to true white to clear without becoming muddy or unstable. When these colors are combined in a single stone, they form as a composite talisman of unique virtue, for the stone is in perfect balance with its various properties. Tourmalines in this configuration may be utilized as both driver and primary. This is the only stone that may harmoniously incorporate many colors without weakening its structural integrity or prejudicing its single focus of energy. It becomes not more dispersed in its workings but more intense in its complex resonance.

Tourmaline works spontaneously and with great virtue, for it draws energy into its negative pole with great strength and transmutes it automatically according to its color nature. Tune tourmalines circumspectly, for their actions will gradually escalate, magnifying from their initial charge setting. This can be of great virtue in the healing process, however, after all channels have cleared in the stone it is difficult to slow this down for reuse. It is wisest to choose a new/unused stone for each use per person. For as a dog will follow one master, so this stone will attune to one harmony. A practitioner may tune the stone to his own harmonic and keep its nature within his own control setting the stone to work independently of his touch upon another person automatically according to its nature but under his direction and guidance. Thus the identity tuning will never need to be changed, just the working charge.

It is most sovereign, in a general sense, as a life stone, but must be most carefully and meticulously selected to closely match the signature pattern of the Spirit, for they have a great integrity of identity structure that can never be completely overridden. Once selected, they will be attuned for life and only the hands of an adept can alter this but never with complete success without the willing participation of the wearer. This is its signature virtue. Tourmaline retains its own characteristic identity pattern to some degree regardless of the use to which it is put. This makes it ideal for a healing stone, because the negativity of the disease or dysfunction will never fully taint the stone. Once it is tuned it will remain focussed on this harmonic. Its nature also allows it to automatically integrate with the full spectrum of the energy system complex. It will weave its virtue through all levels of awareness, aligning them through the energy center to which its nature is keyed. It will manifest its energy through the rational process. This will give the wearer the opportunity to integrate its powers with intelligence.

It should be remembered that tourmaline corresponds to the brow chakra. This is not only the seat of reason, but the center where the spiritual identity is integrated with the concept of time and cause/effect of this universe. Tourmaline can give the wearer a key signature with which to attach to his or her Higher Self and the wisdom and perspective that comes from this connection. It connects this universal awareness and sensitivity to the rational process, allowing the individual to be consciously aware of this connection. This is the conscious individual working in partnership with Higher Self/Higher Mind and when this connection is developed to its fullest potential can activate great harmony and alignment in the individual.

It should also be considered that it is the nature of tourmaline to align itself. When placed within an individuals energy system complex it will begin to function whether it is directed or not. It will integrate with that individual at its strongest level and as this connection grows, its alignment will naturally increase and assist the wearer to increasingly use the energy it presents. This is a constantly building cycle until the stone reaches the natural limits of its capacity. It is this property that allows it to retain its identity as an energy form and, after the initial period of adjustment, it will naturally reject any transient negative states such as illness or depression. The wearer should, therefore, bear in mind that, when charging a new stone, he or she should be in reasonably good health on all levels of the energy system complex if he or she is not going to charge it with a specific intention..

In times of emergency or need, tourmaline may replace any other stone but not necessarily for long duration. In these instances, its color must be most carefully considered, for this will determine its suitability and its ability to hold firm or burn under great stress. When chosen for work within the scope of its capabilities, it will hold in the face of almost infinite load stress and simply grow stronger. But always remember that on completion of the work it may have to be put aside having been opened to the limit of its gradient. One may attempt to re-clear the stone but this will be only temporarily successful. In this it would be wise to consider the procedures used to clear fine steel for the procedures are quite similar in this regard and such methods would be both effective and appropriate. This is because, the flow of energy opens and aligns the structure of the crystal. Once this opening and alignment are accomplished, the stone will not return to its former state. It will remain open and aligned. This can be a very desirable property but it is a powerful one and the practitioner should keep this in mind when applying tourmaline to extended high power applications.

This behavior is closely linked to tourmaline's significant piezoelectric property. That is, when heated it will develop an electric charge and a negative/positive polarity that will cause small particles to be drawn to it. This gives it its self-activating property and a definite strength in alignment with the individual energy system complex.

The colored varieties of tourmaline are as many as the hues of the bright sky bow and as joyous. Often two or more colors are found together in a single crystal. Therefore, take care in their selection for their tone shifts are subtle and the potential harmonic combinations endless in its variety and proportion. In such combinations, the energies of a single stone may manifest as the energies of many stones working in perfect harmony. To the degree that one color is greater in proportion than the other, its energies manifest in strength in that proportion to the other colors within it.

Tourmalines are easily attuned and energized and give great strength and virtue when used with these precepts in mind. These stones are virtually automatic in their activity and, once attuned to the signature charge of its wearer, will respond to that wearer as though by instinct and without intentional direction of the wearer. It should seldom be worn by the untrained or undisciplined, unless the stone is chosen very carefully. But where it is charged fully by the healer or the practitioner, it may be directed to do great work and may be very beneficial especially by virtue of its automatic activities and functions.

TOURMALINE AS PRIMARY

Tourmalines of all varieties make powerful primary stones, but always bear in mind that their nature is automatic and this automaticity will be triggered by the action of the other stones alone and may not wait upon the pleasure of the practitioner. These make good emergency pieces and pieces for the use of those who work in trance and may not have access to momentary modulations of their own tools. But let the charge be closely set by one other than the wearer, so that its activity will be objective and rational rather than subjective to the Dreamer. They may be qualified by any stone of sufficient strength and purpose, but it is suggested that the driver be a stronger stone such as a diamond or sapphire so that the tourmaline does not override them. The metal should be the strongest and purest, whether gold, silver, or platinum. Iron is unsuitable because the combination of iron and tourmaline will over-drive the wearer.

Tourmalines must be activated together as a group to work well as a group. If they have been charged separately, then placed together at a later time, their energies are not likely to blend well unless they are all cleared to the base level and then brought into a charge as a group.

Two different sets of terminology are used to differentiate them. One classifies them according to coloring element and the other classifies them according to color. As with garnets each chemical composition can produce several different colors depending on the precise pattern of combination with the base structure.

Buergerite.............Sodium-Iron
Dravite.................Magnesium................Yellow Brown – Dark Brown
Elbaite..................Sodium-Lithium-Aluminum
Schorl...................Sodium-Iron............Black
Tsilaisite...............Manganese
Uvite...................Calcium-Magnesium

WHITE AND CLEAR (ACRHOITE)

Clear and white tourmalines as primary stones energize and activate the connection between the realization of higher mind and the center that corresponds to the qualifiers placed with them. They act as a connection to bring to bear the articulated spiritual awareness characteristic of the brow chakra into reality via the center to which the qualifier stones direct this energy. Their action is subtle and ethereal making seen what might otherwise only be sensed.

When used as a driver stone it will behave in a similar fashion to moonstone. The openness of its vibration pattern gathers the vibration pattern of any other stones with which it is placed, into a tightly woven complete harmonic, and expresses them in a direct continuity with the wearer's optimal vibrational pattern. White tourmaline as a driver will also have the added benefit that, once charged, the talisman will tend to retain its vibrational harmonic and not be tainted by the negativity or other energy dysfunction of its wearer. This makes it a good driver to use in healing talismans for cases where the illness is cyclical rather than constant. It should be considered, however, that using tourmaline as a driver stone will tend to overwhelm the other stones of the pieces with its characteristic pattern, and if this is not desirable a stone of a different family should be considered.

BLACK (SCHORL) & YELLOW/BROWN (DRAVITE)

The black tourmaline is the strongest and most effective of all the black stones used for grounding, followed by brown and yellow-brown dravite. It will charge immediately and automatically, and then synchronize with the signature pattern of the user. It grounds and purifies virtually without limit and so may be used in cases of even the greatest power load without fear of overloading the stone. This may be of great benefit in that the stone may be placed where its energies may be constantly needed and left there without aid from any person, provided that it is first charged to its purpose. There it will carry forward with its work unaided and unimpeded as long as may be necessary.

There are two varieties of tourmalines that may be considered as truly black, one is known as schorl and is of the gem grade quality. Its appearance is very sleekly black and this stone is most sovereign both for general clearing and grounding purposes and also for specific precision uses. It will carry a definite signature charge of the owner and serve him as a faithful dog would its master even to the end of its capabilities. This stone is of great virtue and strength and may be charged by the owner to any degree of workings within the purview of its abilities. It may be set to work at a distance and may draw the power from any working of which the owner has right knowledge. Therefore, they may be considered a form of distance linkage.

When placed rightly and charged to the specific, schorl tourmaline may be set to retain the filtered charge that may retrieved later by the owner at need. Remember that this will be filtered, charged, and therefore pure energy, and must be respecified to its intended task. There will be no limit to its working unless this limit is specifically stated and charged within it, and thus large pieces may prove a danger to the unwary or weak unless they are used with the proper precautions.

The second type of black tourmaline is known as dravite. It is actually brown containing flakes of golden colored inclusions that serve as a dispersive to its energies and give it a far more gentle-seeming effect than the schorl. Its quality and potential is very similar to smoky quartz, although of far greater potency. It does not retain all energies within itself, but gives back those energies that it has filtered in a cycling action. Thus it may be worn without harm for a greater length of time and will prove of some certain benefit in the cases of hysterical fevers. Both types, and especially this one, may be worn after the workings of great power are completed, so that those practitioners who are in need may gently disperse any retained charges and anomalies caused by fatigue. It may help alleviate confusion, dizziness, and dysphasia caused by lengthy high power usages. Let this wearing for grounding and discharge also be accompanied with the drinking of honey wine in light quantity and a period of rest and quiet so that the cycle can be completed without agitation or instability. In cases where this wine is unavailable, the juice of any clear fruit or berry can be substituted, particularly, where calmative and restorative herbs are steeped in it for the period of a day.

In all things, this stone may prove of great benefit when used carefully, in accordance with the limitations both of its nature, and the nature of the wearer. Its virtue is great and general in all things and is most highly recommended for use.

RED AND ROSE (RUBELITE)

These are excellent stones for healing and energizing the base chakra and therefore of all primal life energies.

They are, however, very strong and whoever undertakes to use them should be prepared in the exercised of balance and discipline. They are more direct that rose quartz and do not have the iron energy commonly associated with red quartz. Their energy centers in the emotional body and integrates easily with the energy system complex. Their uses are similar to that of red garnet – that is, healing to the energy of the vital systems and in keeping with all matters joining the base energies with the heart. Although, being tourmalines, rubelites carry a strong overtone of energy through the rational/spiritual process. They are often given as love charms between those who would join, for they will match pattern for pattern in the passionate energies of both the body and spirit. These pieces may be used to inflame any passion and give energy to the balanced will and are often set beside royal blue sapphires in this enterprise.

Set them in any metal without hesitation but charge them carefully to attune gradually to the wearer.

YELLOW (DRAVITE)

Yellow tourmaline is a great and automatic energizer of the wit and mental faculties, but is even more prone to automatic engagement than the yellow topaz. In the hands of a skilled practitioner, it brings flashes of intuition and insight that can illumine great realms of that individual's life and work. It can lead to greater understanding of him or herself and his or her circumstances or of any difficulty or problem that preys upon the mind. Yellow tourmaline has been known to open the gate of intuitive dreams if worn while sleeping. It has also been known to encourage a sleeping individual to have vivid dreams that bear on certain pivotal life problems that need to be addressed but that may be resident in the unconscious. It would be wise to use this ability intentionally and keep a note pad or journal close by so that any dreams can be written down upon waking.

Because of its automatic nature, it should be subject to conscious control only, and charged to respond ONLY to conscious will lest harm and trouble result from its unchecked activity.

GOLDEN (DRAVITE)

This is the tourmaline that energizes the active ray of both protection and revelation. It can be worn effectively for it's protective influence for the Seer who travels far and is absent from the physical body for long periods. This tourmaline acts to strengthen the spirit and to energize and guard the vacated flesh. In this activity it is unparalleled. Should it be modified to any degree with green, this lessens its quality of protection but reinforces its quality of regeneration and, therefore, care should be taken in the perception and choice of the coloration. For the Seer and Mage this may prove an invaluable aid in the realms of all workings of power and prove a sure and certain defense against the weakness and separation and the debilitation of the flesh that comes through departure of the Spirit.

It may be bound about the brow or worn at the throat. To wear it above the heart will diffuse its influence throughout the entire body rather than centering its influence in the upper chakras to which it is closest akin. It may be set in any precious metal with only the slight differencing in effect.

GREEN (VERDELITE)

The brilliant sea green tourmaline is well known in virtue for it ranks second only to emerald in the pure strength of its green resonant virtue. Its hues are greatly varied and care should always be taken in its selection for the choice of the specific resonance required. It has not the Earth-strength resonance of green garnet, but is rather more unqualified in its energy patterns. As with all tourmalines, its nature is automatic and will escalate its activity to the limit of its frequency and capability. Its nature is restorative to the heart center and indeed to all centers that are drained by heavy strain. Because of this it may be considered a Healer's stone but without the balancing properties of Emerald. It works very well as a restorative and regenerative for those whose work deals with many levels of consciousness simultaneously. For those who must maintain an awareness of the physical world while working it the mental, emotional and spiritual levels, it helps unify the vibrations together, so that the effort is not a strain and so that one level will contribute to the others rather than straining against it.

Its vibration pattern is particularly restorative to those Artisans and Smiths whose craft is both physical and technically demanding. It can be worn along with the stone of their Calling when embarking upon a project that will require great reserves of energy on all levels for great duration of time. This stone will maintain them and its automaticity will refresh them constantly. The Artisans must unify their efforts and bring their intention forth into physical reality. Theirs, like the Warrior's, is a Calling that works on many levels at once, and it is the special virtue of the green tourmaline that it will restore them on these many levels and bring about an internal balance of all levels of awareness. This balance and harmony will communicate itself to the work and will help it be more precise and more in alignment with their initial conception. It will do this while not allowing the continued strain to overtax them.

Its perfect archetypal color is sea green, and care should be taken as to this specific hue. Should the stone be banded let the other colors be noticed and especially taken into account in terms of their specific work at hand.

BLUE (INDICOLITE)

Blue tourmaline comes in many shades from the delicate pastel of the aquamarine to the darkest variety of sapphire. It encourages strengthening the will and power of communication and expression, particularly worn about the throat. It encourages the connection of communication shaped by reason and observation. In its lighter varieties, it will act as a flow stone, but should only be used by those experienced in the disciplines, for its pale color can be deceptive as to its strength. Aquamarine is a better choice for the untrained. However, tourmaline is the stronger stone and is less likely to be overridden or burned out by those individuals of a passionate or impulsive nature. In such cases where automatic force and intense energy are dictated by the circumstances, the blue tourmaline is far better used than a member of the beryl family. It is well worn by females in their rights of passage to hearten them through the dark path of their initiation until they come once more into the Sun of their true abilities.

This stone in its stronger hues is to the Priestess as the citrine and carnelian are to the Warrior and is the footstone of their force. Its energy is best used in the feminine and the masculine energy of the same resonance is the darkest blue sapphire. To the degree that the blue is mixed with green, this energy is added and manifested as a cycling and regenerative force directly into the life cycle energy helix of the being, and this is then keyed to the heart chakra energy signature pattern. In some cases this is highly undesirable as it will override any balance governance otherwise set and work through this heart/will center alone.

The wearer should take care to work with this stone through a balanced harmonic focussing the balanced energy of all the centers together. This can be a stone of marvellous virtue and bring peace of strength to its wearer. In that energy is intentionally cycled through this stone, it is focussed and refined in vibration through intelligent will. These forces are then brought consciously to the use of the wearer, as the reins are brought to the hand of the rider. It is wise to consider accompanying this stone with a strong rose balance, but not true red.

PURPLE (SIBERITE)

True purple tourmaline is known as the Stone of Dominion - sovereign in its sphere above all others. It brings together all other vibrations and orders them according to vibrational hierarchy. It is the unifier of the heart and mind and a focus onto the Earthly plane of all powers of which it is composed. It is the giver of command and, when used by right, no other focused ray may stand against it. It is the stone of reason and rational design. It unifies the voice of spirit with the observation of the physical world bringing the knowledge of each to its vibration without being overwhelmed by either. It encourages the individual wearer to develop objectivity with spirituality and compassion.

It is ideally set in gold that is no less than 75% of its allow (18 karat) or platinum, for these are the ideal metals to direct it energy. Iron in any part will not harm the stone but will hinder its action. Silver will guide its energies to be more generally throughout the energy system complex, but it will limits its nature to the level of the least powerful point through which it is distributed.

When worn in group workings of power, only one participant should wear this at any given time, because, if two are worn or more they will conflict with one another and create unnecessary confusion of energies.

This is a rare and precious stone and in time of need may be temporarily replaced by a perfect carbuncle (ruby crystal) of that unique purple hue. It need not be completely clear but must transmit light. All its faces and angles must be perfectly unflawed where they intersect the termination that must likewise be perfect and unbroken. Do not rely upon the carbuncle for the highest workings of Dominion, for this is not its true purpose and will fail at the end, not being of the exact vibration or truest resonance for the accomplishment of this end. Set the carbuncle in gold (see also section Corundum - Ruby) The ruby should not in this use be attempted by a female unless no other options are available. The work will succeed but at a great cost to the heart. It has not sufficient balance to replace what is expended whereas the tourmaline will strengthen and renew all energies manyfold, and it is her stone to the highest degree.

WATERMELON TOURMALINE

Tourmalines come in a wide variety of colors and shade, often occurring in the same crystal. Many times these are seen layered horizontally with respect to the central axis. However, they are also found layered around the axis like the layers of an onion. When the center is red or rose and the outside is green, this is called a watermelon tourmaline. This particular combination works like nested crystals each perfectly in resonance with the others vibrational energy. The green is restorative and the red pulls energy through the base chakra resonance. Together in this configuration they form an excellent stone for balance the energy system complex. This balance brings together the four levels of the energy system complex and helps them work in harmony with one another to balance and reinforce one another.

This happens with surprising ease and, because these colors are naturally formed in harmony with one another, their action together within the energy system complex is non-invasive and benign. These particular crystals are remarkably versatile and flexible in their uses. They can be used easily in combination with quartz to even further generalize their resonance. They can be set in a variety of metals without limiting the scope of their effectiveness although silver makes a good choice because of its own generalizing and flow properties.

This behavior of multi-colored layering is not restricted to green/red, but extends to as many different color combinations as are possible within the range of tourmalines. It is often wise to examine the base end of the crystal to discover the true nature of the crystal's color structure and thereby get a better estimation of the stones energy properties. Each stone should be taken on its own merits as to the centers and channels it effects. But in all cases the balance between the energies of the colors involved is assured because of the way in which they have been compatibly joined and share their axis vibrations.

DIAMOND

CRYSTALLIZED CARBON (C)

CHAKRA: CROWN

CALLING: PRIEST

ARCHETYPE COLOR: CLEAR

Diamond is the archetype stone of the Stones of Majesty. Its nature is such that, if it is used to its fullest potential, no other stone or crystal will be needed to pursue any cause desired by the Adept. It resonates through the spiritual body as quartz resonates through the physical energy field and its clarity and integral structural alignment provide a resonance bridge with the full potential of higher energy available. Diamond can initialize the cleansing and stimulation of the crown chakra and assist in the opening of the kundalini energy. It can act as the gateway to Higher Self-awareness on a spiritual level and to the development of a universal unity of creation. When the wearer is actively attuned to its vibration it can stabilize and enhance the continuity of the energy system complex as a whole stimulating a more complete harmonic connection of all four bodies/levels. This will lead to a natural clearing of blockages and gaps in the energy complex. For this purpose it should be worn along the central body axis rather than in a ring or broach.

In crystal form, when properly charged, it generates a trinary helix that creates a most powerful center axis charge. This, when combined with its full spectrum potential, makes a most powerful driver stone for all combinations. It is most excellent in focus and allows neither leakage nor nonspecificity in its directive, and, therefore, may be used to insure safe translation of power from all complex energies (talismans) in which it is used. It requires no external directives but is internally driven by its own nature. Take care that any inclusions that may be present do not interfere with the center axis configuration. A secondary benefit to this ability is that it will stabilize and strengthen the energies of all other stones with which it is joined raising the entire piece in energy vibration.

Its color should be pure and blue/white although those diamonds of color take on the specific nature of that color and this does not interfere with the nature of the work, unless it is a purpose of the highest force and power. Those whose hearts are not strong should not wear it over this center for extended periods of time, until the energy system complex has adjusted to its intensity. It may have the tendency to it energize their centers too forcibly and interfere with their regeneration, for this stone will operate to the fullest of its potential once it has been initially charged.

It operates at its best when set in platinum, for this will most perfectly channel and direct its energies. Otherwise, it should be set in gold with as little part of nickel as may be. There is no metal that is unsuitable for the setting of this stone, however, chose carefully that the load level potential of the metal will not interfere with the otherwise desired purpose of the stone.

COLORED DIAMOND

Diamonds form in all colors. The strength of their axial integrity and atomic structure is such that the addition of color in no way impairs or slows its power or focus. Colored diamonds make powerful qualifier stones and work extremely well in this capacity. However, if they are chosen for driver stones, care should be taken in the selection of the other components of the talisman. These stones should be of the highest quality both in terms of color and internal structure. Diamond of any color is sufficiently strong that their direct energy will seek to align all other elements to the maximum possible potential. If the accompanying stones have internal structural anomalies, these anomalies will manifest as weaknesses or resistances and make the piece prone to overload.

Diamonds work well as stones of power and also as life stones because they will encourage the energy system complex of the wearer towards clarity. It is wise to be cautious when using diamond as a healing stone because their strength and direct nature may have a tendency to demand more of a healing energy structure than it is capable of achieving until the convalescence is well along in progress. Diamonds make good personal stones for those both trained and adept in the ways of power and for those who lead active and energetic lives with many varied demands. Diamonds bring the intensity and universal focus of energy and a uniting of all centers with this universal light on a day to day basis. Their activity is pervasive and infused into all levels of the energy system. It should be taken into account that, they integrate so well with the person who wears them that, if this person should be suddenly deprived of them, there will usually be a strong feeling of loss causing anomalies in that person's energy flow. This is due to the fact that diamonds are carbon based as is corporeal life on this Earth and as such they are close akin to the physical life form resonance. Because of this, they are compatible with people with high energy emanations. Diamonds naturally link with these beings once tuned and will make an indispensable tool to the working of many kinds of energy and power. Note however, that should the individual undergo a great change in consciousness or radical change in situation, the diamond will take time and specific attention to readjust its frequencies again with the owner's patterns. It is this very quality of resistance to change that gives the stone its stability. A great deal of attention and consideration should be taken of its virtues in all shades and colors hues. In these colored stones let care be taken in the choosing of the hue and then many great benefits will result from the wearing.

WIDE SPECTRUM CRYSTALS

In addition to stones that correspond in vibratory pattern to the specific energy patterns of the chakras, there are other crystals and stones that correspond to the key signature of the energy system as a whole. These stones key to one or more of the levels of awareness - or subtle bodies, energy fields surrounding and suffusing the physical form. These stones interact with the individual's energy field as a whole and adjust and tune it so that negative and unwanted vibrations are released and the whole system can return to the healthy harmonic that is the individual's true key signature. They are very powerful in healing and adjusting the entire being and can be use in many powerful ways. This is an especially useful property when they are combined with specific use stones.

KUNZITE

LITHIUM ALUMINUM SILICATE

$$LiAl(Si_2O_6)$$

Kunzite has the facility of assisting the emotional body. One of its principal elements is lithium, which activates the crown and heart chakra together by activating the pathway directly between them. This provides a direct pathway for spirit to enter and universal energy to stimulate the higher centers, encouraging the individual to access sources of strength beyond the format of the current physical existence. It promotes a consciousness of universal love that may remain on an unconscious level but will work in the individual for confidence and assurance in the process of putting aside difficulties. An individual who has lived for long periods of time under large amounts of stress and emotional turmoil will have developed layer after layer of coping mechanisms designed to keep the individual functioning during these periods of stress and crisis. These will show in the emotional energy field as sub-fields and extraneous crystallizations in the subtle energy body. These mechanisms often vie with each other to direct the reaction and response of the individual to a given situation. These subfields are tied in with subconscious memories on a stimulus/response basis that is often beyond the individual's specific recognition and, consequently, beyond intelligent control. This will result in inappropriate or extreme response to circumstances and will, therefore, increase the individual's stress level, etc. The resulting whole is a seriously unbalanced system of precariously balanced energy substructures. The fact that this will become an unhealthy situation is self-evident and eventually the individual may wish to dismantle this architecture. There is a very real difficulty of knowing where to begin because, by disengaging one, another is activated.

Kunzite can be marvelously effective in assisting the individual to retain balance and equilibrium during this process, allowing the individual to relax and make real-time decisions and reactions. Its function is to balance, focus, and discharge energies so that a clarified and refined energy field emerges from what was an overloaded and dispersed one. Although this sounds like a drastic and disruptive process, it is perceived by the individual as soothing and gentle. Kunzite maintains the integrity of the individual's personal signature waveform and the continuity of its harmony and balance through the sequential edits and shifts necessary to the changes required. It should be observed, however, that when the stone begins its work and for a length of time depending on the individual's degree of dysfunction, the individual may become drowsy or disoriented until the energy field stabilizes. This can also be beneficial because while the individual is in such a state of semi-sleep, it is easiest for the stone to do its work. It should also be pointed out that this process is not an automatic one and the individual must also take responsibility allowing the stone to do its work, and for recognizing change when it has occurred and not attempting to reconstruct the previous coping architecture.

It is recommended that kunzite be used in the form of a whole crystal, as this is its most powerful and effective form. Although it has some of the same effect when faceted or in cabochon, its benefit is much diminished. It should be worn as close to the center of the energy field as possible, that is, over the heart chakra. We will also add that it is advisable to enter into this process when the individual is in an environment that is conducive to the desired changed. If the individual remains in the harsh and disruptive environment, the balancing process understandably will take much longer. It is to the stone's credit, however, that it can have this desired effect even in the presence of great crisis. This makes it highly beneficial as a stone of passage - a stone used to help an individual though a great difficulty or life changing process. It comes in many different pastel colors such as yellow, green, rose, and clear, that can be indications of its specific effectiveness.

SECONDARY QUALIFYING STONES

Kunzite can be used by itself or in combinations with other stones. By adding a stone with a specific field vibration to kunzite's wide spectrum field, you will be adding a degree of focus and specificity to its purpose that can be greatly helpful in addressing a specific energy center damaged or impaired by constant stress or overload. This can understandably be an effective tool in assisting with the removal of blockages in the chakra system. Kornerupine will add its own distinctive ability to discharge and disperse overloaded energy field constructs and disconnects the source of their reconstruction. The green variety is most beneficial in dealing with seriously impaired heart chakra functions. Green sapphire is also effective in modulating the heart chakra frequencies, particularly if this has resulted in physical impairment of the heart muscle itself. Tourmaline of any color is of a similar strength and is well matched to kunzite's own. Its automatic nature will help the kunzite crystal key in to the source of center that is more effected. Its linkage to the brow chakra will also help the individual bring higher mind and intelligence to the difficulty in question and gain further access to his or her rationality.

DRIVERS AND KUNZITE

It is not recommended to set kunzite with diamonds or clear/ white sapphires because these stones are so specifically focussed in their nature that this will interfere with the wide spectrum nature of the crystal. If a driver is desired, moonstone makes a strong and gentle choice. If something very strong is indicated, white star sapphire is a better choice than a clear one. Star quartz is excellent as it provides great integrity, strength, and direction, adding its strength to the spirit of the individual and its own opening to the celestial consciousness. This strengthens the individual while the kunzite does its healing and reconstructing work.

KORNERUPINE

$$Mg_4Al_6((O,OH)_2/BO_4(SiO_4)_4)$$

Kornerupine works on the energy field as a whole working through the heart center on all levels of the energy system complex. Its primary action is as a discharging agent, releasing overloads of energy in any localized area caused by limiting or counteractive states such as fear, grief, or pain. (This is as opposed to expansive states such as anger or aggression). Generally put, kornerupine releases panic on any level by discharging its built up energy when it reaches a certain level beyond the limits of the harmonic formed by the key signature harmonic of the individual.

Panic can be described as a moment when energy locks up in one or more centers causing backflow and feedback so that the energy cycles out of control beyond the limits of the individual to cycle and balance it. This may be emotional panic such as in extreme states of grief or fear; it can mean mental panic such as excessive stress and anxiety, or it can refer to physical panic such as asthma or hyperventilation. This is not to imply that it will stand in place of appropriate medical therapies or in place of personal discipline and reason. It will, however, dissipate the energy overload and interrupt the feedback cycle so that the individual can then deal appropriately with a situation unhampered by dysfunctional states.

The advantage of this is that, once the panic is relieved, the individual can exert whatever personal disciplines or actions are appropriate to the situation. Panic causes an intense focus of energy/attention of one minute area. Once it is alleviated, this focus of attention can be directed to the issue at hand of whatever nature. Not only will this be effective in mental and emotional states, it will allow the effects of therapy or medication to take effect more quickly and effectively.

SERAPHENITE (GEM CLINOCHLORE)

HYDROUS MAGNESIUM IRON ALUMINUM

SILICATE

$$(Mg,Fe^{+2})_5Al(Si,Al)_4O_{10}(OH)_8$$

Seraphenite is the name for clinochlore in its microcrystalline form. Its color in this state is a dark green. It is also found in crystalline form in a blue-green color. Both of these are varieties of the Chlorite family. We discussed the activity of chlorite inclusions in quartz. The chlorite energies in this case are greatly magnified from the ones found in inclusion in other stones. Here they are found in their own crystalline form. They draw from the immediate earth's life force and weave this energy together with the key signature pattern of the wearer to provide an external energy halo of protection and support that sustains itself and the wearer life force from moment to moment. In this activity all chlorites could be described as Protection Stones.

Seraphenite (gem quality clinochlore) has particular and unique qualities in its own right. It should be used with discretion, for its dense structure makes it very powerful. Its microcrystalline structure is likely to makes its energy field seem mild when first energized, but its effects grow in intensity as the stone interacts with the energy field of the user. It uses the heart center of the general field (rather than the heart center of one particular field) to act throughout the energy system and all levels of the auric bodies. Its effect is to release the causes of blockages and restrictions of energy, in particular those derived from excessive personal controls.

These controls can be caused by personal will to dominate the self and others, or by personal desire to control the self and personal reaction/ interaction. This is applicable to those individuals who resist emotional or spiritual ties with others for fear of pain or loss, or fear spiritual interaction such as releasing of the ego/ temporal personality to communicate with Higher Self and higher energy levels. It is freeing to all flows between all four subtle bodies and will cause the release of dammed up energy in any or all of those levels, whether mental, emotional, spiritual and physical. When using it to facilitate the therapeutic release of physical restriction/control, it can be formed into an extremely effective massage tool that can assist the release of energy stored as impacted tension stored in these areas. This is effective in such cases of storing and impacting pent-up energy in one or more of the muscular/skeletal areas due to stress and frustration. This is known as an energy concretion.

In general, seraphenite deals with control issues of many kinds and on many levels. This control may manifest itself as control over others, in which case it can be instrumental in allowing the user to see the effects of inflexibility and suppression of others. Or it may manifest as the urge to control events and circumstances beyond the scope of human endeavor. In some cases, it can help release fear and anxiety related to phobias, although when used in this capacity the root cause of the phobia may begin to manifest itself. The user should be aware that this will have to be acknowledged and transformed and this process may tend to bring about stress and negative emotion in the course of recognition.

As these blocks are removed, seraphenite serves in its secondary and also powerful capacity in assisting the user to see and reconnect with his

or her chosen purpose or destiny. As it removes the blockages, it allows
the user to connect with the Higher Self to assist the individual to fulfill the
purpose chosen for the present incarnation. It assists the individual to understand, come to terms with, and accept the path or purpose that has been
chosen for this life. This can be very healing when the individual has been
dealing with circumstances beyond this limited understanding. Seraphenite
can help an individual to accept the inevitable, whether in the form of the
death of a loved one, a physical or mental impairment, or a given role in
life. In so doing it encourages that individual to transcend what is perceived as limitations by finding what is given in the way of beauty, resources, strength, etc. This stone can clear the blockages not only to acceptance but also to that acceptance with grace and compassion combined
with a joy in life as it presents itself from day to day.

In its spiritual capacity this may have an added benefit of opening the
individual to channels of conscious communication with spiritual guides
and higher form entities, or to sources of information on the etheric or
akashic register.

KYANITE

ALUMINUM SILICATE

$Al_2O(SiO_4)$

Kyanite is unique in the way it functions in that its principal field is not generated by its axis, but by the ionic bonding of its structure. It is formed from
many hair-like crystals in the way of
mica and some silica forms, layered or
stranded parallel to each other that in-
terlock their exterior energy fields. The nature of the field created by this
interlocking is a composite and created the field for the crystalline structure as a whole.

Kyanite is particularly effective in balancing the energy centers of the
physical body. It can be used in long-term chakra balancing work when
the function of one or more the centers has been impaired and no longer
interacts as part of the harmonic whole. It can also be used in a more
immediate situation of rebalancing and reinforcing the harmony of the
physical system that has been put into imbalance by shock, fatigue, injury, sustained illness or poor diet. It may be used by a practitioner to
recover from heavy demands placed upon the vital energy system as a
whole in the course of his or her work. Kyanite not only works on the
physical energies, but also helps clarify and restore the links of communication between the four principal levels of awareness. It can be a powerful tool to aid in the realization and integration of emotional states,
psychic overloads, etc.

It is recommended that kyanite not be worn for any long duration. This is likely to cause unnecessary dependence in the energy systems. It is far more effective to wear it for a short time while actively engaged in working with it, that is, during meditation, healing procedures, or a day of rest and recuperation from a time of stress and/or anxiety. After such an interval, it should be put aside so that the benefits of its nature can be integrated into the individual's energy system. This way, the individual is actively doing his or her own healing rather than asking the stone to form and hold the healing pattern while the individual continues in the path of unhealthy stress and internal disharmony. The stone will also require a time to reassert its own field integrity.

The Feldspar Group

Sequencing

The group called feldspars is of two similar varieties: those whose principle element is potassium and the other whose principle elements are sodium and calcium. This makes little difference in practice because it is the aluminum silicate in their composition that gives them their distinctive identity pattern. Their activity as a general family or class is one that unifies and focuses energy. They make good driver and qualifier stones for nearly any other stone as primary because their structure is strong and they can take a variety of energy intensities without losing coherence or focus. They can draw together a wide range of energies surprising diversity and weave them together into a pattern of vibration that is useable and agreeable to the human energy system complex. They can also be worn by themselves for the virtue of their individual natures.

When setting them with other stones it is important to pay attention to the direction of their cut. Feldspars often exhibit an optical effect called andularescence. This is due to their lamellar structure, that is, layered in sheets. When they are cut with respect to the grain and direction of the stone, they will often exhibit sheeting of light due to the reflection of light from the layers as the light passes through them. This is a good indication that the stone has been cut with respect to the grain and a good indicator of how to align the stone with others and with a primary crystal. Their behavior with respect to energy is a reflection of this property, because energy links bond these layers together give the stones their coherence and unusual durability despite their lack of physical hardness.

Feldspars can take many elements and weave them into one coherent pattern and hold that pattern in a steady and focused pattern. The key to this behavior is in sequencing, that is, aligning the vibrations with one another so that the form a unified pattern. This implies cause/effect/time and, therefore, identity that is a belly chakra function. They are, therefore, associated with that center. They can greatly help individuals whose energies tend to be dispersed or misaligned to establish a sense of personal perspective. They can also encourage an individual to assert his or her identity pattern when other vibrational elements threaten to overwhelm it.

MOONSTONE

POTASSIUM ALUMINUM SILICATE

$$K(AlSi_3O_8)$$

By its nature, moonstone absorbs energy within itself and then disperses it with force that is both clear and diffusive. It focuses energy of various sorts presented to it and clarifies their wave potential. It then broadcasts this energy, disseminating it across all energy bands. It may be considered at times both driver and also qualifier for its subtle color and density ranges give a most pleasant range of potential qualifications along with its driver nature. but when placed in conjunction with other stones it may draw their different energies unto itself and unify them unto a single purpose.

Its nature is gentle and it integrates its energy and that of the stones with which it is linked compatibly with the human energy system complex. In this aspect it acts almost as a buffer when placed with strong primary stones because it will integrate their natures with one another and with the wearer so that the energies they present are available without being dissonant, overbearing or intrusive.

When moonstone is overloaded its structure will first emit high-range anomalous frequencies and then cease functioning altogether, causing its load potential to backlash and flow back sharply into the other stones. This will cause definite damage and disruption of function and purpose. But if this stone is used wisely, it will serve well and gently for its nature. It should be considered as a flowstone among the drivers, because this is a close description of its function.

Moonstone is best suited to be set in silver or, in special cases, in platinum. When used by itself, it is an excellent stone to be given to a child destined to be an Adept, for its cooling and soothing nature is gentle as well as focusing to the energies. It will give him or her a working tool that will respond in the manner of drivers but will be adaptive to him or her changing nature and identity. It will not lock him or her into one pattern of use to the exclusion of others.

In its clear crystalline and blue flash shades it can act as a Seer's stone, especially when the purpose of the vision is not only to see but to act upon what is seen and this process is to be accomplished by a single practitioner. It is of singular virtue when serving as a "driver", not only for stones but when used rightly to the energy helix of the practitioner. In this capacity in can be used to unify the power stones with the wearer's energy system complex and focus and drive those energies as well to a predetermined purpose. This should not be carried on for long periods of time because it will prove draining to the energies of the wearer and if the stone is overburdened the energy release could be detrimental to the energy system complex as a whole.

Overall, consider that the clearer the stone the stronger its potential. In all its other color ranges it takes on the gentlest virtue of the color manifested. Copper makes an effective setting for it, particularly in its greenish milkier shades. This makes an agreeable woman's charm especially when the copper is worked in the shapes of one of the forms of blessing. Moonstones resonate very well with the female polarity resonance. This has been discussed in the section about carved charms. The stone may be carved and cut without losing any of its potency.

Moonstone comes in a variety of colors including, clear, white, pink, gray, and plum. Each of them is useful according to their color energy compatibility.

SunStone (Aventurine Feldspar)
Sodium calcium aluminum silicate
$$Na(AlSi_3O_8)Ca(AlSi_3O_8)$$

Sunstone is also called aventurine feldspar. This is because the term aventurine applies to all stones that include small glitter-like inclusions within their structure giving them a metallic or sparkling appearance. The type of inclusion differs from one type of base stone to another and in the case of feldspar it refers to inclusions of hematite (iron oxide) or goethite (iron hydroxide). This inclusion of iron with the basic structure gives a strong resonance of both the base chakra and earth force energy. This is a powerful combination and is often a good choice to use in place of carnelian or other strong orange stones. The unifying and sequencing nature of feldspar will allow the power of the iron energy to integrate smoothly with the energy structure complex, but it will not tend toward excessive aggression as might be the case in other stones. The power of sunstone is one of activation of free will, optimism and increased self-esteem. It allows strength in recognizing the validity of the individual identity and its most positive expression. It is also greatly valuable in encouraging convalescence from a debilitating illness or injury.

AMAZONITE

POTASSIUM ALUMINUM SILICATE

$$K(AlSi_3O_8)$$

Amazonite is a milky and translucent green/aqua blue variety of feldspar without adularescence. Sometimes it can be mistaken for jade or chrysoprase. It acts as a general gentle restorative to the levels of consciousness. Amazonite's unifying action in this case is to draw together the energy system complex that has become separated or segmented through excessive trauma to one or more of its levels or through excessive concentration or energy expenditure of one to the exclusion of the others. Its action is very subtle and easy to over ride if the individual does not first withdraw from those activities that caused the disruption. This is a stone of renewal and recovery, not one that will override the effects of continued unbalance.

It is a good choice for carved healing charms because it can be worn for long periods of time without the wearer becoming excessively dependent upon their activity.

LABRODORITE (SPECTROLITE)

SODIUM CALCIUM ALUMINUM SILICATE

$$Na(AlSi_3O_8)Ca(AlSi_3O_8)$$

Labradorite is a brightly iridescent adularia feldspar. Its base structure ranges from clear/translucent similar in appearance to milky moonstone through brown and earthy green. The same behavior that results in the iridescent colors results also in its ability to unify the wearer's personal energy complex to that of natural systems enabling the wearer to draw strength and renewal from these vibrational patterns. It heightens the wearer's sensitivity and alignment to natural cycles and rhythms. As the wearer develops in personal awareness, this sensitivity can extend to universal cycles resulting in a broadening of the individual's increased awareness of him or her self as an integral part of the universal whole. The unifying property of feldspar allows the individual to translate this awareness into conscious identity patterns, blending the energy of the upper chakra register with that of the belly chakra sequencing identity functions.

Its action can be cooling and comforting for individuals who have over worked and need to restore their vital processes as it renews identity and continuity of personality that can be blurred by excessive stress and fatigue. It can also make an effective journey stone because it allows the individual to retain personal continuity through the multiple levels of reality and dimensional existence. As a result of this, it allows the individual clarity of vision without draining the personal energies and resources. It also allows him or her to translate the results of this journeying into articulate reality.

STONES OF CLARITY, REGENERATION AND RENEWAL

IRON SILICATES

PERIDOT, EPIDOTE, ZOISITE & JADE

The group of iron silicates includes Peridot, Epidote and Zoisite as well as the Jade group. The iron silicate base keys its principal energy to the base chakra while emitting its green ray of heart chakra renewal and regeneration. This provides for a stable and clear flow of life renewing energy, while the qualifying agent that gives each respective stone its color, specifies the subtle body through which it acts.

Peridot and Epidote are very much akin to one another occurring in similar color ranges and both being iron silicates. They are both used in the general category of yellow-green and green mid range stones, that is, to enhance recuperation from fatigue and illness, to regenerate and renew the personal energies.

PERIDOT

MAGNESIUM IRON SILICATE

$(Mg,Fe)_2 SiO_4$

Peridot renews and strengthens the channels as is commonly the case with green stones, and its yellow light will also lighten the heart and brighten the mind. It is these combined energies that it integrates gently and kindly with the nature of the entire individual. The magnesium in its makeup causes it to form a harmonic with the brow chakras, bringing a gentle presence of Higher Self to all its acts of healing and renewal. It is a good stone for those who would work with recalling other incarnations, because it enhances true compassion while helping retain objectivity. It encourages the individual to form an alignment channel with the Higher Self energies to be used for healing both others and the self.

At times peridot is called the Evening Emerald because it is often like the emerald though in lesser intensity. Its radiance tends in all things towards the yellowish hue to mix with its pleasant green and, thus, it embodies qualities of both resonances. Its qualities are light although uncommonly strong and it is suitable for many secondary uses.

Peridot is of an appropriate power range to give to children beginning healing work. If the child shows a talent and inclination for this type of work, this stone may be given along with teaching in this craft. But it should be worn only when working and under the supervision of the teacher, then put away. Allow the child to find his own place to store the stone. In this way the child will not only be helped in learning a chosen craft, but will also learn proper treatment and respect for working stones. It is important to remember this gradient of teaching and working. Even though the child may be discerned as a Great Healer reborn and knowledgeable in the work beyond his years, the physical form still immature in the strength and balance of its channels and energies. This must be respected and the energies adjusted accordingly.

When using peridot with other stones in complex talismans, the practitioner should remember and respect its gentle nature. It is not wise to place it with stones that are of a significantly stronger energy resonance than itself, because they will over-drive it and overwhelm its gentle and subtle nature. Peridot may be used to good effect as a qualifier when placed with quartz and worn by novices. In this it may be coupled with a yellow or white driver. Be careful when placing a blue driver with it. This should never be of any other quality or strength than an aquamarine, light blue tourmaline, or other stone of medium range. It will also react well with iolite and tanzanite. It is unwise to use it with any form of sapphire, for this will over-drive it. If it is desirable to have this yellow/green to blue combination, the stones should be more closely matched in power.

EPIDOTE

CALCIUM ALUMINUM IRON SILICATE

$$Ca_2(Al,Fe)_3(Si_2O_7)(SiO_4)O(OH)$$

Epidote occurs in range of yellow, yellow greens, clear gem quality green, to yellowish brown. This color range indicates that its focus of energy centers through the solar plexus and heart chakras. The calcium aluminum in its contents keys it's activity through the mental subtle body enhancing clarity of focus and a general optimism deriving from the ability to see clearly through a situation. It helps the wearer remain centered and flexible in demanding or hectic situations. The iron silicate base makes it kin to peridot in the respect that it enriches the flow of energy through the base chakra and manifests as green coloration linking it to the heart center. Its energy is earthy, compassionate, and intelligent. Epidote will assist the wearer to "see through" difficulties without becoming overwhelmed by them.

Epidote serves much in the fashion of tourmaline and peridot and its power range lies between these two in virtue and strength. This makes a good intermediate stone for one who would be a healer and requires its restorative virtue, needing one stronger than peridot but not wishing the overriding automatics or the intensity of tourmaline.

Its energy is very similar to that of beryls, for its nature is strong and peaceful, clarifying to both mind and spirit. It gently and harmoniously integrates and works within the energy limits of the individual wearer. The epidote may be set in all metals with equal virtue respecting the energy parameters of the individual metal in question. Each will give it a specific quality without overloading it or conflicting with its nature. into iron and lose no virtue and this may serve as a glad and wondrous thing in the binding of weapons especially for those to be used by females and also by children.

ZOISITE

HYDROUS CALCIUM ALUMINUM SILICATE

$$Ca_2Al_3(SiO_{12})(OH)$$

Zoisite is a part of the Epidote group and, as such, has many of its clarifying and restorative qualities. Its color range extends to white, blue, pale green. The presence of aluminum silicate links zoisite in all its forms through the mental body of the individual and resonates through this to link this to the spiritual body. It allows the wearer to put aside self-doubt and self-limitation particularly brought on by feelings of unworthiness. It also allows the wearer to put aside the constraints of karma when they limit the individuals ability to deal with karmic situations and move through them to a more positive and broader personal and spiritual plane of activity. This is done by activating a channel through which the individual can access his or her own Higher Self essence and manifest it into the task or situation at hand.

It sometimes occurs in pink, rose, and deep red due to the presence of manganese and in this case is known as thulite. This gives the stone a powerful connection to the heart chakra essence and magnifies its energy as compassion, including the ability of the wearer to demonstrate understanding and compassion for his or her own perceived shortcomings and personal limitations. It can be a powerful stone for personal growth, particularly as the individual begins a spiritual path. Such a path often leads the individual to deny and reject parts of his or her personality or previous life. Thulite can encourage the individual to resolve this disassociation and to accept all parts of the self as manifestations of the growth experience that has led him or her to the present moment of awareness. In the hands of a skilled practitioner, this can be taken a step farther. When an individual's personality has become disassociated from itself either through trauma or illness in the present life, or through events in other lifetimes that have left personality fragments separated from the individual consciousness stream, this stone can help that individual retrieve and reintegrate those personality elements. It can actuate the healing process of reintegration by allowing the individual to put aside the initial events that caused the separation and allow him or her to accept those fragments with love and compassion.

Zoisite in all its colors is a powerful and much underestimated stone. Its energy works both in an immediate need situation and also in a long-term application allowing the individual to use it for personal growth and awareness.

When ruby and zoisite are found in combination, they bring together their own individual natures to form a powerful and agreeable force to assist the individual to bring together the opposite poles of the inner nature into balance. The stone activates this reunion and translates it into a combined form of higher consciousness while remaining clear and aware of earth plane / physical universe considerations. This can manifest itself in a variety of ways. It can result in the stimulation of the individual's psychic senses either as precognition or as telepathy. It can cause an opening of that individual to a variety of spiritual awarenesses including the intensified awareness and attunement to personal guides and spiritual entities. It can expand the individual's awareness to include sensitivity to his or her own simultaneous existence in other planes, aspects of the self, or perceived time frames. The specific result depends on the nature of the individual.

In its more earthly manifestations it can provide a joining between the separated aspects of the personality – such as the male/female aspects of the personal polarity or between the inner and outer lives of the individual. It can help the individual unite the physical life with the spiritual because it helps build the mental/spiritual bridge between them. It should be recognized, however, that it is the individual who must set these energies in motions. And it is also the individual who must be open to the results that this stone presents. When using zoisite in any of its forms it may be helpful for the practitioner to use companion stones that specify or enhance the purpose for which it is being worn or used.

TANZANITE
CALCIUM ALUMINUM SILICATE
$$Ca_2Al_3(O/OH/SiO_4/Si_2O_7)$$

Tanzanite is the blue-violet dichroic variety of zoisite whose coloring is due to the addition of chromium and strontium in its structure. Like all dichroic stones, its is a gateway stone that can assist the individual to move between the different aspects of his or her own consciousness easily and without disorientation often involved. Tanzanite activates the bridge between the spiritual self and the temporal self. Tanzanite acts to align the energy flow from the crown chakra as it moves downward into the slower moving centers, keeping it steady and clear while minimizing interference. This can manifest itself as increased psychic awareness, but more generally it will show itself as a general feeling of lightness or clarity in the individual allowing expression of this spiritual energy through the intellectual channels and the throat center. This is a delicate and spiritual stone and can be worn comfortably and beneficially by a wide variety of individuals. When putting it in combination with other stones, this delicate nature should be considered. When it is put in combination with stones that are beyond its energy range, they will tend to overwhelm its virtue and establish their own energy patterns as the dominant note of the talisman. It can be used as a accent stone in combination with many stones that contribute to its ethereal and spiritual identity, and in such instances it can greatly expand the parameters of such a piece while helping the wearer maintain his of her energy flow in a consciously coherent pattern.

JADE

JADEITE

SODIUM ALUMINUM SILICATE

$NaAl[Si_2O_6]$

NEPHRITE

CALCIUM MAGNESIUM IRON SILICATE

$Ca_2(Mg,Fe)_5(Si_4O_{11})_2$

ACTINOLITE

CALCIUM MAGNESIUM IRON SILICATE
HYDROXIDE

$Ca_2(Mg,Fe)_5(Si_4O_{11})_2(OH)_2$

Jade is known as the Stone of Peace. Its most commonly associated color is deep green, but it also exists naturally in white, yellowish-white, brown, reddish pink, violet, and black. the term Jade is used interchangeably for related stones including jadeite, actinolite (of which the green variety is called nephrite) and chloro-melanite. Nephrite and actinolite are both related to the group of iron silicates expressing the base chakra connection to the vital fires of earth energy while manifesting through the heart chakra to encourage recuperation from fatigue and illness, to regenerate and renew the personal energies. In certain types of jadeite, the emerald green translucent color is due to the presence of chrome as the pigment, directly resonating it with the heart chakra. In all its shades and hues it settles its gentle benefit throughout the energy system of the wearer with most pleasing effect. Both types of jade will act through the emotional body, in a cooling capacity, helping the wearer find rationality and peace. Their various trace components will determine which center will focus their activity.

Due to this activity these stones can enhance the ability to deal with dysfunctional situations and relationships, to find a middle group of agreeable compromise when dealing with disagreeing parties or individual. It can help to find a common group and build a cohesive group identity. This is result of its ability to reduce resistance in the channels connecting the heart and brow and allow reason and emotion to be joined. The emerald green imperial jades, by virtue of their chromium pigmentation are particularly effective in cooling injuries to the heart center. By doing so they allow the center to release retained energies that could continue to harm the area, which then allows for more wholesome and balanced energies to take effect in this area. Black jade helps individuals who are quick to anger control their fiery natures and allow reason and cooler judgement to prevail. These characteristics can also be expanded to finally enhance the individual's ability to accept love and increase a sense of belonging and security. This includes an expanded awareness of the individual's participation in the essence of divine love.

Jade will take a subtle charge, that is, one on a emotional general wave band and disperse it throughout the system, and that general charge will be retained within its structure as long as the piece stands unchanged. Charms carved from this substance hold the charge throughout generations and this is its one true asset. Jade rarely charges on the specific wave band common to and expected from truly crystalline stones and will not retain a specific charge over a great span of time.

It may be carved in pleasing shapes from charms to complex vessels that extend its cooling and peaceful nature to anything place in them. Its toughness and resiliency makes it general practical for items that are in daily use or wear. It does not have the specificity of chalcedony, but it generates a general field of qualified energy that depends on its color and components as to its specific nature. It is important to observe all the subtle components of each separate stone, because even its trace inclusions give these stones a variety of natures.

Charms of jade may be accompanied with stronger stones even unto diamonds and the jade will add its virtue quietly to the activity of the primary. It is particularly effective when dealing with the energies of typically female nature. It acts subtly and gently on these conditions, adjusting the system as a whole rather than targeting one particularly source of damage or dysfunction. It is effective in treating the traumas of childbirth, miscarriage, shock from rape, or other personal violence done to the female body afflicting its sexuality.

Jades of any color may well be used as a substitute for any of the chalcedony/quartz variety and their charging qualities are very similar to that of jaspers and some agates. Black jade is most sovereign of all stones in the case of women's agitation due to imbalance of the monthly cycle and as a secondary effect will assist her in subtly making peace with her womanhood. Rose and pink jade have often been used in charms to promote healing and also to further sexual love and encourage fertility and this is to some true effect although the greatest strength it has in these matters is in the mind of the possessor. However, in some instances it is more sovereign in these capacities than even rose quartz, for the virtue of its peaceful nature will soothe the energy system complex, while the intensity of the rose will strengthen and hearten all damaged or shocked channels stemming from the base chakra. Therefore, it should be considered when either beginning a process of long duration in which it may be used to initialize the process when other rose stones might be too strong, or to accomplish a short process when those other stones would be excessive in their energies. In either of these cases it should be according to the personal choice of the wearer or the discretion of the practitioner. Its basic nature allows it to respond well with the system energies of its possessor and bring about its effects slowly and with subtlety.

The white is similar in nature to white quartz combined with jade's beauty and peaceful influence. It may be bound with any metal and not lose its virtue but gold is its right companion, for the gold will give unto it a strength and direction that it does not of its own nature possess.

PERSONAL DEVELOPMENT AND TRANSFORMATION

SPINEL & ZIRCON

Although the composition of these two stones is very different, they can be studied together because their energy properties are very similar. They display their energy characteristics through the energy system complex as a whole, making them highly suitable to be placed with other stones that require energy amplification without complicating their initial purpose.

Both spinel and zircon are effectively set in silver and gold. They may be safely set into bronze for accents upon weapons but not where high demands of power will be made upon the piece. They make effective qualifiers and as drivers when applied in the middle ranges of energy demands. When working with these two stones, the practitioner should consider that they are stones of finesse rather than of pure power. They are tools for structuring and guidance, and when these natures are respected make richly effective tools for growth and healing.

SPINEL

MANGANESE ALUMINUM OXIDE

$MgAl_2O_4$

Spinel occurs naturally as clear, red, pink, violet, yellow, orange, dark green (iron bearing), blue and black (chrome and iron bearing). There is also a zinc spinel that occurs in blue, red-violet, and green. Spinel is a stone of the personality. Its manganese nature keying into the warm and loving resonance of the heart/base channel activated by the aluminum in its structure to the mental subtle body. Its clear nature assists the user in clarifying his or her own individuality and becoming aware of his or her own potential. This clarifying property also assists the wearer identifying which of his or her traits belong to him or her alone and which are put upon or accepts from another individual. This can be extremely beneficial in the growth process both in the way of developing and growing into maturity, and as a way of identifying and healing from dysfunctional and/or abusive relationships. Because of this quality, it assists the wearer in making significant life choices. It can also help the wearer isolate which considerations arise form this present lifetime and which arise from unresolved issues in other lifetimes. If a colored spinel is chosen, the color will determine the nature of the specific area or consideration affected.

The clear spinel has been much underestimated in its capacity and ability. No other stone except quartz is so capable of functioning as a broad-spectrum driver. In its crystalline state, it tends to lack a fully delineated center axis through the termination and this will tend to disperse its energy rather than allow it the straightness of the power direction of quartz. For those who wish to accustom themselves to these differences, spinel makes an excellent power stone capable of much full-spectrum diversity. It may be cut as a cabochon and used in places where clear crystal moonstone is unavailable with only negligible loss of specificity and its endurance in this will be long and hardy. It makes a good primary stone in talismans for its nature is well suited to such an activity as it takes well to qualification by other stones. In the cutting of faceted material it loses much of this virtue for it requires its full axis in its whole form to fulfill its functions well. But nonetheless, should the cutting be done carefully and with regard to grain and axis direction this makes as good a driver or qualifier as may be.

ZIRCON

ZIRCONIUM SILICATE

$Zr(SiO_4)$

Zircon is a stone of inner focus and direction. It works through the energy system complex as a whole to assist the wearer to define and align the inner processes. This process can be the manifestation of any of the four levels of awareness or the combination of the levels working together in harmony. It encourages the wearer to gather his or her elements and is of great benefit to those whose forces and personal resources are scattered or dispersed. There is a saying, "Pull yourself together." and it is zircon that can help in this process. Zircon works toward union of the individual throughout the energy system complex, and, if a colored stone is chosen rather than a clear one, the color of the stone determines the level of awareness that needs to be more encouraged in the union.

It exists naturally in clear, yellow, red, green, or brown. Heating some brown ones will produce clear and blue. When clear in this manner or by natural electricity, zircon is a good stone for use by novices or children when beginning their training. It gives a clear vibration, but not too strong for those who are just beginning. This allows them to experiment safely with the manifestations of color energy without fear of overstressing themselves or others. But treated stones tend not to be a stable as those who develop their clarity by natural alignment and each stone should be selected on its individual merits and according to its compatibility with the intended purpose.

Zircon is not a stone to translate heavy amounts of power. It is, rather, a stone of personal development and transformation. It makes a good choice for a qualifying stone when the purpose of the talisman is the growth and unification of an individuals life and potential awareness, because it links all the other stones to this purpose.

When zircon is found in nature, in perfectly clear and crystalline form of whatever color, it should be well and highly regarded, for its true potential should be recognized. It serves as a driver second only to diamond in its tight-band intensity and specificity. It is well and truly used as a focussing stone on talismans of the secondary level and is be much prized for this function as well as for its strength as a qualifier that draws all energies of the talisman into itself and qualifies them with surpassing strength.

Light Reactive Stones

Alexandrite, Tanzanite, Andalusite, & Iolite

Some stones appear to change colors when viewed from different angles or when viewed under different types of both artificial and natural light. Many stones exhibit this characteristic in some small degree. It is called pleochroism. Stones that display a distinct shift between just two colors are referred to as dichroic. This behavior is caused by the differing absorption of light of doubly refractive crystals. We have already mentioned tanzanite as such a stone in connection with its family of Epidote. Other remarkable examples are Alexandrite – a chrysoberyl with a dramatic red-purple to sea green shift – and Andalusite – shifting from yellow and olive green to red-brown and red. Iolite shifts from dark blue to violet. Any of these stones will behave according to the basic tenets of its compositional family and type. They will also demonstrate the quality of being a "Gateway Stone" that will serve the user as a bridge between the essential traits indicated by the color shifts.

Pleochroic stones have a multiple potential and the color that is visible is what is temporarily the predominant energy, while those colors that are temporarily recessive are those that underscore that predominant energy. The true key to understanding the nature of these stones is to remember that they do not tend to "act" on their own. Rather they permit the wearer or practitioner to act by opening a clear channel of energies and accessibilities that would ordinarily be more difficult for him or her to access. Stones placed with them can facilitate, amplify, or augment this behavior. Once again – they are not true "power stones" in that they are not truly suitable to the transference of intense loads of energy, but by virtue of their energy lattice, they act through the energy system complex of the individual to render many things possible.

These stones are best bound with gold or electrum to focus their inherently dispersive nature. They may also be bound with any precious metal and with bronze, but iron should be avoided for its nature suits not well with any of these. However, this is a suggestion not a specific.

ALEXANDRITE

BERYLLIUM ALUMINUM OXIDE

$Al_2(BeO_4)$

Alexandrite manifests a complex color shift of white, magenta and sea green and depending on the nature of the light passing through it. It manifests as regenerative majesty. It opens a gateway through the emotional body to allow the individual to be more confidant and consequently more flexible in demanding situations by helping him or her to access inner reserves of knowledge and strength. This can result in expanded communication or creativity as these are manifestations of confidence and inner knowledge of personal worthiness.

This is a stone that offers an individual a personal gateway to the development of inner energy changes as the energy helix of the age changes. These colors do not always manifest clearly in the spectrum of the human aura. However, as the personality complex evolves with the coming changes, these colors will becomes more in evidence. This is a stone of personal evolution as well as of the evolution of soul groups. It can help the individual retain a present time focus while reintegrating his or her higher consciousness awareness. It can also serve as a useful tool to those who are seeking to reunite with separated elements of soul groups as it allows the openness of the higher radiance of the sea green to expand the heart center.

It was not a coincidence that this stone was first revealed so recently as Humankind was not prepared for this influence until the current century. However, as the development of Humankind accelerates it will be shown to be of more and more value in facilitating this transformation.

ANDALUSITE

ALUMINUM SILICATE

$Al(AlSiO_5)$

Andalusite manifests as the earth energy of the mind and has both a stimulative and calmative effect as it runs through the orange/golden and brown ranges, and this energy may in general be referred to as "encouragement". It allows the individual to develop self-acceptance and the confidence this can bring into all facets of life. Its yellow/olive/brown shifts align with its aluminum mental body linkage to provide a balanced viewpoint and an essence of personal optimism and spontaneity.

IOLITE	The color of iolite shifts from gray through blue to violet. Its structure balances magnesium with aluminum encouraging a balanced communication between the brow, crown, and heart centers. This
MAGNESIUM ALUMINUM SILICATE	
$Mg_2Al_4Si_5O_{18}$	

opens a subtle and gentle gateway for communication with the Higher Self. This presence may not always be on a conscious level, but may manifest itself as leaps in intuition and an awareness of guidance and higher purpose or direction. This can assist the individual in clarifying his or her life purpose as well as being able to articulate this purpose and these intuitive insights. It can be an invaluable tool when the individual is seeking inner guidance and awareness especially when the purpose of that guidance needs to be brought into manifestation through physical acts.

CRYSTALLINE IRON

HEMATITE & MAGNETITE (IRON OXIDES) Fe_2O_3
PYRITE & MARCASITE (IRON SULFIDES) FeS_2

In general, crystals of high metallic content are reactive to the same energy wavelengths as the metal that composes their greatest part. Pure iron resonates with the base chakra and with its connection to the Earth's vital physical energy. As iron is combined with other elements this raises its vibration and enables it to interact with further points on the energy system complex. We have examined this behavior in regards to its combination with silicon, which results in green pigmentation in a variety of stones and resonates this base vital force through the regenerative and unifying energy of the heart center.

Hematite and magnetite (Iron Oxides Fe_2O_3), pyrite and marcasite (Iron Sulfides FeS_2) are all principally composed of iron and, as such, are keyed to the physical level and earth energy complex of the body. These may be considered to be iron in crystalline form and will manifest all energy fields associated with iron, to the degree that they are pure. Pay close attention to this so that you will be aware of this potential, for they are very strong and it may be as though you hold a smaller form of a quartz crystal potential with the iron ray of energy.

Hematite is easily linked with the base energy systems of the body and is extremely useful in establishing the link between the physical body's vital energy field and the vital energy field of the Earth. Both Hematite and Magnetite ($Fe^{+2}Fe^{+3}_2O_4$) act to reinforce the body's field of vitality and its connection to the earth forces that determine health and physical harmony. It is interesting to note that so many recent developments have been made in the field of physical therapy using magnetic energy, both in terms of mapping and viewing the internal process of the body, but also in encouraging the body's own vital field to heal and regenerate itself. As the physical form becomes damaged and particularly in the case of chronic conditions, gaps and inconsistencies can manifest in its energy system complex. The use of magnets and hematite in the affected areas can assist and encourage the body's own vital field to reassert itself. This in turn will encourage its natural healing energies to become activated on many subtle levels. This can encourage healing and regeneration of all vital energies, most especially the nerve impulses – both those that pertain to sensory stimulation and those that act within the tissues themselves. That is also another of these and while it retains the energy potential of the iron that is its base, its crystalline structure is not fully formed and therefore will not hold a charge strongly. It may be used to strike but rarely to retain built up charge and will diffuse any charge set within it colored with the elements of its nature.

Hematite is also considered to be grounding stone. In the accepted sense of rebalancing energies by channeling away excess or by filtering internal vibrational patterns, this is not the case. A better term for its activity could be centering. Hematite acts to connect the body's energy field with that of the earth. This is accomplished by its nature to resonate with both fields simultaneously and establish the harmonic between them. It provides a pathway by which an individual whose energies are weakened or scattered can reunite with each other and the planetary physical energy that both sustains the individual and provides a point of location for the energy vibration pattern. It is useful in working with individuals in the process of retrieving and reconstructing disassociated elements of the spirit/personality complex. Once the separated elements have been located and retrieved, hematite can help the individual reweave them into the present consciousness by providing a cohesive field harmony compatible to all elements.

Pyrite and marcasite are sulfides of iron. They combine the vitalizing energy of iron with the ability of sulfur to reinforce the integrity of the individual's energy system pattern. This gives a protecting and comforting effect allowing for more confidence and expansion in the individual without interference from counteractive vibrational essences.

Any of these stones may be set with any metal and should be dealt with regarding the precepts of metallic entities and behavior of crystalline forms.

NON-CRYSTALLINE STONES OF POWER

As we have seen in the case of micro- and crypto- crystalline quartz, the ability of stones to express energy vibrations is not limited to crystalline forms. Their virtue and power lies in their atomic structure and in the ability to respond to energy fields and produce a signature oscillation. This oscillation or vibrational energy interacts with the human energy system complex and by doing so makes a variety of energy constructs available to the practitioner and wearer.

Many of these stones have been recognized for many ages and treasured as much for their energies as their beauty. Others are just becoming recognized and are coming into their own to interact with the changing energy helix parameters of the parent Earth and its interelationship with the other planes and energies adjacent to it in the continuum of consciousness. Each age brings its own demands and stages of Human awareness, and it is in this present time that these stones are coming to the fore to help individuals awaken and evolve.

These are a few of such stones grouped together by the element that is the principle activator of its nature. As we have often stated, the varieties of stones and their combination in nature is seemingly endless. We offer these listings so that the student may understand the energy qualities represented by both the stones and their significant elements. This should serve as a tool for the student's further exploration of energies and the mineral world.

THE COPPER GROUP

CONNECT PHYSICAL LIFE WITH SPIRITUAL STRENGTH

TURQUOISE, MALACHITE, CHRYSOCOLLA, COVELITE & AZURITE

Turquoise, Malachite, Chrysocolla, Covelite & Azurite are compounds whose key element is copper. They were known far into antiquity and highly valued as much for their beauty as well as their virtue.

Their nature is to stimulate a recognition of the connection between physical life and spiritual essence. They promote an awareness of deity moving in everyday affairs and the awareness that Humankind is but one of the many manifestations of the divine. These stones resonate with the essence of harmony between heaven and earth, creator and created, macrocosm and microcosm but are structured in such a way that this awareness can be interwoven with the awareness of daily life

Their nature varies according to their shades of color but, generally, they are soothing, cooling, virtuous stones. They will aid the gentle side of the nature and activate the spirit will. That is to say, these are stones that resonate well with the connection between the heart and brow chakras and this nature should truly be considered. They are stones that will enhance the wearer's sensitivity to the physical world around him or her and his or her connection to the flow of the planet channel itself when used rightly. Consider closely the nature and necessity of the work. Consider also the presence of trace materials such as matrix and inclusions for these will also impart a virtue according to the kind and nature.

Their natural resonant metals are silver and copper and they will respond most graciously when bound with them. They cease to function adequately when touched and bound with iron. Electrum is most pleasing in its effect, for its elements enhance one another, and enhance the virtue of the stones with good potential. It is unwise to make vessels from these materials, because they are porous and a will instill their contents with toxic substances. When making elixirs the same caution holds true, but elixirs can be made from polished or sealed stone.

Each of these stones is slightly different in composition and will be taken in turn for a study of their differences and similarities. However, their natures are so similar and so compatible that they often form together with one blending into the other and becoming indistinguishable from it.

Azurite forms with malachite combining the celestial clarity and objectivity of the azurite with the earth wholeness of inner balance between the physical and emotional bodies.

TURQUOISE

COPPER CONTAINING BASIC

ALUMINUM PHOSPHATE

$$CuAl_6((OH_2/PO_4)_4$$

Turquoise has been prized by Humankind for the beauty of its sky blue color since the most Ancient Days and much is connected with it in terms of racial and karmic memory. Take this into account in the consideration of charms and carvings. Some of its virtue will arise from the racial/cultural associations that each individual has with them. This may be stimulated on a subconscious level. The practitioner should be aware that these stones were prized in Egypt, Mesopotamia, China, Meso-America, and the American Southwest. Stones of this nature were worn in ancient Atlantis.

The rich blue color associates both turquoise and azurite in the collective mind with the higher vibration of the sky. This perception is enhanced by the nature of their composition that links them with the spiritual body. Combining with the base/heart harmonic of copper, this allows them to be an excellent stone to raise the personal vibration to establish a constant connection with the spiritual vibration while maintaining close touch with physical universe reality. This indicates that turquoise and azurite particularly are stones of personal inner balance.

AZURITE

BASIC COPPER CARBONATE

$$Cu_3((OH)_2/(CO_3)_2)$$

Azurite raises the vibration of turquoise and further assists the individual to dispel negative vibrations from his or her energy system complex. It provides for alignment of the heart with the spirit allowing the individual to release the spiritual results of unpleasant situations and move forward with his or her higher life purposes. Azurite expands the personal outlook and viewpoint. This encourages objectivity while retaining compassion. This allows the energy system complex to become clarified.

CHRYSOCOLLA
HYDROUS COPPER SILICATE
$$CuSiO_3.2H_2O$$

The activity of chrysocolla centers around the physical center of the energy system complex and connects the heart chakra to the clarifying effects of the copper base. This is a useful stone in promoting creativity and self-expression. The elevating effects of the copper can also help the individual process and rise above excessive negative emotions by demonstrating a pathway to a "better place". For the individual who wishes to reach beyond depression, self-doubt, or grief, chrysocolla provides a tool for the healing process by opening avenues that reinforce the individual's sense of personal sense of beauty and harmony.

Chrysocolla is also known in its translucent form as gem silica. In this form its significant virtue is that it activates the release for negativity that has collected in any of the subtle energy bodies. As this energy releases, it can come to the individual's attention and is available to be evaluated, processed and released. This will allow for the individual to turn the energy processed into more positive and expansive avenues.

EILAT STONE

Eilat stone is a particular formation of copper compounds found in the Middle East where chrysocolla combines turquoise and malachite. These stones can be very beautiful as well as possessing the vibrations of all three variations in balanced harmony. In ancient times they have been credited with a wide variety of powers and virtues, most especially that of granting the possessor great wisdom and clarity.

MALACHITE
BASIC COPPER CARBONATE
$$Cu_2((OH)_2CO_3)$$

Malachite brings the celestial energy into connection with the physical universe. Its green color has led many people to associate it with physical prosperity and personal abundance. It is useful in working with clearing the energy system complex because, as harmful or conflicting vibrations are moved away, malachite can set up an energy complex to hold the vacant place until the individual can reharmonize the system for him or her self. This is a useful tool, because it often happens that as negative or entangled vibrations are processed, they leave vacant places in the energy system. In a healthy system, these will be filled in time as the natural harmony and balance of the individual is restored. However, in a recovering individual it often happens that the individual seeks to fill them with vibrations similar to those that have been removed, because these are familiar and feel appropriate. The practitioner should be aware of this tendency and provide what support is possible to bridge these gaps until the individual is capable on his or her own to establish a healthy balance and rhythm. Malachite is particularly helpful when concerns of the physical universe are involved, of personal abundance, creativity, bodily health, and fertility.

COVELLITE

COPPER SULFIDE

CuS

Covelite is similar in nature to pyrite in that it is a metallic sulfide. Covelite is, in many respects an important tool in many kinds of energy work and personal transformation. Its nature is essentially to assist the individual in work that has been begun by the personal desire and will rather than to initiate change by its own vibration. As the copper and sulfur are joined together they permit a resonance that helps the individual transcend the harmful structures of ego. It assists the individual to resolve and cast off the energy concretions from the spiritual aura when the individual has been excessively centered in the present time personality and in the concerns of the physical world. We mean that materialism in whatever form it may take has the result of rendering the spiritual body less permeable to the regenerative and restorative energies of the Celestial planes to which it is naturally connected. This happens in the same way that an excessive denial of the needs and energies of the physical body will weaken its vitality. Use of covellite can help the individual reassert his or her own natural "lightness".

Covelite can also help the individual release the effects of energy implants, especially those carried over from previous lifetimes or assumed in this lifetime because of karmic concerns. It resists the effects of both self-imposed limitations and the limitations imposed by others because these often appear as energy concretions and implants.

MANGANESE GROUP

RHODOCHROSITE & RHODONITE

Rhodochrosite and rhodonite are unusual in the microcrystalline families because, although their appearance as whole crystals is rare, their microcrystalline form has unique and powerful properties that make them powerful and agreeable working stones. Their potency comes from the manganese element in their structure that is the same agent that gives rose quartz its color. Even the black intrusion in rhodonite carries this potency being made of manganese oxide. Manganese is the element that links a stone directly to the vibratory love energy of the heart.

RHODOCHROSITE
MANGANESE CARBONATE
$MnCO_3$)

Rhodochrosite carries the full range of healing properties notable in rose stones, and has a full range of correspondences to the base, heart, and crown chakras. It works well in long term healing work such as convalescents from traumatic physical injury as well as extreme personal loss and emotional injury. It should be used after the initial damage is dealt with and the healing process is begun. It will help strengthen the overall spirit on all levels so that the healing can take place. Rhodochrosite is particularly helpful in this because, as it enables a harmonic to resonate between the three chakras together, it opens the way for the individual to see the truth of the situation, accept it, and deal with it in the most positive light possible. In this aspect it can be called the Stone of Hope, because it encourages the individual to see what is in its most constructive and positive light so that the individual can create new life and new reality from this center of truth. Its action is supportive and reassuring, which is an important quality when such critical work is involved.

It also allows the wearer to use information from past lives and integrate it into the current situation. This does not necessarily have to be on a conscious level. Many individuals are not ready to remember past circumstances that have a strong bearing on the current situation. Rhodochrosite can allow this information to be assimilated on an unconscious level and integrated into the healing and growth process in a positive and strengthening way.

Rhodochrosite that is banded with white and paler pink although beautiful can be structurally unstable when channeling a highly level of energy or energy that has sudden variations in its intensity. It is generally more effective to use rhodochrosite as the center or principle stone of a talisman using moonstone as a focus stone and a secondary stone that is specific to the nature of the healing or meditation work at hand. Silver makes a good carrier for this talisman. Gold may also be used if it is specific to the task although it will have a tendency to over-drive the stone. If gold is use the driver/focus stone must be of the first quality with as few flaws and anomalies as possible. The purer and darker the color of the rhodochrosite, the stronger it will be and the most constant and regular its benefit. It is recommended that only the true raspberry red color be used when the work involves any true intensity.

RHODONITE

MANGANESE METASILICATE

$MnSiO_3$

Rhodonite is a valuable stone for healing and sustaining people under constant stress, particularly those individuals who must use psychic or metaphysical gifts in a stressful or highly stimulative environment. The black inclusions of manganese oxide give it its own naturally harmonic grounding capacity that will help clarify and stabilize sensitive energies.

Its activity is centered principally in the heart chakra where it helps bring stability and a feeling of well being and love. It is especially useful to those practitioners whose primary karmic task is to live their life in service as healers, seers or health care professionals, because it will greatly help them from becoming damaged by the energies they must deal with on a constant basis. It can be worn constantly as a personal talisman allowing its nature to work steadily and consistently over time, or it may be worn in periods of rest to give the practitioner a much-needed break from the demands of the environment or work. Rhodonite can be set with either silver or gold equally well. This choice should be made by the individual who is going to wear the charm according to their taste and nature of the work for that the stone is intended.

STONES TO REBALANCE THE ENERGY SYSTEM COMPLEX

CHAROITE, SUGULITE & LEPIDOLITE

Charoite, Sugulite & Lepidolite are linked by their similar abilities to resonate through the crown chakra and bring a wholesome and vigorous connection with the Higher Self into the present consciousness. Each manifests this property in a slightly different form, but all three can be effectively used in addressing imbalances between the subtle bodies. Each in its own way can assist the practitioner or individual to integrate the activities of the four subtle bodies into a whole and balanced energy system complex.

SUGULITE

COMPLEX MANGANESE SILICATE

$$KNa_2Li_3(Fe,Mn,Al)_2Si_{12}O_{30}$$

Sugulite is the higher consciousness stone whose resonance is seated in the heart via the emotional body by virtue of the manganese in its structure. The black marbling presents an oxide of manganese that provides a grounded resonance similar to that found in rhodonite. Through the lithium in its structure it connects the higher consciousness awareness through the heart center. This makes its energy accessible through the entire energy system complex as well as through the secondary axis (arms and hands) in a healing vibrational flow. It can encourage the wearer to connect with healing and reinforcing vibrations from other levels of consciousness as well as to energize his or her own healing energies and the energy system complex' own nature to seek healthy coordinated balance. In the case of sugulite, this activity is coordinated through the heart center.

Sugulite can also be of assistance in doing out of body or trance work involving karmic repercussions. It can help the wearer sustain the level of trance necessary to bring about successful conclusion to the work while reinforcing the intellectual clarity to process the information gathered. As such, when carved into the appropriate charms, this can serve as a powerful shamanic journey stone.

CHAROITE

CALCIUM POTASSIUM SILICATE

$K(Ca,Na)_2[(OH,F)|Si_4O_{10}].H_2O$

The calcium in charoite links its higher consciousness action through the mental body and the brow center. Its action is very similar to that of sugulite but of a much lighter mental tone. It encourages the wearer to seek a balance of his or her energy system complex by actuating the balance of the spiritual and mental levels. This stone can assist the wearer in "lucid dreaming" that is, participating in an active role in one's dreams to direct their course. This provides a pathway by which spirit can encourage the individual to access sources of strength beyond the format of the current physical existence. Its activity is both relaxing and clarifying, because by the balance it initiates it constructs the means by which the individual is constantly renewed and connected to his or her higher resources. This often results in a personal consciousness of universal love.

LEPIDOLITE

BASIC FLUOSILICATE OF LITHIUM, POTASSIUM, AND ALUMINUM

$KLiFeAl[(F,OH)_2/AlSi_3O_{10}]$

Sometimes found with rubelite tourmaline, lepidolite acts through the physical and emotional bodies. As in both kunzite and sugulite, the lithium in its structure activates the crown and heart chakra together by activating the pathway directly between them. This can be a powerful tool for working with the physical body complex to relieve conditions with emotional roots that manifest as physical disorders and disabilities. It can rebalance and harmonize the physical manifestation with the higher vibrations of the other subtle bodies providing a healthy template for energies to renew and restructure. The rubelite tourmaline helps connect the individual to the life giving energies of the base chakra as it resonates through the heart center. This is an excellent stone for those seeking to rise above the limits of physical limitation and find their own breadth of expression.

THE SEER'S STONES

LAPIS LAZULI & SODALITE

LAPIS LAZULI

SULFUR CONTAINING SODIUM ALUMINUM SILICATE

$$Na_8(Al_6Si_6O_{24})S_2$$

SODALITE

CHLORIC SODIUM ALUMINUM SILICATE

$$Na_8(Cl_2Al_6Si_6O_{24})$$

Lapis lazuli and sodalite are cousin stones, being but slightly different in their basic structures and natures, lapis lazuli having the stronger nature of the two because of the sulfur in its structure. This sulfur in the structure of lapis lazuli provides the element that encourages energy field integrity, allowing the wearer's energy field complex a steady resonance of balance not provided by sodalite. This sulfur also manifests in the presence of pyrite "stars" across the deep blue field of the lapis lazuli. These are highly desirable for their stabilizing influence as well as for their beauty.

Lapis lazuli and sodalite are Seer's stones. They activate through the mental body and the throat and brow channel to open the gates of perception for the individual in order to take out of body journeys or to act as a visionary seer. They also facilitate the ability of the individual to return from the trace work and remember and communicate what was seen. Their nature is easily accessed enabling the user to travel in consciousness beyond both time and space to access whatever information is necessary. It should be used with caution, however. Its structure allows it easy access to the energy system complex. Before wearing the stone, the individual or practitioner should experiment with the individual's reaction to it to determine the extent of its influence.

Under no circumstances should you make any drinking vessel from lapis lazuli, for its nature is porous and will taint the drink. If such a vessel is necessary, sodalite should be used, being harder and not as porous. Sodalite is equal to blue chalcedony in the fashioning of the Dreamer's

Cup, although it is more powerful and may prove too strong for the nature of the Dreamer. This must be judged according to each individual who would use it. Their true power lies not in the basic stone matrix, but in what gives it its intense blue color, and to the degree that their color is deepest indigo without vein or flaw, so they are valued and respected most highly.

Pendants of lapis lazuli and sodalite should be worn above the breastbone between the heart and throat Chakra. If a headband is worn to match, it is advisable that the stones of both pendant and band were cut from the same rough block. This will allow them to be as closely keyed as possible to one another. If this is not possible, their color and consistency should be as close as possible, for they must resonate together at the same pitch and frequency. See that their settings match as well in proportion of metallic content. Silver, gold or electrum or combinations of them, may be used as long as the same proportions for both are the same for the best results.

These stones (often mistaken for one another) have ever been known as the Talismans of the Wise and the Strength of the Mage and have justly been treasured and prized throughout the ages for the aid that is given to the mind and the will. When they are tuned and bound properly, they are a sure and certain aid to those who go forth seeking wisdom in many realms and are of inestimable virtue in the retrieval of such knowledge and visions when the seeker does return. They are a valued tool in workings of power, for they bring out all the strength of the higher will force in conjunction with the pure white light force of the highest power center.

THE CALCIUM GROUP

MENTAL ACTIVITY & FOCUS

FLUORITE, APATITE, CALCITE, SELENITE,

ALABASTER & MARBLE, DIOPSIDE

This is a group of crystals and rocks that are much softer than the stones we have been discussing. Generally speaking, such soft stones do not have the structural integrity to withstand strong demands of power even including the normal energy surges consistent with extreme emotional states that are involved with everyday living. This is not to say, however, that they are not useful. Their axial structure and crystalline makeup are often very regular and consistent.They make excellent teaching tools for experiencing different natures, colors, and structures. They are easily charged, cleared and recharged and will take on a wide range of charge natures and contents both specific and nonspecific. Spar (optical calcite) and fluorite particularly will take on sensory programming and mood charges with pleasing results.

The low hardness and density of these stones does not allow them to hold a charge for any great length of time. They will gradually dissipate any charge placed upon them. Their axis frequency can be accelerated to cycle charges, that is, to take in, alter, and emit charge, but even this will eventually slow and cease until it has returned to its natural level unless this acceleration charge is maintained and renewed on a regular basis. This quality can be of great virtue and benefit when used according to its nature, for within these stones messages, qualities and various charges may be placed that can be clearly read and then can easily be deactivated or will vanish in a relatively short span of time. A healing charge may be placed upon them that will release its benefit and gradually, as the healing process takes place and as convalescence proceeds, will reinforce this process. Then the charge does not linger when its work is accomplished that also has the added benefit of preventing dependency upon the stone. Fluorite clusters and singular octahedrons are ideal for this as they also come in a wide range of pleasant and appropriate colors.

None of these stones should be worn about the body for extensive periods of time except by children who may wear and use them prior to their formal training for their casual delight and experimentation. This is for two main reasons: the first is that their physical structure is fragile and an inadvertent change in this structure will cause an inadvertent charge anomaly in their activity and interaction. They are, in this, subject to gradual physical and, therefore, axial erosion that will prove unfortunate. The second reason is that they cannot bear the sudden intensities of energy that even the most latent experience.

Bind them, if this is necessary, with silver, bronze, or occasionally with copper for the natures of the other metals will, in and of their own strength, override and overburden them, rendering them useless.

FLUORITE

CALCIUM FLUORIDE

CaF_2

The regular structure of fluorite octahedral crystals makes it an excellent tool for those who are new to crystal meditation to experience the lattices of a regular crystal structure. Its colors include yellow, blue, green, and violet. The pigments causing the coloration are bonded regularly with the atomic structure so that they are easily visualized and experienced by the student. In general fluorite makes an excellent tool for clearing the mind during meditation. It is not a stone of power, but rather one that reminds the user to release all concerns and clear the consciousness. Its nature is cooling and objective. This also makes it a good healing crystal for those who are convalescing, because it encourages them to leave their physical concerns and draw from the richness of the spirit body. It should be stressed that it is not wise to use fluorite for active healing or any work that requires specific intention. It encourages such things to be put aside and the energy demands on the energy system complex allowed to rest and restructure themselves on a healthy basis.

APATITE

CALCIUM FLUORO- AND CHLORO- PHOSPHATE

$Ca_5(F,Cl,OH)(PO_4)_3$

Apatite is one of the gentlest of the mentally reactive stones and well suited for the process of the training of the novice. Its colors range from pale transparent yellow/ green, brown and occasionally blue. Its nature is often like clear spring water in its nature. It is often found with slight rainbowing in the cleavage lines that should be taken wisely into account when considering whether it is appropriate for use in the novice's state of inner development. These rainbows may sometimes indicate internal stress fractures and should be considered closely, for, insofar as these interrupt the central axis, so they cause modulation anomalies that may be unsuitable for the untutored.

Nonetheless, these are gentle stones and may be used to stimulate the budding processes of the novice and to aid in the integration of powers and forces through the age of puberty. They act generally throughout the mental level of awareness to encourage its energy patterns to be coherent and smooth and to act in harmony with the other subtle bodies. Apatites may serve as a restorative to those whose mental functions have been injured in the course of life, especially those who have lived as latents and have been damaged in the exercise of power through the channels of their latency. In this latter case, care should be taken to teach these individuals basic disciplines and powers. This will help such injuries from recurring. If this teaching is not done, it is likely that similar injuries will happen again. This is because they cause an area of weakness in the mind that will not fully regenerate unless there is exercise to that portion to develop its strength. This stone may be given to children to stimulate mental awareness in all phases of life, but let care be taken that balance should be maintained.

Silver suits apatite well as a setting allowing its influence to permeate gently and with balance. Gold or electrum may also be used should the occasion warrant and will cause no harm or stress to the individual who wears it. It should not lightly be taken as a Life Stone for there is a tendency for dependency to occur unless this is used by someone who is otherwise impaired and requires its constant stimulation.

CALCITE

CALCIUM CARBONATE

$CaCO_3$

Calcite clusters and singular crystals have an earthy grounding nature and are best set to nonspecific general charges. They make excellent short duration linkage stones as they are capable of handling surges of some intensity for short spans of time. Its seemingly endless variety makes it optimal for a wide variety of purposes and it may also be worn about the body of the non-developing latent in times of stress, for it will have a steadying quality. Its calcium nature causes it (along with apatite and selenite) to work through the mental body of the individual and on a physical level translate its energy field close to the energy levels of the neural pathways of the human body. This makes it convenient to use in the healing work of recovering from injuries and damage to the nervous system. It can be energized to interact with the regenerative physical helixes to encourage the nerves to reconnect correctly and completely.

Spar (optical calcite) is self-contained in its energy structure and requires no ground or base structure, thus it is well used as an environmental or message stone with tactile or emotion carrier wave on the charge. Its properties are greatly similar to fluorite in these respects.

SELENITE (CRYSTALLIZED GYPSUM)
HYDROUS CALCIUM SULFATE
$CaSo_4.2H_2O$

Selenite rods are most appropriate for specific direction of short duration, low to mid-range charges, but will cloud and shatter if overloaded. However, as a specifying booster they may save the practitioner much labor and effort. They will not emit a stronger charge than their load limit permits and, consequently, are excellent governors when used in healing children and small animals as they will not permit inadvertent overloading of the energy systems. Also, selenite will retain no charge of disease from its object and will act as a noncontaminative buffer for the practitioner and is also easily cleared for reuse. Its disadvantage, however, is in its fragile structure and its virtue will gradually degenerate with constant use, as will all these softer stones, until it becomes unstable and inadequate and must be replaced. Selenite found in rod form, and especially those with contained water inclusions, make excellent directing wands provided that their structure is sufficiently regular through their length.

Its calcium base will cause its effect to be linked principally through the mental body harmonizing through the brow and belly centers. It can encourage the appropriate sequencing of neural stimuli and can serve as an amplifier for gaps in the energy field complex until the body/mind/spirit has regenerated to return to normal balance and function.

Setting a rod with silver bands close to the termination of each end connected with bands or wires running the length of the rod will lengthen its life span and increase its ability to transfer and direct and higher level charge.

ALABASTER (SEE ALSO SELENITE)
HYDROUS CALCIUM SULFATE
$CaSo_4.2H_2O$
& MARBLE (SEE ALSO CALCITE)
CALCIUM CARBONATE
$CaCO_3$

Alabaster is a finely grained variety of gypsum and retains the general qualities of selenite. Its nature is amorphous rather than crystalline, however, resulting in any charge placed on it being general rather than specific in direction. The nature of its gypsum base makes it unsuitable for storage of liquids for any length of time and its practical use should be restricted for storage containers and statuary. In these functions it creates an excellent generally charged field for the storage of charged objects. Objects put in these containers will absorb the field charged to the alabaster. Statuary and small carvings will take on the essence of a charge and gently emit its vibrations to the holder. This can be useful in healing charms or charms for confidence. the nature of the charge will be general rather than specific and will gradually dissipate over time to be replaced with the user's own response and belief in their virtue. This gradually encourages the user on a subconscious level to create his or her own healing vibrational matrix of energy.

Alabaster and marble are unique in that they are the only products of such amorphous composition that will retain a truly defined charge. Their virtue is similar to that of white chalcedony although their potency is not as great. Their primary virtue is similar to that of chalcedony. Containers, vessels, and charms can be made from them that will impart a certain charge to their contents. However, this is not strong and will not be as lasting as the charge in true chalcedony. An interesting function of these stones is in the fashioning of lamps, for the heat generated will more strongly activate their potential charge and add great virtue as their function. Take care in choosing of the stone that it not be grained heavily, its color should preferably be more uniform for it to work ideally. However, in the making of carved charms this grain may be used to some advantage to enliven the artistic virtue of the piece and may add a connotation that is pleasing and connective to the desired charm.

DIOPSIDE

CALCIUM MAGNESIUM SILICATE

$$CaMg(Si_2O_6)$$

The calcium in diopside links this stone to the energy system complex through the mental body while its magnesium nature activates the brow/crown connection. This is a stone of mental focus occurring in many shades of green from very light to brilliant grass green and very dark shades containing chromium. It is also found in clear or lemon yellow. The purple-violet shades are called violane and their color is due to their manganese content.

Star Diopside or Cat's Eye Diopside may be used as a Grounding / Seer's stone in the same manner as black sapphire, and will function as well or better especially in the case of a Novice or the Initiate. It exhibits much of the same qualities and its power is gentle due to its grounding ability that will steady the mind and senses of the Seer. Visibly the difference will be that the star of the sapphire will have six rays while the star of the diopside will have four. It does well also as a general calmative. This is because it both grounds naturally, and its colors and patterns are pleasing to look upon. It will help the individual put aside distractions and confusion by providing a directed focussed energy that will engage and balance the mind. It will assist the wearer in seeing the humor in things by making inconsistencies visible.

The simple focus and directness of Diopside's nature make it a very good choice for either a driver or qualifier stone. Diopside agreeably harmonizes with stones of both more and less powerful constitution and allows its qualities to be distributed throughout the talisman's vibrational structure.

Always set this stone in silver, so that the natural flowing action of the metal will aid it in its activities. This stone may be worn in any position but is most beneficial when worn upon the breast as a pendant or upon either hand in rings or bracelets that its gentle star may serve as a guide to focus the thoughts and the spirit.

Take care in its setting, for due to its structure its surface is fragile and easily scuffed or marked and then part of its benefit will be lost. Do not rely too heavily on its power, for it is not a strong stone nor one with tightly integrated grain structure. It will not serve at all as a vehicle for great sendings, but its nature is such that when rightly used, it allows the strength in its wearer to be able do so if all other trainings and disciplines are also there. It may be charged to a single purpose and that charge will hold true. It may be charged to answer only to a single wearer and this will hold as well to the degree that in the breaking of that charm the stone's virtue will also be broken.

It has been well set in the bottom of silver scrying bowls as a focus through the medium and such are known as treasured relics where they reside. Their surface may also be polished as a mirror and this used as a seeing vehicle as well. When the back of the mirror or the border of the cup are set with other stones of virtue, to strengthen and aid the working of the piece great is its potency and power.

LIFE FORMS & FOSSILS

AMBER & JET – CORAL & PEARLS

FOSSIL ANIMALS & PLANTS

AMBER

Amber is the petrified resin of certain ancient trees. It is unique among the stones of power, for it is not a mineral but organic matter that has undergone sufficient stress and change within the Earth to become as stone and achieve a crystalline nature of sorts. Its uniquely powerful nature derives from the fact that it is conductive of static electricity and may become easily integrated into the body's own electric field. This electrical nature is easily seen when the stone is rubbed briskly with wool or similar material. It will generate a small field that will draw bits of lint to it, and in the dark one may see it give off sparks and small flashes of light owing to electrical discharge. By this electrical nature, it achieves a true companionship with the living organism. Its basic structure was formed of tree resins and plant pollen and it brings to the individual attuned to it the blessing of the fruitful earth. Its nature will vary slightly depending on the type of tree or plant the resin came from – whether pine or palm, etc.

It is extremely powerful in discharging and rebalancing the body's electrostatic field. This quality makes it very helpful in treating shock that has occurred from raising intense levels of energy to which the individual is not accustomed, especially in the cases of great duress. Often, this will be too intense a charge to be adequately discharged through the body's system. Amber can be very effective in discharging it, for the stone will gather into itself this self same electrical discharge and dispose of it according to the natural processes of dispersal and dissipation.

In many ages amber has been worked into charms and figures to suit the beliefs and fancies of many peoples. It has been greatly prized as the Stone of the Sun for its glowing color and its trait of growing warm with the flesh of the wearer. It often contains bits and particle of organic matter that may give the context of the stone additional meaning and significance to the wearer. In many ancient cultures, amber was regarded as the charm specific to females and their nature according to their religious beliefs. It has been long used with great effect in aiding the strength of the mother at the time of birth and her healing afterwards. It has also been thought to have some power in the treatment of the debility that comes with age and disease, to ease pain, calm fevers and aid in the restoration of the body's strength. In this case, however, its benefit is most often transitory since the physical system does not have the strength to sustain such energies even should they be temporarily restored. In the Eastern Nation, it is often thought of as the Dragon's Charm, as it retains within itself the power of the young Earth in fullest flower and it is believed, and with some truth, that through its virtue this energy may be tapped upon great need. Charms carved in this fashion are highly prized in that place.

Great care should be taken when cutting the rough stone so that it should not be over heated or stressed, for its properties are delicate and easily marred. It is better set in gold than in any other metal for the essential nature of gold will enhance its beneficial properties to the best extent possible and thus it will prove stronger in cases of great need. Also, the gold, which is the best electrical conductor, will augment its functions and direct its purposes to the finest extent. It should also be noted that this stone and no other is unique to this planet and is found in no other place.

JET

Jet is a type of bituminous coal of sufficient hardness to allow it to take polish. Its primary substance is carbon, which allows it to access the physical mechanisms of the body. Its general vibration is calming and balancing. It is effective in addressing emotional disorders that affect the physical health such as excessive worry or emotional excess. Because it is the compressed and transmuted remains of ancient forests, it is possible to use jet as a key to the energy of this ancient age when doing trance or Seeing work.

CORAL & PEARLS

Coral and pearls are by-products of living marine organisms. And, while they contain mineral compounds that give them certain resonance of energy, they also contain traces of the living ocean from which they came. This includes microscopic amounts of trace minerals as well as the energy resonance of the marine environment. This is extremely harmonious to some individuals and disruptive to others and it is wise for the practitioner to observe their effect before using them extensively for talismanic work. They are also not as dense or tightly structured as mineral and crystals that have formed geologically. Therefore, their activity is to enhance and fulfill an energy rather than to assert a separate distinctive one. When the limitations of their organic nature are understood and accounted for, they can make a significant contribution to the field of talismanic healing and energy work.

All life on this planet evolved from the ocean and a large percentage of the human body is composed of seawater. It is therefore not surprising that coral and pearls can contribute significant subtle energies to the energy system complex in receptive individuals.

CORAL

Red coral is composed of calcium carbonate ($CaCO_3$) which is the same composition of calcite, but of a different structure. Its works through the mental body of the individual and on a physical level to help strengthen and regenerate the energy field close to the energy levels of the neural pathways of the human body. This makes it convenient to use in the healing work of recovering from injuries and damage to the nervous system. It is helpful in encouraging convalescence from emotional, mental and physical trauma and extended illness. Its color can range from white through the palest rose pink to deep blood red depending on the nature of the marine organism who inhabited them and the elements present in the waters where they grew. These elements respond in varying degrees to the emotional level of the individual so that the result is a balancing between the mental and emotional bodies. Coral can contribute sentimentality, tenderness, and joy to an individual.

Blue and black coral are composed of organic matter similar to pearl. They activate the exterior of the body's surrounding energy field to repel and negativity and discordance in the environment.

PEARLS

Pearls are also composed of calcium carbonate ($CaCO_3$) arranged in plates formed like aragonite and covered with an organic substance (conchiolin) as the surface skin. In this case, the structure of the calcium carbonate gives them the potential to assist the individual to be more centered direct and focussed. It is this gentle activity that gives them the capability of reflecting negativity and realigning energy entanglements that present confusion to the individual. Their calcium carbonate structure aligns directly with the mental body to allow the individual to accept this influence gracefully and move through situations on a moment to moment basis without becoming bogged down in a limited viewpoint or the stress of the pressure of the desires of others.

FOSSIL ANIMALS & PLANTS

Fossils are formed when organic matter is replaced by mineral matter. This mineral matter takes the shape of what was once organic, but the essential organic matter disappears leaving only the mineral matter in its form. This gives the fossil a dual nature. First the nature of the replacing mineral should be understood. This will give the stone its power and focus. But the second part of the nature is also important. The fossil will retain a form of the energy resonance of the organic matter that gave it its shape – whether animal or plant, land or marine animal, compressed fern in coal or agatized "petrified" wood. A small piece of animal bone will resonate with the essence of the creature of which it was once a part. It will also contain an energy essence pattern that will allow the Seer to access the archetype of the species of creature. When combined with other stones to give this essence focus and direction, this can create a particularly dynamic shamanic charm and personal talisman.

APPENDIX A

STONE TYPE	COMPOSITION / COLORING ELEMENT	COMMENTS
QUARTZ	Silicon Dioxide SiO_2	**GENERAL HARMONIC OF ENERGY SYSTEM COMPLEX**
MACROCRYSTALLINE		
Clear		
White	structural anomalies / gas & water bubbles	See also Microcrystalline, White
Black (Morion) & Smoky	natural radiation	
Red (Ferrifinous Quartz)	hematite inclusions	
Rose	manganese or titanium	
Orange (Citrine)	natural heating or colloidal iron hydrates	
Green		
Green Quartz	chlorite inclusions – see also chlorite	
Blue – Siderite	tiny rutile, zoisite or tourmaline inclusions	also called Blue Aventurine
Violet (Amethyst)	trace amounts of ferrous iron	
Black Amethyst		
Rutillated		
Star Quartz	axially oriented silimanite inclusion - aluminum silicate dioxide	Similar to sapphire
Cat's Eye Quartz	axially oriented rutile	
Rutillated clear, smoky & amethyst	rutile crystals – titanium oxide	
Tourmalinated	microcrystals of tourmaline	
MICROCRYSTALLINE (CHALCEDONY)		
Onyx		

STONE TYPE		COMPOSITION / COLORING ELEMENT	COMMENTS
	Green Aventurine	scales of green mica inclusions (fuchsite), goethite or hematite	
	Prase	Actinolite inclusions	See also Jade
	Moss Agate (not a true agate)	inclusions of horneblende or iron & manganese oxides	
	Chrysoprase	traces of nickel	
	Carnelian	emtite	
	Sard & Sardonyx		
	Heliotrope (Bloodstone)		
	Tiger's Eye (Yellow Brown), Hawk's Eye (Blue)	asbestos fibers replaced by quartz / crocodilite fibers	

AMORPHOUS (CRYPTOCRYSTALLINE)			
	Opal (SiO_2)	cristobalite spheres in a silica gel / microspheroids of hydrous silica	
	Fire Opal		
	Fire Agate	Opalized Chalcedony	

GARNET		BASE CHAKRA	
Black (Melanite)		black andradite var. of grossular	
Red (Pyrope)		magnesium aluminum silicate $Mg_3Al_2(SiO_4)_3$	Red & Rose
Orange (Spessarite)		manganese aluminum silicate $Mn_3Al_2(SiO_4)_3$	
Yellow (Grossular)		calcium aluminum silicate $Ca_3Al_2(SiO_4)_3$	Pale milky green Emerald Green (containing chromium) Tsavorite Yellow Reddish Brown to Orange (containing iron)
Green (Uvarovite)		calcium chromium silicate $Ca_3Cr_2(SiO_4)_3$	emerald green

STONE TYPE		COMPOSITION / COLORING ELEMENT	COMMENTS
Andradite		calcium iron silicate $Ca_3Fe_2(SiO_4)_3$	
	Melanite - red, brown, black		
	Yellow – Topazolite		
	Demantoid – Emerald Green		
Purple (Almandine)		iron aluminum silicate $Fe_3Al_2(SiO_4)_3$	Red to violet-purple
Spessartite		Magnesium aluminum silicate $Mn_3Al_2(SiO_4)_3$	orange to red-brown (cinnamon)

ZINC GROUP		BELLY CHAKRA	
Zincite		Zinc Manganese oxide $(Zn,Mn)O$	
Hemimorphite		Hydrous basic zinc silicate $Zn_4((OH)_2/Si_2O_7).H_2O$	
Smithsonite		Zinc Carbonate $ZnCO_3$	White/Clear – pure pale blue-green –copper bright yellow – cadmium pink-violet – cobalt or manganese brown – iron hydroxide

TOPAZ		SOLAR PLEXUS CHAKRA	
Clear		hydrous aluminum silicate $Al_2SiO_4(F,OH)_2$	
Smoky			
Pink/Rose			
Yellow/Gold			
Pale Green			
Blue			

BERYL		Aluminum beryllium silicate $Al_2Be_3(Si_6O_{18})$	HEART CHAKRA
Clear (Goshenite)			
Pink (Morganite)			
Yellow (Heliodore)		Uranium oxide (radioactive)	
Green (emerald)		chrome (sometimes vanadium)	

STONE TYPE	COMPOSITION / COLORING ELEMENT	COMMENTS
Pale Blue (Aquamarine)	iron	
CORUNDUM GROUP (SAPPHIRE & RUBY)	Aluminum oxide Al_2O_3	**THROAT CHAKRA**
Clear		
Red (Ruby)	chrome	
Orange (Pad Parajah)	chrome	
Yellow	iron	
Green	iron	
Blue (Sapphire)	iron & titanium	
Violet	vanadium	
Star Rubies & Sapphires	axially oriented 3 dimensional streaks of rutile cause the stars seen in star quartz & star corundums – see also Metal-Based Crystals – Rutile (Titanium oxide)	
TOURMALINE	aluminum borate silicate (complicated and changeable composition) $(NaLiCa)(Fe_{11}MgMnAl)_3Al_6((OH)_4(BO_3)_3(Si_6O_{18})$	**BROW CHAKRA**
Clear (Achroite)		
Rubelite (Red)		
Dravite (Brown & Yellow)	magnesium	
Verdelite (Green)		
Indicolite (Blue)		
Siberite (Purple)		
Schorl (Black)	sodium-iron	
Elbaite	sodium-lithium-aluminum	
Buergerite	Sodium-Iron	
Tsilaisite	Manganese	
Uvite	Calcium-magnesium	
DIAMOND	crystallized carbon (C)	**CROWN CHAKRA**

STONE TYPE		COMPOSITION / COLORING ELEMENT	COMMENTS
WIDE SPECTRUM CRYSTALS			
	Kunzite	Lithium aluminum silicate $LiAl(Si_2O_6)$	Crown/Heart channel – rebalance as emotional body cleanses & rebuilds
	Kornerupine	$Mg_4Al_6((O,OH)_2/BO_4(SiO_4)_4)$	Discharging – anti-panic
	Seraphenite	Hydrous magnesium iron aluminum silicate $(Mg,Fe^{+2})_5Al(Si,Al)_4O_{10}(OH)_8$	Releases control issues
	Kyanite	Aluminum silicate $Al_2O(SiO_4)$	Align chakras – rebalance energies – physical body

FELDSPAR			**SEQUENCING**
	Moonstone	Potassium aluminum silicate	Purity, focus, dissemination
	Amazonite	$K(AlSi_3O_8)$ Adularia/Adularescence	Restorative – reunifying
	Labradorite (Spectrolite)	Sodium calcium aluminum silicate	Awareness of natural cycles
	Sunstone (Aventurine Feldspar	$Na(AlSi_3O_8)Ca(Al2Si_2O_8)$	Free will, optimism, self-esteem

IRON SILICATES			**CLARITY, REGENERATION & RENEWAL**
PERIDOT		Magnesium iron silicate $(Mg,Fe)_2\ SiO_4$	Renewal through connection with Higher Self – brow chakra – mental body

EPIDOTE			Solar Plexus/Heart channel – compassion and intelligence
	Epidote	Calcium aluminum iron silicate $Ca_2(Al,Fe)_3(Si_2O_7)(SiO_4)O(OH)$	
	Zoisite	Hydrous calcium aluminum silicate $Ca_2Al_3(Si_3O_{12})(OH)$	Access to Higher Self Essence Green - Anyolite or Zoisite Amphibolite (also Ruby in Zoisite) Pink – Thulite - Manganese
		Tanzanite (pleochroic)	Calcium aluminum silicate $CA_2AL_3(O/OH/SIO_4/Si_2O_7)$	Unify diverse elements of life & personality Blue-violet - chromium & strontium

STONE TYPE		COMPOSITION / COLORING ELEMENT	COMMENTS
JADE			**STONE OF PEACE**
	Jadeite	Sodium aluminum silicate $NaAl[Si_2O_6]$	Deal with dysfunctional relationships – accept love & sense of belonging – heart/brow channel – union of reason & emotion
	Nephrite	Calcium magnesium iron silicate $Ca_2(Mg,Fe)_5(Si_4O_{11})_2$	Base/Heart Channel
	Actinolite	$Ca_2(Mg,Fe)_5(Si_4O_{11})_2(OH)_2$	
LITHIUM & POTASSIUM			**REBALANCING ENERGIES**
	Charoite	Calcium potassium silicate $K(Ca,Na)_2[(OH,F)|Si_4O_{10}].H_2O$	Mental Body through brow center – balance of mind & spirit – lucid dreaming
	Sugulite	Complex manganese silicate $KNa_2Li_3(Fe,Mn,Al)_2Si_{12}O_{30}$	Connect with healing vibrations across planes of higher self
	Lepidolite	Basic fluosilicate of lithium, potassium, and aluminum $KLiFeAl[(F,OH)_2/AlSi_3O_{10}]$	Balance crown/heart channel – heal physical condition with emotional source
PERSONAL DEVELOPMENT & TRANSFORMATION			
ZIRCON		Zirconium silicate $Zr(SiO_4)$	Inner focus & direction
SPINEL		Manganese aluminum oxide $MgAl_2O_4$	Personality, individuality Dark green (iron bearing) Zinc spinel - Blue, red-violet and green Black (chrome and iron bearing)
LIGHT REACTIVE STONES (PLEOCHROISM)			**GATEWAYS**
	Alexandrite (Chrysoberyl)	Beryllium aluminum oxide $Al_2(BeO_4)$	White-magenta-green Emotional body – confidence – personal evolution
	Tanzanite (Epidote - Zoisite)	Calcium aluminum silicate $CA_2AL_3(O/OH/SiO_4/Si_2O_7)$	Blue – Violet – strontium & Chromium Unify diverse elements of life & personality
	Andalusite	Aluminum silicate $Al(AlSiO_5)$	Yellow-brown-olive Mind - encouragement

STONE TYPE	COMPOSITION / COLORING ELEMENT	COMMENTS
Iolite	Magnesium aluminum silicate $Mg_2Al_4Si_5O_{18}$	Brow/Crown/Heart channel – Guidance Blue-Lavender

CRYSTALLINE IRON		PRIMAL ENERGY
Pyrite & Marcasite	FeS_2 Iron sulphide	Reinforce energy system pattern
Hematite	Fe_2O_3 Iron oxide	Connect body's energy – align with primal earth energy
Magnetite		Reinforce & regenerate body's energy field – stimulate physical healing

THE COPPER GROUP		CONNECT PHYSICAL LIFE & SPIRITUAL STRENGTH
Turquoise	Copper containing basic aluminum phosphate $CuAl_6((OH)_2/PO_4)_4$	Balance spiritual awareness of physical life – personal inner balance
Malachite	Basic copper carbonate $Cu_2((OH)_2CO_3)$	Bridge gaps in energy complex as negative elements are released
Chrysocolla (Gem Silica)	Hydrous copper silicate $CuSiO_3.2H_2O$	Reinforce sense of personal beauty & harmony
Azurite	Basic copper carbonate $Cu_3((OH)_2/(CO_3)_2)$	Dispel negativity – Encourage objectivity –personal inner balance
Covelite	Copper sulfide CuS	Crystalline Copper Release effects of energy implants

THE MANGANESE GROUP		HEALING & RENEWAL THROUGH COMPASSION
Rhodochrosite	Manganese Carbonate - $MnCO_3$	Base/Heart/Crown Channel Truth with compassion Hope
Rhodonite	Manganese metasilicate - $MnSiO_3$	Strengthens heart center under stress – grounding through heart center

STONE TYPE	COMPOSITION / COLORING ELEMENT	COMMENTS
SEER'S STONES		**OPENING INTUITIVE FACULTIES**
Lapis Lazuli	Sulfur containing sodium aluminum silicate $Na_8(Al_6Si_6O_{24})S_2$	Throat/Brow Channel through mental body Sulfur – energy field integrity
Sodalite	Chloric sodium aluminum silicate $Na_8(Cl_2Al_6Si_6O_{24})$	

THE CALCIUM GROUP		**MENTAL ACTIVITY & FOCUS STRUCTURES OF SECONDARY STRENGTH**
Alabaster	Hydrous calcium sulfate $CaSo_4.2H_2O$	General dispersive charge on objects & containers
Selenite		Mental body – harmonize brow/belly channel – neural sequencing
Calcite	Calcium Carbonate $CaCO_3$	Wide spectrum capability of charge focus
Marble	Metamorphic rock – calcite based containing a variety of other minerals in varying amounts	General charge on containers qualified by secondary elements present
Fluorite	Calcium Fluoride CaF_2	Flexibility – Objectivity Gentle energy
Apatite	Calcium fluoro- and chloro- phosphate $Ca_5(F,Cl,OH)(PO_4)_3$	Wit-Mental clarity
Diopside	Calcium Magnesium Silicate $CaMg(Si_2O_6)$	Calming – Clarifying – scrying stone

FOSSILS & LIFE FORMS		
Amber	Petrified tree resin	Treat shock & excessive energy states – energizing to physical senses & body's energy field
Jet	Bituminous Coal Carbon	Calming to emotional excess
Coral	Calcium Carbonate $CaCO_3$	Through mental body assist regeneration
Pearls		Reflect negativity
Fossils	Various	Combined energy of mineral and life force essence

INDEX

A

Actinolite 336
Adept 209, 269, 319, 329
Adularescence 330
Adularia 330
Agate 254, 267, 270, 273, 278
Agate, fire 278
Akasha 138
Alabaster 62, 245, 355, 359, 360
Alexandrite 341, 342, 343
Aluminum 265, 266, 272, 290, 308, 321, 324, 327, 328, 329, 331,
    332, 333, 335, 336, 339, 342, 343, 346, 352, 355
Amazonite 330, 331
Amber 362, 363
American Southwest 347
Amethyst 69, 88, 89, 104, 105, 107, 186, 187, 216, 226, 227, 263,
    264, 265
Analogy of the Rose 28, 35, 79, 166
Andalusite 341, 342, 343
Apatite 355, 357
Apprentice 229, 231
Aquamarine
    69, 82, 85, 86, 103, 187, 194, 256, 263, 296, 301, 316, 332
Aragonite 364
Archetype 106, 111, 113, 203, 209, 217, 249, 255, 279, 287, 290,
    293, 296, 302, 308, 319, 365
Arm bands 234, 235
Armor 233, 247, 249
Arsenic 96
Arthur 250
Artisan 71, 200, 204, 206, 207, 209, 211, 214, 215, 217, 218, 227,
    267, 279, 315, 316
Ascension 138
Asteration 103, 104
Asterism 266
Atlantis 192, 266, 290, 293, 347
Aura 43, 44, 70, 71, 238, 342, 349

Aventurine 329
Aventurine, blue 272
Aventurine feldspar 329
Aventurine, green 272
Axis 100, 101, 102, 103, 104, 105, 107, 108, 109, 118
Azurite 191, 346, 347

B

Base 206, 214, 216
Bell 130, 168, 211
Beryl 69, 71, 76, 97, 98, 101, 108, 110, 157, 179, 182, 271, 296, 297,
    298, 299, 316, 333
Black Man 224
Blade 236, 237, 238, 239, 240, 241, 242, 269, 276, 292, 300
Blockages 282, 287, 297, 319, 323, 325, 326
Blood 163, 164, 169, 177
Blood sugar disorders 65
Bloodstone 267
Bowl 246, 248
Box 243, 245, 246
Boxes 268, 269
Bracelet 234, 235
Bran the Blessed 250
Bronze 74, 164, 166, 168, 169, 209, 239, 247, 248, 278, 293, 300,
    304, 338, 341, 356
Brow 212, 216, 217, 234, 248, 249, 263, 272, 274, 286, 293, 300,
    301, 312, 315, 332, 336, 343, 353, 354, 359, 360
brow 216
Brow band 248

C

Cabochon 181, 182, 188, 190, 265, 271, 280, 291, 303, 322, 339
Cadmium 288
Calcite 106, 355, 358, 359
Calcium 311, 327, 328, 331, 332, 333, 335, 336, 353, 357, 358,
    359, 360, 364, 365
Calling 121, 126, 129, 189, 194, 199, 200, 201, 202, 203, 204, 205,
    206, 209, 211, 212, 215, 216, 217, 218, 219, 220, 224, 225, 230,
    231, 255, 279, 287, 290, 296, 302, 308, 315, 319
Calling, Artisan 71
Calling, Monarch 88
Calling, Seer 31

Calmative 257, 258, 281, 292, 313, 342, 360
Candle 246
Candleholder 246
Cap 102, 184
Carbon 320, 363
Carbonate 289, 346, 349, 351, 364, 365
Carbuncle 226, 317
Carnelian 227, 247, 261, 267, 269, 275, 316, 330
Cat's-Eye 273
Cause and effect 26, 27, 28, 38
Centering 11, 13, 14, 15, 16, 17, 18
Central axis 56
Chakra 13, 21, 22, 23, 24, 25, 28, 29, 30, 31, 32, 33, 36, 37,
    38, 41, 43, 46, 69, 70, 71, 73, 78, 79, 82, 83, 88, 90, 117, 126,
    127, 132, 136, 138, 139, 141, 142, 143, 144, 157, 159, 188, 192, 193,
    194, 196, 197, 199, 200, 201, 206, 207, 209, 211, 212, 215, 216,
    217, 218, 224, 225, 230, 232
  base 23, 24, 26, 27, 33, 36, 38, 56, 66, 70, 71, 73, 131, 139,
      141, 166, 188, 192, 206, 207, 210, 218, 260, 271, 280, 281,
      282, 283, 284, 285, 287, 292, 298, 303, 318, 330, 331, 333,
      336, 337, 343, 353
  belly 28, 38, 41, 73, 141, 169, 207, 209, 210, 212, 214, 216,
      217, 218, 247, 262, 269, 284, 287, 289, 304, 328, 331
  brow 32, 33, 38, 39, 71, 77, 82, 84, 88, 188, 263, 264, 272,
      309, 312, 323, 346
  crown 23, 24, 32, 33, 36, 38, 62, 70, 90, 139, 141, 188, 192,
      199, 214, 216, 217, 218, 219, 263, 265, 319, 335, 352
  heart 14, 15, 16, 18, 21, 27, 28, 29, 30, 33, 36, 37, 38, 41,
      42, 43, 69, 79, 126, 129, 139, 141, 142, 149, 157, 165,
      166, 179, 183, 188, 189, 196, 210, 211, 212, 217, 224, 225,
      242, 259, 271, 272, 273, 283, 286, 287, 296, 299, 300, 306,
      315, 316, 321, 322, 323, 324, 325, 331, 333, 334, 336, 342,
      343, 346, 348, 351, 352, 353
  solar plexus 29, 31, 40, 42, 69, 189, 211, 247, 290, 304, 333
  throat 31, 40, 69, 82, 189, 210, 215, 216, 264, 302, 305
Chakra Talisman 192, 194, 196, 225
Chalcedony 159, 186, 244, 245, 257, 261, 267, 268, 269, 270, 274,
    275, 278, 337, 354, 360
Chalcocite 168
Charge 93, 95, 96, 105, 106, 108, 109, 114, 115
Charging 99, 108, 110, 114, 115, 116, 235, 236, 237, 238, 239, 240,
    241, 242, 243, 244, 245, 246, 250, 252, 255, 257, 268, 269, 270,

271, 274, 277, 278, 283, 287, 291, 308, 309, 310, 311, 312, 313, 314, 319, 337, 344, 356, 358, 359, 360, 361, 362

Charoite 91, 353

Chi 11, 13, 15, 247

Child 256, 257, 258, 261, 268, 270, 271, 275, 280, 282, 283, 290, 293, 294, 299, 304, 329, 332, 333, 340, 356, 358, 359

China 347

Chlorite 103, 105, 261, 324

chlorite 261, 324

Chloro-melanite 336

Chromium 68, 299, 303, 335, 336, 360

Chrysoberyl 341

Chrysocolla 166, 346, 348

Chrysoprase 189, 267, 271, 330

Citrine 209, 227, 247, 248, 260, 261, 262, 269, 316

Citrine, green 262

Cleansing 239, 244

Clearing 108, 109, 110, 111, 113, 115

Clinochlore 324, 325

Coal 363, 365

Cobalt 289

Collar 247, 249

Color

    black 61, 62, 64, 65, 66, 69, 79, 103, 108, 109, 188, 189, 198, 224, 226, 257, 264, 268, 269, 277, 281, 306, 307, 308, 311, 312, 313, 336, 337, 339, 350, 351, 352, 360, 364

    blue 30, 31, 32, 33, 34, 69, 71, 82, 83, 85, 86, 109, 120, 171, 172, 175, 182, 188, 189, 191, 198, 204, 206, 214, 215, 217, 218, 226, 227, 244, 264, 272, 273, 276, 288, 290, 295, 296, 297, 298, 301, 302, 303, 305, 307, 314, 316, 319, 324, 329, 330, 332, 333, 335, 339, 340, 341, 343, 347, 354, 355, 357, 364

    brown 189, 256, 257, 270, 273, 281, 289, 290, 311, 312, 313, 330, 333, 336, 340, 341, 342, 357

    golden 28, 43, 76, 77, 189, 191, 211, 227, 261, 273, 277, 284, 285, 290, 293, 294, 295, 313, 315, 342

    green 28, 30, 31, 65, 66, 68, 69, 71, 72, 76, 78, 79, 80, 82, 120, 157, 166, 167, 180, 186, 188, 189, 191, 204, 214, 226, 238, 247, 248, 260, 261, 262, 270, 271, 272, 274, 276, 280, 283, 285, 286, 288, 290, 295, 296, 297, 298, 299, 300, 302, 305, 315, 316, 318, 323, 324, 330, 331, 332, 333, 336, 339, 340, 341, 342, 343, 348, 357, 360 indigo 32

lavender 173, 276

orange 28, 73, 74, 169, 209, 247, 260, 269, 284, 287, 304

pink 71, 72, 120, 289, 290, 302, 329, 334, 336, 337, 339, 351, 364

purple 32, 33, 34, 68, 69, 90, 91, 188, 189, 192, 217, 218, 225, 226, 227, 230, 264, 280, 286, 298, 303, 306, 308, 317, 341, 360

red 26, 27, 34, 49, 69, 70, 72, 120, 163, 174, 192, 198, 206, 217, 258, 259, 270, 273, 275, 276, 277, 279, 280, 281, 282, 283, 284, 288, 296, 298, 302, 303, 313, 314, 317, 318, 334, 339, 340, 341, 351, 364

rose 26, 27, 71, 72, 79, 90, 120, 188, 189, 259, 260, 265, 272, 280, 281, 283, 290, 292, 293, 294, 298, 303, 313, 314, 317, 318, 323, 334, 337, 338, 350, 364

smoky 186, 256, 257, 265, 269, 290, 292, 313

violet 32, 33, 34, 69, 88, 89, 104, 188, 189, 218, 226, 255, 263, 264, 281, 286, 289, 298, 302, 306, 335, 336, 339, 341, 343, 357, 360

white 61, 62, 66, 76, 77, 109, 111, 113, 114, 115, 166, 172, 173, 174, 175, 181, 187, 188, 189, 198, 201, 204, 217, 218, 225, 226, 228, 256, 261, 263, 264, 268, 269, 276, 277, 278, 286, 288, 293, 303, 308, 312, 319, 323, 329, 332, 333, 336, 338, 342, 351, 355, 360, 364

yellow 29, 30, 69, 75, 76, 77, 120, 189, 191, 211, 214, 275, 276, 284, 288, 290, 293, 296, 297, 299, 302, 304, 311, 312, 314, 323, 331, 332, 333, 339, 340, 341, 342, 357, 360

Colored glass 96

Conchiolin 364

Concretion 349

Copper 71, 80, 166, 167, 168, 169, 171, 204, 212, 235, 239, 247, 260, 265, 283, 284, 286, 287, 288, 292, 293, 297, 299, 300, 301, 329, 346, 347, 348, 349, 356

Coral 362, 363, 364, 365

Corundum 170, 173, 182, 186, 187, 302, 317

Counterpoise 249

Covelite 168, 349

Cristobalite 276, 277

Crocidolite 272, 273

Crown 207

Crowns 233

Crystals 6

Cup 212, 214, 243, 244, 245
Cup of Joining 245, 268
Cup of Life 250

D

Dance 9, 10, 11, 16, 235, 247, 248
Dancer 207, 210, 211, 214, 216, 217, 218, 226, 227, 235, 247, 249, 285, 290, 292
Destiny 123, 134, 137, 138, 139, 150, 151
Diamond 76, 109, 164, 170, 173, 181, 186, 188, 198, 218, 226, 227, 230, 263, 298, 306, 319, 320, 323, 337
Dichroism 335, 341
Diopside 360
Diopside, Cat's Eye 360
Diopside, Star 360
Dizziness 13, 16
DNA 250
Double helix 23
Double terminated 102, 103
Dragon 228, 272, 363
Dragon's Back 16
Dravite 281, 311, 312, 313, 314, 315
Dream 262, 276, 284, 314, 353
Dreamer 186, 244, 311
Dreamer's Cup 244, 276, 355
Dreamer's Talisman 186
Driver 179, 181, 182, 183, 184, 185, 186, 187, 188, 189, 193, 196, 197, 198, 204, 206, 217, 256, 257, 277, 286, 291, 303, 308, 311, 312, 319, 320, 323, 327, 328, 329, 332, 339, 340, 351, 361
Dyslexia 13
Dysphasia 13

E

Earth Opal 186
Egypt 145, 166, 347
Eilat stone 349
Electricity 255, 310, 340, 362
Electrum 173, 216, 226, 239, 265, 278, 286, 287, 341, 346, 355, 358
Electrumtrum 173
Emerald 69, 80, 103, 109, 166, 182, 189, 197, 198, 212, 214, 226, 227, 283, 295, 296, 298, 299, 300, 301, 303, 305, 315, 332
Emotional body 45

Energy system complex 46, 136, 143, 181, 184, 192, 193, 197, 201,
        206, 220, 243, 247, 262, 264, 266, 273, 280, 281, 282, 286, 287,
        288, 296, 297, 305, 306, 309,310, 314, 317, 318, 319, 320, 324,
        327, 328, 329, 330, 337, 338, 339, 340, 341, 343, 344, 345,
        347, 348, 352, 353, 354, 357, 360, 364
Epidote 331, 333, 341
Ethics 122
Evening Emerald 332
Excalibur 250

F

Facet 181, 265, 280, 303, 322, 339, 342
Feldspar 182, 327, 328, 329, 330, 331
Fetching 153
Fire agate 198
Fish 8
Fluorite 106, 355, 356, 357, 358
Fluorites 100
Fowl 8
Frankincense 130

G

Gaia 271
Garnet 65, 69, 70, 71, 91, 100, 166, 185, 186, 197, 198, 206, 226,
        227, 247, 248, 279, 280, 281, 282, 283, 284, 285, 286, 287, 311,
        314, 315
Gateway Stone 341
Ghosting 104, 105, 107
Girdle 249
Goethite 272, 329
Gold 71, 72, 74, 76, 77, 80, 91, 170, 171, 173, 211, 226, 230, 239,
        260, 263, 265, 278, 280, 283, 287, 292, 293, 297, 299, 300, 301,
        304, 311, 317, 320, 338, 341, 351, 355, 358, 363
Gorget 247, 248, 249
Goshenite 297
Grail 250
Grand Talisman 196, 224
Great Gathering 205, 220, 221, 225
Grounding 62, 65, 66, 69, 257, 312, 313, 344, 351, 358, 360
Guardian 151, 210, 250, 263, 300
Gypsum 359
GyrLyon 169

H

Harmonic Resonance, Law of 97, 154
Hawk's Eye 273
Headache 16
Headdress 235
Healer 80, 95, 99, 114, 126, 127, 129, 130, 155, 156, 158, 171,
     200, 207, 210, 212, 213, 214, 216, 217, 219, 226, 227, 238, 263, 271,
     276, 296, 300, 304, 305, 315, 332
Healing stones 94
Heart 66, 109, 114, 116, 117, 118, 157, 158, 159, 204, 207, 209,
     210, 211, 212, 214, 216, 217, 218, 219, 234, 235, 238, 239, 240,
     242, 247, 249
Heirlooms 250, 252
Heliodore 69, 76, 182, 296, 298, 299
Heliotrope 267, 276
Helix 36, 37, 42, 264, 358
Hematite 65, 165, 265, 297, 329, 343, 344
Hemimorphite 288
Higher Mind 266
Higher Self 121, 122, 133, 138, 202, 203, 264, 288, 289, 309, 319,
     325, 326, 332, 334, 343, 352
Hopi 151
Horizontal axis 42, 43
Hornblende 270, 272, 273

I

Implant 139, 140, 262, 283, 349
Implement 207, 209, 211, 214, 215, 216, 218
Incense 13, 130
Inclusion 98, 103, 104, 105, 107, 111, 254, 256, 261, 267, 268, 272,
     273, 275, 281, 282, 305, 306, 313, 319, 324, 329, 337, 346,
     351, 359
Indicolite 316
Instinct 29, 44
Interactive 132, 133, 138, 143, 146, 147, 151
Iolite 88, 173, 332, 343
Ionic bonding 56, 57
Ionization 109, 114
Iron 71, 80, 163, 164, 165, 169, 203, 204, 206, 239, 242, 247,
     270, 272, 278, 280, 287, 289, 292, 293, 297, 300, 301, 302, 305, 311,
     314, 317, 324, 330, 331, 332, 333, 336, 339, 341, 343, 344, 346

Isis 145

J

Jade 62, 65, 66, 71, 72, 186, 263, 271, 272, 330, 331, 336, 337
Jadeite 336
Jasper 267, 274, 275, 276
Jasper, green 276
Jasper, red 275
Jasper, yellow 275
Jesus 145
Jet 362, 363
Jewelry 233, 235, 236, 239
Jonquil 299
Journey Stone 272, 295

K

Karma 39, 43, 79, 94, 98, 122, 123, 132, 133, 134, 136, 137,
    138, 139, 141, 142, 143, 144, 146, 151, 200, 202, 204, 207, 250, 251,
    288, 333, 347, 349, 351, 352
Key signature 46
King 166, 171, 173, 216, 217, 226, 227, 300, 304
Kornerupine 323, 324
Kundalini 280, 287
Kunzite 321, 322, 323, 353
Kyanite 182, 326, 327

L

Labradorite 330
Lamp 218, 243, 246
Lamps 267
Lapis Lazuli 190, 194, 276, 354, 355
Lepidolite 353
Levels of Awareness 229
Life Stone 80, 94, 114, 358
Lion 29, 260, 261, 270
Lithium 321, 352, 353
Luck stones 94

M

Macrocrystalline 256
Macrointeractives 145, 147

Mage 121, 128, 129, 130, 131, 209, 224, 228, 229, 315, 355
Magnesium 324, 332, 336, 343, 360
Magnetite 343, 344
Malachite 66, 166, 191, 346, 347, 348, 349
Manganese 68, 69, 259, 270, 287, 289, 311, 334, 339, 350, 351, 352, 353, 360
Marcasite 165, 343, 344
Mask 233, 249
Massage 95, 243
Master 151, 238, 240, 241
Master Talisman 205
Melanite 281
Mental body 45
Mercury 96, 290
Meso-America 145, 347
Mesopotamia 347
Metallic crystals 65
Mica 272, 326
Microcrystalline 180, 256, 260, 264, 267, 273, 274, 278, 324, 325, 350
Middle East 348
Mirror 215, 246
Monarch 207, 210, 212, 214, 216, 219, 308
Moon 301
Moonstone 172, 181, 182, 186, 187, 188, 189, 204, 263, 264, 286, 293, 298, 312, 323, 328, 329, 330, 339, 351
Morganite 296, 298
Morion. *See* See Quartz, smoky
Moss Agate 267, 270
Mother Goddess 244
Mother's Daughter 270
Myrrh 130

N

Naval 234
Nephrite 336
Nickel 271, 306, 320
Nightmares 261, 288
Noble Houses, Talisman of 250
Novice 276, 360

O

Obsidian 181, 226, 227
Oil 95, 243, 246
Onyx 65, 181, 187, 188, 226, 227, 267, 268
Opal 110, 166, 186, 187, 197, 198, 276
Opal, common 277
Opal, fire 277
Opal, precious 277
Opalescent 181
Orb 236, 238
Osiris 145

P

Pad Parajah 74, 209, 304
Pale colors 120, 171
Panic 324
Parallel Resonance, Law of 98, 154
Pearl 362, 363, 364, 365
Pecos Diamond 258
Pectoral collar 235, 249
Pectoral collars 249
Peridot 80, 166, 189, 198, 271, 283, 331, 332, 333
Phantom 258, 259
Phoenix crystal 182, 204
Platinum 71, 72, 173, 198, 203, 204, 218, 239, 278, 286, 293, 304,
    306, 311, 317, 320, 329
Potassium 272, 327, 352, 353
Pre-menstrual syndrome 65
Priest 200, 207, 210, 212, 214, 217, 218, 225, 226, 227, 230, 244,
    286, 293, 300, 319
Priestess 172, 212, 216, 218, 225, 226, 227, 230, 283, 286, 316
Primary 179, 180, 181, 184, 185, 186, 187, 188, 189, 190, 192, 193,
    194, 196, 197, 204, 205, 206, 209, 217, 219, 220, 224, 274, 291,
    297, 308, 311, 312, 324, 327, 328, 337, 339, 351, 360, 363
Prince 304
Prism 22
Protein 8
Pyrite 65, 165, 343, 344, 349, 354

Q

Qualifier 102, 179, 180, 181, 182, 183, 184, 185, 186, 187, 188,

189, 191, 192, 193, 198, 204, 205, 206, 219, 220, 224, 225, 258, 265, 274, 278, 291, 298, 312, 320, 327, 328, 332, 338, 339, 340, 361
Quartz 55, 56, 59, 62, 66, 69, 71, 72, 80, 97, 98, 101, 103, 104, 105, 107, 108, 110, 115, 119, 120, 156, 157, 159, 167, 179, 184, 185, 186, 187, 188, 190, 191, 192, 193, 196, 198, 203, 204, 205, 224, 225, 255, 256, 257, 258, 259, 260, 261, 264, 265, 266, 267, 268, 269, 270, 271, 272, 273, 274, 277, 278, 280, 285, 292, 299, 313, 314, 318, 319, 323, 324, 332, 337, 338, 339, 343, 350
Quartz, green 186, 261, 270
Quartz, smoky 257
Quartz, white 159, 256, 257, 264
Queen 166, 167, 171, 173, 216, 217, 225, 226
Quetzalcoatl 145

R

Racial consciousness 151, 152
Rainbow 22, 256, 266, 267, 276, 277, 302, 357
Restorative 260, 271, 272, 276, 284, 286, 300, 301, 305, 313, 315, 318, 330, 333, 349, 357
Rhodochrosite 350, 351
Rhodonite 350, 351, 352
Ring 235, 247, 250, 251
River of Life 10, 14, 16, 117, 165, 175, 214
Rod 237, 268, 269, 359
Rome 145
Rubelite 70, 71, 227, 280, 282, 314, 353
Ruby 70, 71, 72, 91, 103, 109, 189, 192, 198, 206, 226, 227, 247, 258, 280, 282, 286, 302, 303, 306, 307, 317, 334
Rutile 103, 107, 265, 266, 272

S

Salt 109
Salt water 109
Sandals 167, 169, 235, 248
Sandalwood 13, 130
Sapphire 65, 74, 82, 103, 109, 173, 181, 186, 198, 215, 226, 227, 228, 230, 266, 286, 298, 302, 303, 304, 305, 306, 307, 311, 314, 316, 323, 332, 360
Sard 269
Sardonyx 267, 269
Scepter 216, 236, 238, 242

Scrying 172, 238, 246
Sea water 109
Seer 121, 128, 129, 172, 186, 187, 190, 194, 207, 210, 212, 214,
    215, 217, 219, 222, 226, 227, 242, 244, 246, 249, 258, 273, 296,
    302, 315, 329, 354, 360, 365
Seeress 301
Seer's Stone 82
Seer's Talisman 190, 194
Selenite 355, 359
Seraphenite 324, 325, 326
Sexual activity 9
Sheilding 18, 20
Shielding 124, 125, 126, 127, 128, 129, 130, 131, 222, 224, 228,
    229, 232, 237, 242, 243, 247
Siberite 91, 225, 308, 317
Siderite 244, 272, 273
Silica 326, 348
Silicon 256, 274, 276, 343
Silimanite. *See* Star Quartz
Silk 240
Silver 63, 71, 72, 74, 76, 80, 86, 88, 91, 113, 118, 120, 159,
    170, 171, 172, 173, 176, 190, 191, 198, 204, 215, 226, 239,
    247, 260, 263, 264, 265, 278, 280, 283, 286, 287, 292, 293,
    297, 299, 300, 301, 306, 311, 317, 318, 329, 338, 346, 351,
    355, 356, 358, 359, 361
Smith 169, 204, 206, 207, 218, 227, 238, 239, 241, 242, 279, 315
Smithsonite 288, 289
Sodalite 244, 276, 354, 355
Solar plexus 207, 210, 211, 212, 214, 216, 217, 219, 290, 293, 295,
    304
Solitary One 224, 226, 227, 229, 249
Spar (Optical Calcite) 356, 358
Spectrum 22, 23, 26, 27, 30, 55, 57, 61, 68, 78, 85, 88, 91, 199,
    200, 201, 205, 212, 214, 255, 256, 257, 260, 265, 266, 271, 277,
    278, 286, 288, 298, 302, 308, 309, 319, 323, 339, 342
Spinal column 23, 280, 287
Spinel 338, 339
Spiritual body 46
Staff 236, 238
Star 103, 266, 273, 280, 295, 307, 323, 354, 360, 361
Star Quartz 266, 273, 323
States of awareness 43, 44, 46

Steel 163, 164, 165, 169, 174, 175, 176, 203, 204, 206, 239, 240, 242, 247, 280, 287, 300, 304, 310
Stone of Dominion 225, 317
Stone of Fidelity 302
Stone of Peace 336
Stone of the Mother 270, 272
Stone of the Sun 362
Stone of the Will 305
Stones of Majesty 186, 225, 319
Stones of the Callings 225
Strontium 335
Sugulite 91, 352, 353
Sulfide 349
Sulfur 344, 349, 354
Sun 170, 202, 260, 261, 269, 270, 275, 284, 290, 293, 294, 304, 316, 362
Sunstone 74, 329
Sword 74, 209
Sword of Will 250

T

Tale of the Golden Lion 261
Tale of the Warrior's Torch 294
Talisman 57, 66, 80, 86, 88, 93, 94, 96, 97, 98, 101, 102, 105, 107, 163, 166, 168, 171, 172, 173, 175, 178, 179, 180, 181, 182, 183, 184, 185, 186, 187, 189, 191, 192, 193, 196, 197, 199, 201, 202, 203, 204, 205, 206, 219, 220, 224, 225, 226, 233, 234, 236, 237, 239, 243, 248, 250, 251, 252, 262, 266, 274, 280, 286, 289, 293, 294, 297, 298, 299, 305, 306, 308, 312, 319, 320, 332, 335, 339, 340, 351, 361, 365
Talisman of Dominion 286
Talisman of the Healer 271
Talisman of the Seer 258
Talismans of Noble Houses 250
Talismans of Power 96
Talismans of Togetherness 220
Tanzanite 332, 335, 341
Teacher 151, 200, 215
Termination 100, 101, 102, 107, 110, 112, 120, 183, 184, 186, 191, 192, 196, 198, 236, 237, 257, 291, 317, 339, 359
Thought forms 149, 150, 151, 152, 153, 154
Throat 207, 210, 214, 215, 216, 217, 219, 235, 247, 248, 249

throat 216
Thulite 334
Tiger 169
Tiger's Eye 273
Time 23, 24, 25, 26, 28, 32, 33, 34, 38, 39, 40, 42, 46, 47, 122,
    124, 127, 132, 138, 141, 142, 143, 146, 147, 151, 207, 215
Tin 168, 169
Titanium 103, 265, 302, 305
Titanium oxide 265
Topaz 76, 77, 198, 211, 227, 235, 247, 248, 284, 290, 291, 292,
    293, 294, 295, 296, 299, 314
Topaz, smoky 66, 80, 82, 85
Tourmaline 65, 66, 69, 70, 71, 76, 80, 82, 85, 91, 97, 98, 103,
    108, 109, 159, 188, 192, 225, 226, 227, 230, 256, 265, 276,
    280, 281, 282, 283, 286, 293, 298, 308, 309, 310, 311, 312, 313,
    314, 315, 316, 317, 318, 323, 332, 333, 353
Tourmaline, dravite 65
Tourmaline, schorl 65, 66
Tsavorite 197, 226
Turquoise 166, 346, 347, 348
Twins 102, 103, 186

V

Vajra 198
Vajra Talisman 197
Vegetarian 8
Verdelite 315
Vertical axis 42, 43
Vessel 243, 245, 246, 267, 354
Volcanic glass 181

W

Wand 236, 237, 238, 268, 359
Warded space 130, 131
Wards 129, 130, 131
Warrior 27, 29, 74, 121, 141, 165, 169, 205, 207, 209, 210, 211,
    214, 216, 217, 218, 221, 227, 239, 242, 247, 248, 249, 258, 261, 262,
    270, 287, 294, 295, 300, 303, 304, 316
Watch Towers 229
Water 95, 96, 97, 109, 240, 243, 246, 277, 278, 357, 359
Watermelon tourmaline 318
Wine 244, 245, 246, 313

Z

Zinc 168, 169, 287, 288, 289, 339
Zincite 74, 209, 287
Zircon 338, 340
Zoisite 272, 331, 332, 333, 334, 335

- About the Author-

Maya Heath is an internationally published author of works on divination and personal empowerment. She has appeared on television and radio and has lectured and taught on divination, metaphysics, energy and crystal work.

Her first book, The Egyptian Oracle published by Bear & Company, a unique divination system based on ancient Egyptian myths and magic. It offers a multifaceted tool for self-awareness and personal transformation.

Her first release from Merlyn Press, Ceridwen's Handbook of Incense, Oils and Candles, weaves together the many metaphysical elements of essential oils and aromatherapy, color, planetary and lunar influences, tarot and ritual to provide an excellent summary reference guide to the basics of ritual sympathetic magic for self-development and consciousness expansion.

Energies: A Book of Basics is a unique book that opens the complex and sometimes confusing world of metaphysics and esoteric practices to the beginner. Energies explores the world of meditation, chakra work, colors, crystals, the four elements, the seven planets to awaken the reader's true powers of intuition and healing, and to unlock hidden inner resources to reshape the reader's life. This is an illuminating tour through the energies that surround and empower the human spirit that connect us all with the greater universe.

As the design artist and co-owner of Dragonscale Jewelry, Maya combines an abiding interest in metaphysics and higher consciousness studies with her life-long passion for art and history. She uses her skill as an artist and art historian to fabricate images which stimulate and make an inner bridge between the seen and the unseen - the Higher and Lower aspects of the self and the other worlds which surround us. Her love of the past transforms into her vision of the future in her elegant designs for the archetypal jewelry.

When not travelling, she lives with her husband, Bob, her daughter, Adrienne, spiritual extended family, many happy cats, dogs and assorted other creatures in a log cabin in the green rolling hills of the Missouri River valley in northwestern Missouri.

If you or your organization would like information regarding personal appearances, lectures, and workshops on energy work or developing your personal intuitive process; or if you would like information about archetypal jewelry and related materials, your letter can be addressed to:

ENERGIES
P. O. Box 12212
Parkville, MO 64152-0212

The author would welcome your questions and comments and will make every attempt to answer correspondence that she receives. However, due to her travel schedule and the volume of correspondence this may not always be possible, but thanks you for your time and interest.